Founding the ACC

Founding the ACC

The Origins of a Major Collegiate Athletic Conference, 1951–1953

ROBERT B. MCCORMICK

McFarland & Company, Inc., Publishers
Jefferson, North Carolina

This book has undergone peer review.

Library of Congress Cataloguing-in-Publication Data

Names: McCormick, Robert B. (Robert Bradley), author.
Title: Founding the ACC : the origins of a major collegiate athletic conference, 1951-1953 / Robert B. McCormick.
Description: Jefferson, North Carolina : McFarland & Company, Inc., Publishers, 2023. | Includes bibliographical references and index.
Identifiers: LCCN 2023024567 | ISBN 9781476689944 (paperback : acid free paper) ∞
ISBN 9781476649696 (ebook)
Subjects: LCSH: Atlantic Coast Conference—History. | Southern Conference—History. | College sports—Southern States—History.
Classification: LCC GV351.3.S684 M44 2023 | DDC 796.04/30975—dc23/eng/20230523
LC record available at https://lccn.loc.gov/2023024567

British Library cataloguing data are available

ISBN (print) 978-1-4766-8994-4
ISBN (ebook) 978-1-4766-4969-6

© 2023 Robert B. McCormick. All rights reserved

No part of this book may be reproduced or transmitted in any form or by any means, electronic or mechanical, including photocopying or recording, or by any information storage and retrieval system, without permission in writing from the publisher.

Front cover images © 2023 CSA-Archive/iStock and RetroClipArt/Shutterstock

Printed in the United States of America

*McFarland & Company, Inc., Publishers
Box 611, Jefferson, North Carolina 28640
www.mcfarlandpub.com*

For Mom, Dad, and PaPa

Table of Contents

Acknowledgments	ix
Preface	1
Introduction	3
1. The Schools and Men Who Built a Conference	9
2. Reform in the Era of National and Local Scandals	41
3. Banning Bowls	64
4. Southern Conference Football and the 1951 Bowl Crisis	75
5. The Everett Case Invitational: Southern Conference Basketball, 1951–1952	112
6. Conference Struggles and Ineffective Reforms in 1952	125
7. A Reduced League: Southern Conference Football, 1952	137
8. The Last Was the Best: Southern Conference Basketball, 1952–1953	156
9. The Atlantic Coast Conference Is Born	171
10. ACC Football: The First Season	207
Conclusion	221
Chapter Notes	227
Bibliography	245
Index	251

Acknowledgments

Unbeknownst to me, this project began when I was a child. I grew up in eastern North Carolina, and it is hard to remember a time when the Atlantic Coast Conference was not a part of my life. In that regard, I wish to thank sports broadcasting pioneer C.D. Chesley and his broadcasting team of Jim Thacker, Billy Packer, and Bones McKinney for providing me with a great love for ACC sports. C.D. Chesley, a national pioneer in sports broadcasting, brought ACC basketball games into my house, a big deal when there were only three channels. I cannot imagine my life without hearing the phrase "This was a C.D. Chesley Production." Likewise, I can still hear Jim Thacker at the beginning of each basketball broadcast saying, "This is Jim Thacker, along with Billy Packer." Those words meant that an exciting ACC basketball game was ready to commence, one in which the broadcast often was as entertaining as the game. It was an extra treat when Bones McKinney joined them in the booth.

In the same vein, broadcasters such as Wally Ausley (NC State), Gary Dornburg (NC State), Woody Durham (North Carolina), Jim Phillips (Clemson), and Gene Overby (Wake Forest) were wonderful voices for the schools they represented, painting elaborate and vivid pictures through the spoken word. With few ACC football games televised in the 1970s, I was fully dependent on these men to describe the games. With flair and love for the institutions they represented on the air, these figures brought the ballgames to me and thousands of others.

Furthermore, I am thankful for the great ACC athletes and coaches who compelled me to follow ACC sports with great fervor. I could never list the enormous number of athletes I enjoyed watching and following for so many years. I marveled at their abilities and appreciated incalculable moments vicariously through their achievements. None of these athletes heard me scream or saw me jump in joy. Likewise, they never saw me shed tears in defeat or in a particularly weak moment throw something at the television. Nevertheless, I am enormously thankful for having been a tiny part of their games.

Archival assistance was essential to making this project a reality. I am immensely appreciative of the help I received from archival staffs at Clemson, Duke, Maryland, North Carolina, North Carolina State, South Carolina, Virginia, Virginia Tech, and Wake Forest. They provided invaluable assistance, especially considering that archival materials for athletic departments are often "hit and miss" during the time frame of this study. Many records were simply thrown away and never preserved. Nonetheless, I always was conscientiously and skillfully steered in the right directions by these outstanding staffs of archivists.

My colleagues, past and present, in the History Department at the University of South Carolina Upstate always have been supportive of this project, having listened to me speak much too much about the founding of the ACC. I have learned a great deal about American history, especially southern history, in the late 1940s and early 1950s from invaluable conversations with them. I am appreciative of my home university for providing a sabbatical and travel funds that were necessary to complete the manuscript. Furthermore, many thanks go to Gary Mitchem and the team at McFarland for enthusiastically supporting my manuscript and offering wise and helpful advice.

My wife Cindy and daughters Mary and Anna have cheerfully listened to me talk about this book, even when I knew that they did not wish to hear any more about the ACC's founding. They have been a font of love, support, and encouragement, integral to everything I have done. My mother, who was a sports fan since even before her high school basketball days at Saluda (SC) High School, has been a source of great inspiration and affection. Ron Montesano of the Nichols School in Buffalo, New York, helped a great deal with this manuscript, reading chapters and simply offering encouragement. He, along with my other fraternity brothers from Sigma Nu at Wake Forest, offered consistent inspiration and all-around good cheer. My dear friend, Rabbi Yossi Liebowitz, provided constant support throughout the research and writing process. His friendship and encouragement helped make this book possible.

Invariably in a project of this scope, there are errors of judgment and interpretation as well as mistakes in everything from grammar to citations. For these, I, alone, am responsible.

Preface

The founding of the Atlantic Coast Conference has garnered little attention, often ignored even in works about the history of college athletics in general or more specifically the history of college football and basketball. The Big Ten, which was the most powerful voice in the NCAA, and to a lesser extent other leagues like the Southwest and the Southeastern conferences, have received the lion's share of focus. For example, John Sayle Watterson's fine volume, *College Football*, which examines how the game became a juggernaut, does not address the league's founding in any appreciable manner. Murray Sperber's *Onward to Victory*, which carefully studies the development of big-time sports in the 1940s and 1950s through the lens of scandal and corruption, does not examine the establishment of the ACC, focusing its attention far more on Notre Dame and the Big Ten.[1]

Most histories of collegiate sports have allotted more consideration to the Big Ten or the Southeastern Conference (SEC), in part because there is a strong contrast to be drawn by comparing these two giants.[2] This is understandable, especially considering the healthy enrollments of universities like Minnesota and Ohio State, as well as the large populations that these state universities served. Although most Southeastern Conference schools resided in small cities and did not approach the enrollments or distinction of Big Ten schools, their sports programs, especially football, were oversized and nationally powerful. The Southern Conference was academically and athletically much different from either of these leagues.

A significant portion of this book studies how the Southern Conference responded to scandals and corruption in collegiate sports. Ronald Smith's *Pay for Play* adroitly illustrates the role that alumni and boosters played in forcing the creation and development of big-time collegiate sports. John R. Thelin's *Games Colleges Play* remains an indispensable work about the growing power of athletics on college campuses, despite scandals and corruption. Reform never gained traction considering the powerful constituencies that supported big-time athletics, sometimes including university presidents, a position outlined in Brian Ingrassia's *The Rise of Gridiron University*. Ingrassia demonstrates that some presidents and professors enjoyed the attention and money that collegiate football brought to their institutions.

ACC-centric works such as K. Adam Powell's *Border Wars* or J. Samuel Walker's *ACC Basketball* devote limited attention to the league's founding. Even Bruce Corrie's history of the ACC, *The Atlantic Coast Conference, 1953–1978*, moves quickly through the league's establishment but provides a good discussion of the conference's early development.[3] To have a fuller picture of the landscape of athletics, especially as interpreted by smaller state and private schools, an examination of the ACC's founding is important.

Recently, Kurt Kemper's *Before March Madness*, an examination of college basketball at mid-century, shows us the competitive gap that developed between larger universities and small colleges and the choices that were made with the increasing pace of commercialism and professionalism. The Southern Conference, with smallish liberal arts colleges and military schools attempting to compete on the same terms with state universities or better financed private schools, in some ways complements his study. The sentiments of the original ACC institutions, however, demonstrate that even among those wanting to play big-time collegiate sports, there was a strong current of academic and athletic leadership that was wary of sports slipping away from academic control.

By featuring the words of many prominent sportswriters in the conference's four-state region, this work complements Michael Oriad's *Reading Football*. Although centered on an earlier era, Oriad's view that the game was given an enormous boost through the vivid and exciting columns featured in papers across the country was true in the Southern Conference's region and during the early 1950s as well. Nonetheless, it is important to note that there was a variety of opinion among these writers, including some who were concerned about the direction of college athletics, such as Dick Herbert, even while writing compelling pieces about college athletics.

In the 1950s, many colleges did not have archiving policies and university documents were preserved only by the good work of staffs or individuals with the foresight to conserve them. Often, athletic departments had an earned reputation for not being good custodians of their documents. At some schools, athletic department documents were simply pitched in the trash after their usefulness had passed. While researching this book, I discovered that countless documents were missing from university archives simply because they were never preserved. For example, there is a pronounced shortage of documents from major figures such as Eddie Cameron at Duke, North Carolina's Chuck Erickson, and Rex Enright at South Carolina, all of whom played significant roles in forming the ACC. The lack of many documents leaves countless questions unanswered.

Introduction

"It was a fast death. Practically painless, sharp, and clean. One big sudden sweep of the axe and the old bulky and unpractical 17-member Southern Conference died."[1] With those words, Bob Williams of the *Rocky Mount Evening Telegram* described the establishment of the Atlantic Coast Conference on May 8, 1953. For several years, the Southern Conference, an unwieldy grouping of 17 institutions over five states, struggled to maintain cohesion as the landscape of college athletics changed. Having endured significant internal turmoil, especially over bowl game participation and the growing commercialization and professionalization of collegiate sports, the conference fractured. The new league, not named until June 1953, included Clemson, Duke, Maryland, North Carolina, North Carolina State, South Carolina, and Wake Forest.[2] Virginia was admitted as the eighth member in December of 1953.

This was not the first split in the Southern Conference. In 1932, the league faced travel and competition issues that compelled 13 schools to withdraw and form the Southeastern Conference. These institutions, spread over seven states, wished for geographic cohesion and wanted to play more competitive games in a league that could anoint a clear champion on the football field.[3] With only 10 schools remaining in the Southern Conference, the league expanded in 1936, inviting six colleges, four of which were private and none of which had the athletic cachet of the institutions that left to form the SEC. Those six were The Citadel, Davidson, Furman, Richmond, Wake Forest, and William & Mary. In addition, their inclusion meant that the Southern Conference was an even more diverse association of state universities, military academies, and private institutions. There were significant differences in resources and athletic ambitions, with some schools well placed to compete on a national level. Likewise, there was a variety of opinion about the role of athletics on college campuses and the relationship between academics and athletics. The league's membership was unlike the Big Ten, the Southeastern Conference, or any of its other peer conferences.

The Southern Conference, never the most stable or united of organizations, began to show notable competitive division with the hiring of key figures who changed the paradigm of competition within the league. Historically, basketball was a sport without much distinction in the Southern Conference. Instead, it was seen as an urban game played at the highest levels mostly in northern cities, such as New York and Philadelphia. That view started to change in 1946, when Everett Case, an enormously successful Indiana high school coach, was hired at State College to change the athletic fortunes of Wolfpack basketball. Case's extraordinary success, including unparalleled dominance in the Southern Conference Tournament and the Dixie Classic, forced other schools, especially those in North Carolina's Big Four (Duke, North Carolina, State, and Wake

Forest), to develop their basketball programs to compete with Case. Gradually, this led to a recognizable split in the conference between those institutions that wanted to challenge State for basketball excellence and those not willing or able to take that step. There were exceptions, such as Furman and George Washington, but a distinction began to develop that was punctuated in the 1952–1953 season.

On the gridiron, it was Maryland's Jim Tatum, hired in 1947 to lead the Terrapins to football glory, who changed football's dynamics in the Southern Conference. Tatum transformed the Terrapins into a dominant and nationally recognized football team in the early 1950s, running roughshod over the Southern Conference and winning a national title. Tatum's success in the collegiate sport that was most popular in the region and in the country forced other schools to elevate their programs or be left behind. With football being an expensive sport with large numbers of players, it was difficult for smaller institutions to maintain a competitive balance. Maryland, therefore, separated itself from most of the conference members except for Duke and Clemson and staked a claim to big-time collegiate sports. Like Case at State, Tatum forced a reckoning. The successes enjoyed by both men compelled a reinterpretation of the role of college athletics on Southern Conference campuses. Some schools were willing to develop big-time athletic programs and others were not willing or did not have the resources to follow that path.

Complementary to coaches like Tatum and Case was a unique collection of administrative leaders and faculty members who realized that the Southern Conference no longer served their purposes. The league was notorious for division between larger and smaller schools, especially on issues such as freshman eligibility, recruiting, and scheduling. These disagreements hindered reform and inadvertently worked to enhance commercialism and professionalism. Furthermore, the divide held back schools that sought to play athletics at a higher level than some of their brethren. Leaders such as President Gordon Gray at North Carolina, Duke's president Hollis Edens, and President Harold Tribble at Wake Forest among others believed that they had an opportunity to stop corruption in collegiate sports, reform its sins, and place it in a proper relationship with academics. These goals could not be reached, they believed, in a 17-team league that featured institutions as different as The Citadel and the University of Maryland. In addition, they understood that they had an opportunity and an obligation to contain the evils of intercollegiate sports, in part by placing presidents and other academic leaders at the forefront of reform and even conference leadership. In its first years, the ACC would subscribe to academic leadership over league operations.

It is important to appreciate the political, economic, and social landscape of the early 1950s to understand why the new conference formed. Postwar American higher education, heavily influenced by the G.I. Bill and growing economic prosperity in the South, brought enormous changes in the early 1950s. State universities that were small in the 1930s, with many serving children of elites, became dynamic and growing campuses after World War II. Schools like South Carolina and North Carolina experienced significant enrollment gains in the years immediately after the war which brought a new crop of students to their campuses, compelling change in the traditional curriculum. Elitism was declining as the universities served larger and broader populations. Some returning veterans enjoyed athletic opportunities and made the most of them, bringing excellence to collegiate sports and winning large numbers of new fans. The level of athletic competition increased, and the public was attracted to collegiate sports in numbers never predicted. Indeed, collegiate sports grew in significance, in part because more southerners, many for the first time, had extra income to spend on entertainment. Heading to a ball game at Duke Stadium or Reynolds Coliseum, a cavernous and impressive venue for the time, became something that more people could do.

Adding to these changes was the growing prominence of the sports page in morning and evening newspapers. Newspapers covered college sports very closely and with great zeal, offering several pages of coverage each day and even more on Sunday. Sports columnists such as Bob Quincy of *The Charlotte News*, *The Greensboro Daily News*' Smith Barrier, Chauncey Durden of *The Richmond Times-Dispatch*, and *The State*'s Jake Penland among many others wrote engaging columns that generated devoted readers for newspapers while growing fan bases for colleges. Radio broadcasts of games and the emergence of television, which only broadcast a small slate of contests, forged additional emphasis on athletics. The growing interest in collegiate sports among the general public, including many who had no affiliation with any college, was a trend redefining the relationship between collegiate athletics and the public. Presidents, coaches, athletic directors, and faculty athletic representatives had to respond to these new pressures.

The drive to reform athletics, often through demands to de-emphasize them, felt more prescient than ever considering the scandal ridden collegiate sports landscape of the early 1950s. Point fixing and academic scandals placed pressure on administrators and faculty members to respond and ensure that their own houses were in order. The point-shaving scandals at City College of New York, the University of Kentucky, Long Island University, and other institutions captivated the nation and accelerated questions concerning the proper context of athletics at academic institutions. Gamblers understood that basketball was an easy game to fix and there were players willing to take money to adjust the point spread. Organized crime had infiltrated collegiate basketball, calling into question leadership on campus as well as whether games were being decided by honest play.

Likewise, the shocking cheating scandal at West Point in 1951 that ensnared the football team, followed by news of significant levels of academic dishonesty at William & Mary, a Southern Conference school, influenced leaders to respond to charges of academic dishonesty in college athletics. The country was surprised to learn that Red Blaik's Army team, a paragon of virtue and sportsmanship, had succumbed to academic dishonesty on a stunning level. If it could happen at Army, it was believed, it must be happening almost everywhere. When news of William & Mary's scandal erupted soon afterward, it appeared to be, again, confirmation that football was a corrupt game, tarnishing the mission and goals of academic institutions.

With scandal and corruption being discussed at home and work, the term "de-emphasis" became a lightning rod derided by some and praised by others. In some ways, the debate over the role of athletics at Southern Conference schools was a debate over maintaining or redefining the relationship between academics and athletics. Were the league schools willing to favor and support big-time athletics, or did they wish to refocus athletics in a strongly subordinate position to academics? Should colleges be in the entertainment business? Was a middle ground achievable? Could conference division be the method for reforming athletics? These and other questions formed part of the foundation for establishing a new league.

Like the adage that the Battle of Waterloo was won on the playing fields of Eton, there was a sense in the Southern Conference footprint that collegiate athletics were about far more than simply competition. They, in part, were about defeating the Soviets in the Cold War. Some coaches and some academic leaders believed that collegiate athletics, conducted in a proper environment, taught lessons that extolled American values and traditions. Football and basketball, in particular, were not simply sports but tools for separating capitalist American culture from the Soviet Union. The more fit Americans were and the more focus that was placed on winning, the stronger America could become, some maintained. Others, like football coach Bill Murray at Duke, did not focus on the international political aspect. Instead, he wanted to preserve sportsmanship and amateur competition, arguing that these elements were essential to building a better America. Sports, conducted properly, taught the proper lessons for young men to live better lives while exalting American virtues of hard work, teamwork, and sportsmanship, Murray and others believed. It was essential, then, for athletics to be a significant part of the college experience.

This is the story of how in the early 1950s a group of college presidents and professors, believing that they could control and limit professionalism and commercialism, joined hands with coaches and athletic directors, hoping to preserve and enhance athletics, to leave the Southern Conference and form the Atlantic Coast Conference. The establishment of the ACC came about via a perfect storm that combined forces that often opposed one another. Academic leaders and athletic leaders favored the new league for very different reasons that were, at times, in direct conflict with one another. The presidents, by and large, saw the league as a grand opportunity to control the commercialism and professionalism of collegiate sports while keeping college athletics subordinate to academic interests. The new league, therefore, included schools of generally like-minded approaches to athletics, concerned with maintaining athletics under the academic umbrella. Some athletic officials supported the new league for some of these reasons but for some contrary ones as well. Almost all athletic officials saw secession from the Southern Conference as necessary for the development of athletic programs. The Southern Conference was filled with too many schools of varying sizes and missions with a widely disparate commitment to athletics. The conference did not have the athletic consistency of the SEC or the Big Ten, conferences which, by and large, were composed of large state universities. By forming the new league, the seven schools separated themselves from others that did not have the resources or commitment to play college athletics at a national level. Coaches like Jim Tatum of Maryland, Clemson's Frank Howard, and South Carolina's Rex Enright understood that competing at a national level would be difficult in a conference that included small institutions like Davidson and Washington and Lee. With a small and unified league comprised of the larger Southern Conference schools, a legitimate football champion could be crowned, one that was clear and undisputed, and schedules would include teams of similar quality. Rivalries could be created and current ones intensified. Costs could be cut by the compact nature of the league, a very important component for coaches, athletic directors, and presidents. Furthermore, the new conference held the promise of gaining national stature, something that the Southern Conference could never fully achieve.

Apart from Maryland's president Curly Byrd and perhaps Clemson's Frank Poole, the leadership among the seven founding schools as well as at Virginia believed that they were forming a league that would preserve and grow what was best about college athletics while containing or even eliminating the ills that had plagued collegiate athletics since their founding. Administration and faculty as well as most of the athletic leadership at schools like Duke, North Carolina, North Carolina State, Virginia, and Wake Forest viewed the new league as a positive step for maintaining academic rigor in athletics. Forging a competitive balance while balancing the books was a popular concept as well, but reform, based on keeping athletes closely aligned with the overall student population, was a significant theme in the months and years prior to the league's establishment.

These leaders failed to fully achieve their goal, but they did take a step toward crafting a prominent and influential athletic league. Within only a few years, their views of the relationship between athletics and academics appeared quaint as the snowball of big-time athletics marched inexorably toward the commercialism and professionalism that we see today.

1

The Schools and Men Who Built a Conference

The Schools

The institutions that formed the Atlantic Coast Conference were almost as varied as those in the Southern Conference they left. The seven schools that seceded in 1953 included two religious institutions, three land grant universities, and two state universities that were among the oldest in the country. They resided in urban and rural areas and varied greatly in size, resources, and mission. The oldest, North Carolina, dated to 1789, and the youngest, Clemson, was founded in 1889, barely over 60 years old. Each of the schools had fielded athletic teams for decades, but their performances were as diverse as the institutions themselves.

The University of North Carolina received its first students in 1795, six years before the University of South Carolina was established. The Chapel Hill school played a significant role in the early development of North Carolina, and the institution grew rapidly in the 19th century, even with the disruption caused by the Civil War. Though North Carolina was a poor state, it enjoyed the luxury of a distinguished state university that became a leading American institution in the 20th century, breaking free from its regional identity. It had a long history of academic excellence and by the early 1950s was part of a three-campus consolidated system. In particular, the school was fortunate to have enjoyed strong and visionary leadership that helped place the institution within the mainstream of American higher education.

The second oldest institution was the University of South Carolina, originally known as South Carolina College. Founded in 1801, the Columbia institution was one of the finest schools in America, prior to the Civil War. The war and the state's poor economy afterward savaged the college, and it struggled to regain even a semblance of its pre–Civil War reputation, lagging far behind its northern neighbor in Chapel Hill. The school was not favored by state political leadership, and it clashed with a state government whose leadership often looked to the past and not the future. It was not until the end of World War II when South Carolina began to emerge as a major academic institution.

The two denominational-based institutions were Wake Forest and Duke. Wake Forest was established as a manual labor school in 1834 by Samuel Wait, during an era when Christian denominations had a fever for planting colleges. Founded to train Baptist ministers, Wake Forest Manual Institute, as the school was first called, remained small and financially challenged for much of its early development. Although it enjoyed support from alumni and North Carolina Baptists, Wake Forest grew slowly, barely surviving the Civil War. Even in the early 20th century the college maintained its focus on educating Baptist ministers, mostly for North Carolina. The school's trajectory changed forever when it accepted a lucrative financial offer from the Z. Smith Reynolds Foundation to relocate to Winston-Salem. On the surface, though, it appeared to be more like the smaller schools in the Southern Conference than one of the big players.

Following on the heels of Wake Forest, Methodists and Quakers in North Carolina established Union Institute in Randolph County in 1838. In 1851, the school was chartered by the state as Normal College and by 1859 it changed its name to Trinity. Like Wake Forest, Trinity struggled to craft a firm financial foundation, and its leaders believed that its rural location was a hindrance to its development. In 1892, Trinity left its Randolph County home for Durham and financial incentives offered by the City of Durham and Washington Duke, a tobacco magnate and lifelong Methodist. After receiving the Duke Endowment from James Buchanan Duke, Washington's son, the institution changed its name from Trinity to Duke. With financial resources the envy of almost all colleges, Duke quickly developed a national reputation, becoming the wealthiest and the most prestigious university in the Carolinas with nationally prominent undergraduate, graduate, and professional programs.

In nearby Raleigh, North Carolina College of Agriculture and Mechanic Arts, as today's North Carolina State University was first known, was one of the three land grant universities to be charter conference members. The school's founding in 1887 was influenced by young North Carolinians who were on the forefront of modernizing the state by embracing science and technology as a part of modern North Carolina. With this energetic and progressive thinking, State held its first classes in 1889, rapidly growing as a favorite institution for children of North Carolina farmers, but quickly expanding its footprint. Its commitment to agricultural education grew rapidly to include textiles, engineering, and the broader sciences, but it disliked being viewed as secondary to its sister campus in Chapel Hill. It would take years of strong leadership and numerous conflicts in state government for the school to gain the identity that it deserved.

Although State enjoyed growth in enrollment and reputation, it was plagued by problems with its name. When the conference was formed, the school went by the awkward name of North Carolina State College of Agriculture and Engineering of the University of North Carolina. There was a reason why almost everyone called it State College.[1]

In the same year when State's first students began attending classes, the state of South Carolina established Clemson Agricultural College. The institution was formed by a generous gift from Thomas Clemson, who left his estate to support the formation of a school dedicated to agricultural education. Different from its land grant neighbor to the North, Clemson was a military college, with enrollment in the corps of cadets mandatory until 1955. Clemson followed to the letter the Morrill Land Grant that mandated military training. The first students arrived in 1893 in the rural and remote campus in far western South Carolina. The school grew steadily, because of regular financial support from the state, but the military component, at times, deterred students from attending. Women were not allowed to matriculate until 1955, limiting enrollment as well. With membership in the cadet corps mandatory, very few veterans wished to attend Clemson under the G.I. Bill.

Perhaps it was appropriate that Maryland's flagship institution, the most northern of the schools, had origins that differed somewhat from its brethren. Charles Calvert, a planter and politician, wanted an institution, with a corps of cadets, to teach modern agricultural methods. In 1859, on the cusp of the Civil War, Maryland Agricultural College, located on land formerly owned by Calvert, began operation as a private institution. Maryland joined the land grant college ranks in 1864, two years after the Morrill Land Grant law was enacted. The school was rechartered as Maryland State College with the absorption of a number of professional schools that traced their ancestry to the founding of the Maryland College of Medicine in 1807. In 1920, the school was renamed the University of Maryland, a comprehensive institution that had been founded as an agricultural school but now housed extensive professional schools and graduate schools.

Although Maryland was a large university in the immediate postwar era, it had an inferiority complex. Neighboring schools such as the University of Virginia and the University of Pennsylvania gained more accolades. Maryland had grown rapidly but academics had been kept on a tight leash with significant financial investment going toward buildings and athletics.

The eighth ACC member that joined later in 1953 was the University of Virginia. The Charlottesville school held the distinction of being founded by Thomas Jefferson in 1819, but it did not enroll students until 1825. The former president took an exaggerated role in crafting the college, from choosing faculty to establishing curriculum. Before the Civil War, Virginia had a comprehensive curriculum and had carved an identity as one of the best schools in America. It continued to flourish in the early 20th century, but it was viewed as a college for the elite, not friendly to the rank-and-file Virginians. It enjoyed a strong faculty and an array of programs, similar to those found at North Carolina and Duke. Like Clemson, the school was all male, not allowing women as undergraduates on the Charlottesville campus until 1970. Prior to this change, women undergraduates attended Mary Washington College, the female undergraduate campus for the University of Virginia.

Athletically, these schools and the remainder of the Southern Conference were outside of the dominant collegiate sporting landscape. The towns and cities where these institutions resided, by and large, were small and did not have a large media presence. Only Maryland was close to a large city, and Washington was not a major American city in the early 1950s. Consequently, they did not receive the kind of attention that institutions like Ohio State, Michigan, Notre Dame, or even Ivy League schools garnered.

Only Maryland had an enrollment that approached the leading institutions in the Big Ten. It was by far the largest school, having increased its enrollment from 3,400 in 1935 to a whopping 15,700 in 1954.[2] Wake and Duke were small schools and the remaining state institutions had enrollments hovering around 5,000 or fewer. In addition, resources at these southern institutions, save Duke, lagged behind universities in more economically advanced states. The lingering effects of the Civil War and the Depression still were felt throughout the South.

The Southern Conference members were unlike their Southeastern Conference friends in many ways as well. The conference did not have an institution, except perhaps Duke, that enjoyed a long period of national success on the gridiron. They did not have football programs to compete with the ones found at Tennessee, Alabama, and Georgia Tech, for example. Southern Conference schools did not play many intersectional games, except for Duke, North Carolina, and Maryland. The only time other schools played intersectional contests was to balance the athletic department's budget by playing away games at large stadiums. The contests were not for prestige.

World War II

World War II brought enormous change to America's higher education landscape, and Southern Conference members were no exception. With young men entering the service, enrollments were badly harmed, especially institutions that were all male. In 1942, Wake Forest opened its doors to women students, in hopes of shoring up its staggering loss of male students. Although not a member of the Southern Conference, in Virginia's College of Arts and Sciences, enrollment plummeted 70 percent during the war.[3] Fortunately for athletics and academics, the United States Navy and the Marine Corps provided tremendous help. Their V-12 program, a consolidation of previous V-1 and V-7 training programs designed to train naval aviators, was a boon for college campuses as well as athletics, because participants in the programs were allowed to partake in campus activities, including athletics.[4] V-1 and V-7 reservists completed their degrees at their home institution, if it had a V-12 program. If not, they could transfer to a campus with one.[5] With the home institution heading the academic program for the Navy and students allowed to participate in athletics, strong teams could be constructed, even with the traditional male students having flocked to military service. The lenient transfer policies within the program allowed for the construction of powerful teams. Within the Southern Conference, V-12 programs were located at Duke, Virginia, North Carolina, Richmond, and South Carolina.

Wake Forest was an exception to the above schools in that it did not have a V-12 program. Instead, the Army Finance School occupied the campus from 1942 to 1944, very much helping the institution get through those difficult times. The federal assistance came at the right time, considering that Wake's enrollment levels dropped to numbers last seen in 1904.[6]

The V-12 program was a tremendous opportunity for players and coaches to share athletic experiences and game strategies. It allowed for outstanding athletes to continue competition and helped the game to evolve after the war. Good collegiate players often burnished their skills under a fine array of coaches from around the country. Schools without a V-12 program usually suffered mightily during the war years, often shuttering athletic programs, especially football. In 1941, there were 650 colleges and universities playing football. Two years later, the number had dropped to 167.[7] This was despite urgings for Americans to increase their fitness which often led to the strengthening of intramural programs. Young men were putting their education and their athletic ambitions on sabbatical in favor of wartime service.

Some schools within the Southern Conference eliminated athletic teams. Ten of its 16 schools continued to field athletic teams, but some of these had reduced the number of sports in which they competed.[8] Many coaches, Wallace Wade for example, were called into the ranks, placing further strains on athletic programs. In general, athletic programs were led by older coaches or those who were 4-F, medically unfit to serve.

Some institutions did not suffer from declines in enrollment. At North Carolina, for example, enrollment did not drop, but the traditional makeup of the student body changed. There was a surge in female students and military students. At nearby North

Carolina State, there were declines in enrollment, but there was a spike in female engineering students, complemented by servicemen as well. The wartime experience was different at each institution, but larger schools, in general, were able to manage the wartime challenges better than small institutions.

At some colleges, athletics, especially football, remained popular, even under wartime rationing restrictions. At Virginia, for example, football remained a draw, but the fans and players were different from the pre-war era. The team was dominated by men from NROTC and the V-12 Program while fans now consisted of older students and students who were very unfamiliar with the university and Charlottesville.[9] Many of the naval cadets knew precious little about the school and certainly were unfamiliar with university traditions.

The Japanese attack on Pearl Harbor significantly altered the football landscape in North Carolina by forcing the removal of the January 1942 Rose Bowl from Pasadena to Durham. Duke lost on a rainy afternoon, but never had the state of North Carolina received so much national attention for football. Although the war interrupted big-time college athletics, the Rose Bowl game signified that the Southern Conference could field teams that competed on a national level. As Duke Coach Wallace Wade went to war, he was the toast of the state.

Postwar Transformation

The end of the war and the passing of the G.I. Bill created an initial surge in enrollments, the reestablishment of athletic programs, and remarkable growth in academic programming. Many institutions were modernizing at a speed never envisioned. Part of the optimism that fueled change rested with the political and economic environment that had been altered by World War II. To a large extent, there was a sense of opportunity and optimism in southern states where the Civil War's legacy had been hard to shake.[10]

Around the country, many football and basketball programs featured large numbers of returning veterans, eager to take advantage of the G.I. Bill, while participating in athletics. Outstanding players such as Notre Dame's Johnny Lujack and Penn's Chuck Bednarik were only two examples of great postwar players who had served in World War II.

It was not surprising that North Carolina institutions in the early 1950s felt confident to embark on a new athletic conference while bidding goodbye to their long-term friends in the Southern Conference. Like many other states, World War II accelerated the modernization of the Tar Heel State, giving a strong boost to a transformation that had been slowly developing for several decades. When Governor W. Kerr Scott entered the Queen Anne–style governor's mansion in Raleigh in 1949, North Carolina was the leading industrial state in the Southeast, widely hailed for its New South economic dynamics. Although agriculture remained a dominant feature of the state's landscape and in many places tobacco ruled as it had for decades, the evolution to a more diversified economy based on good roads and good schools was progressing. North Carolina lagged in educational opportunities, especially the number of students attending college and economic opportunity in other parts of the country compelled people to leave.[11] Nevertheless, the state was charting a course that was separating itself from many of its southern neighbors. The "Rip van Winkle" state of the early 1800s was little found in growing cities like Charlotte, Raleigh, and Greensboro, as piedmont economic development gained the upper hand.

Governor Scott wasted no time inaugurating a program of reform called "Go Forward." This moniker may have sounded out of step coming from an Alamance County farmer who had graduated from State College with a degree in agriculture, but it was in line with his belief in modernizing the state. Scott appealed to the "everyman" in North Carolina, in part due to a homespun personality and in part due to his desire to elevate Tar Heels. He worked to increase electrification and telephone access while recognizing the need to provide women and African Americans with more opportunities.

Optimism abounded and the state legislature approved $200 million for road construction, an allotment desperately needed, especially in rural regions. School construction and renovation was driven by an increase in the gasoline tax, salaries for teachers increased, and the University of North Carolina opened the first dental school in the state.[12] Baptists were watching Wake Forest undertake an audacious and optimistic new direction by accepting a lucrative financial offer from the Reynolds Foundation to relocate their campus to Winston-Salem. Although most in the state opposed the federal government's order that UNC accept qualified African American applicants to their professional, graduate, and medical schools, integration was underway.

As much as North Carolina was emerging as a progressive state within the mainstream of the country, South Carolina remained more connected to its past. In many ways, the Palmetto State continued to be outside of mainstream America, preferring to continue its agricultural tradition at the expense of modernization. Charleston's Judge Julius Waring ruling in a 1947 civil rights case may have said it best, writing, "It is time for South Carolina to rejoin the union."[13]

Like North Carolina, World War II changed South Carolina, almost forcing it to emerge from a past in which it was so deeply mired. The Upstate of South Carolina was more industrious than other parts of the state, housing most of the state's industry, especially textiles. Textiles dominated cities like Spartanburg and Greenville which served as leading industrial centers, having more in common with textile centers in North Carolina than much of the Palmetto State. After many years of suffering, the Upstate had flourished during World War II, because textiles received guaranteed and lucrative contracts to equip the armed services. Featuring Fort Jackson, state government, and the state university, the city of Columbia had done well in World War II. Much of South Carolina, however, remained as it had been decades prior: rural and poor. Simply put, the state did not possess the New South vigor of its northern neighbor.[14]

Strom Thurmond was elected governor in 1947 and spent much of his time in the governor's mansion gaining leadership in the States' Rights Democratic Party and finding ways to extricate himself from the party after 1950. Thurmond dug in his heels in opposition to civil rights for African Americans, sometimes stating that it was a Trojan horse for communism. Thurmond's politics put South Carolina level with states of the deep South rather than some in the upper South.

The G.I Bill, as it was in many places, became one of the key engines for forcing change in the state's higher education policies. Although the University of South Carolina was a small institution, some state legislators hoped to lead South Carolina in a new direction of national prominence. In some ways like what was being discussed at Wake Forest and what had been done at Louisiana State in the 1920s, they proposed moving the university out of downtown Columbia to a suburban site of 1,200 acres. Although the plan failed to gain approval at the 11th hour, it indicated a new and creative way for thinking about improving the state university.[15]

Significant change was underway in many parts of Virginia, signaling progress and modernity, although sometimes it was hidden by Senator Harry Byrd's Organization that controlled Virginia politics. The previously sleepy capital of Washington, D.C., had expanded in the war with a significant overflow of development in Northern Virginia. In a few years after World War II, this region almost became unrecognizable from its past. The Tidewater saw remarkable economic development during World War II, especially in shipbuilding in and around the naval base at Norfolk. These two regions were separating themselves from many other parts of the state with their economic vitality.

Former governor and U.S. senator Harry Byrd remained the dominant force in Virginia politics in the 1950s, with very little of consequence happening in the state without his approval. Like Strom Thurmond in South Carolina, Byrd was an outspoken segregationist strongly opposed to school integration and a powerful voice against the modernization of the South. He was the architect of "massive resistance" to school and social integration, a position that strongly damaged the commonwealth. Virginia's governors, in the late 1940s and early 1950s, were anti-integration and did little to improve education or broadly speaking modernize the state. Even with powerful segregationist forces, the University of Virginia was required by a federal court to admit Gregory Swanson as a law student in 1950, thus compelling the school to accept small numbers of black students to graduate and professional schools. Change was coming, regardless of political intransigence.[16] This was not fully evident in the early 1950s, because the Byrd machine had dispatched all liberal challenges. Nevertheless, there were elements of change in the state that were inspired by Virginia's economic awakening.

At the University of Virginia, the postwar surge of students was remarkable for its size and pace. For the fall of 1946, enrollment was 40 percent higher than its previous peak which occurred in 1939.[17] Two-thirds of those enrolled had been fighting the Nazis and the Japanese one year earlier.[18] With a student body above 4,000 students, the university was a very different place that challenged the elitist notions of its pre-war days. The university's president, Colgate Darden, vowed to curtail Virginia's elitism and reliance on private school students, striving to make it more accessible to Virginians by encouraging the enrollment of students from more humble backgrounds.

Postwar Maryland focused enormous energy on infrastructure improvements, especially road construction, and education on all levels. The election of Theodore Roosevelt McKeldin as governor in 1951 symbolized energy and enthusiasm for Maryland's future. McKeldin was born to a working-class family and had worked his way through college and law school at the University of Maryland by diligence and perseverance. He symbolized American success and energy when he became governor. His unveiling of the Chesapeake Bay Bridge in 1952, a marvel of engineering, was a tangible indication of Maryland's future. As the state's population grew and Marylanders become more economically prosperous, McKeldin presided over the construction of new school buildings and the growth of a more affluent suburbia which became a significant trend for Washington and Baltimore. Infrastructure improvements, especially road building, became a symbol of a new and modern state. As Robert Brugger termed it, Maryland was now the "land of pleasant living."[19]

The ambitions of the University of Maryland appeared to reflect the broader feeling throughout the state. Maryland experienced an onslaught of veteran students like few other institutions. In 1946, 4,400 of Maryland's overall student population of 7,300 were veterans attending on the G.I. Bill.[20] These veteran students were changing the trajectory of the University of Maryland and the state.

Postwar political and economic developments in Maryland, North Carolina, and even South Carolina and Virginia influenced academic and athletic officials with a sense of optimism about the future. Even with old more conservative regimes clinging to power, academic leaders realized that their institutions had newfound opportunities for growth and development that would place them in the mainstream of American higher education. Their attitudes reflect what John Thelin and others have called "a golden age" for higher education.[21] Coaches and athletic administrators seized upon the same optimism, believing that their success on the court and the gridiron was a source of regional and institutional pride, critical to success in the postwar world.

The Leaders

Gordon Gray at North Carolina: The Reluctant President

In 1950, Gordon Gray assumed the presidency of the University of North Carolina, a position for which he believed he was not well suited. Gray's personal background in North Carolina associated him closely with the university in Chapel Hill as well as Wake Forest College, and he and the broader Gray family played a significant role in the fates of both institutions. Gordon Gray was the son of Bowman Gray, Sr., the president and chairman of the prosperous R.J. Reynolds Tobacco Company. Reynolds was a major economic engine for North Carolina, especially Winston-Salem, and a well-respected company. Its 21-story Art Deco headquarters in downtown Winston-Salem, a design on which the Empire State Building was based, was a testament to the company's strength and influence. Gray Sr., a man who started his career as a Wachovia bank teller, was a great philanthropist for the state but especially for his beloved Winston-Salem. His sudden and premature death of a heart attack in 1935 was a great shock and a tremendous loss to the community and the state. Gray Sr. passed away while on vacation cruising around Norway with his wife and two sons.[22] The family mantle passed to his eldest son, Gordon Gray.

Gray was born on May 30, 1909, in Baltimore. At the age of three, his family moved back to Winston-Salem to the impressive, Norman-styled Graylyn Estate where young Gordon grew up in wealth and luxury. He attended primary and middle school in the twin cities. Gordon was a dutiful young man when he entered Woodberry Forest in Virginia, where he excelled academically. Upon graduation, he enrolled at the University of North Carolina, where his father had attended for one year. Gray was a stellar student, serving as president of the Phi Beta Kappa chapter and graduating first in his class. With a Yale law degree in hand by 1933, Gray, after briefly practicing law in New York City, returned to Winston-Salem in 1935, in part to help take care of his mother. Following in his father's footsteps, he threw himself into public service. For two years, he was a lawyer in Manley, Hendren, and Womble, but the legal possession was unappealing to him.

Already a busy man, Gray married Jane Boyden Craige, a Vassar graduate, in 1938 at St. Paul's Episcopal Church in Winston-Salem. Eventually, they had four sons. A year earlier, the young Gray purchased the *Winston-Salem Journal* and the *Twin City Sentinel*, the latter the afternoon paper, for about $1 million. His media purchases also included WSJS radio in Winston-Salem which was owned and operated by the two newspapers. Never content, Gray was elected to the North Carolina Senate in 1939 and was reelected in 1941. He even found time to serve as president of the Winston-Salem Community Chest (Chamber of Commerce).[23]

At his death, Bowman Gray, Sr., left $750,000 in a trust to Winston-Salem to be used for a "charitable endeavor."[24] No one was certain how to spend this impressive gift. While considering an appropriate initiative for the money, there was an intensive, national movement to transform two-year medical schools into more comprehensive four-year programs. North Carolina and Wake Forest operated two-year schools, but both institutions realized that they needed to expand to four years as soon as possible, if their programs were going to remain nationally viable. Since 1923, Winston-Salem was home to North Carolina Baptist Hospital, but higher education opportunities were limited in the industrial town. Winston-Salem's civic leaders believed that the city needed a medical school to correspond with its hospital and UNC was first approached to move its medical school to Winston-Salem. With North Carolina's leadership not interested in relocating out of Chapel Hill, Wake Forest was approached. In August 1939, Wake Forest accepted the offer of $750,000 to move their medical school to Winston-Salem and transform it into a four-year degree program. Bowman Gray's funds allowed the school to open in 1941 at Baptist Hospital, a natural fit for the Baptist college. The new Bowman Gray School of Medicine was a major step forward for the manufacturing city of Winston-Salem and became a magnet for the Reynolds family to attract Wake Forest College to Winston-Salem. Gordon Gray was intimately involved in all these negotiations.

World War II interrupted Gray's life, as it did for millions of Americans. Gordon Gray began service in World War II as a private but ultimately attained the rank of captain, serving in Europe as part of the Twelfth Army Group. Returning to Winston-Salem after the war, Gray and his brother established two trusts of $125,000 each to support the establishment of neuropsychiatry and preventive medicine. Even though his Forsyth County constituents reelected Gray to the North Carolina Senate after the war, he was quickly tapped for service in the federal government. He was appointed assistant secretary of the Army in 1947, and two years later, Gray was promoted to secretary of the army, a post he began on June 29, 1949. On February 6, 1950, Gray left Washington and returned to Chapel Hill as the new president of the consolidated University of North Carolina System. Many in the administration hoped and believed that Gray would run a tight ship and straighten up Chapel Hill's operations. He was well known to the presidential search committee and had many friends among its members; however, he did not have the enthusiasm for the position or see himself as possessing the qualities of a college president. Gray's commitment to service, especially North Carolina, led the talented young administrator to accept the position. In 1951, Gray remarked to a friend, "This is a post which I did not seek or for which I did not see myself qualified and which I should be happy indeed to relinquish to someone else."[25] Duty had called Gray to the presidency, not excitement or enthusiasm for the presidency.

What also drove Gray's unrest in the president's office was that he remained involved in the federal government. When Gray had served only a year as president, Truman convinced him to become director of the Psychological Strategy Board, a unit that was charged with developing, on the basis of non-military Cold War issues, working relationships among the growing number of government agencies.[26] As a hard-core anti-communist who had associated union activity with communism, Gray was the popular selection for the task.

Gordon Gray was inaugurated president over three days on three campuses in October 1950. In Greensboro at the Woman's College of the University of North Carolina, Harold Tribble, the new president of Wake Forest College provided the sermon. Most likely, it was the first meeting between the two newly tapped presidents.[27] It is certain that neither man imagined that they and their institutions would play integral parts in establishing a new athletic league.

Gray was very much unlike his predecessor, Frank Porter Graham, affectionately known as Dr. Frank. Graham was an outspoken liberal and an advocate for social causes, who caused conservative North Carolinians to look upon him with suspicion. He used his voice as president to influence North Carolina to adopt more progressive views and policies and saw the university's role as essential to modernizing the state and strengthening its educational system. Graham, furthermore, was not detail oriented, operated an unorganized office, and depended heavily upon a few important staff members like William "Billy" Carmichael. He often relied on his gut feeling and his great popularity and engaging personality. Most people thoroughly enjoyed Frank Graham's company, even though he was often out of step with state politics. Students adored him and enjoyed visiting with him in his house on Sunday evenings. He was a man known for compassion and good will.[28]

In contrast, Gray was a serious man, not prone to joking or laughing, and he ran a very tight ship. Gray believed the university needed a more corporate structure and a strong bureaucracy. Although he was an accomplished man, he was difficult to know and never felt comfortable as a university president. Policy

Gordon Gray (shown here in 1951), president of the Consolidated University of North Carolina, eagerly sought reform in college athletics (courtesy North Carolina Collection Photographic Archives, Wilson Library, University of North Carolina at Chapel Hill).

and detail were important to Gray and were hallmarks of his presidency. An ardent anti-communist and anti-unionist, the new president was not keen to promote any causes deemed radical or outside of the mainstream.[29] He could never see himself leading progressive causes like Graham.

This is not to say that Gray was a man of stone. He was a good man but a private one. He was formal but not uncaring. Bill Friday, Gray's closest advisor and later president of the North Carolina system, spoke glowingly of Gray as a person and as an administrator.[30] The death of his wife in 1953, at the young age of 39, was a terrific blow to him. The pair had four sons and the weight of raising the boys without their mother descended upon him.

Essentially, Gray would have been more comfortable in the Northeast than in postwar North Carolina, but his family had contributed much to the state that called him for service. Gray lived in aristocratic circles, having relationships with the most prominent families in North Carolina. He was never a man of the people and that did not bother him as long as he had figures like Bill Friday to run interference for him. In this manner, he contrasted mightily with Bob House, the chancellor in Chapel Hill.

Over his years as president, Gray depended more and more on Bill Friday for assistance, a man at home at country stores or in boardrooms. Gradually, Gray realized that he needed Friday to soften him and provide some homespun charm that was still very much required in early postwar North Carolina.

Gray inherited leadership over the consolidated University of North Carolina system. The consolidation took place in 1931, and included the Chapel Hill campus, North Carolina State College of Agriculture and Engineering (known as State College to most people), and the Woman's College of the University of North Carolina.[31] Each of these universities maintained a chancellor who served under the leadership of Gordon Gray. This was a large and complicated organization that greatly influenced the politics of the state. Leading it effectively was a tall order for anyone, including Gray.

Robert Burton House: A North Carolina Favorite

Many of the leading figures in the Southern Conference and in the early years of the Atlantic Coast Conference were from small, rural spots and Robert Burton "Bob" House was no different. He was a native of Thelma, North Carolina, a tiny community in rural Halifax County. House, raised a Methodist, graduated North Carolina in 1916 and Harvard the following year with a master's degree. He spent World War I as an army infantry lieutenant in a machine gun company in France before returning to North Carolina as an archivist for the North Carolina Historical Commission in 1919, quickly rising to the post of executive secretary. In 1926, House returned to the Chapel Hill campus as executive secretary for the university, a complex job that involved him in many aspects of university life. From 1934 to 1945, House was dean of administration at the University of North Carolina, working closely with President Graham.

Bob House, while serving as dean of administration, prior to the position being renamed chancellor in 1945, was a great complement to Frank Graham. As mentioned, Dr. Frank did not concern himself with the minutiae of policy implementation or even the daily operation of the campus. Those duties fell to House. Fortunately for Graham, he had House leading the Chapel Hill campus. From 1945 to 1957, House was chancellor of the University of North Carolina, the first person to hold that position. He handled the details of policy implementation and the daily operation of the campus, and in those duties Graham trusted him completely. House was a popular and trusted administrator, possessing calmness and a keen intellect; he was an immensely popular figure at the university.[32]

The harmonica-playing and pipe-smoking House was a well-liked, some may say adored, figure on and off campus and often invited to speak around the state. He had an engaging personality, and all enjoyed his grand sense of humor. He was such a good speaker that Gordon Gray and Frank Graham used him to warm up audiences for them. When examining his correspondence, it is easy to see that House loved jokes and was ready to pen a funny or ironic line whenever he could. House was popular with students and always wore a smile on his face. His rural upbringing in a poor North Carolina county influenced him a great deal throughout his life, from his literary output to his desire to expand the curriculum at UNC to help serve the interests of the citizenry. Many North Carolinians identified with House's rural childhood and saw within him an inspiration for their children to attend the university and perform well in the classroom.

Very unlike Gordon Gray, House relished his job and held an unbridled affection for the Chapel Hill campus that started when he was a freshman in 1912.[33] Becoming the first chancellor of the Chapel Hill campus was a crowning achievement, but House, along with Billy Carmichael, the university's controller, operated much of the university's day to day affairs for years while President Graham was more deeply involved in larger issues.[34]

Bob House oversaw enormous changes to the Chapel Hill campus, from a healthy increase in enrollment to the expansion of the medical school from two years to four years. Furthermore, he unveiled a building campaign that erected structures like Morehead Planetarium and new dormitories. He even presided over the federally mandated but tension-filled admission of four African American law students to the school of law in 1951. All of this was underscored by a genuine belief that the university was a beacon for the state and was an institution that needed to serve the state's citizens as best as it could.[35]

Regarding football and athletics in general, House had a moderate to positive opinion of its role on college campuses. House called recruiting "very much out of control," but he had "no criticism of the public's interest in this spectator sport, and certainly the institution benefits so long as this public enthusiasm is not misguided or betrayed by an institutional betrayal of its responsibility primarily for the welfare of the athlete as a student."[36] House believed that football was "educative" and credited it with a very useful public relations role as well as important to student morale. He even admitted that it could play a part in developing morality, but House believed that the current state of collegiate football did not do much for cultivating moral behavior.[37] Like most academic leaders, his attention was on preserving and encouraging the athlete's academic welfare, placing him within the mainstream of many of the academic leaders that founded the new league.

Colonel John W. Harrelson: A State Man

Another native of rural North Carolina was House's colleague at State College, John W. Harrelson. A Cleveland County native, from the Double Shoals community,

Harrelson graduated from State, a very young institution at the time, at the top of his class with a mechanical engineering degree in 1909. Growing up near the Double Shoals Cotton Mill may have influenced the young Harrelson to study engineering. After graduation, Harrelson accepted a math professorship at State and completed his master's in mechanical engineering in 1915. Ultimately, Harrelson was promoted to professor of mathematics at his alma mater. Meanwhile, Harrelson embarked on a lifelong military career. His first service was as a lieutenant in the coast artillery of the North Carolina National Guard. Like so many men of his generation, Harrelson served in World War I, spending much of his times as a general staff officer in Washington, D.C. Soon after the end of World War I, he was promoted to lieutenant colonel and remained a part of the military for the rest of his life, reaching the rank of colonel. Many on the campus simply called him "The Colonel."[38]

With solid managerial experience, Harrelson's star rose quickly. When he returned to State after World War I, he remained at the university, except for four years leading the North Carolina Department of Conservation and Development. In 1934, Harrelson was named dean of administration, an odd title that required its holder to conduct duties of a chancellor. He succeeded Eugene Clyde Brooks, a post he had held since 1923. Harrelson was a welcomed selection, and he became the first State graduate to lead the Raleigh school.

Harrelson's position was difficult and required a man of tact and skill. It was hard to coordinate the operation of three campuses under one university-wide system, and at this time State often was considered secondary to Chapel Hill. State's loyalists were deeply annoyed by Chapel Hill's financial dominance and how it perceived State as a "little brother," a condescending view that even was present in the state legislature. Assuming leadership of the agricultural college in the middle of the Great Depression was a challenging task as well. State's budget was very tight and there was precious little money available to develop the school's academics or its facilities. After World War II, Harrelson was an enthusiastic supporter of a new State College that welcomed veterans in large numbers. New housing and new classroom facilities were constructed, and a building boon reached the Raleigh campus.

One of the great achievements of Harrelson's time in office was the building of the first nuclear reactor planned, constructed, and operated by a university. The R-1 reactor began operation in 1953, after four years of planning and development. Although it was controversial for some North Carolinians, the reactor was a symbol of State's emergence as a modern and important research university.[39] State had bested Chapel Hill, and the reactor was a symbol of the school's independence from North Carolina's traditional dominance. There was no question that the Raleigh school had ambitions to be a leading national university, and Harrelson had helped position the school in that manner.

Hollis Edens: The Unconventional President

Thirty miles from Raleigh, Hollis Edens came to Duke with an unconventional background and in an unconventional manner. The son of a Methodist minister, Edens was born in Willow Grove, Tennessee, but was reared in Clay County, Tennessee, along the border with Kentucky. He was another son of the rural South. As a youth and as a young man, Edens had much experience with hard labor working as a lumberjack and in an Akron rubber plant. He even had found time to minister at several churches when he was not delivering mail. Edens graduated Emory University at the age of 29, having earlier served as a teacher and principal at Cumberland Mountain School. He remained at the school until 1937, when he became associate dean at Emory Junior College in Valdosta, Georgia. This was his first foray into higher education administration. Even without a Ph.D., Edens' talent for administration was quickly identified and he enjoyed a meteoric rise. In 1942, he moved to Atlanta, accepting the position as associate dean of the Emory undergraduate college. Two years later, Edens was associate professor of political science. Again, he was drawn to administration, being named dean of administration at Emory. In 1947, Edens became vice chancellor of the Georgia university system while the following year he was named associate director of the Rockefeller Foundation's General Education Board.

With his great success, Duke wanted Edens for its next president, but his lack of a Ph.D. was an issue for many professors. Edens, who held a master's from Emory and Harvard, finished his dissertation and graduated Harvard in 1949 with a doctorate in public administration. He now had the credential to lead Duke University. It had been an unlikely rise to prominence for a son of rural Tennessee, but he was a very good fit for Duke.

During his inaugural address, Edens made clear his positions on education. He praised educational advancements in the South and urged for greater educational

Pictured in the 1950s with his Gothic campus behind him, Duke's president Hollis Edens was a strong voice for reforming college athletics (courtesy A. Hollis Edens Collection, David M. Rubenstein Rare Book and Manuscript Library, Duke University).

opportunities and an expansion of research in the region. He cautioned about the dangers of too much government sponsored research, fearing that it would hinder more broad-ranging and far-reaching research. Like so many other educational leaders, Edens attacked communism as the enemy of freedom of inquiry and accused it of being a stifling ideology.[40] In 1953, Edens, Virginia's Colgate Darden, and Gordon Gray signed an Association of American Universities statement banning the employment of communists as faculty members, stating that it was incompatible with the values of American universities.[41]

Edens was a tall man with a personality that most found very pleasing. He did not have the presence of a Bob House and was not going to impress a large audience with after dinner remarks, but he was a caring and compassionate man, who had a calm maturity about him. Edens did not chase headlines, but he was driven by a deep desire to improve the educational experience at Duke. Edens was a quiet visionary and like Dr. Frank at UNC a man not inclined to focus on details.[42] Nonetheless, his human touch was critical to his leadership success, and for several years, served him well in Durham.[43] Edens was a conservative leader, not prone to rash decisions, who was a good fit for a very conservative board. He was the right man to lead Duke in the post-war period.

Curly Byrd: Maryland's Architect

Harold C. "Curly" Byrd deserved his nickname.[44] The tall, handsome Byrd, with his black curly hair that turned a brilliant gray as he aged, was a dominant force from childhood. Born in 1889 and growing up in Crisfield, Maryland, a small town on the Chesapeake Bay along Maryland's Eastern Shore, the young Byrd worked with his father in the oyster industry while starring as a baseball player at Crisfield High School. He left Crisfield for College Park and entered the college in 1905 at 16.

Attending Maryland Agricultural College as the modern University of Maryland was then known, Byrd quickly established himself as an accomplished athlete in track and baseball, but especially on the football field. On his first day at football practice, in his first year at Maryland, it looked as if Byrd's playing career had ended before it began. Trying out for the football team and in line to receive his football gear, the 139-pound Byrd was sent away by Coach Frederick Nielson for being too small to play. Byrd responded by purchasing second hand gear and a new jersey, eager to dispense with the notion that he was not big enough for the team. He attended a later practice in his full kit, looking much larger than his height and weight denoted. Soon, the young man was first string for the Terrapins.[45] Perhaps more telling about Byrd was that he played in the same pair of used pants throughout his gridiron career.[46]

Byrd majored in civil engineering and graduated second in his class before going to graduate school where athletes usually could persist with athletics. Ringers were a common part of college football in its early days, and most schools had few rules about eligibility. While studying at Georgetown, George Washington and Western Maryland College, Byrd continued to participate in athletics. He even was an accomplished baseball player who had an opportunity to play for the Chicago White Sox. Because of his athletic ability and perseverance, Byrd, most likely, would have starred in professional baseball, if he desired.

Byrd was hired by Maryland in 1913 to teach English and physical culture, but it was in sports that he earned his reputation. He coached baseball, track, and football and served as athletic director on many occasions. It was apparent to almost everyone he met that he had tremendous leadership skills and a unique love for his alma mater. He exuded confidence and dominated gatherings. It was hard to take your eyes off such an imposing man. Maryland's administration put his stature and his leadership skills to use years before he became president. Byrd, for example, was a substantial figure in helping Maryland increase its funding from Annapolis to modernize the College Park campus.[47]

Byrd led the Terrapins to a 119–82–15 record in football, coaching his final season in 1934, but Byrd's vision for the school went far beyond football. He saw a distinguished future for Maryland, stepping beyond its agricultural roots. He had supported the creation of the University of Maryland, a consolidation of the Agricultural College and the professional schools under one umbrella, which was established in 1920. It was a significant step in elevating the reputation of the rather undistinguished College Park institution. Byrd was a powerful advocate for Maryland's membership in the Southern Conference, joining the league in 1922. He developed strong relationships with the more dominant schools within the league. He became acting president of the University of Maryland in 1935 and president the following year, holding this position until 1954, when he sought an ill-advised move into politics.

No one has influenced a college campus more than Curly Byrd. Essentially, he created the modern University of Maryland, building a large chunk of the campus, expanding enrollment, developing, and deepening academic programs, as well as improving athletics. A staunch segregationist, Byrd fought against integration while leading Maryland's enrollment growth that made it the largest university in the Southern Conference. Faculty were not terribly important to Byrd and were seen as interchangeable cogs. But buildings and athletic success were major parts of Byrd's plan to elevate the university from a small agricultural college with little distinction to a modern university with a national reputation for excellence. Under his leadership, the campus constructed 23 major buildings and 18 dormitories.[48] Rarely has a figure left such an impressive stamp on a university.

Always a supporter of Terrapin football, President Curly Byrd (shown here in the 1950s) transformed the University of Maryland into a modern university (courtesy University Archives, AlbUM, University of Maryland).

By 1950, everyone had an opinion about Byrd. Some saw him as an authoritarian, a dictator of sorts, while others viewed him as a visionary and an effective campus leader. All understood that Byrd was a political genius who crafted miraculous deals in Annapolis and Washington to have buildings constructed on the campus or programs and research funded. No one questioned his ability to influence politicians and donors to support causes at Maryland. And no one doubted his devotion to Maryland football and the athletic program in general. Otherwise, opinions varied throughout the state and beyond.

After Byrd resigned from the presidency, *Harper's Magazine* published a blistering assault on Byrd's tenure. Drawing from a report completed by the Middle States Association of Colleges and Secondary Schools that was released in 1954, the magazine savaged Maryland's president. The report criticized Byrd's "dictatorship" and the exclusion of faculty from administrative decision-making. They criticized low faculty salaries and a pitiful library that could only seat 305 students. In contrast, Maryland had one of the finest football stadiums in the nation. Its athletes received generous scholarships that totaled 54 percent of all scholarships awarded at the school.[49] This was the type of criticism that was consistently leveled against Byrd, especially in the era of Maryland's greatest gridiron successes.

As a former football coach, Maryland's football fortunes were close to Byrd's heart. Byrd Stadium, his namesake which opened in 1950, was a tangible reminder of his desire to have winning athletics.[50] The Terrapins did not field terrible football teams, but there was a lack of consistent winning and too many losing seasons. The program needed long-term successful coaching. In 1947, Byrd had seen enough heartbreak and disappointment when he turned to Jim Tatum to lead the Terrapins. That decision forever changed the fortunes of the Southern Conference.

Harold Tribble: The Man Who Made Wake Forest

Sometimes it is good for the first choice to turn down a job. Dr. Harold Tribble was not the first choice to replace Thurman D. Kitchen as president of Wake Forest College in 1950. The board of trustees wanted George Modlin, president of the University of Richmond, but he rejected the offer, choosing to remain at his Baptist college in Virginia. Modlin had only been president for four years when he was approached to relocate to North Carolina. Most likely, the removal of the college to Winston-Salem, a herculean task that inevitably would leave hurt feelings, was too much for his liking.

The second choice was Harold Wayland Tribble. Although well known in Southern Baptist circles, Tribble was following Thurman Kitchen, an institution in North Carolina and at the Baptist college where he had served as president for 20 years. A native of Scotland Neck, North Carolina, Kitchen was a Wake alumnus who earned a medical degree from Jefferson Medical School in Philadelphia. In 1930, Kitchen's selection as president had not been a popular choice among some Baptists and some faculty at Wake Forest. Although the Kitchen family was influential in North Carolina, he was a medical doctor and not known as a devout religious leader. Many questioned his liberal arts acumen, predicting trouble for the humanities. Kitchen, however, was devoted to his alma mater and a good politician and administrator.

Tribble was cut of different cloth. He was a highly educated Baptist minister deeply immersed in Christian theology and the liberal arts. Tribble's father, Henry Wise

Tribble, was a Baptist minister and president of the all-female Rawlings College when Harold was born. Harold's formative years were spent in Lake City, Florida, where his father served as president of Columbia College. After two years at his father's institution, he transferred to Richmond College, later the University of Richmond, graduating in 1919. Interestingly, Tribble, who often was accused of being opposed to college athletics, played basketball at Richmond. He could have never imagined the role collegiate sports would play in his later life.

Tribble was ordained a Baptist minister in 1919 and matriculated at Southern Baptist Theological Seminary where he earned a Th.M. and a Th.D., graduating summa cum laude. He served as a professor at Southern from 1925 until 1947, educating a generation of Baptist ministers. Later, he earned a M.A. in philosophy from the University of Louisville before embarking on extensive study abroad at the University of Edinburgh, where he earned a Ph.D., the University of Bonn, and the University of Basel. Tribble had the distinction of studying with famed theologian Karl Barth, arguably the most influential religious thinker of the 20th century.[51]

Christianity was woven into Tribble's being. Throughout the 1930s and 1940s, he was an active minister, and a popular speaker. In 1947, Tribble made a significant change in his life, moving from Louisville, Kentucky, to Newton, Massachusetts, to become president of Andover Newton Theological School.[52] Three years later, he was president of Wake Forest College with a daunting task in front of him. Tribble was hired to move the college from the small town of Wake Forest to Winston-Salem. Furthermore, he was charged with elevating the college's reputation through proper management of the Reynolds family gifts. These were enormous duties, making it easy to appreciate why Modlin declined the job. Rarely has a new president faced the type of significant tasks that Tribble tackled.

The announcement of Tribble as president was met with enormous praise from Baptist ministers and laypeople. Ministers were happy that the new president was an ordained minister while many others were deeply impressed by Tribble's powerful academic credentials.[53] Advocates of the liberal arts believed they had a great ally and friend in the president's office.

At Tribble's inauguration, Gordon Gray, the new president of the consolidated University of North Carolina system, provided a warm welcome and greeting, full of praise for the Baptist school as well as Tribble.[54] Gray was well acquainted with the role Wake Forest was playing in drastically altering his hometown. The two men had had two opportunities in 1950 to get to know one another better, both involving their presidential inaugurations.

With the medical school in Winston-Salem, the Reynolds family had seen an opportunity to attract the college, which always seemed short of money, to one of the burgeoning industrial cities in the South. The Z. Smith Reynolds Foundation offered the college a package that it could not reject, no matter how painful the initial move would be. Wake Forest's economic pressures, almost endemic to the school for over 100 years, would be relieved with a new campus of 14 buildings constructed on land donated by Mary Reynolds Babcock. When Tribble accepted the presidency, he realized that he was walking into a divisive environment with not all convinced that the move to Winston-Salem was a good idea. It demonstrated the mettle of the man that he successfully relocated the school as painlessly as possible while elevating it to levels of prominence it had never known.

Wake Forest president Harold Tribble, standing before a model of the new Georgian-styled Winston-Salem campus (likely in 1950 or 1951), believed college athletics had grown beyond their proper place on a college campus (courtesy University Archives Photographic Collection [RG 10.1], Special Collections & Archives, Z. Smith Reynolds Library, Wake Forest University).

R.F. Poole: Clemson's Athletic Advocate

Frank Poole, known to many as "Sarge," loved Clemson athletics, and he never shied away from it. A native of tiny Gray Court in Laurens County, South Carolina, Robert Franklin "Frank" Poole was born December 2, 1893. As a young man, he matriculated at Clemson graduating in 1916. He served in World War I as an aerial photographer, specializing in examining aerial photography, a field in its infancy. He served in France and in postwar Germany as a sergeant in the United States Expeditionary Force. After Poole's military service, he matriculated at Rutgers, earning a Ph.D. in plant pathology in 1921. In 1926, Poole joined the faculty at North Carolina State where he worked in plant diseases and served as an associate professor. Poole remained at State until he accepted the Clemson presidency in 1940.

Although State and Clemson were founded as agricultural training schools, they were very different institutions. He left urban Raleigh for rural Clemson and a co-educational school for a military campus. The distinction of returning to South Carolina to lead his alma mater and becoming the first Clemson graduate to lead the institution must have been a strong incentive to leave North Carolina's capital city.

Poole was a popular figure on the campus, navigating the university beyond the difficult years of the Depression. Students were very fond of him, and he worked well with the school's board of trustees. Under Poole's presidency, the foundation for Memorial Stadium was begun, emphasizing Clemson's desire to develop its football program, but he also began the process of modernizing the college, emphasizing the hiring of talented and respected faculty members. Clemson received few returning veterans under the G.I. Bill, and the school's enrollment declined after World War II, forcing Poole to lead Clemson toward radical change. Those changes were ending mandatory membership in the cadet corps and admitting women, both instituted in 1955. In some ways, Poole was responsible for fueling what became the modern Clemson University.

Poole had played football at Clemson and held a deep affection for the game, like his predecessor. Although he chose not to have a heavy-handed role in football, his experience on the gridiron as well as his fondness for sports made him a natural ally with Curly Byrd.

Norman M. Smith: Wrong President, Wrong Time

The least popular president involved in the founding of the new league was in Columbia, SC, at the University of South Carolina. Born in Williston, South Carolina, in 1883, Norman Murray Smith followed the very popular James Rion McKissick in 1945.[55] Smith was raised in rural Barnwell County, and attended the U.S. Naval Academy. Later, he graduated Rensselaer Polytechnic in 1909 studying civil engineering. Pursuing a naval career, Smith rose to prominence as the chief civil engineer in the Navy. Retired Rear Admiral Norman Smith was chosen mainly because there were plans in place to remove the university from downtown Columbia, its location since 1801, to a more suburban setting near the Veterans Hospital several miles from the inner-city Columbia campus. It was believed that Smith had the organizational skills and government connections to make the relocation happen.[56] Smith, however, did not enjoy ringing endorsements. According to board member Sol Blatt, Secretary of State Jimmy Byrnes as well as Governor Olin Johnston had called Smith "all right" and little more. In a later interview after Smith's death, Blatt, when speaking about Smith, bluntly remarked, "He could not do the job."[57]

Smith started on the back foot. He was not a gregarious person, being very direct and serious. As historian Dan Hollis commented, Smith was completely honest and hardworking, but never adjusted to the academic environment, having numerous problems with students and faculty.[58] Meanwhile, the G.I. Bill quickly transformed the university as former troops flocked to Columbia. Smith, however, was not popular with the students, in part because many wanted to separate themselves from anyone associated with the military. Smith stepped down in 1952, with the board of trustees having enough votes to remove him from office. After a two-month interim regime under longtime dean Francis W. Bradley, an enormously popular and respected figure at the university, Donald Russell assumed the presidency. Ironically, Bradley was responsible for allowing Russell to matriculate at South Carolina in the 1920s, an action that led to Russell assuming the presidency decades later.

Colgate Darden: Governor and President

Colgate Darden never wanted Virginia in the ACC, and he caused the league a fair amount of anxiety in its first few months of existence. Darden was an important figure in Virginia politics when he assumed the presidency of the state's flagship university. Colgate

Whitehead Darden, Jr., was a Virginia native, growing up in Southampton County in the southeastern part of Virginia that adjoined North Carolina. He graduated Virginia in 1922, but he began his career at the university in 1914. Service in World War I interrupted his studies. With war raging in Europe, Darden with two friends, Douglas Bolling and Clark "Plug" Lindsey, teamed up with Bobby Gooch, a UVA Rhodes Scholar, to join the American Ambulance Service. There was no delay in getting into the action, because Darden found himself sent to Verdun.[59] Later, Darden became a U.S. Navy pilot and a lieutenant in the United States Marine Corps. Darden completed his law degree at Columbia University in 1923, after spending time at Oxford, having won a Carnegie Fellowship in International Law. The young man returned to Virginia as a worldly fellow with a good understanding of international and national politics. As a young lawyer in Norfolk, he rapidly embarked on a political career. After serving in the Virginia legislature, Darden quickly moved to the U.S. House of Representatives in the later 1930s, becoming governor of the commonwealth in 1942. As the wartime governor, Darden spent most of his energies modernizing the commonwealth's infrastructure and improving education and access to higher education. Many parts of Virginia, like other southern states, faced crushing poverty and feeble educational opportunities. Darden's time in office helped begin the process of moving Virginia beyond its Civil War past. Although knowing that some faculty would have reservations about a politician becoming the third president of the University of Virginia, he happily and eagerly assumed the presidency of UVA in 1946. It is likely that Darden turned his back on a Senate career to take the position in Charlottesville, but the former governor believed that he could develop the traditionally elitist Virginia into a university that would attract a broader array of students.[60]

Although a Virginia alumnus, his view of the school was colored by his previous state-wide service. The new president was determined to destroy the private club mentality at the school and replace it with the understanding that it was a university open to a greater number of Virginians, especially those who did not attend private schools. In addition, Darden, as governor, had fought for all commonwealth schools and was devoted to serving his native state. Now, he was representing a single university, but it was the most significant educational institution in the commonwealth. Nonetheless, many of his views on academics and athletics at UVA were influenced by the desire for all Virginia colleges to flourish.

There was concern from students and faculty alike about how a Darden presidency would change the institution. His lack of academic background and alleged opposition to fraternities caused him some initial problems. But it was not long into Darden's presidency when college athletics emerged as an enormous issue for his university. Darden was not an enemy of athletics; instead, he believed that it should be placed subservient to the university's academic mission. He would wrestle with this issue throughout his tenure in Charlottesville.

Coaches and Directors

Jim Tatum: Football's Voice

Sunny Jim or Big Jim—no matter what he was called, James Moore "Jim" Tatum was a leader in forging the new conference. On the football field, he transformed Maryland football, taking the Terrapins to a level of achievement that fans had never imagined possible. Tatum hailed from the little town of McColl, South Carolina, a remote place between Laurinburg, North Carolina, and Bennettsville, South Carolina, on the border between the two states. A high school star, Tatum, a giant of a man for the time, joined the football program at North Carolina, quickly becoming a star tackle. He helped bring winning to Kenan Stadium, along with his teammate George Barclay, who later coached the Tar Heels. When Coach Carl Snavely left North Carolina for Cornell in 1936, Tatum, having graduated North Carolina, followed as an assistant on his staff. Under Snavely, Tatum learned how to coach and how to win. The Tar Heel state, however, was never far away from Tatum—his wife was from North Carolina—and he returned to Chapel Hill as an assistant coach from 1939 to 1941. He received the opportunity to lead the Tar Heels for the 1942 season, guiding the team to a 5-2-2 record, before his military service began. Until joining the Navy in World War II, Tatum, like Wake Forest's Coach Peahead Walker, spent summers playing minor league baseball with Tarboro and Snow Hill of the Coastal Plain League. This was a rather common endeavor for coaches needing to make a little extra money during the off-season.

During World War II at Iowa Pre-Flight, Tatum had the career-changing opportunity to learn the split-T offense from its originator, Missouri's Don Faurot. A Mountain Grove, Missouri, native who spent almost his entire college and professional life at the University of Missouri, Faurot was a great offensive innovator as well as one of the most likable and highly regarded coaches in college football history. Out of necessity, Faurot unleashed the split-T against a far more powerful Ohio State squad in 1941. Although Missouri lost the contest, Faurot had pioneered a new offense destined to become one of the most dominant offenses in football. Using the split-T, Faurot's Missouri Tigers won the 1941 and 1942 Bix Six championships.[61] Young Jim Tatum was anxious to learn this new and effective option offense from Faurot when both were assigned to Iowa Pre-Flight School in 1943. Faurot did not disappoint, leading the military squad to a 9–1 record, while providing Tatum with an education.[62]

After a stint at Jacksonville Pre-Flight, Tatum found himself in Norman, Oklahoma, in January 1946, leading the Sooners with the yet-to-be-great Bud Wilkinson as an assistant and Darrell Royall, the future illustrious Texas head coach, at quarterback. His first and only squad at Oklahoma was filled with ex-servicemen, making for a very fit and mature team. Tatum went 8–3 in a tumultuous stint on the plains where he garnered a great deal of attention by flaunting all traditional standards for recruiting, tryouts, and out of season practices. Tatum finished the year with a Gator Bowl victory over State's Wolfpack. Highlighting the year, the Sooners demolished Oklahoma A&M, their biggest rival, by 61 points with a final score of 73–12. But Tatum had made countless enemies in Norman. He ran a financial deficit that reached $113,000 and was alleged to have paid players.[63] According to Buddy Burris, Tatum had distributed clothing coupons and money to players when they were at the Gator Bowl.[64] Oklahoma's administration was almost apoplectic from Big Jim's habits and was happy to see his car leave Norman, Oklahoma, for good.

Tatum had spent only one season in Norman before moving to Maryland in 1947 where President Curly Byrd was anxious to field consistent winning teams, as part of his plan for making Maryland a powerful, national institution. Byrd had experienced a falling out with Bear Bryant who only coached the Terps for the 1945 season. Bryant did not like Byrd's micro-management of the football program and left College Park for the

University of Kentucky. Byrd turned to Clark Shaughnessy, who had previously coached at Maryland prior to World War II. Although a great coach and one of the game's most inventive minds, Shaughnessy's Maryland team performed poorly, and he resigned in early 1947. Byrd looked to the Sooner state and gave Jim Tatum a $12,000 per year salary for five years and appointed him athletic director. Geary "Swede" Eppley was athletic director but was keen to drop those duties while retaining his duties over student life and as a close advisor to Byrd.[65] Many within the Oklahoma community were very happy to wave goodbye to the hard-driving and brash coach with questionable policies. Quickly, Bud Wilkinson was promoted to head coach. No one could have predicted how Tatum's departure and Wilkinson's promotion would change the trajectory of Sooner football.[66]

When Tatum arrived at College Park, he was given latitude by President Byrd to transform the Terps into a winner. While Tatum's Sooners finished 8–3, Maryland stumbled to a disappointing 3–6 under Shaughnessy. Tatum quickly turned the Terrapins into a feared club. In his first season, the Terps compiled a 7–2–2 record that included a 20–20 tie in the Gator Bowl against Georgia. This was Maryland's first appearance in a bowl game. Tatum's split-T offense had only just begun paying dividends for the Terrapins who were on the cusp of their greatest era of gridiron success.

Big Jim, only 33 years old, quickly turned his recruiting emphasis on Pennsylvania and was very successful in the Keystone State. When hired in 1947, Maryland only had 14 high schools playing football. He had no choice but to look out of state for talent.[67] High school players and their parents liked Tatum, with his southern drawl, a great deal. He had a commanding presence and a big personality, but he was a task master who never shied from making himself clear. Winning was most important for Tatum, and his players understood that.

Very little mattered more to Sunny Jim than football. It was his life. Seemingly, Tatum always had a bold retort for anyone who criticized college football or college athletics in general.

Some people saw him as the symbol of everything wrong in college athletics, a brash, demanding, and loud coach, while others praised him as a gridiron genius, teaching young men how to live better lives. According to the *Saturday Evening Post*, "He has been variously described as ruthless and softhearted, shrewd and tactless, candid and hypocritical. Actually, all of these adjectives apply."[68] Tatum was the firebrand for supporters of college athletics as well as those seeking de-emphasis.

Eddie Cameron: The Real Blue Devil

Eddie Cameron and Jim Tatum had little in common, but they were both giants in creating the new league. For much of the 20th century, Eddie Cameron's name was synonymous with Duke athletics. A native of Irwin, Pennsylvania, Edmund McCullough "Eddie" Cameron graduated high school from Culver Military Academy in Culver, Indiana, where he starred as a fullback on the football team. It did not take long for Cameron to make the South his home, where he would leave an indelible mark. With several friends heading to Washington and Lee, Cameron decided to tag along to the Lexington, Virginia, school. Although he played football and basketball, he excelled the most on the gridiron where he was an All-Southern Conference fullback in 1923 and 1924. Cameron was a good athlete who as a senior captained the basketball and football teams.

After spending one year as an assistant coach at Washington and Lee, Cameron's boss, Jimmy DeHart, was offered the head football position at Duke, in part due to Cameron campaigning for him. Cameron, in 1926, followed DeHart and became freshman basketball coach and a football assistant. He did not take these posts until he had coached one year at Greenbrier Military Academy in West Virginia to prove himself to Duke's administration. Meanwhile, DeHart had some mediocre years until 1930 when his team broke through with an 8-1-2 record. Southwestern College in Memphis, Tennessee, offered DeHart their head coaching position, and he left Duke for Southwestern (now known as Rhodes College).[69]

Meanwhile, Cameron became head basketball coach for the 1928-1929 season. His time on the court was very successful, compiling a career 226-99 record for the Blue Devils. Cameron's success influenced the administration to move the Blue Devils out of Duke Gymnasium, later named Card Gymnasium, a facility built in 1930. In January 1940, the Blue Devils opened Duke Indoor Stadium, the largest of its kind south of Philadelphia. It was a showplace that deeply impressed North Carolinians and other Southern Conference schools who played in the arena. The facility would later bear Eddie Cameron's name.[70]

Cameron's hardcourt coaching career established Duke basketball as an important part of Duke University's identity. He compiled a schedule that included teams well beyond the South, expanding Duke's identity. Realizing that the rural South produced very few top tier basketball players, he recruited in the North, drawing players from Washington, Philadelphia, and the like to Durham. He was an outstanding coach, who also enjoyed the luxury of a tremendous financial resources that provided him with the finest facilities of any Southern Conference school, until State built Reynolds Coliseum. This was an extraordinary advantage when enticing young men to play basketball or football at Duke. For the sake of comparison, basketball facilities at South Carolina and Clemson were exceedingly poor.

In 1942, Cameron switched to the gridiron to coach Duke in place of Wallace Wade who left for military service. He did not miss much of a beat, leading the Blue Devils to four straight winning seasons and an overall 25-11-1 record. This success was achieved while guiding Duke's Navy V-12 program and managing Duke athletics. With Wade back on the sidelines, Cameron shifted to an administrative role as director of physical education and athletic director.[71] He remained on the sidelines, though, as backfield coach on Wade's staff. Cameron continued to coach with Wade until the end of the 1950 season, his last two years serving as the defensive coach (coordinator).

By 1951, Cameron's time at Duke had been littered with victory in football and basketball, the marquee sports. Of all Southern Conference schools, Duke enjoyed the greatest athletic stature, having been successful for over two decades, much of it due to Eddie Cameron. He was a likable man, very popular with students and athletes. Unlike many coaches he was calm during games and was slow to excitability. His personality crafted confidence that permeated his relationships. Cameron used these tools effectively when helping create the new league.

Wallace Wade: Football Genius

Cameron's contemporary at Duke was William Wallace Wade, one of the country's best football coaches. Duke's gridiron dominance in the 1930s and 1940s was due to Wade.

A man of enormous coaching gifts and a strict disciplinarian who smiled little, Wade was born in Trenton, Tennessee, a small town about halfway between Nashville and Memphis. Wade played guard at Brown University where he featured in the first Rose Bowl in 1916. After graduating Brown in 1917, Wade returned to his home state to coach football at Fitzgerald and Clark Military School. His success was recognized by Vanderbilt where he served as an assistant coach, helping lead the Commodores to two undefeated seasons.

Wade was a hot commodity when he landed in Tuscaloosa ready to change the football culture. His hard-nosed practices and seriousness were a great departure from the previous Alabama coach Xen Scott. Wade was an immediate success, completing a surprising 7–2–1 record in his first season. The best was yet to come. In 1925, Wade led the Crimson Tide to an undefeated campaign that ended with an invitation to the Rose Bowl, something believed unthinkable, considering the low regard that southern football maintained in other regions of the country.

Wade created Alabama's football tradition, winning the 1926 Rose Bowl versus Washington State, 20–19, one of the most important games in college football history. The victory brought southern football to national prominence, transforming the game and its relationship to southerners. He tied in the Rose Bowl the following year and won the game for a second time in 1930. He had coached Alabama to three undefeated seasons when he left Tuscaloosa for Duke. When he departed the Crimson Tide, his career coaching record stood at 61–13–3, an amazing mark.

Wallace Wade arrived at Duke earning the princely sum of $12,500 per year, far more than the highest paid full professors were making.[72] Most likely it was good for Wade that his salary was private at Duke. He easily was the highest paid coach in the Southern Conference.

Fans were shocked that Wade left Alabama for Duke, but the magic that he implemented in Tuscaloosa transferred to Durham. It took him only three years to win the Southern Conference title and by 1936, he had assembled a juggernaut. His teams rarely played close games, usually winning in blow-outs. In the 1936 season, his only loss was by two points at Tennessee. His famed 1938 "Iron Dukes" did not surrender a point in the regular season, and only allowed seven points in a Rose Bowl loss to Southern California. This type of domination continued until he left for the Navy in 1942.

After the war, Wade could not reestablish the dominance that he had enjoyed in the '30s. The landscape of college football was changing, and Duke faced other schools with athletic resources that could challenge it. Furthermore, the oversized role that returning veterans played on football teams at many schools in the late 1940s was a steep hill to climb. In 1950, he stepped away from coaching to become the first commissioner of the Southern Conference. It was the right move.[73]

Rex Enright: The Gentleman Coach

The University of South Carolina might never have been a part of the new conference without the coaching acumen of and the deep respect held for its football coach, Rex Enright. The Gamecock leader came to Columbia in 1938, after serving the previous six seasons as an assistant football coach and head basketball coach at the University of Georgia. As the new head coach, Enright took over a mediocre South Carolina football program that had never won more than five games in three seasons under previous headman Don McCallister. McCallister was an unheralded high school coach in Ohio when hired to lead the Gamecocks. Surprisingly, he had no college experience, something almost unthinkable today. McCallister was an inexpensive coach, another example of the financial weakness in South Carolina's athletic department as well as across the university. The campus was chronically short of funding from the state and private sources and hiring in the Depression made choices even more difficult.

With Enright, South Carolina was moving in a very different direction. He was an accomplished former player and coach who had starred as running back under the famed Knute Rockne at Notre Dame. That alone provided an almost unmatched pedigree, but the young Enright also had played basketball for the Irish. A native of Rockford, Illinois, he was a football and basketball star for the Rockford High School Rabs. After graduating, he headed to South Bend, Indiana, and enjoyed a fine career at Notre Dame, although he sat out a year because the Four Horsemen dominated playing time.

After two seasons playing with the Green Bay Packers, Enright headed to a warmer climate as an assistant football coach at North Carolina on Coach Chuck Collins' staff. Enright and Collins were friends, with Collins having played end at Notre Dame with the Four Horsemen. After only one year with the Tar Heels, Enright moved in 1931 to Athens, Georgia, to join Harry Mehre's football staff and to coach basketball. He quickly earned a reputation as a fine coach and a well-liked and highly respected person, valued for his judgment and sportsmanship.

Upon his hiring at South Carolina in 1938, there was hope that Enright would make the Gamecocks more competitive. Immediately, he won university and community support, in part due to his engaging personality as well as his record of accomplishments and success. As board member Sol Blatt stated, Enright "was a perfect gentleman and a very capable fellow."[74] Enright had little time to develop the Gamecock program, because World War II service intervened. He spent 1943 through 1945 in the Navy, returning to the South Carolina sideline in 1946.

Regardless of his won/loss record, Enright was well respected in the Southern Conference and by the early 1950s considered one of the great men of the game. His words and opinions carried weight and were destined to play a leading role in the new league.

Frank Howard: Mr. Clemson

Few coaches have fit their environment as well as Clemson's Frank J. Howard. Another son of the rural south, Howard was a native of Barlow Bend, Alabama, a small community northeast of Mobile. After graduating high school, he matriculated at Alabama, playing under Wallace Wade. Howard started on Wade's 1931 Rose Bowl team, his last season leading the Crimson Tide, that defeated Washington State 24–0. When Jess Neely, who held a law degree from Vanderbilt, was hired as head football coach at Clemson, he brought Frank Howard with him from Alabama as an assistant coach. Neely left Clemson for Rice in early 1940, leading to Frank Howard's promotion to head coach.

Howard was an immediate success, winning games and winning fans. He, along with his close friend Clyde "Peahead" Walker at Wake Forest, formed a dynamic pair who were highly sought banquet speakers and interviews. Howard spoke in a thick drawl and emphasized his rural upbringing in Alabama. He reveled in folksy expressions and enjoyed chewing tobacco, and the Clemson fans loved it.

What satisfied students and alumni the most was his success on the field. In 1948, he led the Tigers to an undefeated season and a one-point victory over Missouri in the

Clemson's head football coach Frank Howard (center) celebrates the 1951 Orange Bowl championship with his players and fans. A great advocate for football, Howard guided the Tigers to many great victories in his 30 years as head coach (courtesy Clemson University Photographs, Special Collections and Archives, University Archives, Clemson University).

Gator Bowl. This was followed by an undefeated season in 1950 that was only marred by a 14–14 tie to rival South Carolina. It annoyed Howard, that Rex Enright had a knack for having the Gamecocks play their best football against the Tigers.

By 1951, Howard was well on his way to being an institution in South Carolina. He was an advocate for college football and bowl games, believing that the sport was operating within the academic mission of the university. His popularity brought legions of South Carolinians into the Clemson fold, something well understood by the Clemson administration. Howard had a strong relationship with President Frank Poole, an invaluable part of Howard's success. Being in a remote location, without good road connections, one of the only ways for Clemson to attract attention and students was through sports, in particular football. Howard was the perfect man to fit this role in the football-crazed state. If Eddie Cameron was the original Duke Blue Devil, Frank Howard was the original Clemson Tiger.[75]

Chuck Erickson: The Quiet Leader

Chuck Erickson began his college career far from the Tar Heel State. A native of Oak Park, Illinois, a Chicago suburb, Erickson crossed the northern border to attend the University of Wisconsin. North Carolina's football coach, Chuck Collins, saw Erickson play in the Badger backfield and convinced the young man to leave Madison for

Chapel Hill. Collins' recruiting changed the direction of North Carolina athletics and the future of college sports throughout the South.

Erickson played for the Tar Heels for two years while earning a degree in engineering. By 1933, he was working in the athletic department, where he held numerous posts that allowed him to gain a broad knowledge of how athletics functioned. With Bob Fetzer's retirement in 1952, Chuck Erickson, who had served as Fetzer's assistant for years, was the natural choice to assume the post of athletic director, a position he held until 1968.

Erickson was a shy and reserved man, characteristics that seemed to exempt him from being a successful athletic director. It was appropriate that he was a fine golfer who was at home playing with friends or alone on the links. Nonetheless, he was a man of vision who had the right friends to help develop Tar Heel athletics. Erickson's friendship with Rand Kenan, Jr., one of the wealthiest men in the state, was essential for creating North Carolina's athletic physical plant. Kenan's money improved the football stadium, built the field house, constructed Carmichael Auditorium, and assisted in all aspects of athletics.[76] Later in his career, some liked to call Erickson the "Knute Rockne of North Carolina." It was a good moniker.

Roy Clogston: A Northerner Down South

With so many southerners in Southern Conference leadership, Roy Clogston was another exception. Clogston was a native of Ballston Lake, New York, but his career in Raleigh earned him lasting recognition. Clogston graduated Springfield College with a bachelor's degree in physical education, followed by studies at New York University where he was awarded a master's in physical education. Clogston spent many years at St. Lawrence University as a football coach and athletic director, even finding the time and energy to coach wrestling and golf. After service in the Navy during World War II, Clogston moved to Raleigh, assuming the duties of athletic director on August 1, 1948.[77] He came with glowing recommendations from Paul Brown and Frank Leahy, two of the most important figures in athletics during this era. There was little doubt that part of the appeal of State lay in the construction of Reynolds Coliseum and the growing dominance of Everett Case's basketball program.

Clogston understood that there was a great deal of potential at the Raleigh school. Riddick Stadium required a lot of work, but the framework for Reynolds Coliseum was in place and the facility was only a year away from opening. Furthermore, Everett Case was destined to pack the coliseum with rabid Wolfpack fans. This was a foundation on which other sports programs could build.

A big man, Clogston became a popular figure in Raleigh, interested in building all sports at State, not just football and basketball. His faith in State was evident when he accepted the position in Raleigh without ever visiting the campus or the city. Clogston was a key cog in supporting and developing State into a basketball power, fully appreciating the importance that it played on and well beyond the Raleigh campus.

Jim Weaver: Wake Forest's Athletic Savior

A North Carolina native, Jim Weaver was born in Rutherford County. His father, who held a Ph.D. from Johns Hopkins, was president of Rutherford College. James Harvey "Jim" Weaver attended Emory and Henry College where he was a talented athlete playing football, basketball, and baseball. After a brief stint at Duke, he graduated Centenary College in biology, where he starred on the gridiron as well. After teaching high school in Nacogdoches, Texas, he returned to the east coast, taking a position at Oak Ridge Academy near Greensboro in 1928. He coached basketball and football at the school which also served as a junior college, when, in 1933, he was selected to coach football and golf at Wake Forest.

A large man, Weaver was hired to make Wake Forest more competitive in football, but his first season was a winless disaster. By year three, however, the Deacons had a winning record. Stepping off the field, Weaver was selected as director of physical education and athletics in 1937. Wake Forest's athletic program, always short of resources, desperately needed the managerial skills of a man like Weaver.[78] When Weaver became head coach in 1933, the athletic department did not even possess a telephone.

Weaver's tenure was an enormous triumph. He placed the athletic department's finances in better order and led a program that was very successful in football, basketball, and baseball, far exceeding expectations. He founded Wake's golf program that brought Arnold Palmer to campus. With a gravelly voice and a deceptively gruff demeanor, he was a man of sound judgment and was close friends with many league members, especially Roy Clogston. Like his basketball coach Murray Greason, Jim Weaver was an avid outdoorsman, eager to talk about hunting and fishing. But athletic administration was his specialty, and all who worked around him recognized it. In the second year of the ACC's existence, he was selected its commissioner.

The Academics

James T. Penney

Few would have thought that a biologist who conducted research and published regularly on freshwater sponges would have the interest or the inclination to be involved in major college athletics. James T. Penney was the exception. Penney was a Charlotte native, born in 1900. He received his B.A., M.S. and Ph.D. all at the University of North Carolina. He arrived at the University of South Carolina in 1929 as a biology professor in a small, underfunded department. The spectacled Penney was an active scholar and a popular professor, quickly earning a strong reputation on campus for his scholarly research and his interest in the history of naturalists in South Carolina, as well as freshwater sponges. In March 1953, Penney co-authored an inventory of reptiles, amphibians, and fish in South Carolina through the university's research council.[79] For decades it remained an essential publication on the topic.

Penney was more than a biologist. He and his wife were deeply involved with Columbia's Town Theatre, and Professor Penney, at times, could be seen acting on stage. Perhaps some of his acting ability led him to athletics at South Carolina, where he was chair of the university's athletic council, managing and advising the university on athletic issues. ACC leadership was so impressed with Penney's skill that he would be tapped as the first conference president.

Forrest Clonts

Working closely with Penney was a history professor at Wake Forest with the unforgettable name Forrest Clonts. Clonts was the dean of Demon Deacon athletics. A 1920 graduate of Wake Forest, Clonts taught European history to almost countless students at Wake Forest from 1922 to 1967. Like Penney, he was an avid supporter of athletics and a beloved professor. An erudite and cultured man, he had an engaging personality and was well liked by almost everyone. A fashionable dresser and an avid cigar smoker, "He could breathe life and spirit into the dry bones of history," a student remarked. "He taught with an enthusiasm that was contagious; he communicated his own excitement and pride and curiosity; he made the process of learning an exuberant pilgrimage into the past."[80]

It was no great surprise that Clonts was popular among Southern Conference leaders. Over the years, he became one of the leading voices for college athletics in the Southern Conference, serving as an active member in league leadership while crafting a good relationship with athletic director Jim Weaver. His friend Weaver served as ACC commissioner from 1954 to his untimely death in 1970.

Oliver Cornwell

Oliver Cornwell was much more than a physical education professor. He was a missionary for physical education, transforming the discipline at the University of North Carolina as well as for public school children in the state. From South Charleston, Ohio, Cornwell graduated from Wittenburg College. After working in public schools, he completed his graduate work at Ohio State. Having served several years at Wittenburg, Cornwell was offered a position at Ohio State. Initially, he accepted the post, but he was convinced to head to North Carolina when the Chapel Hill school offered him a professorship that included the opportunity to lead and develop a modern physical education program. In 1935, Oliver K. Cornwell assumed leadership over North Carolina's new department of physical education. Two years later, physical education and athletics were merged into the same unit. In 1952, Cornwell's career changed when he was named chairman of the Department of Physical Education and Athletics, a position that was vacated when Robert (Bob) Fetzer became executive secretary of the Morehead Foundation. Chuck Erickson became the new athletic director, but Cornwell was tapped to lead the combined physical education and athletics program, essentially in charge of the academic wing.[81] It was a different relationship than found at other schools.

Unlike his friends at South Carolina and Wake Forest, North Carolina's Oliver Cornwell was professionally involved in athletics as a professor of physical education. Cornwell was a virile man, physically fit, and even imposing by his size. He was an outstanding and beloved teacher and speaker who pioneered the use of film for athletic events and physical training. He convinced the North Carolina government to invest in film equipment in its public schools. Essentially, Cornwell built UNC's physical education program from a barely existent program to a nationally recognized program that influenced much of the state.

Cornwell was the right man at the right time. He had participated in Southern Conference business since his arrival at North Carolina and was a recognized authority on college athletics. He was an indefatigable worker, focused on his civic duty to better his adopted state.

Lee Milford

Lee Milford was not a traditional academic, like so many of his colleagues in the Southern Conference. Although he played a similar role as other academics in conference affairs, Milford was Clemson's physician, not a traditional professor. Instead of lecturing and grading, Milford dispensed medical advice and prescriptions. He was the college physician for the general student body as well as athletics, a department of the campus where he projected much of his energy. Remarkably, Milford even found time to enjoy his hobby of fishing and operate a practice of general medicine for the Clemson community.

An Anderson County, South Carolina, native, Milford graduated from Furman before attending medical school at Emory University. Milford came to Clemson in 1926, as a physician for the school. Quickly, he became an essential cog for the athletic program, especially football. Unlike his colleagues, Milford, not holding a traditional faculty position, unconventionally served as chair of Clemson's Athletic Council. In that role, he became a key figure in the Southern Conference, serving as president on three occasions. He was a consistent supporter of Clemson athletics, but he also played a significant role in bringing Furman and The Citadel into the Southern Conference.[82]

The Southern Conference

The neo–Romanesque Piedmont Hotel in Atlanta, Georgia, was the setting for the founding of the Southern Intercollegiate Conference on February 25 and 26, 1921. The 10-story hotel opened in 1903, immediately becoming a local landmark and a popular site for entertainment and meetings. The Piedmont resembled structures in northern cities and in some ways helped define Atlanta's economic and cultural progress which was drawing the city more into mainstream America. It was the ideal arena for founding a new athletic conference.

Alabama, Alabama Polytechnic Institute (Auburn), Clemson, Georgia, Georgia School of Technology (Georgia Tech), Kentucky, Maryland, Mississippi Agricultural and Mechanical (Mississippi State), North Carolina, North Carolina State College (North Carolina State), Tennessee, Virginia, Virginia Polytechnic Institute (Virginia Tech), and Washington and Lee left the unwieldy Southern Intercollegiate Athletic Association which was comprised of 29 members. These institutions were eager to create a league of like-minded schools that agreed to basic principles of college athletics, but one that was easier to manage.[83] Georgia's Dr. Steadman V. Sanford, namesake of the university's Sanford Stadium, and an outspoken advocate for college athletics, was the driving force behind the creation and operation of the Southern Conference. Sanford was the faculty athletic chairman at Georgia from 1907 to 1932 and a respected voice in athletics throughout the South.[84]

After its founding, the Southern Conference quickly began to suffer from the same problems that plagued its predecessor. By 1929, eight additional schools had joined the Southern Conference including private schools Tulane, Vanderbilt, and Duke. Meeting in Knoxville, Tennessee, on December 8 and 9, 1932, the conference faced secession, again due to its bloated size. With Sanford leading the way, 13 schools said goodbye to the Southern Conference and formed the Southeastern Conference. Those schools were Alabama, Auburn, Florida, Georgia, Georgia Tech, Kentucky, Louisiana State, Mississippi, Mississippi State, Tulane, University of the South, and Vanderbilt. The Southeastern Conference was more geographically attuned and included a good number of schools that felt a similar way about the importance of athletics and athletic policies. In general, that meant strongly supporting athletic programs, especially football, and going as far as to openly endorse full athletic scholarships, a policy established in 1935. These schools were determined for athletics to assist in crafting an identity for them that could not be easily achieved through academics.

The remaining members of the Southern Conference were a strong group but a little more hesitant about the growing commercialism and professionalism in college athletics. Clemson, Duke, Maryland, North Carolina, North Carolina State, South Carolina, Virginia, Virginia Military Institute, and Virginia Tech were very different schools, but they were spread out over only four states, thus the league remained geographically close-knit. The conference voted to expand to 16 teams and invited The Citadel, Davidson, Furman, Richmond, Wake Forest, and William and Mary to join on February 7, 1936. All accepted membership into the conference, but the league now consisted of many disparate schools, from military academies to small denominational institutions, to state universities. That variety was to prove difficult to manage.

On the positive side, there were outstanding rivalries within the league. The Big Five in North Carolina (it was starting to be termed the Big Four, with Davidson's declining fortunes), the Big Six in Virginia as well as South Carolina and Clemson and North Carolina and Virginia were keen rivalries. What enhanced and deepened them was that many fans and graduates of these schools were neighbors or worked with folks from competing institutions. Even within families, the rivalries often were present. All of this worked to craft a tight league, regardless of its size and the impossibility of crowning a legitimate league champion in football. To some, championships simply were not very important; sometimes victories over instate competition or a rival counted more than a mythical football championship.

A year later, in 1937, conference leaders were disappointed when Virginia withdrew to restore itself as an independent. Although Virginia was an independent, they continued to play their traditional Big Six schedule; therefore, not much had changed in the Old Dominion. Five of the Big Six schools in the commonwealth remained Southern Conference members. They were Richmond, Virginia Military Institute, Virginia Polytechnic Institute, Washington and Lee, and William and Mary. They had enjoyed years of rivalry dating back to the late 1800s. Likewise, in North Carolina all the Big Five were league members. They included Davidson, Duke, North Carolina, North Carolina State, and Wake Forest. Davidson stood a bit outside of the other four, but all these schools had contested against each other for decades. Although Clemson and South Carolina were the major draws in the Palmetto State, games against Furman and The Citadel were significant events. Only Maryland was left without an in-state rival. The Southern Conference survived the SEC's secession and performed well, although rarely fielding a football team to match the best in the SEC.

As 1951 dawned, the seven seceding schools had strong and, in some cases, visionary leadership at the executive level and within athletics. Most boasted careful leaders, seeking the betterment of their institutions, working to bring about athletic reform that reflected more fully the ambitions of their colleges. There were wildcards like Jim Tatum and at times Frank Howard, as well as Curly Byrd, but by and large, there was a consensus that athletics should be subservient to academic leadership. Scandals far away and close to home provided challenges for the conference's leadership that eventually created the foundation for division.

2

Reform in the Era of National and Local Scandals

On January 6, 1951, Gordon Gray, heading to the NCAA convention in Dallas, had the hypocrisy of college athletics on his mind. Gray was very familiar with the Graham Plan, his predecessor's hope to gain academic control over athletics, which had suffered a quick death at the hands of alumni, boosters, and sportswriters. Although the plan, a noble attempt to confront corruption in college athletics, had damaged North Carolina president Frank Porter Graham's reputation, Gray was a supporter of the principles espoused by the progressive North Carolina president. Gray had no patience with college athletic corruption, but he understood that the Sanity Code, originally known as the Purity Code, was unworkable and, in some ways, created a more corrupt environment.[1] He had gone as far as to admit that North Carolina and State College were not in compliance with the Sanity Code.

Instituted in 1948, the Sanity Code was unenforceable and hypocritical. Many schools, especially in the South, objected to it, arguing that they could not field competitive teams with the code in place. There was a lot of truth to that assertion. On the surface, the code sounded high-minded and progressive, but it had numerous problems. It called for limiting scholarship aid to tuition and fees, excluding room, board, and a small stipend. In addition, it required that athletic aid be disbursed through the university and based on need. It even created an NCAA Compliance Committee, the first of its kind for the organization. To most schools in the South, the code was deemed unfair, and was established to strengthen northern and western schools, especially in the Big Ten, who were losing athletes to southern institutions who provided athletic scholarships. The SEC had been issuing athletic scholarships since 1935, an attractive enticement for good athletes. The Southern Conference adopted the athletic scholarship model three years later.[2]

The Big Ten schools, for many years the leaders of the NCAA, allied with the Pacific Coast Conference to favor the Sanity Code. They encouraged student athletes to obtain jobs to help pay their necessary college expenses. These jobs were on and off campuses but opened the door to athletes being employed in phony jobs and being paid exorbitant salaries. Southern schools rebelled against this notion, especially military academies or colleges with a corps of cadets. Virginia Military Institute, The Citadel, and Virginia Tech argued that it was impossible for their athletes to obtain jobs when they held additional duties in the cadet corps. The Citadel was so angry with the Sanity Code that they resigned from the NCAA in January 1950 but remained a member of the Southern Conference.

The most famous of the dissenters were known as the Seven Sinners, four of whom were Southern Conference members. The seven were Boston College, The Citadel, Maryland, Villanova, Virginia, Virginia Tech, and Virginia Military. Virginia had been the first of these schools to reject the Sanity Code, arguing that it was impossible for their students to play sports, earn their education, and work part-time. President Colgate Darden emphasized that Virginia intended to continue providing athletic scholarships, essentially ignoring the Sanity Code, and would withdraw from the NCAA if the code persisted.[3] Darden believed that without athletic scholarships, athletes would be unable to successfully pursue their studies, thus damaging their academic careers.[4]

Maryland's Curly Byrd was another one of the early leaders in the campaign against the Sanity Code and what he saw as growing NCAA power. The Maryland leader openly supported athletic scholarships and fully supported Coach Jim Tatum's distribution of them. Byrd charged that northern schools, like Michigan and Ohio State, often maintained they were following the Sanity Code, although they had created many mechanisms for avoiding it. For example, Byrd alleged that Ohio State did not need scholarships, because they had a vast system for providing jobs to athletes. Big Ten schools, he argued, were wealthy and lined up donors to support their athletes through jobs. He smartly played on Southern animosity toward northern dictates, which was how some saw the Sanity Code, and skillfully leveled a blow directly at the Big Ten and their presumed leadership over the NCAA.

The Sinners were providing athletic scholarships that included room, board, and laundry money. This was a violation of the Sanity Code. After failing to dismiss these seven schools from the NCAA in 1950, the Sanity Code became an unenforceable policy. Indeed, it was ignored by many schools, not simply the Seven Sinners. It remained, however, NCAA policy. The showdown in January 1951 was to decide if the Sanity Code, on life support, would survive.

Gordon Gray thought that the NCAA was damaging its own cause by crafting an unworkable policy. Writing to Clarence Houston of Tufts, chair of the NCAA Constitution Committee, Gray explained, "Once athletic ability was recognized as justification for some financial aid, the authorization of tuition and fees, accompanied by a denial of other necessary educational expenses, is an arbitrary grounded on neither logic or morals."[5]

Gray saw only two ways to get the athletic house in order. One was for the NCAA to retreat and allow athletic conferences and non-conference schools to police the financial aid process. This was a position that had been favored by Southern Conference members, especially considering a weak NCAA. The other option was for the NCAA to alter its by-laws to expand scholarships to include room, board, and a stipend.[6] Gray supported the first option with his conference brethren, but he believed that the second option was the better alternative, because it promised the opportunity to forge some national standards. Furthermore, it would decrease the financial abuses in intercollegiate athletics by providing all that was necessary for an athlete to attend. Lastly, he hoped it would treat the athlete like other students, something that harkened back to the days of the Graham Plan.[7] The ultimate hope was to restore integrity to athletics by placing it in a proper relationship with academics.

Everyone knew that the Dallas meeting had the makings of a donnybrook. The issues facing the NCAA were many, headlined by the Sanity Code and the Korean War, but television and athletic scholarships, controversial matters, were part of the docket as well. A united front that included all schools in the Southwest Conference, the Southeastern Conference, and the Southern Conference, with a smattering of eastern colleges, particularly Catholic institutions, defeated the Sanity Code by a 130–60 vote. Not only did the vote indicate that the Big Ten's dominance was shaky, it also relegated the NCAA to a body that left enforcement and a great deal of policymaking to conferences and schools outside of leagues. The NCAA was a deliberative body, at least for the time being. The Sanity Code very much split college athletics and became a critical element in shifting athletics toward the design that we see today.

The code was a victim of the postwar educational environment, and, in part, the increasing confidence of southern colleges and their athletic programs. They were not going to take a back seat to the powerful Big Ten. It was a relic of a previous era when schools were small and catered to an elite. The Sanity Code harkened to a time when supposed amateurism reined at colleges. Its focus on retaining the myth of amateurism, a concept born in the United Kingdom among well-heeled athletes, did not fit. There was no real amateurism in American collegiate sports in the 1950s. Once schools entered the business of funding athletes to attend, the concept of amateurism was mortally wounded. It was an ideal that had long since lost meaning due to scholarships that compensated students for athletic performance. In postwar America, some coaches, including George Barclay at Washington and Lee, and administrators even believed that the time was right to pay athletes a small, uniform stipend.[8]

A Southern Conference Commissioner

The new Southern Conference Commissioner, Wallace Wade, had worked hard to end the Sanity Code. Before January 1, 1951, the Southern Conference had never employed a commissioner. As Easley, South Carolina, native Wilton Garrison of the *Charlotte Observer* put it, "The conference hired him [a commissioner] for one important job—to curb the evils of recruiting…. The conference wants competitive bidding for athletes stopped. It wants everyone put on an equal basis and leave it up to the athlete to pick his own school."[9] This was a tall task for any commissioner. Recruiting had placed such enormous pressure on some coaches that they desired a commissioner with authority to gain control over it. Many coaches believed that recruiting was damaging their employment prospects, making their jobs difficult, and harming collegiate athletics.

The league members knew that a commissioner was necessary, but the selection of a leader had caused division and had languished for a year. Some wanted Wake Forest's athletic director Jim Weaver, a very popular leader who had worked wonders at the Baptist college. Weaver's popularity was so great that he would take the reins of the conference in 1955, leading it until his death in 1970. Others favored Washington and Lee's athletic director Cap'n Dick Smith, an equally admired figure. Meeting on December 9, 1951, at Charlotte's Hotel Barringer, Duke's famed head football coach, Wallace Wade, 58 years old at the time, was elected commissioner on a 12–5 vote, the minimum votes necessary for him to earn the position.

A four-man committee led by Colonel D.S. McAlister of The Citadel had worked for months to locate a commissioner and to ensure that only one name, unanimously supported by the committee, was nominated. McAlister was assisted by North Carolina athletic director Bob Fetzer, Gerry Eppley of Maryland and George Washington's Max

Farrington. Conference members were feeling the pressure to appoint a commissioner, in part because the Southern was the only major conference without one. Essentially, the league operated with an elected president, but no central figure devoid of attachment to a particular school leading and managing the conference. Of the major conferences, it seemed that the Southern Conference needed a commissioner more than others.

Uncertainty as to how many young men would be drafted or would volunteer for the Korean War almost stopped the election of a commissioner. In a razor thin vote that had West Virginia casting the deciding ballot, the conference chose to move forward with the commissioner's election.[10] The debates illustrated that some schools were concerned that athletics could be entering a difficult period, like the World War II era that badly damaged college sports programs.

No one was sure how powerful the commissioner's office would become, but the conference did provide enough financial support for it to function properly. Wade was allotted a $12,000 yearly salary, a good deal more than some schools were paying their coaches. In addition, he was provided $18,000 to operate the Southern Conference office in a city not yet named.[11] By standards of the era, this was a substantial investment.

Although the transition from football coach to commissioner, doubtless, was bittersweet, Wade could take some solace in having scored a 7–3 victory over North Carolina in his last game. The Duke coach had elevated Blue Devil football to heights most thought unreachable, but Wade's postwar teams had not been as successful as his squads from the 1930s, and he may have been relieved to step away from the competitive pressures. Carl Snavely's UNC squads of the late 1940s, for example, had surpassed Duke. Wade realized it was time to alter his career path.

Max Farrington and the Southern Conference

Working closely with the first conference commissioner in 1951 fell on the shoulders of Max Farrington. Unlike so many Southern Conference officials, Farrington was a Midwesterner, a native of a major city, who spent most of his professional life in Washington, D.C. This almost made him a foreigner to most key figures in the Southern Conference. A native of St. Louis, Farrington graduated Westminster College in Fulton, Missouri, before earning a master's degree in physical education at George Washington. Most likely, Farrington did not envision spending the next 40 years as a faculty and staff member at GW, but that became his path. In 1929, he served as baseball and freshman football coach. His leadership talents were noted by the administration who gradually expanded Farrington's duties to include far more than coaching and teaching.

Farrington was promoted to athletic director in 1939. Serving in the Navy during World War II, he returned to his former post with the Colonials after the war. Tirelessly, Farrington worked to place George Washington in a strong position within the Southern Conference, a difficult task due to the school's location, its lack of athletic resources, and the growing challenge from Maryland athletics and professional sports. He had the added weight of keeping George Washington fully engaged with a collection of southern institutions, except for Maryland. That alone was a challenge in the early 1950s when southern identity was a significant component of campus cultural life at most southern schools.

Southern Conference remembers respected Farrington for his achievements and viewed him as a solid leader. Some complained that he was a bit long winded, but that was a mild rebuke. He had a tough job.

Virginia and the Southern Conference

Meanwhile, the University of Virginia, where academics and athletics had an uneasy relationship, was making noise about applying for reentry into the Southern Conference, the league it had left in 1936. President Colgate Darden, in mid–January, was quoted saying, "I'm in favor of Virginia being a member of a conference. I don't like this lone wolf business."[12] While this statement appeared emphatic, Darden remained wary of committing Virginia to conference membership. It appears that Darden and athletic director Norton Pritchett had decided on this action after the Sanity Code was rejected by the NCAA. Southern Conference members had been in the forefront of fighting the policy and George Washington's Max Farrington had issued the motion at the NCAA Convention that dispatched the Sanity Code.[13]

If Virginia rejoined the league, the Southern Conference would consist of 18 schools, adding to an already cumbersome collection of institutions. Virginia, however, would have the benefit of continuing its contests with its in-state rivals, but in the context of a conference. With 18 members, it was difficult to see how the league could remain united, and some sort of split rapidly would occur, even if it were simply a division into two units of the same conference.

Although Darden had expressed his desire to join the Southern Conference, it was far from certain that the Cavaliers would pursue conference affiliation. Virginia's president, often, was inconsistent regarding his statements towards athletics. Darden was not as interested in athletics as some other presidents, and there was a strong movement for de-emphasis of athletics on the campus. This would come to a head with the publication of the Gooch Report, an internal evaluation regarding the future of Virginia athletics, released in October 1951.

Freshman Eligibility and Korea

Discussion about freshman eligibility was never far from the lips of Southern Conference coaches and administrators, and there had been little unity on the issue throughout the years. Smaller schools consistently favored freshman participation, because they could not field substantial football teams, unless these students were allowed to play. Larger schools opposed it, arguing that a student needed a year of seasoning on campus, before athletic rigors began. There was some truth to that, but they also knew that it helped give them easy victories versus smaller schools.

The beginning of the Korean War in June 1950 elevated the importance of freshman eligibility. In the Southern Conference, most schools, even the larger ones, feared that the war would sap their numbers, leading to badly weakened football squads which in turn would damage the product on the field and harm gate receipts. The Southern Conference polled its members to determine how to proceed. There was resounding support to play freshmen. Many schools made legitimate and compelling cases. State College's football Coach Beattie Feathers, for example, said that he needed about 12 freshmen to play, or his Wolfpack squad would be in trouble. Davidson was concerned that football would be suspended without the help of freshman participation. Similar issues were found at schools such as Furman.[14] None of this was a concern to schools with a cadet corps, such as Virginia Tech, Clemson, VMI, or The Citadel. These students were enrolled in ROTC programs and could not be drafted.

On the other hand, the shortage of players combined with freshman eligibility fostered a heated recruiting environment, more passionate than normal. It served to highlight the problems that existed within recruiting, from paying players to promising them jobs. The race for athletes was even more intense, because the two-platoon system, enacted in 1942, remained in effect. Two-platoon football began when rules were altered to allow unlimited substitutions. Quickly, it spelled the end to the all-around player who played offense and defense. With two-platoon football, schools had to recruit many more players to compete effectively, costing colleges more money and exerting great pressure on recruitment. This situation was counter to everything that reform-minded presidents desired.

The Role of Presidents

With the Sanity Code removed and conferences enjoying the authority to manage their athletic affairs, there developed a desire by some presidents to take the lead in reforming athletics. Gordon Gray believed that a meeting of the presidents of Davidson, Duke, North Carolina, North Carolina State, and Wake Forest was needed to discuss the status of athletics at their institutions, and in the Southern Conference, with an eye for developing policies for how to reform and manage athletics. A meeting of four of the five North Carolina members of the Southern Conference was held in Chapel Hill on January 27, 1951. Davidson did not send a representative, but at the gathering, it was agreed for Gordon Gray to establish a meeting of all the conference's presidents to be held at Morehead Planetarium on March 3, 1951, again in Chapel Hill.[15]

Davidson's absence was not a major distraction, in part because the Wildcats had fielded some weak teams over the recent years and discussions about deemphasizing football were rife on the campus. In 1950, the Wildcats had won three football games. They defeated Presbyterian, Richmond, and Erskine. It was Erskine's last year playing football before reestablishing a program in 2021. In the previous year, Davidson scored only two victories, besting a woeful Wolfpack squad in Charlotte and dropping Rollins College. Over the last two basketball seasons, Davidson had fallen well off the pace, especially as basketball in the conference was improving steadily. The Wildcats had chosen a different course, and the Big Four of Duke, North Carolina, North Carolina State, and Wake Forest stood as the dominant force in North Carolina collegiate athletics.

Gray was the natural selection to lead this drive. He had a sincere concern about the oversized role of athletics in the collegiate environment and was eager for the presidents and chancellors to play a larger part in regulating college sports.[16] In addition, he held great prominence in the state, leading three institutions in the consolidated University of North Carolina System and was highly regarded for his managerial abilities and his professionalism. All of this worked in Gray's favor, providing him with a large platform with which to voice athletic reform in North Carolina and throughout the South.

Gray, however, was dealing with far more important matters than athletics in early 1951. The first steps toward desegregating the UNC medical school were underway, occupying much of his attention. Gray, like his predecessor, was a gradualist, supporting a slow process of integration. That conflicted heavily with many who steadfastly opposed any integration; this included a large number in the state legislature and members of the university's board. His chancellors, Bob House and John Harrelson, also found themselves on the forefront of integration at their schools.

The meeting agenda for March was full, designed to discuss the pressing issues that the Southern Conference and most athletic programs faced. At the top was the role of university presidents in the operation and administration of athletic programs and what issues were most important for them to monitor and manage. With collegiate sports having a long history of entrance requirement violations, it was natural for the agenda to include the question of establishing minimum entrance requirements for all who received a grant-in-aid based on need. Furthermore, they were to discuss Southern Conference compliance versus NCAA compliance, a topic of enormous importance considering the Sanity Code's defeat.[17] The presidents even discussed "trust and mutual confidence" as necessary for increased presidential involvement.[18]

At Gray's urging but with the support of at least two presidents, the UNC president asked if an invitation could be extended to President Colgate Darden at the University of Virginia to attend the March meeting of presidents. All the presidents endorsed Darden's presence. In this era, it was not uncommon for many different guests to attend Southern Conference meetings. Most likely, the idea for inviting Darden originated with Gordon Gray and was supported by Curly Byrd who was interested in establishing a rivalry with the Charlottesville school.

North Carolina and Virginia played football every season and had enjoyed an intense rivalry since their first contest in 1892, a game won by the Cavaliers 30–18. This rivalry, for years the highlight of both schools' schedules, and sometimes called the South's oldest rivalry, was established two years before the beginning of the North Carolina series with State. The game had assumed great prominence in the teens and twenties. The competition between the Cavaliers and the Tar Heels went far beyond athletics, because the two schools competed for national prestige, something that was a distant dream for most southern universities. Furthermore, the competition reflected the historical natures of both states with North Carolina viewed as a humbler state compared to Virginia and its oversized role in early American history.

Most presidents were not well versed in athletics and realized that they would need assistance in making athletic policy. The presidents, often turned to coaches, faculty athletic representatives, and athletic directors to advise them. Even with this help, presidential involvement in athletics was a minefield. Most presidents came from academic backgrounds, some quite distinguished, and focused almost all their energies on strengthening the academic offerings at their institutions. Athletics was a distraction, but one that garnered attention because of alumni and boosters who put enormous emphasis on the won/loss record. At Duke, for example, Hollis Edens sought the opinions of Eddie Cameron and Charles Jordan, chairman of the Athletic Council and vice president for University Relations, as to the agenda items.[19] These were trusted hands who could brief Edens about what was good for Duke athletics and college sports in general. This type of situation existed at all league schools.

State's Hilbert A. Fisher, North Carolina's A.W. Hobbs, and Duke's Charles Jordan, all essentially in the modern role of faculty athletic representative, supported the movement for presidents to get more involved in collegiate sports. Most of their colleagues in the conference felt the same way. Fisher told his friends at North Carolina and Duke, "We have let it get into the hands of the coaches."[20] Like so many other academic officials, Fisher thought that it was best for the coaches to coach and the presidents and academics to administer. Fisher, in particular, detested the constant recruiting competition with schools, and objected to how coaches repeatedly visited players. The problem was how to stop it. There were not many good options, but getting the presidents more involved in athletics was, at minimum, a good sign.

The *Richmond Times Dispatch* urged action at the meeting. To support their views, the editorial board featured some important remarks made recently by Dr. Jay B. Nash, chairman of the Department of Physical Education and Health at New York University speaking before the southern district meeting of the American Association for Health, Physical Education, and Recreation. Nash was a nationally known advocate for physical education, spending most of his professional life crafting the discipline into a legitimate and important field of study. Nash condemned the abuses in college athletics. "Equally guilty with these [basketball players in point-shaving scandals] were a lot of people in respectable positions who can and will dodge their responsibility and deny their guilt. College and university presidents and boards of directors must share their responsibility with the few players who accepted a few paltry dollars. Most of these chancellors and presidents have lost their intellectual and moral leadership."[21] These words, coming from a scholar of Nash's pedigree, were a stinging indictment and a call for the Southern Conference presidents to do more than provide minor reforms to a broken system.

One must be careful not to be too hard on college presidents. Many of these men were good leaders and academics who directed their schools with distinction. In general, most differed from men like Curly Byrd who viewed winning athletics as essential to the construction of a nationally prominent university. They were not opposed to college athletics, none of them wanted to end college sports, but they wanted to ensure that athletics was positioned within the context of the far more important academic mission. Academics, sometimes in a very pure sense of the term, was their chief interest. These leaders were expanding their campuses and bettering their academic programs, regardless of the scores on the playing fields.

Southern Conference Presidents Meet

The meeting on March 3 gathered some of the most important academic leaders and athletic officials in the Southeast, with all 17 schools in attendance. Because of his previous leadership, Gray was the logical choice to serve as the presiding officer. Max Farrington, president of the Southern Conference, a thankless task, accepted the role of secretary.

In the new, sparkling Greek Revival styled Morehead Planetarium, the first planetarium in the South, Gordon Gray could proudly exhibit one of the university's proudest achievements. In numerous ways, the $3 million building, which linked science, Christianity, and education, was a symbol of a thriving and modern campus. It was the envy of all who attended.

Not long after the 10:00 a.m. meeting time, President Irvin Stewart of West Virginia

University made the motion to approve the first agenda item which stated that conference presidents needed to take an active role in studying and managing athletic programs in a similar fashion as they did academic programming on their campuses. This was unanimously approved, but it meant a great change in direction from how many presidents handled college athletics.[22] It sounded like an innocuous agenda item, but, if fully implemented, it denoted enormous change for presidents and athletic departments.

North Carolina Chancellor Bob House proposed that the presidents affirm that their institutional policies and actions be in line with Southern Conference by-laws. A vote was not taken, but the motion was approved by acclamation.[23] This was another step toward establishing uniformity within the 17-member conference, but it was a recognition as well that it had not been finalized whether NCAA policies trumped Southern Conference policies.

"Trust and Mutual Understanding" was a topic of significant discussion raised by Curly Byrd of Maryland and President Frank Poole of Clemson. For the presidents to successfully conduct their duties of effectively managing college athletics, Byrd made a motion, approved unanimously, that each Southern Conference president be apprised of key athletic meetings on their campus and attend enough of them to become proficient about the issues facing college athletics. This was not hard for Byrd, who, unlike many of the other presidents, was a former football player and coach as well as a strong advocate for athletics who kept a careful watch over Maryland's sports. Frank Poole, a keen advocate of collegiate athletics, provided additional ammunition, saying that presidents needed to work together more closely to handle and solve problems related to intercollegiate sports.[24] All of this was true. College athletics needed careful monitoring to contain its growing stature, but could presidents do the job?

As was seemingly always the case, the ills of recruiting and what could be done to stop impropriety was discussed. With only one dissenting vote, most likely The Citadel, the conference supported a motion from President Poole at Clemson asking that the league collectively support current NCAA recruiting regulations.[25]

Complementary to the recruiting issue was Eddie Cameron's plea to establish uniform entrance requirements as well as enforcement of high school graduation as a prerequisite for university matriculation. This was a persistent concern at Duke. University entrance requirements were a prickly issue for Southern Conference members, in part because the schools differed greatly in size and purpose with varied ambitions as well. Discussion swirled for some time about the difficulties of establishing a unified entrance policy. Although not mentioned in the minutes, the presidents were deeply worried about instituting policies that separated athletes from the broader student body. Ultimately, they decided to instruct conference officers to enforce high school graduation as a minimum requirement with an additional recommendation to consult with accreditation bodies as to what may function as a minimum standard.[26] Obviously, much more work was needed on this controversial topic, but it was going to be hard to find a standard which all Southern Conference schools would accept.

With the always ubiquitous rumors swirling about the conference's future, often fanned by sportswriters, George Washington's Max Farrington, foreseeing the future of conference athletics, recommended that the conference be divided, for football, into a northern league and a southern league with a championship game played two weeks after the season. Revenue from the game would be divided by thirds, with the participating schools receiving one-third each, and the conference treasury receiving one-third.

Farrington's proposal was inspired by public and private discussions concerning the future of the league and its competitiveness. Dividing the conference would help solve the problem of establishing a clear conference champion, a dilemma throughout the league's history. A motion to partition the conference in this manner was not made, but discussion on the issue took place.[27]

The conference's baseball teams already played in two divisions. The basketball coaches one day earlier had formed a committee of five to study dividing basketball into two leagues within the conference. The coaches envisioned a northern division that included teams from Virginia, Maryland, Washington, and West Virginia. The southern loop would field teams from the Carolinas. The top four teams from each league would play in the Southern Conference Tournament.[28] Something of this sort was desperately needed in basketball and football, where schedules had enormous variety.

Towards the end of the meeting, there was a discussion of out of season football practices, a continuous source of controversy in the conference and around the nation. Allan W. Hobbs, a mathematician and dean of liberal arts at North Carolina, made a motion to abandon all out of season practices. There was no hope of this motion passing, and it failed to obtain a second. Any full abandonment of out of season practice would provide non-conference foes with a substantial advantage over Southern Conference squads. Not willing to abandon the entire idea of curtailing these practices, Davidson and George Washington moved that the Southern Conference abandon these practices if and when other conferences abolished them. If the full conference passed this motion, the commissioner was charged with alerting other conferences of this action.[29] The hope to contain the growth of football was very much prescient among Southern Conference leaders.

The last item at the meeting came from Geary Eppley at Maryland, who, on the recommendation of Curly Byrd, proposed that the presidents meet at least yearly, and that Gordon Gray be tapped as the chairman for the presidents. This passed unanimously.[30] It was a clear statement that presidents needed to be involved in collegiate athletics, but by mandating only a yearly meeting, it also indicated that Byrd did not wish the presidents to be too deeply involved in athletics.

By and large, this first meeting of Southern Conference presidents was a success. Simply gathering all of them in one location was a herculean task, but there was a commitment to cooperate on the most difficult athletic issues. None of this meant that they had the answers, but at least they recognized that they needed consistent involvement in athletics. It was in their benefit.

Dropping Football

While presidents were concerned with Southern Conference football, athletic de-emphasis advocates were pleased to see that Georgetown University dropped football in March 1951. Georgetown's president, the Rev. Hunter Guthrie, declared that the university needed to allocate money to other student activities that benefited a larger portion of the student body.[31] Guthrie did not see a relationship between football and the academic mission of the university, and the cost of football gave him a legitimate opportunity to terminate the program. Georgetown had played football for over 60 years and as late as 1949 had made an appearance in the Sun Bowl, but the postwar era led to a decline in attendance and interest. More importantly, the program was losing money.

Georgetown was playing their games off campus at Griffith Stadium, a cavernous facility for a school Georgetown's size. Griffith was a multi-use stadium, used for baseball and football. It never provided a home field advantage for Georgetown, and the Hoyas shared it with George Washington University, the Washington Redskins, and the Washington Senators. Even Maryland spent a year, 1948, playing home games in the facility while Byrd Stadium was under construction.

The Catholic school's decision, mercilessly attacked by some alumni, was in line with a spate of schools who ended their football programs in 1950 and 1951. These included Duquesne, Niagara, St. Mary's, Tusculum, and Milliken.[32] St. Mary's, a small California college, was a powerhouse in the 1930s and 1940s, but it could not compete within the postwar environment. Gael football did not have much of a presence in dynamic postwar California. Their final game was in 1950 against Villanova.

In North Carolina, High Point and Atlantic Christian College suspended football, in part due to the Korean War, and in part due to the extreme difficulty fielding competitive teams. In the Palmetto State, Erskine, in tiny Due West, dropped the sport as well.

Georgetown's announcement, however, was major headline news around the country. Few expected a prominent school of Georgetown's pedigree to end its football program. With many small schools in the Southern Conference, all of this was a call to place their houses in order lest they follow this pattern.

The shuttering of these programs also indicated that it was appropriate for Southern Conference schools to clarify their ambitions and goals in college athletics. It is worth noting that even large Southern Conference schools struggled with the economics of football. NC State, for example, with a healthy enrollment and growing stature, was habitually running deficits in the athletic department, mostly because its football team could not generate enough revenue. In 1951 and 1952, there were rumors that State was considering dropping its football program. The program ran on overdrafts in 1951, reaching over $60,000 at one time. In the past the athletic program even had borrowed money from local banks.[33] As late as 1953, things looked bleak for State athletics. The athletic program was losing money, with a deficit of $55,000 predicted by September 1.[34] It was far from certain that State could continue to play football, but the athletic council believed that football could continue, if radical changes were made. State may have been the largest of conference schools in this predicament, but other Southern Conference colleges, especially the smaller ones, were having financial difficulties as well.

May 1951 Southern Conference Meeting

All of this formed the backdrop to the May 1951 Southern Conference meeting at the John Marshall Hotel in Richmond. As usual, the executive committee met a day prior to the main meeting, this time on Friday, May 4, to discuss the final agenda for the meeting scheduled for Saturday. Rumors that the Richmond gathering was designed to end the Southern Conference were refuted by Eddie Cameron who stressed that the Blue Devils were happy within the league and were not aspiring to a different athletic arrangement.[35] Considering Duke's longtime success in the league, especially in football, this was a strong confirmation that the Southern Conference was solid, but there was no doubt that Cameron and his colleagues at Duke had considered a different conference arrangement for many years. Any new league would have to take Duke, the wealthiest school in the conference, with them. Duke had athletic aspirations that were well in excess of what many Southern Conference foes could reach. The Blue Devils were balancing their national ambitions with a league that included schools that never could hope to compete with Duke.

In some ways, the conference meeting in Richmond was called into order with renewed confidence. Many of the league's schools had been on the forefront of defeating the Sanity Code, pledging that schools and conferences should decide athletic rules, especially as they pertained to the finances of college athletics, and not the NCAA. With Virginia's Norton Pritchett attending the meeting, it appeared that the table was set for conference expansion as well. There was confidence in that the league had successfully fought the NCAA, strengthened conference sovereignty, and could focus on persuading Virginia to join. The future looked bright.

On the morning of May 5, the *Richmond Times-Dispatch* editorial page urged the Southern Conference to "take the lead" in reforming college athletics and to rid it of commercialism and corruption.[36] The editorial noted that J. Edgar Hoover, before a Senate subcommittee, had attacked colleges for being, in part, responsible for the corruption scandals in basketball that had been investigated by the FBI. Although not providing a course of action, the Richmond paper explained that firm and direct action was needed and that the conference could no longer make minor changes hoping for the best. A clear moral approach was necessary, they argued.[37]

Commissioner Wallace Wade echoed these opinions when speaking at Davidson College's Athletic Banquet. Wade told the young men to stress "fair play" and "sportsmanship."[38] To the former Duke coach, college athletics formed part of the "foundation of the country" by teaching sportsmanship. Some in the Southern Conference, however, were not excited to hear remarks that smacked of de-emphasis.

The meeting, like so many Southern Conference gatherings, did not accomplish all that was hoped. A keen observer of the Southern Conference, Shelley Rolfe described the meeting in this manner. "The Southern Conference people expended something like seven hours, 51 pitchers of ice water, and 11 cartons of cigarettes yesterday discussing the going wage for blocks and tackles. It was a day to try men's patience, and when the last gavel had been banged by Wallace Wade, the conference commissioner was looking frayed and wilted."[39]

With the Sanity Code defeated, the Southern Conference could pen its own recruiting standards, including enforcement policies. Although enjoying more conference sovereignty, the representatives in Richmond failed to take advantage of the situation and delayed crafting recruiting policies, postponing things until its December meeting. They could not draft any language providing the conference commissioner the ability to punish institutions for violating recruiting policies. It made one wonder the purpose of having a commissioner. All of this was a notable abdication of duty.

On the bright side for conference members, Virginia's Norton Pritchett, acting as an observer, did nothing to dispel the idea that Virginia would rejoin the league by the end of 1951. With so much discussion and very little movement, one wonders why Virginia considered rejoining a conference that had as many issues as the Southern. Nevertheless, Pritchett's attendance was a good sign.

On July 17, 1951, the University of Virginia was stunned and saddened by the death of Norton Pritchett, its longtime athletic director. Pritchett died at Presbyterian

Hospital in Charlotte from pulmonary embolus. He had become ill while attending his son's graduation at Davidson College, where he previously had been an English professor and the athletic director. Pritchett had led Virginia's athletics since 1935, carving out a career of distinction, especially pertaining to keeping athletics within the mission of the university.[40] Pritchett had transformed the Cavaliers from an also-ran outside of the Southern Conference to a school with a competitive football program, that appeared eager to rejoin the league. He had laid the foundation for Virginia to take the next step.

Racial Integration

Although athletics dominated a lot of headlines in 1951, racial integration in higher education captured many headlines. Several university leaders found themselves trying to balance racial integration with segregationists, a balance that held no hope. The University of North Carolina offers an interesting example of the integration struggle.

North Carolina had been forced to accept a black medical school student in 1950, because there was no medical school in the state designated for African Americans. The UNC system in 1951 was dealing with the pressures of desegregation, especially in graduate schools. Gray and his chancellors were directed to conform to board of trustee policy enacted on April 4, 1951. The board stated that "non–Caucasian" students could be considered for admission, if the program to which they applied was not available at an African American school in North Carolina. Standards for admission were supposed to be the same. The board mandated that only medical school acceptance be considered, maintaining the barrier to the undergraduate matriculation of black students. African Americans were prohibited from summer school, the law school, and graduate programs which were offered at a black college or university. By June, the board was forced to relent on law school admission.[41] The policy, though, made it clear that no out-of-state African Americans would be considered for admission in any programs.[42]

In the summer of 1951, the University of North Carolina School of Medicine accepted four African American students for classes in the summer. In the fall semester, the university chose to mandate that black students be banned from sitting with white students at ball games. The issue came to a head in October 1951. Chancellor Bob House decreed that there was a distinction between academic integration and social integration, believing that the university was responsible only for academic integration, hence standing by the policy of denying five black law students the opportunity to sit with white students at athletic contests. Regardless of House's stated position, on November 2, 1951, four black students were allowed to sit in the previously white student section.[43]

Although integration was a hot-button issue at almost every southern school, it was never perceived as an athletic issue. Most administrators could not anticipate a day when African American student athletes would be participating on teams at southern schools. Although some Southern Conference schools, on occasion, played against colleges with African American players, the games had not caused an uproar, and the conference had not established a policy towards playing teams with black players.

Basketball Scandals

From 1949 through 1951, basketball point shaving formed the backdrop to athletic reform, but in the South, they did not carry the weight of football scandals. Nevertheless, basketball corruption in 1951 rocked the athletic world and was featured on front pages across America, giving the public a sense that there was a lot of rot within basketball programs. In the Southern Conference, basketball, traditionally, was secondary to football, although the sport was gaining an audience in the years after World War II. Many in the rural south had little connection with the game, seeing it mostly as a city sport. New York City was the unofficial capital of college basketball. The country's largest city housed the cavernous third incarnation of Madison Square Garden, and it featured a large number of collegiate games matching up some of the best teams in the country. The undistinctive building sat over 18,000 for basketball, making it the most important basketball arena in the country and one of the places where many college basketball players dreamed of competing. It also attracted gamblers and con men.

Basketball was easy to manipulate, thus making it a choice selection for gamblers who believed they could prey on naïve college athletes. With only five players per side, one or two athletes could have an enormous effect on the point spread. Although 1951 appeared to be the apex of basketball fixing, the practice was old, with many games having the stench of fixing draped over them. Regarding the Southern Conference, George Washington had endured a scandal as late as 1949, when four gamblers were charged for bribing co-captain David Shapiro to fix a game against Manhattan in New York City.[44]

Unsurprisingly, New York was the scandal's center with squads from Manhattan, City College, and Long Island University being implicated in fixing games. The biggest name was City College of New York, because they featured a dominating team that had won the NIT and NCAA tournaments in the 1949–1950 season. In early 1951, the nation's leading scorer at LIU was arrested for fixing games and news of the scandal went mainstream. Quickly, it was apparent that fixing was not only a New York City problem. It was found all over America. The University of Toledo and Bradley University were implicated and even the powerful University of Kentucky under Adolph Rupp was involved in fixing games. Rupp had declared that his players were immune from gambler intimidation, but he was wrong.

To Southern Conference members, it was Kentucky's implication that caused the greatest concern. Kentucky was the most heralded team in the land and was covered closely by media whether playing in Lexington or at Madison Square Garden. In addition, the Wildcats were viewed as a southern team, and received support from many southerners when they played northern schools. News that Alex Groza, Dale Barnstable, and Ralph Beard were involved in fixing games in the 1948–1949 season was a sensation. It was followed by charges that Adolph Rupp had associated with gamblers while being involved in aiding boosters in paying players after games. Kentucky's involvement in point shaving felt close to home.[45]

No Southern Conference school was implicated, but media stories about the scandal were featured in almost every American paper. One could not escape the scandal and the dereliction of duty that came from so many people from coaches to athletic directors and from trustees to presidents. It was hard to have faith that games were being played honestly. In the final reckoning in 1951, "thirty-five active and ex-players were accused of accepting $50,000 to fix eighty-six games. Sixteen players reported that they had spurned bribe offers totaling $22,900. Twenty-one gamblers and go-betweens were also implicated."[46] Colleges had to respond to such damning activities, especially after the statements of the presiding judge in these cases.

When sentencing convicted offenders, Judge Saul Streit, a former New York assemblyman, took the opportunity to vociferously attack basketball and football corruption in a 41-page document. He spared no one, maintaining that bribery, fraud, immorality, and the like pervaded every aspect of college athletics, all the while under the purview of presidents, boards, alumni, and coaches who ignored it or were culpable in promoting it. Oddly, he attacked Maryland's football program, associating it with Tennessee, Oklahoma, Southern Methodist and others.[47]

Although not calling for a suspension of intercollegiate athletics, Streit unambiguously voiced his concerns about the environment of college sports in 1951. He energetically wrote:

> Commercialism and over-emphasis in intercollegiate football and basketball are rampant throughout the country.... Intercollegiate football and basketball are no longer the sport of amateurs.... Professional coaches are engaged at salaries far exceeding professional pay.... Scholastic standards are evaded and resorts are had to trickery, devices, frauds and forgery.... The responsibility for the sports scandal must be shared not only by the crooked fixers and the corrupt players, but also by the college administrations, coaches and alumni groups who participate in this evil system of commercialism and over-emphasis.... Commercialism and over-emphasis contaminates everything it touches.[48]

Maryland's Curly Byrd, whose university was not a part of these criminal charges, was angered that Streit chose to use the sentencing portion of the case to assault college athletics and to attack Maryland in particular. Byrd accurately charged that Streit had no qualifications to speak about collegiate sports.[49] Never one to be quiet, Jim Tatum defended his Terps and college athletics, saying, "There are more fixed judges and jurors than there ever have been college athletes."[50] He even charged Streit with searching for headlines. The Maryland coach made his opinion clear on a television program where he was featured along with Dick Harlow, famed coach at Harvard and Penn State.

All around the country, athletic department leaders and coaches defended their programs and often attacked Streit. These responses came from schools such as SMU, Oklahoma, and Texas, among others. Although Streit did not know a lot about how college athletics functioned, he had drawn attention to age-old problems that plagued intercollegiate athletics.

At Kentucky, President Herman Donovan, a Rupp supporter, tried to find dirt on Judge Streit, especially communist affiliations. He asked Senator Thomas Underwood to help in this endeavor. Donovan even appealed to Curly Byrd, for information about Streit that he believed Maryland's president had obtained.[51] To his credit, Byrd's response was concise and direct, and perhaps saved Donovan's career. Byrd wrote that Maryland had "checked up" on Streit, but the board had decided that the proper course of action was to "make no reference to him, whatsoever."[52] He urged Donovan to follow Maryland's strategy and to step back from engaging Streit. Sound advice.

The ever-popular Red Smith of the *New York Herald Tribune*, featured in newspapers around the country, supported Streit's opinions, arguing that the biggest culprits in college athletic corruption paid no penalty. "Regrettably, there is no law that can reach the educators who shut their eyes to everything except the financial ledgers of the athletic department, the authorities who enroll unqualified students with faked credentials, the professors who foul their academic nests by easing athletes through their courses, the diploma mill operators who set-up classes for cretins in Rope-Skipping IV and History of Tatooing VII, the alumni who insist on winning teams and back their demands with cash, the coaches who'd put a uniform on Lucky Luciano if he could work the pivot play."[53] Smith even expressed his dismay with "mature men" defending the indefensible in collegiate athletics, many saying that Streit had no business speaking about college athletics and coaches.[54]

West Point Scandal

On August 4, 1951, just weeks prior to the beginning of the football season, Americans opened their newspapers expecting to read about the Korean War and perhaps peace negotiations. Most were shocked to learn that a large number of football players at West Point, heirs to those leading troops in Korea, had been expelled for cheating. This was unthinkable to most Americans. Army football was viewed as a paragon of virtue in collegiate athletics, dedicated to honesty and fair play on the field and in the classroom. To almost everyone's surprise an organized cheating ring had been in place at West Point since 1949. How could the institution that had produced many of the leaders that guided the Allies to victory in World War II fall prey to an athletic scandal? It was simple. Winning football had become more important than academics at West Point. What also stung so badly was that the cheating involved large numbers of cadets who operated an organized and systematic system for cheating. Ninety cadets, some of whom were tutors, were accused of academic dishonesty and expelled. The school, however, refused to provide names for those who had graduated but who were implicated in the scandal. Likewise, they did not offer the names of the current perpetrators. With these expelled student athletes looking for universities where they could continue their athletic and academic careers, names became public very soon.

Since his hiring in 1941, Coach Red Blaik had led Army to a string of enormously successful seasons, the envy of any college football program. These included five undefeated seasons, the last in 1949. The 1949 squad had won games by enormous margins with the closest scrape a 14–13 victory over a strong Pennsylvania squad on November 12. For the entire season, Army surrendered only 68 points while scoring 359. It was one of the most dominant seasons in college football history, and another example of Army's gridiron excellence.

Part of West Point's football mystique was because Red Blaik was the perfect man to lead Army. An army veteran who had played at West Point, Blaik was a hard-nosed, no-nonsense coach who inspired respect and admiration from almost all who met him. His previous coaching record at Dartmouth from 1934 through 1940 had been remarkable and featured a 22-game winning streak, something unheard of at the school. After leaving Dartmouth for Army, he posted a 32-game unbeaten streak and won two national championships.[55] It was hard to believe that such achievement would be tainted by corruption, especially given the reverence that many displayed for the military academy.

As the scandal became public, Blaik had to think deeply about the academic and athletic relationship that he had forged at West Point. His son, Bobby, an outstanding junior quarterback, had been charged in the cheating scandal, personalizing the corruption in almost an unthinkable way. The demands of major college football, Blaik argued, caused West Point to make accommodations for athletes and ultimately led to cheating. West Point, for example, had a "cram course" paid for by private individuals that allowed talented athletes to prep for the entrance examination for free. The coach said that West Point could not field a competitive team without such a course.[56] He blamed travel commitments and a punishing "physical and mental load" for leading cadets down the wrong path.[57]

The *New York Herald Tribune* placed the West Point scandal in its proper context, saying that the point-shaving scandal in basketball did not elicit the same kind of shock as what transpired at West Point. A reexamination of the relationship between athletics and academics was necessary, they said, but the most concerning aspect was that no player had demonstrated, at least publicly, remorse for their actions. "Everybody does it," a phrase we often hear associated with contemporary athletics, was the accepted explanation. The paper blamed West Point and all big-time football schools for lowering moral standards.[58]

The *Christian Science Monitor* was far more direct in damning the role of athletics at West Point and many other institutions. Pulling no punches, they charged that the scandal "had many of its roots in today's extravagant commercializing of America's college athletics."[59] Firing a salvo at alumni and boosters, the editorial board noted that "Academic integrity all too often bends before the persistent onslaughts of perpetual adolescents among the alumni."[60] They were complimentary as to how West Point handled the scandal, but strongly chastised the national environment that made the scandal possible.

Hubert O'Keef of the *Durham Morning Herald*, considering the West Point scandal, polled the Big Four to determine how they were managing the relationship between academics and athletics. Harold Tribble and Hollis Edens did not respond, but Bob House and Harrelson did. State's John Harrelson commented that recruitment was one of the greatest evils in college athletics and suggested that coaches or a representative from the university be allowed only one visit with potential recruits. State's head man maintained that a coach should not be paid more than the maximum allotted to full professors. This was already exceeded at UNC where Carl Snavely's salary was equal to the governor's.[61] Harold Tribble at Wake Forest was, no doubt, in agreement with Harrelson. He had let Peahead Walker leave, in part, because he did not believe a coach should earn more money than the highest paid faculty member.

Questions abounded about the scandal, especially as to the players involved, the two-month investigation, and football's future role at West Point. Politicians called for sweeping change. Arkansas senator J. William Fulbright, for example, proposed eliminating football at West Point and Annapolis, even though the Midshipmen were not involved.[62] The academy, unsurprisingly, closed ranks with Coach Blaik unavailable for comment as well as everyone in the football and athletic offices ordered to be tight-lipped.[63] Blaik's job was in peril, but he was retained as coach, in part because he was not implicated in the cheating scandal. Nevertheless, he was fortunate to retain his job. Blaik's 1951 squad, however, featured a badly depleted roster, devoid of much veteran talent. The team finished the season with only two wins versus seven losses. The only victories came against The Citadel and Columbia. In some ways, the season was Blaik's best as a coach. With little experience and few good players, the team was competitive for the entire season.

Even with a good showing in the 1951 season, considering the difficulties, the damage was done to college football and West Point. The public realized that if cheating occurred at Army, then it was rife at other schools around the country, no matter their academic reputation. The pursuit of victory, it was presumed, had surpassed everything else. The Army scandal was good fodder to everyone who believed that college football was a destructive force in academic institutions. Although a long way from New York, the scandal was an undercurrent for reform in the Southern Conference.

Small School, Big Scandal

South of West Point, another scandal was building in the Tidewater of Virginia. William & Mary joined the Southern Conference in 1936 in a wave of expansion necessary due to the withdrawal of schools who left the league to form the Southeastern Conference. Although in a league with some significant athletic programs, the Williamsburg school had a modest athletic tradition and was a lightly regarded institution, even considering its pedigree as the second oldest college in the country. It gained little attention, even in Virginia, and had a significant female student population that provided the school with the reputation as a school for women. This feminine reputation was a significant problem to the Board of Visitors, which saw athletic prowess as a way to masculinize the campus.[64] Something had to be done to elevate the school's reputation, which was far behind schools like the University of Virginia within the commonwealth, and to make it a solid choice for young men.

Following the blueprint of using athletics, especially football, to craft a new image for the institution, a strategy pioneered by President William Rainey Harper at the University of Chicago, William & Mary hired Carl Voyles as football coach in 1939.[65] President John Stewart Bryan, an enthusiastic supporter of the athletic initiative, selected Voyles from Wallace Wade's staff at Duke where he coached ends. Voyles was highly regarded by Wade and helped coach many of Duke's finest football teams. When the Oklahoman arrived at William & Mary, the situation was far removed from what he had experienced in Durham. The Indians had suffered through some tough seasons on the gridiron, with the program reaching a nadir in 1936, posting a 1–8 record. Although they rebounded to four wins the following season followed by a three-win campaign, there was no reason to think that much would change without a new hire and a full commitment to winning football games.

Voyles quickly found his footing and reeled off a series of very successful seasons. In his first two years, he finished with identical 6–2–1 records. In 1941, William & Mary completed an 8–2 campaign which set the stage for a Southern Conference Championship in 1942 with a 9–1–1 season. William & Mary finished the year with a 14–7 victory at Oklahoma and a number 14 ranking in the AP Poll. This was an incredible run of success, far greater than William & Mary had ever enjoyed. These achievements did not go unnoticed, and Auburn University offered Voyles $12,000 to leave Williamsburg for the plains of Alabama. With a 50 percent raise in salary, Voyles packed his bags and headed to Auburn and the SEC.[66]

President John Pomfret, who took the helm in 1943, continued the bold and dangerous athletic policy, but he was not a vocal advocate of athletics like most of the Board of Visitors and many alumni. Pomfret, who had served as a history professor at South

Carolina from 1935 to 1937, was a prominent historian of colonial America and was the author of several books, especially notable for his work on colonial New Jersey. He was a scholar with limited interest in athletics and completely unprepared to deal with athletic corruption or an athletically aggressive board. It was certain that he was going to feel uncomfortable with a board that was fully dedicated to winning athletic contests and had even stated so in its minutes in 1946.

With Voyles's departure, Ruben McCray, one of Voyles's assistants, was selected as head football coach and athletic director. A former player at Kentucky Wesleyan, McCray was a popular selection as the successor to Voyles, at least on the field. McCray enjoyed several outstanding years, continuing the best period of football success the institution had known. The 1947 edition of the Indians finished the season with only a 13–7 loss to Charlie "Choo Choo" Justice's powerful North Carolina team marring their record. Although they lost to Arkansas 21–19 in the Dixie Bowl, William & Mary football was earning a national reputation. The following year, the Indians enjoyed another outstanding season, losing only to Wake Forest and St. Bonaventure. They punctuated their year with a 20–0 Delta Bowl victory over Oklahoma A&M.[67]

With the full support of the Board of Visitors as well as the favor of the faculty athletic committee and the scholarship committee, William & Mary was gaining a great deal of attention for its athletic prowess.[68] But how was the tiny college competing against major football powers with far greater resources? It was cheating. In the 1949–1950 academic year, it became clear to a young dean, Nelson Marshall, that Ruben McCray, the football coach, and the athletic director, as well as basketball coach Barney Wilson, were operating corrupt athletic programs. High school transcripts were changed to allow entry into the college and fraudulent grades were assigned to athletes who needed good marks to remain eligible. To win at a high level, entry requirements were lowered and all efforts possible were made to keep players eligible. To assist these players, McCray even taught a course that provided struggling athletes with stellar grades.[69] Adding to this list was an intimidation scheme whereby Barney Wilson forced secretaries, undergraduate women at the college, to provide him with 10 percent of their wages.[70] In May 1951, the boyish Nelson Marshall, a marine biologist, presented Pomfret with a report detailing the corruption rife throughout the football and basketball programs. The charges were extensive, illustrating a defined pattern of academic dishonesty. He even had evidence of a typewriter used by the athletic department to alter transcripts. President Pomfret recognized the gravity of the charges but was slow to move, in part because the Board of Visitors was an ally of athletics. Pomfret could not believe that McCray, a friend of his, had stooped so low to win games. In the final analysis, Pomfret was not prepared to deal with an athletic scandal, certainly not one of this magnitude that struck at the fundamental elements of academics. Trying to maneuver his way through the mess, he kept his promise to elevate McCray to full professor, a curious and bizarre move that caused a great deal of uproar when it became public.

With no response from Pomfret, Dean Marshall, on June 11, provided the president, again, with details of athletic corruption. Nothing much was done, except Pomfret convening a faculty committee to investigate athletics. This was unnecessary, considering the amount of evidence that Marshall had accumulated.

Pomfret, seemingly, was trying to keep the scandal quiet, but rumors spread throughout campus and in Williamsburg that something was brewing in the athletic department. On August 10, under pressure, McCray and Wilson resigned their posts.

Wilson stated that his intention was to enter private business in Kentucky while McCray said little about his immediate plans, but he clearly wished to coach.[71] Pomfret resigned as well, after having been held responsible for the scandal, a largely unfair charge. The real blame fell at the feet of the Board of Visitors who wanted to win at all costs.[72]

Throughout the crisis, Pomfret appeared paralyzed, even avoiding public comments. He was hoping to leave William & Mary and become the director of the Huntington Library. The last thing he wanted was for the scandal in Williamsburg to jeopardize his opportunity in San Marino, California. His resignation was a surprise to most, but welcomed by the board, who never much warmed to his academic bearing. With the resignation, they now had someone to blame. Pomfret was a fine academic who was steam rolled by an athletic scandal not of his making and beyond his abilities to manage.[73]

Meeting in Richmond in mid–August, the Board of Visitors preferred to castigate the president rather than admit wrongdoing on its behalf. Even though McCray and Wilson had resigned, clearly due to their corrupt actions, and the school's president was ready to move 3,000 miles away from Williamsburg, there was no recognition on the part of the board that they had done anything incorrect. They closed ranks, even though newspaper stories about the scandal littered Virginia papers.

Obviously, the faculty was outraged and, after not being allowed to have their voices heard by the board, created a powerful document addressing their concerns about William & Mary sports. They argued that "The fundamental cause is an athletic policy which at William & Mary, as at many other American colleges and universities, has proceeded to the point of obscuring and corrupting the real purposes of an institution of higher learning."[74] The faculty did not detail the violations, as there was no need at this point, but stated, "Steadily and inevitably the intercollegiate athletic program has usurped a dominating position in the College. Instead of a healthy and indispensable extra-curricular activity, it has become a commercial enterprise demanding winning teams at any cost, even the cost of dishonest academic practices."[75] The faculty statement identified all of the ills of college athletics, stressing that academic standards were reduced to enroll athletes, scholarship money was redirected from academic achievement to athletic ability, course schedules were gerrymandered, easy classes were embraced, and athletes were directed away from strenuous academic programs. They charged that the college's honor system was shabbily treated, and key administrators were actively violating the basic tenants of the college's mission. The economic stress of attempting to field nationally competitive teams was also mentioned as a great drain on resources that would be better directed to important elements of the school's academic mission.[76] In its manifesto, the faculty did not call for the banishment of athletics but demanded for it to be subordinate to the overall mission of the university.

Faculty recommendations for change, if fully enacted, would have ended William & Mary's membership in the Southern Conference. Without athletic scholarships and donor gifts to the athletic department, the Indians had no hope of competing with the larger schools in the conference or even those who usually were on the fringes of victory. Membership in the Southern Conference was not mentioned in the resolution, but it needed to be part of the overall discussion of William & Mary's academic and athletic goals.

Charles Karmosky, the sports editor for the *Newport News Daily Press*, feared that the faculty statement on athletic reform might trigger an overreaction that would savage William & Mary athletics. Like many other sportswriters, Karmosky favored reform in college sports, especially football, but he feared that "revenge" might destroy college sports.[77] Abolition was not the answer, but reform was, he argued.

Meanwhile, the Board of Visitors issued their report on William & Mary's problems and found little fault in their behavior. The influential *Richmond Times-Dispatch* attacked the Board of Visitors saying that they had released an insufficient report on the scandal, leaving key questions unanswered. They were right. The report was designed to be general and avoid speaking of any responsibility from the Board of Visitors.[78] But Virginians deserved to hear the full story from Williamsburg. The school's leaders had allowed an aggressive athletic program to compromise its academic reputation. The paper charged the Board of Visitors as being the primary culprit in creating a big-time sports program at William & Mary. There were other questions concerning the behaviors of Marshall and Pomfret, but these were secondary.[79]

The Richmond *News Leader* produced a scathing indictment of the Board of Visitors. The editors wrote:

> It was the Board of Visitors that laid down a perverted "athletic policy" for the Williamsburg school. It was the Board of Visitors that hired coaches, administered the funds of the athletic association, spurred the team on to great victories. It was the Board of Visitors that directed the administration to field teams that would "win more games than they lose." It was the Board of Visitors which laid formal emphasis on successful teams. It was the Board of Visitors that laid down a policy in 1946 and reaffirmed it in 1951 of demanding that William & Mary's football be conducted on a sound financial basis. Members of the Board of Visitors entertained Coach McCray in their homes; they sat on the bench with the players; they visited the locker rooms. They gave every indication that they wanted big-time football. They never once objected to the schedules arranged for William & Mary. They now have hired a new coach, at a salary far above that provided for veteran professors, and their unsatisfactory report of September 8 (in which all the blame was laid on the administration and none on the board itself) gives a revealing indication of how much de-emphasis may be expected from the board.[80]

Rarely has a newspaper so accurately and clearly explained the administrative problems at a college or university.

The *New York Times* complimented William & Mary's faculty and stressed the need to think deeply about the faculty's judgments which were very different from the relative silent response at West Point.[81] The board, however, had no interest in listening to the faculty. Acting without consultation with the faculty, they quickly moved to appoint Admiral Alvin Duke Chandler as president, hoping like many college boards, that a military figure would use his military bearing to whip the faculty into shape. Pressure from alumni in addition to significant decreases in giving, however, forced William & Mary's hand. Athletics had to be de-emphasized.

The scandal at William & Mary was a devastating embarrassment and humiliation for the Williamsburg school, but more importantly it did not provide the clarity about college athletic abuses that many desired. Supporters of big-time college athletics could say that the problem rested with rogue coaches and spineless administrators. Those wishing for de-emphasis, including most of the faculty, argued that the root of the problem was the Board of Visitors, boosters, and big-time athletics, not people like Pomfret and Marshall. They were casualties of the drive to gain a national reputation through performance on the field and the court.

As a member of the Southern Conference, the scandal at William & Mary resonated with conference members in a way that the West Point scandal did not, especially among the other Virginia schools. Although a school of only about 1400, the depth of the scandal was astonishing. Essentially, the board, heavily focused on athletic glory, created an environment whereby coaches were allowed to run roughshod over established academic policies. This was all in the name of winning. It was not a coincidence that presidents of the Southern Conference later in the same year began to be more proactive in attempting to contain the corruption of big-time college athletics. Even with a significant scandal, Southern Conference members did not punish William & Mary. There was no probation or conference suspension. The leadership let the school clean up the embarrassing scandal.

The corruption caused a change in William & Mary's athletics, no matter the desires of some on the board who wanted to continue with big-time sports. There no longer was much interest in playing Oklahoma or other national programs. No new league wished to touch the school, especially in an era of scandal. Furthermore, the instability caused by the turmoil scared away potential coaches who wanted to work at a school where the relationship between academics and athletics was better. The scandal and its fallout had made athletic decline almost inevitable.

William & Mary, badly needing some stability in the football program, promoted its line coach, Marvin Bass, to the head position. Bass had starred at the Williamsburg school and had won the Southern Conference title in 1942, as an All-Southern Conference tackle. Bass, known as Big Moose, was well liked by his players and was one of the few coaches interested in coaching for a program whose future was unknown. He was the only surviving coach from the previous year's staff. Although it was late in the year to be hiring a football coach, they could have done much worse than Bass, who was highly regarded for his time on the staffs at UNC and William & Mary.[82] Even with a coach of Bass's pedigree, this was the beginning of a decline in William & Mary's athletic ambitions.

West Point Transfers

As schools started their fall semester in 1951, the West Point scandal began to directly affect some Southern Conference members in an unanticipated way. Hollis Edens reported that West Point coaches had approached Duke's coaches as to the possibility of expelled West Point students being accepted at Duke to play football. Edens had no desire to tell other member institutions what to do but explained that Duke's policy was not to accept these students. The obvious issue was whether this was to be a permanent bar from a college education or only a prohibition on participation in college athletics. Nevertheless, Edens urged that other conference members bar West Point's expelled students from collegiate athletics even if they chose to accept them as students.[83]

Presidential responses to the transfer question provide a good indication of the variety of institution within the Southern Conference. The Citadel's president, Charles Summerall, was quick to endorse Edens' position, explaining that the former West Point students could not be accepted at the Charleston school.[84] Davidson's J.R. Cunningham felt the same way and noted that they had been approached by an influential donor to accept an expelled West Point student.[85] North Carolina State had a policy towards transfers that banned the university from accepting an expelled transfer student if their former school would not accept them.[86] This was essentially the same position held by

Furman. State's John Harrelson agreed that any student expelled for academic dishonesty should be banned from collegiate sports. To no great surprise, John Pomfret at William & Mary, who was dealing with the emerging athletic scandal, reported that his institution already had decided not to accept any of the former West Point students.[87] Clemson agreed to barring the students from athletic participation, but not from the opportunity of earning an education.[88]

Virginia Tech's Walter Newman provided a more nuanced policy for dealing with students who were expelled. Although agreeing that expelled students should not participate in collegiate sports, he explained that Virginia Tech had accepted, conditionally, students who had been expelled from other institutions. To his knowledge, they had in general performed well. At times, he had encouraged other Virginia schools to give VPI students a second chance as well. Newman argued that it was best to deal with these cases on an individual basis instead of with a blanket policy and that the passage of time before readmittance provided a good source of evidence as to the suitability of a student's readmittance.[89] As usual, Newman offered good judgment and a wise course of action.

West Virginia took a position similar to that of Virginia Tech. Irvin Stewart explained that they already had accepted one of the former cadets at West Virginia and were perhaps expecting another two additional applications. Stewart interpreted the acceptance as part of the civic duty associated with operating a state university. He saw no reason that these ex-cadets should be barred from athletics, unless one conference member was gaining an advantage by actively recruiting large numbers of these student-athletes to their school.[90]

By September 11, Maryland, a logical destination considering the success that Jim Tatum was enjoying on the football field, had received seven former West Point applications but had rejected all of them in what was called standard practice.[91]

The differing opinions on West Point transfers underscored the huge variety of schools within the Southern Conference. Opinions ranged from Duke's full rejection of these students to West Virginia's willingness to offer a second chance on the football field and in the classroom. It was another example of the unwieldy nature of the Southern Conference and the struggles to craft consistent policies with so many different schools with varying missions, sizes, and ambitions.

The year was a turning point for schools nationally and in the Southern Conference. Scandals unleashed a wave of reform enthusiasm that emboldened Southern Conference presidents and academic leaders. There was a widespread belief that the time was right for the presidents to lead the Southern Conference toward reform efforts. Nonetheless, reform efforts faced strong headwinds from sportswriters, boosters, and alumni. Gordon Gray was the linchpin for reform, but it was a role he did not cherish. The dutiful Gray was about to take a step that would change the course of the Southern Conference in a profound manner.

3

Banning Bowls

In the academic year, the summer always provides time for administrators and faculty to think boldly and widely, sometimes unrealistically, about the future. The summer of 1951 was no different. With sports schedules dormant and most students away, the first serious indications of an actual conference split appeared. In the context of a forthcoming conference meeting in September, Curly Byrd told Gordon Gray that he wished to "have a meeting of the larger institutions in the conference. In my opinion, the time has come when we should have a more closely knit organization, an organization in which there would be only institutions of similar resources and interests."[1] Byrd had a new conference on his mind, and the invitation indicated that he was ready to move on from the Southern Conference. With presidents more interested in managing athletics, the time was appropriate for Byrd to convince other presidents that the Southern Conference no longer worked for some of its schools.

Before the William & Mary scandal attracted attention and perhaps with Curly Byrd's invitation on his mind, Gordon Gray called another meeting of the presidents and the faculty chairmen of the Southern Conference schools for September 28. Athletic directors were asked to attend as well, but they were to be excluded from participating in the meeting. They only held observer and advisor status. Transparency was fully recognized, because the presidents agreed for the press to attend and hear all the discussion, a policy that would be changed as collegiate sports grew larger.[2] It was unclear to most participants that this September meeting would have great consequence for the Southern Conference's future.

Two weeks prior to the meeting, *Life* magazine, influential and widely read, published a scathing article about collegiate football bluntly titled "Football Is a Farce."[3] Attacking college presidents for shirking their duty to instill and defend ethics and morality on their campuses, the editorial staff wrote:

> The college president will say that he doesn't really sell the tickets—that in fact he has nothing whatever to do with football. Maybe not, Mr. President, but someone is certainly committing the crime in your name. In fact your football team is violating all the ethics that you are trying to teach in your classrooms. Whether you are an active conniver in this fraud or just the victim of a camel under the tent you appear equally guilty to any casual bystander.[4]

With an exceptionally large readership, *Life*'s comments, directly confronting presidential leadership, formed an important backdrop to how the Southern Conference presidents conducted their business.

Curly Byrd was unable to make the September 28 gathering, but he did provide Gordon Gray with his positions on the agenda items, offering an indication of his opinions on the most contentious issues facing college athletics and the conference. Unlike many of the other presidents, Byrd did not have a problem with off-season practices as long as they were standardized across the different conference members. He strongly opposed the conference's ban on transfers, but Byrd understood that there was little chance of movement on that issue. On the matter of bowl game participation, Byrd, always a supporter of football, emphasized that universities should have the right to play in bowls. Toward the end of the memo, Byrd urged that there should be minimum requirements to participate in college athletics, such as having graduated high school, and that athletes should be legitimate and regular students. His absence at the meeting, most likely, made a significant difference.[5] Gray was the leader of Southern Conference reform and the movement for de-emphasis of college athletics. He detested the term de-emphasis but that would be the outcome if Gray's ideas were implemented. His ally, Hollis Edens, was a powerful voice as well. The only president who could challenge Gray, especially in athletics, was Curly Byrd. Not only had Byrd transformed Maryland's flagship university, but he also had a nationally recognized football team with a coach who some at UNC desperately wanted.

Gray, nonetheless, saw opportunity. He believed that the upcoming meeting held great promise for comprehensive athletic reform. When meeting with the chancellors at North Carolina and State College on September 10, 1951, Gray asked the chancellors if they would support a proposal to end all off-season practice in sports. House and Harrelson "agreed and urged it."[6] It was more of an indication that something substantial was possible.

The September 28 meeting, again at the Morehead Planetarium, was a momentous event for the future of the 17-school league. At 10:30 a.m., Gordon Gray called the meeting to order and his trusted advisor, Bill Friday, the holder of an undergraduate degree from State and a law degree from Chapel Hill, began taking minutes.[7] Recognizing that the scandal-ridden year had led many to suspect that this gathering was called to get the conference's house in order, Gray explained that the presidents had met in March and were collectively discussing issues within collegiate athletics well before the recent scandals.[8] That was true, but the year's headline-making events had influenced presidents, and Gray's words would do little to end speculation. Simply put, the role of collegiate athletics had been featured in newspapers and magazines around the country. It could not be ignored.

Commissioner Wallace Wade was asked to present a resolution that recently had passed at a meeting of the National Association of Collegiate Commissioners. The resolution declared that there were "undesirable trends" in collegiate athletics that sacrificed the student's academic duties on the funeral pyre of regimented athletic requirements. The commissioners recognized that out of season practices were a growing problem as well as too many games played within a season. Athletics, they argued, were becoming so pervasive in their demands for improvement that they "interfere with the basic concept of athletic activity as only an incidental part of college life and experience."[9] The resolution criticized the growing pressures that were placed on the student-athlete, arguing that universities and colleges needed to quickly move to contain the excesses of college athletics to readjust it to its proper relationship with academics and the broader aspects of college life.[10] With this insightful preamble outlining some of the most significant problems in college athletics, the commissioners urged conferences and colleges to limit or eliminate off-season practices, particularly in football and basketball.

They recommended a reduction in the number of games played in a season and favored attempts to stop the overlap of seasons in major sports. The commissioners encouraged colleges to control the amount of influence from outside forces, especially alumni and boosters, an almost impossible proposition. Lastly, the public needed to appreciate that the retention and flourishing of college athletics required "the maintenance of a sane and sound balance in the life of the student athlete under which he must be a student primarily and an athlete incidentally."[11] Although the resolution did not provide a detailed outline of the many changes that were needed to control the professionalization and commercialization of college athletics, it was an excellent summation of the general problems faced by colleges and universities. Using the term incidental to describe the relationship between athletics and academics cast athletics in a different light, one clearly subservient to the academic mission.

Wade explained that the commissioners wished for athletic conferences to adopt and support their recommendations as fully as possible. The presidents attempted to pass the entire resolution as a recommendation to their representatives to the Southern Conference, but they failed, because the formation of the agenda prevented such action. Instead, it became much more of a piecemeal process, another indication of the difficulties to craft reform in a 17-team league.[12] Essentially, these recommendations were to be passed to athletic directors and faculty athletic representatives for more consideration.

Freshman participation in varsity sports, again, was discussed. The argument that freshmen were needed to fight in the Korean War was broached but rejected. Although the war had begun the previous year, it in no way had placed the type of strain on academic and athletic programs that World War II had done. It could not be used to justify the need for freshman participation. Furman's president John Plyler wanted to retain the current freshman policy, allowing participation for another year, but the University of Richmond's president George Modlin's recommendation that the conference study freshman academic performance before establishing a policy won the day.[13]

Academic control over athletics was an issue since the beginning of college athletics and the Southern Conference presidents revisited the topic with a resolution presented by Davidson's president John Cunningham, a Presbyterian minister. The motion requested a change to the Southern Conference by-laws stating that a vote could be delivered by a president or administrative officer or a faculty member whose chief duties were outside of athletics. This was a strong indication that academics were needed to keep a check on athletics. As expected, there was vigorous discussion, because the resolution was affecting the most sensitive issue surrounding college athletics. Was academic leadership going to take a vigorous role in athletics or should it be allotted to athletic administrators? What would be the long-term consequences for athletics if the academic officials exercised increased authority? The motion passed.[14] Southern Conference presidents appeared serious about retaining academic control over athletics.

The two-platoon system was an issue on which most coaches, sportswriters, fans, and academics could unite. The presidents failed to discuss the elimination of the two-platoon system, which would need agreement from other leagues. Most presidents were deeply concerned that fielding a platoon for offense and a platoon for defense simply cost too much money and required too much specialization. From Hollis Edens' notes of the meeting, for instance, he strongly favored a single platoon and capping football teams at 35 players.[15] This action, not voted upon, would have made a significant difference in containing some of the corruption in football, but for it to be practical other conferences had to follow suit. Even supporters of wide-ranging reform did not want to place their teams at a significant competitive disadvantage.

The question of post-season football was now brought to the floor by Chancellor Bob House of UNC. House proposed eliminating the phrase "except by the consent of the conference" from section 3 of article 4 of the conference's by-laws. This was the caveat that mandated conference members approve any institution's participation in bowl games. House presented this motion expressing his full agreement with UNC's faculty, which was on record opposing North Carolina's future participation in bowls. Most likely, Gordon Gray had persuaded House to bring the motion to the floor, because Gray was the presiding officer of the meeting and House's boss. Everyone in the room knew that Gray was a strident opponent of bowl participation. The motion was seconded by Walter Newman of VPI, and Duke's Hollis Edens jumped aboard as a co-sponsor of the motion with House. It does not appear that there was much discussion, because Bill Friday, recording the minutes, only reported that it passed.[16] Gray knew he had the votes to win passage, and Byrd's absence simply made approval easier. But this was far from the end of the matter.

Wallace Wade, perhaps caught off guard by the rapid approval of what was destined to be a very controversial item, asked that the presidents provide an indication of whether they would charge their conference representatives to vote for or against a conference member's participation in a bowl game for the current season. President Stewart made a motion stating, "The Presidents present record their intention to vote against the request of any member of the Conference to accept any bowl bid if offered to any member institution this year."[17] The motion was seconded by Bob House. Of the 17 members present only Clemson voted that it would not ban bowl participation. State, Washington and Lee, and Maryland did not cast a vote. Therefore, 13 conference presidents signified that they would instruct their representatives to ban a conference member from participating in a bowl game at the conclusion of the football season.[18]

North Carolina chancellor Bob House, pictured with his famous harmonica (likely in the late 1940s or early 1950s), loved Tar Heel sports but was concerned about the growing commercialism and professionalism (courtesy North Carolina Collection Photographic Archives, Wilson Library, University of North Carolina at Chapel Hill).

It was not surprising that Clemson supported bowl game participation. The Tigers had played in three bowl games, the latest in January 1951 in the Orange Bowl. Furthermore, Frank Howard was fielding a good team in 1951. Maryland's pass was a bit surprising considering that

Jim Tatum had led the Terrapins to an outstanding early season run. It is worth remembering that Curly Byrd was not in attendance, thus depriving Maryland of its most powerful and persuasive voice.

There were other pressing issues to debate, but they were too late to add to the agenda and would have taken a great deal of time. These related to recruiting practices in and around "all-star" football and basketball games and the role that collegiate coaches played in these contests. Subsidizing athletics was the second issue that did not make it to the floor. Regardless, a subcommittee was formed to study these items.[19]

Of the issues discussed at the Chapel Hill gathering, the bowl ban was an immediate lightning rod, seemingly an indication that the Southern Conference had decided to de-emphasize athletics, most notably on the gridiron. With the ban having been initiated by Gordon Gray and Bob House, Smith Barrier in the *Greensboro Daily News* asked if the University of North Carolina was de-emphasizing football. The United Press judged that the meeting passed measures to "de-emphasize big-time" college sports.[20] It appeared to many outside observers that the Southern Conference had made a strong statement designed to constrain college sports.

Further complicating issues was that this action was taken while the season was underway. No one knew how the football season would unfold, but all the presidents were aware that Maryland had a powerful football team, with a great opportunity to end the year as the top team in the land. There was a strong likelihood that the Old Liners would be invited to a prestigious bowl game that garnered national attention. How could a bowl ban withstand that type of enormous pressure?

The September meeting was a red-letter moment in the history of the Southern Conference. The presidents were dealing with the fallout from a series of series scandals that held the possibility of spreading to their institutions. William & Mary, one of their own, was reeling from their scandal. The role of college athletics in the life of higher education required careful and detailed study and always had been controversial. By accepting the recommendations of the commissioners' report, the conference was moving in the direction of controlling some of the devilish problems that had plagued college athletics; however, they also had taken a step toward conference fragmentation by banning participation in bowl games beginning in the 1951 season which was underway. The Southern Conference had not been this unsettled since the Southeastern Conference's split from the league almost 20 years earlier. It was looking like the December Southern Conference meeting would be a donnybrook.

The editorial pages of papers in the Carolinas and Virginia praised the presidents for their actions, desiring that they follow through with their attempts at reform. The *Rocky Mount Evening Telegram* was jubilant that bowl game participation would end. The editors saw the games as revealing a bloated and unseemly side of college athletics that deserved reform.[21] Praising the prohibition, the *News and Observer*, for example, wished for the presidents to take additional steps, such as prohibiting out of season practices.[22]

Editorial boards, by and large, favored presidential involvement and reform in college athletics. Knowing that their actions, especially on bowl games, caused a significant uproar among fans, alumni, and sportswriters, Gordon Gray attempted, unsuccessfully, to quell the flames. Gray commented, "This is no fire alarm meeting, no chopping block for the coaches and athletic officials. We feel that collegiate athletics has a place in the educational picture and we want to place it in the proper perspective in the whole scheme of university life."[23] Smith Barrier emphasized that it was Bob House of North Carolina who made the proposals to ban bowl games and freshman participation in sports, underscoring North Carolina's leadership in what he believed to be a de-emphasis campaign.[24] Furthermore, Barrier stressed that the bowl ban was for the 1951 season and the roll call vote made certain that each institution realized that the ban was approved.

The *News and Observer*'s Dick Herbert offered a more nuanced approach to the banning of bowls. In North Carolina's capital city, it was difficult to speak about sports without the conversation turning to Dick Herbert. A native of Harrisburg, Pennsylvania, Herbert graduated from Duke University in 1935. His long career with the *News and Observer* started in 1942 and lasted until 1974. Herbert's duties accelerated in the postwar period as the Big Four matured into major universities of regional and national standing. Herbert was an insightful writer, not prone to hyperbole, who was concerned about commercialism and professionalism in college sports.

Herbert pointed out that the conference which had fought the Sanity Code was now the conference that banned bowl competition. Herbert trusted that the presidents believed that their actions were proper, but he suggested that they could be the death knell for major college football within the Southern Conference.[25] This would be true, he argued, if spring practice were disallowed, something he thought the conference leadership would demand. Herbert believed that the great evils of bowl games could be mitigated if restrictions were placed on "the number of bowl games sanctioned by the conference and then turning in all receipts above expenses to the conference office."[26] That would reduce the desire of individual schools to commit ill deeds to win bowl games.

Herbert thought that the meeting was a significant moment in reducing the power of athletic directors and coaches while placing athletic matters in the hands of presidents and their faculties. He encouraged that those voting needed a strong background in athletics, but he did not express the gloomy views of so many other sportswriters. Herbert believed that the presidential actions were positive and held the promise of helping reform college athletics.[27]

The *Charlotte Observer*'s Wilton Garrison, one of the early supporters of stock car racing, was concerned that the Southern Conference was moving too far away from mainstream college athletics in its prohibition of bowl games. Viewing the situation very differently than his colleague in Raleigh, he regarded the college presidents as the problem, by delving too deeply into athletics, an area in which they were not well versed. Garrison had no problem with reforms such as a standard admission policy or limits on recruiting; however, his concern was that Southern Conference presidents, driven by scandals, felt compelled to demonstrate that they oversaw college athletics. Football's over emphasis, Garrison argued, was the chief threat to college athletics, but most fans and colleges did not believe that over-emphasis was a problem. Regardless, reform had to be conducted uniformly around the country. If the Southern Conference conducted widespread reforms alone, it would be at a terrible disadvantage when facing squads from conferences like the Southeastern, where de-emphasis was not a factor. Somewhat like Dick Herbert, Garrison wanted a slower approach to reform, one that did not strip the conference of its ability to compete on a national basis.[28]

To no great surprise, Bob Quincy hammered the Southern Conference presidents for acting in what he believed was a draconian manner that would do nothing to reform football. A North Carolina graduate, Quincy flew bombing missions over Europe with the 8th Air Force during World War II. Ending the two-platoon system, he argued, would do much more good than eliminating bowl participation. At least, it would help reduce some of the emphasis on recruiting. Although he admitted the presidents had some good intentions, they were all misplaced. "At the coming Richmond meeting, let me go on record as suggesting the addition of Queens College, St. Mary's, and Sweetbriar for an even 20 members."[29]

Even with Gray attempting to silence unrest, media members wanted to gauge the relationship between academic leaders and college athletics. The *News and Observer* asked Southern Conference presidents to provide them with statements about the importance of football and its proper relationship with academics. The Raleigh paper, which heavily covered the Big Four, was certain that this was to be a story of great interest, especially when published at the end of the season, when bowl talk was at its highest.[30]

In his typical terse manner, President Norman Smith at South Carolina responded saying that the presidents were essentially in agreement about all matters related to college football and that responses from other academic leaders would be the same.[31] He had no intention of providing any detailed information about his opinions, but his answer was off the mark.

State's Chancellor Harrelson took the request seriously and conferred with H.A. Fisher to provide a precise and thorough response. Regarding coaches, Harrelson and Fisher believed "a coach's tenure and protection should be predicated on the coach's value to the young men of the college and not on his table of wins."[32] That was an unpopular position, as pressure on winning increased with each passing year. Harrelson opposed all freshman participation on varsity athletic teams and did not want them hanging out with varsity squads as well. Spring practice needed to be banished, he argued, a position that all leaders in the North Carolina system supported. "All post-season games should be eliminated with the exception of basketball tournaments on the conference level."[33] Harrelson, like so many other presidents, favored limiting seasons to designated months, to reduce emphasis on athletics. Season creep was a problem. Lastly, conference voting members, he insisted, needed to be presidents or someone they had designated. This was another strike against the power that coaches and athletic directors had exercised in forging conference and institutional policies.

Harrelson engaged the question of recruiting, widely recognized as the most serious problem in intercollegiate athletics. "The competition between institutions is one of the worst features of the whole intercollegiate program. Only one visit should be made by a football coach or athletic representative, of any college or university, to talk athletics to any high school player."[34] Once the decision was made by the student, he suggested it be final. In general, Harrelson wanted college athletics to be on the "same level with physical education, intra-mural athletics, fraternities, debating teams, or any other general activity open to all students."[35] Alumni and boosters would have a great deal to say about that.

Fisher concurred with his boss's assessment and even went a step or so beyond him. As a faculty member in mathematics, Fisher wanted only "bona fide" faculty members voting on Southern Conference policy.[36] Policy should not be left to athletic directors and football coaches. This was a widely accepted concept within the league.

Recognizing the huge costs in athletics and State's habitual debt, Fisher condemned

President Gordon Gray, left, enjoys a conversation with State's chancellor John Harrelson, a man exasperated by athletics, in his Raleigh office, sometime between 1950 and 1953 (University Archives Photographic Collection, People, Special Collections Research Center, NC State University Libraries).

the platoon system which "requires more of everything."[37] The platoon system demanded more athletics, more equipment, more time, more specialization, and much beyond this. Fisher's comments on the two-platoon system found support throughout most of the conference, at Duke, North Carolina, and Wake Forest in particular.

Faculty chimed in as well. The UNC chapter of the American Association of University Professors gave a resounding endorsement of the decisions made by the presidents. They passed a resolution congratulating House and Gray on their effective leadership to regain control of college athletics.[38] Not all faculties were as politically motivated as the one at North Carolina, but it is likely that many other faculties within the Southern Conference felt much the same way.

The Daily Tar Heel solicited comments from Gray about his opinion of the September presidents' meeting. Resoundingly positive in his remarks, the UNC president defended the decision to ban bowl games arguing, "outlawing postseason athletic participation would eliminate a distinctly non-educational distraction for students, both players and otherwise," because "the games are primarily commercial ventures and contribute nothing to the real values of intercollegiate athletics."[39] Gray was exceedingly hopeful that this action would begin to rid college football of some of its foundational problems while recasting the game's relationship with academics in a proper light. He understood that the ban was not a panacea, but he accepted that it was a good step.

Although it appears not to have been released, a draft of a joint statement from the presidents regarding bowl games was written. A draft with a few corrections on it appears in the Hollis Edens Papers at Duke. In an articulate and thoughtful statement, the justification for banning bowl participation was aggressively argued. The presidents underscored that college athletics was an accepted and healthy practice on campuses, but that its place within the academic mission was out of kilter, needing correction. Because athletics was a part of the academic life at universities, the presidents emphasized that it fell under the purview of presidential leadership, because if the athletic house was not in order, it damaged academics university wide. Presidents, therefore, needed to establish appropriate and uniform policies to keep athletics in its proper perspective.[40]

"Commercialism in college sport" was the chief problem, they maintained.[41] Bowl games, operated by private entities in cities far from the participant campuses, were the primary factor in the growing commercialism in football. Many students believed that a bowl game was the most important event of their collegiate career and, often ill-advisedly, spent large amounts of money to attend bowl games, they contended. This put an additional financial stress on students and parents. Because bowl games extended the football season, they drew emphasis away from other college sports that deserved attention. They even distracted students from vacation time away from studies and athletics. A bit contrary to Gordon Gray's words, the statement made it clear that scandals in basketball, at West Point and at William & Mary, had had an effect. "We have noted with equal distaste other encroachments of commercialism (and its by-products the pressures it exerts) in college sports. The Madison Square Garden scandal merely underlines the problem. Further, the evidence of excessive pressures at our military establishment at West Point, emphasizes how such pressures have resulted in dishonesty."[42]

William & Mary and De-Emphasis

In less than a month after the presidents voted to prohibit bowl game participation, William & Mary took reform to the next step. With angry faculty and many alumni choosing to no longer financially support the school, President Alvin Chandler announced in October that the Indians would not participate in bowl games. This statement indicated that William & Mary's position was policy, regardless of the Southern Conference's policies. In addition, the Indians would play only schools in its region, mainly from Virginia and within the Southern Conference. Schools like Oklahoma would not be on the schedule. Chandler was quoted as saying, "We don't intend to get out of our class."[43] Demonstrating the gravity of the sports scandal, his announcement was made in a convocation before over 800 students and faculty.

Chandler did not wish the Indians to limit themselves to only Virginia schools, however. He wanted to play schools that had de-emphasized or controlled football's growth. That could mean a refocus of competition toward schools in the Ivy League or similar institutions where de-emphasis was occurring. William & Mary's athletic goals were different, after the scandal, regardless of the Board of Visitors' desire to ignore their responsibility for the transgressions.

The *Richmond Times-Dispatch* hailed William & Mary's actions as a great step forward in bringing "sanity" back to college football. There was no declaration of victory over football zealotry, but there was a recognition that this was an important action for William & Mary as well as the other Virginia schools.[44]

The Gooch Report

Almost simultaneous with Chandler's announcement at William & Mary, the University of Virginia's faculty voted 68–9 to endorse a plan to de-emphasize athletics. The plan, months in the making and with the potential to redefine Virginia athletics, was known as the Gooch Report. Athletics at Virginia had had an uneasy relationship with academics and the Gooch Report was controversial. It recommended that UVA abandon athletic scholarships to de-emphasize sports, particular football.[45] The de-emphasis of the Gooch Report dovetailed somewhat with Colgate Darden's well-known opposition to bowl games.[46]

Robert K. "Bobbie" Gooch was a political science professor at UVA, a former star athlete who had played quarterback on the 1914 and 1915 Cavalier squads. He was a Roanoke, Virginia, native who had distinguished himself in World War I, after graduating UVA in 1914 with a B.A. and 1915 with a M.A. With the world at war, the young political scientist enlisted as an ambulance driver in France, beginning in 1915. After the war, Gooch was able to pursue his Rhodes Scholarship at Oxford studying politics. A cosmopolitan man, he returned to Charlottesville in 1924 as a faculty member in political science, having served two years on the faculty at William & Mary. His career at Virginia was marked by distinction as a scholar, in particular his studies of Japanese politics, and by his service during World War II with the Office of Strategic Service and the Department of State.

When he agreed to chair a committee examining the role of athletics at UVA, the future report gained gravitas that other athletic studies would not have earned. The report, released on October 10, 1951, from what became known as the Gooch Committee, divided the university and the community. It called for the end of scholarships associated with athletic ability. Instead, scholarships needed to be awarded based on need and academic merit. Faculty were to have great control over athletics, a position outlined by the Southern Association of Colleges and Schools and reinforced in the report. The outcome was a divided campus, community, and alumni.[47] Gooch's conclusions caused such great consternation that Colgate Darden issued a statement of support for athletics, saying that athletic ability was not the sole criterion for scholarship awards and even met with the football team.[48]

Aggressively written, even including unsubstantiated charges against athletics, the Gooch Report was a salvo fired against football and the growing stature of college athletics. The committee believed and stated in the report that a growing number of alumni were disappointed with the role athletics were playing at Virginia. Gooch may have judged that President Darden was on his side, having the feeling that the time was right to strike. Contemporaneously, the Ivy League was actively de-emphasizing football, eliminating athletic scholarships, and forcing Pennsylvania, the strongest program, to decide their football future. If ever there was a chance to control college athletics, it was to act in 1951. Gooch wanted a restoration of faculty control over athletics. Faculty only held three of the nine seats on the athletic council with three reserved for students, and the last third controlled by the athletic director.[49]

Considering their relationship, most likely, Gooch held a fairly clear understanding of Darden's views on college sports. Darden was keen to keep growing professionalism and commercialization out of college sports, by in part limiting the role of football at the Charlottesville school. He wanted the Cavaliers to play its traditional in-state rivals as well as Ivy League schools, when the opportunity arose.[50] The president wished for most players to hail from the Old Dominion and for educational ambitions to be foremost. He held no love for scholarships, but Darden understood that they were a part of the current college football environment and had defended them during the Sanity Code controversy.[51]

The editorial staff of the *Richmond Times-Dispatch* was giddy about the Gooch Report, fully endorsing its recommendations and praising that Virginia and William & Mary were leading the nation in football reform. The editors believed that there was a chance for all Virginia colleges to adopt these reforms, making the Old Dominion the national leader in suppressing commercialism and professionalism.[52] There was cautious optimism that the general public had reached a breaking point making reform possible. The paper pointed to articles in the *Atlantic* and the *American Magazine* as well as the suspension of football at Georgetown as evidence that de-emphasis had momentum.[53]

The editorial staff and the faculty were misjudging the public and the academic administration. Sports, particularly football, had influential supporters. By late November, the Gooch Report was in trouble. Alumni rallied in support of football and professors in the Department of Education rejected it. There was fear that if the recommendations became policy, they would destroy the other sports at Virginia that depended upon football revenue. The Gooch Report and its goal of crafting a strictly amateur athletic environment were doomed.

With the animosity that erupted with the bowl game ban and the difficulties seemingly inherent in managing sports in an academic environment, State's John Harrelson was exhausted by athletics. In a letter to an acquaintance, he remarked, "I am about to despair of any hopes of remedying the intercollegiate athletic situation, especially football. [Johns] Hopkins may be showing us that we can turn the calendar back fifty years or more. My long experience with intercollegiate athletics has about brought me to the point of believing that the whole of it should be abolished."[54]

4

Southern Conference Football and the 1951 Bowl Crisis

The 1951 Southern Conference gridiron season began with a great many questions, mainly springing from the arrival of new coaches at five conference schools. The coaching changes were highlighted by Wallace Wade's departure from the sidelines at Duke to the Southern Conference commissioner's role. It was a highly coveted job, and many candidates were advanced for the Duke post, including the very successful Charley Caldwell of Princeton, who may have turned down the Duke position, and Ace Parker, a former football team captain under Wallace Wade and a Duke assistant.[1] Georgia's Wally Butts and Virginia's Art Guepe were considered candidates as well. Paul "Bear" Bryant's name was mentioned with some hoping to pry him from Kentucky. Many put their money on Eddie Cameron to be the next coach, because he had led Duke when Wade was in the military during World War II. Wyoming's Bowden Wyatt visited Duke and appeared, briefly, to be the top candidate for the job.[2] Bowden was a former Tennessee player who had led Wyoming to a Gator Bowl victory over Washington and Lee. Brown was one of several candidates to visit Duke. Another name tossed about for the position was Clemson's Frank Howard, one of Wallace Wade's players at Alabama. Howard's success at Clemson was well known and admired, but the question was whether he would fit at Duke, a far cry from Clemson. Clemson supporters, for example, reveled in his country demeanor. Howard visited Duke's campus in early January 1951, but a job offer did not appear to be in the mix. The tobacco chewing Howard was a perfect fit for the rural Upcountry of South Carolina, but he would have struggled to be accepted by faculty and alumni at Duke.

In what was a surprise to most observers and fans, Bill Murray, a Rocky Mount, North Carolina, native, was tapped to fill the very large shoes of a legend. Eddie Cameron had contacted Murray, who had not applied for the position. It was not surprising that Cameron was deeply impressed by the Delaware coach. Born in Rocky Mount in 1908, William David "Bill" Murray had starred in the backfield at Rocky Mount Senior High School before entering Duke as a celebrated athlete in 1927. Jimmy Simpson, a former Duke (Trinity) star was his coach and encouraged young Bill to play at Duke. As one of the many outstanding players at Duke in the late '20s and early '30s, Murray may have been the best. In his senior season, Murray rushed for over 1,000 yards, a significant achievement, and was the team's most valuable player as well as an All-Southern Conference halfback. Beyond football, Murray was student body president and the recipient of Duke's Robert E. Lee award for the most outstanding student. The smallish Murray was a fine coach and principal at the Methodist Children's Home in Winston-Salem before being selected to lead a floundering University of Delaware program. Murray's football teams at the Children's Home finished a remarkable 69–9–3 over nine seasons. This run included a 36-game winning streak and three undefeated seasons. In the college ranks in 1940, Murray quickly brought a level of success never enjoyed by the Blue Hens. In 10 years at Delaware, excluding three years absent for military service, Murray went 49–16–2 with three undefeated seasons, including a great unbeaten 1946 squad. He even amassed a 32-game winning streak for Delaware.[3]

Murray was the perfect choice to lead Duke. He was a devout Methodist, widely respected by his coaching peers and well known as a contributor to his community. Most importantly, Murray had the confidence and personality required to follow Wallace Wade. He was an imminently likable man, often wearing a pleasing smile, who enjoyed a great rapport with players. A committed Christian, Murray often led his teams in prayer, always after a game. He was an unrivaled sportsman who wanted to keep collegiate football in its proper place in relation to academics, while encouraging the development of sportsmanship in his young men. Murray believed that the lessons drawn from competition and sportsmanship were of utmost importance and should not be lost in the continued march for professionalism and commercialism in football.

Murray contrasted with Wade, a good quality when replacing a great coach. Wade often was unapproachable, not interested in speaking much to reporters, and distant.

Duke head football coach Bill Murray is carried off the field on the shoulders of his victorious players after defeating North Carolina in 1952. Note UNC's bell tower in the background (courtesy North Carolina Collection Photographic Archives, Wilson Library, University of North Carolina Chapel Hill).

Bob Quincy depicted Wade in this manner. "Wade, the master strategist, was hard to approach. He was near impossible. This is not out of disrespect for the man, but merely a confession of the situation that most newsmen agreed upon, but few mentioned in print."[4] Quincy respected Wade but described the former Duke coach as aloof. It was a bit easier to write about Wade in this manner in the early 1950s, because his postwar Duke teams had not been as strong when compared to his success in the 1930s.

Unfortunately, Murray's tenure continues to be unfairly placed in the shadow of Wallace Wade. Murray reversed Wade's declining football fortunes, leading Duke to successful seasons in an era when it was much more difficult for the Blue Devils than in the 1930s. It was hard to follow someone of Wallace Wade's stature, but Cameron's choice was a remarkable successor. Perhaps it is somewhat due to his modesty that Murray does not enjoy the stature that he fully deserves on the Durham campus.

It was going to be hard for Tom Rogers to replace Peahead Walker, another conference stalwart. Although replacing Wallace Wade was difficult, it was going to be impossible to step into Peahead Walker's shoes. Being a legend throughout the South for his huge personality as much as his coaching acumen, Walker would be hugely missed for his humor as much as for his coaching. Walker enjoyed great success at the small Baptist college where so many others had struggled. The Alabama native had given Wake the confidence to be giant killers and spoilers, often winning games in which they were underdogs. He had forced other schools to respect Wake Forest football. Walker's football success was very much responsible for Wake Forest making its way as a founding member of the Atlantic Coast Conference.

Peahead Walker did not leave Wake Forest willingly. The issue was money. Having performed brilliantly as a coach, Walker believed he deserved a raise. Walker was paid $7500 per year, much less than his chief rivals. The athletic council was prepared to pay him $9,000 per year on a four-year contract, but Harold Tribble balked at the number. The new president was willing to increase his pay to $8,000, but nothing beyond it.[5] To Tribble, it was a battle between the role of academics and athletics at the college. When it was clear that Tribble would not budge, Walker left for Yale University where he received a $2,000 raise to coach under his close friend, Herman Hickman. Ultimately, Wake Forest offered close to $9,000 for Walker to stay, but he already had committed to Yale.

Without much hesitation, Tom Rogers was promoted from assistant coach to the head position. Like Murray, Rogers was a star at Duke, playing for Wallace Wade after Bill Murray graduated. The Hinton, West Virginia, native was an assistant under Walker for six years and was a popular choice to lead the Deacons, but he had none of the experience of a coach like Bill Murray.

There were some at Wake Forest, its more conservative elements, who thought it was good to see Walker leave. They argued that he was too rough-hewn for the college. Walker had been known to enjoy parties in Raleigh and sometimes cursed in practices and during games. These practices were frowned upon, even though he was enormously successful on the football field and beloved by his players.[6] Nevertheless, the hiring of Murray and the resignation of Walker were indications that Duke and Wake wanted their football programs to conform to the academic and cultural traditions of their campuses.

At William & Mary, the rebuilding task was on the shoulders of Marvin Crosby "Moose" Bass. A former William & Mary star tackle and team captain, Bass, who graduated in 1943, was trying to win football games while placating a very angry faculty, embarrassed by the recent scandal, as well as a divided alumni base. The Petersburg, Virginia, native, who had been coaching linemen, had an unenviable task of leading a greatly depleted team, albeit a talented one. The Indians simply did not have enough players to endure a long, tough season.[7]

Virginia Tech convinced Alabama native Frank Moseley to build a football program that had reached its nadir. Moseley did not apply for the position, but was courted by Virginia Tech athletic leaders and its president who were genuinely impressed by the Kentucky assistant. It took considerable imagination for Moseley to see what was possible for VPI. Tech had won only one game in the previous three years, beating Richmond in 1949. The 1950 season had been a disaster, with the Hokies only scoring in double digits in two games. It could not get much worse.

As an assistant on Bear Bryant's staff, Moseley helped coach the Kentucky Wildcats to a Sugar Bowl victory over previously unbeaten Oklahoma 13–7. An Alabama halfback from 1931 through 1933, Mosely had spent much of his career with Bryant, and the two men were good friends. They played one year together at Alabama and Mosely was on Bryant's staff for his only year at Maryland before moving on to coach Kentucky for eight years. Obviously, hope was in the air, because Moseley's background brought new life and an outstanding pedigree to Blacksburg. The Gobblers were not disappointed. Mosley was a solid hire who, over many years of service as coach and as athletic director, significantly elevated Virginia Tech's athletic programs.

As in all seasons, there was great inconsistency in the number of players on each team. Fall practice usually brought very healthy numbers that were winnowed down as the practices grew more intense. By the time the season started, some teams had many more players on the sidelines than others. For example, South Carolina was hoping for 55 players to begin fall practice while the powerful Maryland Terrapins were expecting 97.[8] It was not uncommon for some Southern Conference teams to field fewer than 40 players for each game. The playing field was far from level.[9]

The Season Begins

For many fans and sportswriters, it was Maryland's year. Maryland was the favorite to win the conference and to gain laurels at the national level, perhaps competing for a national championship. Among southern sportswriters, however, they were in no way the prohibitive favorite. Some thought that Carl Snavely's North Carolina team was at the point of returning the Tar Heels to the glory that they enjoyed in 1949. On paper, he had a strong football team, but 1950 had been a significant disappointment. North Carolina had the building blocks for a very successful season, and many hoped that the previous year's struggle was an anomaly that Snavely would correct. The Gray Fox, as some called Snavely, did not generate much enthusiasm for his case. His dour personality did not help, especially compared to Jim Tatum's boosterism campaigns for Maryland football. Although he enjoyed great success at UNC, especially in the late 40s, there was a feeling of sadness around him. Snavely's only son, Carl, had been killed in the Pacific during World War II.

Even though North Carolina was seen as a rival for conference dominance, it was Maryland that looked ready to control the league. Jack Scarbath was the Terrapins' unstoppable star quarterback. Scarbath held the distinction of scoring the first touchdown in newly constructed Byrd Stadium, a structure he helped build by raking concrete in 1949. The game was a 35–21 win over Navy. The blond-haired signal caller from Hamilton, Maryland, had not been a high school star while prepping at Baltimore Polytechnic. Scarbath was lightly recruited as a high school player in Baltimore, but Jim Tatum saw something he liked in the young man. Entering the year as a junior, Scarbath, who wore number 62, had developed into a fine field general in which Tatum had complete faith.

Scarbath was fortunate to have the luxury of a fantastic backfield that featured Ed "Big Mo" Modzelewski at fullback as well as Chet Hanulak and Ed Fullerton. Bob Ward, at age 24, was a dominant force on the line, one of the great anchors for the Terps. All were outstanding players. The son of a Pennsylvania coal miner, Ed Modzelewski was a powerful and feared runner between the tackles. His brother Dick anchored a defensive juggernaut and would win the Outland Trophy in 1952. This was a powerful group, difficult to contain. With a strong offensive line and a smothering defense, Jim Tatum, in his fifth year at Maryland, was poised to win the conference championship and make a splash nationally.

Because of wildly different schedules, there was a chance that VMI could win the conference title in 1951. The Keydets were predicted to have a good team, but their conference schedule held no significant competition. They played William & Mary, Davidson, The Citadel, and Virginia Tech, with only the Indians fielding a competitive team. If VMI could defeat these clubs, they would be undefeated in the conference and be in the

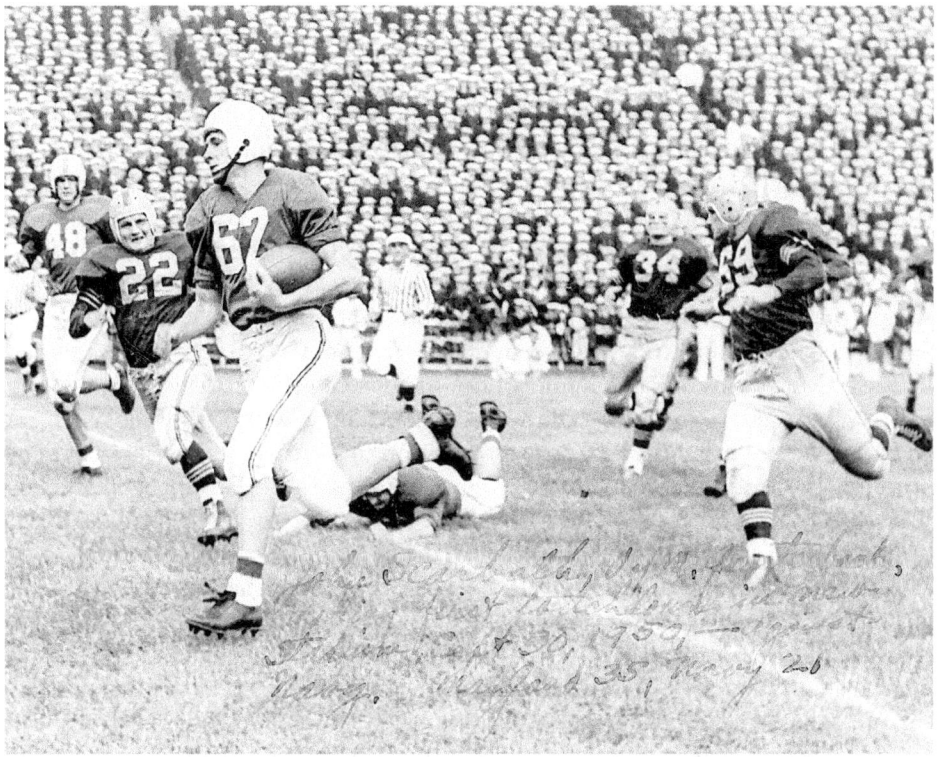

Maryland's star quarterback Jack Scarbath (#67), scoring one of his many touchdowns for the powerful Terrapins, in 1950 (courtesy University Archives, AlbUM, University of Maryland).

position of at least sharing the conference title.[10] This scenario was a significant problem for the Southern Conference.

Maryland traveled to Washington and Lee for the first game of its 1951 campaign to take on the Generals at quaint Wilson Field, a small facility on the Lexington campus. Although the Generals had won the Southern Conference the previous year playing a pedestrian schedule, they were no match for the men from College Park. Maryland blistered Washington and Lee 54–14, confirming to some that the Lexington school's weaker Southern Conference schedule the previous year had been complicit in their winning the league championship.

On the same day, William & Mary, in its first game since the academic scandal broke, was pasted by Oklahoma, 49–7, in Norman. In another poor showing among Old Dominion teams, Virginia Tech lost to Davidson, 32–20, continuing Tech's misery from the previous winless season and confirming that Moseley had a herculean task in front of him. Although Moseley most likely expected a loss, the Davidson defeat was more intense because the Wildcats had dropped their opener the week earlier to Lenoir-Rhyne. Things got worse for Tech on October 7, when they were crushed 33–0 by Virginia.

Maryland followed its victory over Washington and Lee with another easy win. The Terps beat a heavily over-matched George Washington club, 33–6, at the new and spacious Byrd Stadium, which had a capacity of almost 35,000. With two games under their belt, Maryland had not been tested, but they had manhandled inferior competition. To keen observers, it was a telling sign that the Southern Conference was too disparate when it came to gridiron quality.

Duke, with their new coach Bill Murray, headed into the season as somewhat of a mystery. Murray was installing a new offense, the split-T, and Blue Devil fans believed that it would take a few games for Duke to hit its stride. Nevertheless, the Blue Devils started the year in full stride, whipping the South Carolina Gamecocks 34–6 in Columbia on September 22. Even on a very hot day, Duke was ready to play and immediately alleviated some of the concerns about Murray. His 1950 Delaware squad had finished with a disappointing 2–5–1, seemingly an indication that his coaching was slipping. Against the Gamecocks in this 2:30 contest, however, everything worked well. Steve Wadiak, the Gamecock's star running back, was held in check, while Duke's backfield and defense demonstrated a level of quality that South Carolina could not match. Although sportswriter Jake Penland spoke of South Carolina's 1931 upset of Duke in Wallace Wade's first year, the 1951 edition replicated it in no way.[11] It now looked to many that Duke had not missed a beat in the transition to Murray, and perhaps were even better than some of Wade's squads, while Rex Enright's South Carolina appeared to be much weaker than anticipated.

South Carolina faced The Citadel after its drubbing against Duke. The rivalry game with the Bulldogs had added emphasis, because The Citadel had defeated the Gamecocks the previous year. In this evening contest, the pressure was on the Gamecocks, but they pulled through with a 26–7 win in Columbia. The Enrighters, as *The State*'s Jake Penland often called the Gamecocks, exploited Steve Wadiak's running skill to control the game. A bit of optimism returned to Columbia, but there was a long season ahead.

With freshman Jerry Barger successfully calling the signals in the opener at Columbia, Duke fans hoped that their season was destined to be a tremendous success in the tradition of the Wallace Wade teams of the past 20 years. The impression that

Duke's coaching transition was seamless seemingly was confirmed the following week when Duke traveled to Pittsburgh to take on the Panthers. What followed was a second road win, this time 19–14. Pitt was not a strong test, however. The Panthers, playing as an independent, had only won one game in 1950, the Backyard Brawl versus West Virginia. Even with all the football talent in western Pennsylvania, Pitt was fielding weak squads. Nevertheless, Duke had won two road games to start the season. It was looking rosy for the Blue Devils.

The season quickly changed when Duke dropped its next game to Tennessee 26–0. The 90-degree afternoon contest against third-ranked Tennessee in Knoxville at Shields-Watkins Stadium demonstrated that Duke was not ready to compete with teams like Coach Neyland's Volunteers. Although the game was penalty ridden, with 20 called in the first half, Tennessee dominated the Blue Devils, especially the Volunteer defense.

Hugo Germino of *The Durham Sun* always had a knack for summing up a game. In this case, he wrote, "The Volunteer line was as tough as a stone wall…. Tennessee had too many guns for Duke. That's the simple truth."[12] A learning curve from Wallace Wade to Bill Murray, with his new split-T formation offense, was destined to have a few bumps, and this was the first one of the season.

Meanwhile in Chapel Hill, hopes were high that the gray fox would reestablish Tar Heel dominance and prove that he remained the right man to lead UNC. A 21–0 victory over State in the season opener appeared to confirm this. The game, played before 43,000 at Kenan Stadium, was seen as a good omen, but the Wolfpack football program was weak and far from an appropriate measuring stick. The Tar Heels were expected to beat State.

The next week, North Carolina faced the Bulldogs from Athens, Georgia, coached by Wally Butts. The series was renewed, in part because of UNC's controversial loss to Georgia in the 1947 Sugar Bowl 20–10. Two calls by the officiating staff heavily influenced the Georgia victory. Before that contest, the schools had not met since 1934. This was a test for Snavely's Tar Heels, although Butts was bringing one of his weaker sides to Chapel Hill. In a hard-fought contest in which UNC's defense stifled the Bulldog rushing attack, Georgia used a strong fourth quarter to defeat North Carolina 28–16 in Kenan Stadium. Georgia's quarterback Zeke Bratkowski used his arm to craft a Bulldog victory. Fans could accept this type of loss, because they were not expecting to beat Georgia. Cautious optimism remained with this 1–1 start to the season. Nevertheless, it was disturbing that Georgia had exercised its will in the fourth quarter, scoring two touchdowns in 2:35 to take control of the contest.

As the Tar Heels were wrestling with the Georgia Bulldogs, Wake Forest, a team not predicted to be at the top of the league, was tussling with the Wolfpack in cozy Riddick Stadium in Raleigh. Regardless of won/loss record, this game always was highly anticipated because it had a long history of hard-fought, tight contests. Although State had lost to North Carolina, they had an opening game victory over Catawba College, making the game more intriguing. The Deacons used a strong second half to defeat the Wolfpack 21–6, before over 20,000 fans. New coach Tom Rogers enjoyed a good start to his first season replacing the legendary Peahead Walker. Rogers' victory in Raleigh was preceded by a convincing win over Boston College at Chestnut Hill 20–6. The game in Boston was one of the many road games designed to turn a profit for Wake Forest football and its broader athletic program. Having allowed only 12 points in two road contests, the Deacons were surprising fans and sportswriters alike. In the third week of the season, Wake Forest took apart the Richmond Spiders 56–6 in Wake Forest at Groves Stadium. In the second quarter, the Deacons scored three touchdowns in three minutes against a listless Spider side. Wake was favored in the game, but this type of victory was fully unexpected. The season was progressing well for the Deacons.

In comparison, coach Beattie Feathers was struggling to satisfy the Wolfpack fans. His Wolfpack opened the season with a 34–0 victory over Catawba, but the next two weeks were losses, as the quality of competition increased. State did not score against UNC and only put six points on the board at home against the Deacons. The season was quickly going south for the Wolfpack and Feathers, a popular coach. The pressure on him was growing. After five wins the previous year, hopes had been high that a returning 22 lettermen would lead the Wolfpack to a strong season. With the season spiraling out of control, all the goodwill Feathers had accumulated the previous year was dwindling. The State faithful wanted to win.

Coming off an excellent undefeated season in 1950, Clemson continued its winning ways in Frank Howard's 12th year on the sidelines. They started the year whipping Presbyterian College 53–6. It was tradition for the Tigers to play a weak team in the season's first game, usually an in-state rival. That warm-up game was followed by a trip to Houston, Texas, to take on the Rice Owls. Rice's Jess Neely was Clemson's head coach when he hired Howard as an assistant, and the two knew each other very well. The 1951 Rice squad was an average team, with little expected of them. In 1950, they finished 6–4, having lost both of their biggest games to SMU and Texas. Clemson was their opener in 1951, and the Tigers were victorious 20–14.

On October 6, 1951, Clemson traveled to Raleigh to face the struggling Wolfpack. On a warm and humid afternoon, Feathers' Pack almost pulled off the upset, battling valiantly all day in a 6–0 loss. Clemson was held to a 0–0 halftime score, but they took the kickoff and scored a touchdown on the first possession of the second half. The Tigers increased their winning streak to 16. State's defense held Clemson star Billy Hair to a lackluster afternoon, but the Tigers did just enough to leave Raleigh with a victory.

The following week, the Wolfpack played another hard-fought contest against Duke. Entering the fourth quarter, surprisingly, State posted an eight-point lead 21–13. The Pack had held the Blue Devils scoreless for the second and third quarters and appeared to be in position to defeat the Blue Devils in front of 23,000 at Duke Stadium. Duke wore down the undermanned Wolfpack who tired as the game drew to a close, scoring a 27–21 victory. Although State lost, it was another example of Feathers' ability to rally his troops when they were out-numbered and out-classed.

Autumn had not reached Columbia, South Carolina, on October 6, when a small crowd of about 12,000 braved the heat and humidity to watch the Gamecocks defeat the Purples, as many sportswriters called Furman. South Carolina controlled the game from the beginning, but it did not tell much about how good the Gamecocks could be. Steve Wadiak, the Gamecock star running back, and the South Carolina rushing attack were too much for Furman.

On the same weekend, Wake Forest dropped a disappointing 7–6 decision to scandal-ridden William & Mary in a game played at City Stadium in Richmond. Wake had numerous opportunities to win, but they played a mistake-ridden game. The game was an important reminder that although the academic scandal had caused considerable pain among the William & Mary team and their followers, the Indians still retained very good players. William & Mary would complete the year 7–3, including wins against Duke and Penn, before losing their finale to Virginia 46–0.

Over the same weekend, State reached the victory column for a third time, with a 31–0 win over a weak Davidson team. This was the Wolfpack's last victory of the year, having tamed Virginia Tech 19–14 in Blacksburg on October 27. Davidson was on the fringes of the Southern Conference, especially in football, and their defeat was not a great surprise, even against a struggling Wolfpack. The Wildcats suffered the loss before only 7,000 fans in Charlotte's Memorial Stadium, one of its smallest crowds since opening in 1936. The following week, State traveled to Maryland where they lost to a powerful Terrapin team 53–0. The Red and White of State finished the year with only three wins.

In Chapel Hill, restlessness was intensified when the Tar Heels were beaten badly by Texas, 45–20, in Austin. Snavely, however, rallied his team, and the following week they scored an unexpected 21–6 victory over South Carolina in Kenan Stadium. Steve Wadiak did little in the contest for the Palmetto State club, but Larry Parker, starting at quarterback for the Tar Heels, was the spark that carried them to victory. This October 13 win would be the last bright spot for what would become a miserable year for Snavely's squad.

The Tar Heel offense sputtered badly, and North Carolina dropped the final six games of the season. Over this skid, they scored a total of 42 points. It did not look bleak at the beginning of the losing run, however. Before over 31,000 in College Park, North Carolina faced an undefeated Maryland Terrapin team sporting a number seven national ranking after they had dismantled and embarrassed Georgia 43–7. Not much was expected from the Tar Heels, but they played admirably versus Maryland, losing 14–7, while frightening the Terps. The Heels had a chance to win late in the fourth quarter, but UNC's Goo Goo Gantt could not hold on to a pass in the end zone. The stifling North Carolina defense held Maryland scoreless in the second half, something no one else achieved in the 1951 season. The game was a "wake up call" for the Terrapins who were much too overconfident entering the game.

The belief that Snavely's team had turned a corner was dispatched the following week, October 27, when Wake Forest plastered UNC at Groves Stadium 39–7. In the homecoming contest, the Deacons dominated the game from the beginning, passing and running at will on a listless Tar Heel club. North Carolina only earned 55 yards on the ground while completing only 4 passes. Dick Herbert summed up the game in this manner. "The Deacons were great. That helped to make Carolina look bad—and the Tar Heels were very bad. It was no contest from the start."[13] The victory was Wake's largest against UNC to that date in the history of the series, which was first played in 1888.

It only got worse for the Tar Heels the following week when UNC was shut out at the hands of an impressive Tennessee squad 27–0 in Knoxville. Those two away games placed Snavely in the crosshairs of many fans. Losing to Tennessee was not surprising, but being embarrassed by Wake Forest, one of the Big Four but a much smaller school, was almost too much. Some alumni and boosters had the knives out and sharpened, hoping that Coach Snavely soon would depart Chapel Hill. The Tar Heels limped to an embarrassing 2–8 record. The great 1948 season when they only suffered a tie to William & Mary and a loss to Oklahoma in the Sugar Bowl seemed a distant memory.

As the Tar Heels were struggling against the Volunteers, Duke visited Atlanta on November 3 to play Georgia Tech, one of the nation's powerhouses. Tech had crafted a national reputation on the gridiron that far exceeded that of their rival in Athens,

Georgia. The previous week, Duke had been manhandled by Virginia 30–7, surprising almost everyone, but demonstrating that Virginia played good football. The pressure was on the Blue Devils to recover from the poor outing.

In a hard-fought contest that was not decided until the last play of the game, the Blue Devils and the Jackets ended with a 14–14 tie. It was Tech's first tie since 1938, and was a sign that Bill Murray was the right coach for Duke. The game was played with such intensity that after the final whistle, the benches for both squads were cleared as fights erupted on the field. Even some fans got involved in the melee. Fortunately, order soon was restored, and tempers subsided, but Murray's charges had equaled one of the best teams in the country.

The game was a coming-out party for Ed "Country" Meadows, Duke's fierce lineman. Bobby Dodd, highly complimentary of Duke's performance, was deeply impressed by Meadows, who already had gained a reputation among North Carolina sportswriters for outstanding performances. Playing on one of the biggest college football stages in Atlanta awakened national writers to big number 70.[14]

Another Big Thursday arrived in the Palmetto State on October 25, 1951. Ten days earlier, Clemson had lost to a good Pacific team in Stockton, California, by a 21–7 final score. The Pacific Tigers finished the year 6–5, losing in the Sun Bowl to Texas Tech. Frank Howard's team, still running the single-wing offense, was eager to get the taste of defeat out of their mouths, and there was no way better to do that than defeat a mediocre South Carolina side. Rex Enright's Gamecocks entered the contest with a 2–2 record, having lost the previous week 21–6 in Chapel Hill to a poor and struggling Tar Heel team. It was a humiliating affair for South Carolina, who invariably struggled against North Carolina. Surprisingly, the Gamecocks dominated the Tigers 20–0 before 33,000 in Columbia. It was South Carolina's defense that was the star, according to sportswriters, but the Gamecocks played a complete game on both sides of the ball. The Gamecocks' Billy Stephens scored on a 74-yard punt return to pace South Carolina to the victory, but it was South Carolina's defense, led by Harry Jabbusch, that stifled Clemson's running attack and controlled the game. Rex Enright, regardless of his futility against North Carolina and Duke, always had his team ready against Clemson. For Clemson, it was a very disappointing game. Frank Howard did not mince words. "We got the hell beat out of us," he bluntly stated.[15]

With the Big Thursday loss behind them, Clemson had time to prepare for its next game against Wake Forest. The Tigers recovered from their Big Thursday defeat to beat the Deacons 21–6, in a tilt in which Wake was favored. Clemson's Billy Hair played a fine game, and its defense stymied the Deacons until the fourth quarter. By that time, it was much too late for Wake Forest to attempt a comeback against a rowdy sell-out Clemson crowd in Memorial Stadium. As was often the case with their small roster, the Deacons were running out of steam as the season reached its final hurdles.

Meanwhile in the capital city, the Gamecock squad may have enjoyed their previous victory against Clemson much too much. In a surprising game, George Washington used an outstanding passing attack, especially in the final three minutes of the contest, to post two scores and win 20–14 over a bewildered Gamecock side. The Colonials were led by tiny Bino Berreira, a mere 150 pounds, who caught nine passes for 160 yards. It was a significant upset win for GW but a crushing loss for the inconsistent Gamecocks. It was the kind of result that plagued Rex Enright throughout his long tenure with South Carolina.

Recovering from their loss to Clemson, Wake Forest, on November 10, won the Big Four title, an important distinction, with an exciting win over Duke by the score of 19–13. The Deacons built a 19–0 lead at half but had to stifle a furious Duke rally to obtain the victory. Wake often was second to Duke, but this year big Bill George, the Deacons' tackle, played every minute of the game, 60 minutes, to solidify victory. In particular, it was George's punt coverage in the fourth quarter that made the difference, as Wake was holding on for all it was worth. Ed Listopad, George's mate on the line, never left the contest either. Both were keys for the Deacons. Duke Coach Bill Murray called George the best lineman he had seen the entire season.[16] He probably was right. George entered the NFL Hall of Fame in 1974, for his fearsome linebacker play for the Chicago Bears.[17]

The loss was Duke's first in the Southern Conference, but with Maryland and Clemson winning, it most likely prevented the Blue Devils from claiming the Southern Conference title. The victory was massive for the Deacons, providing them with a second state title in a row and a shoulder ride for new head coach Tom Rogers, a former Duke player. The game was one of the season's highlights, with 30,000 fans in Durham witnessing the contest.

The same weekend was good for Palmetto State teams. Playing at home, Clemson dominated Boston College 21–2 in another game where Billy Hair starred. The talented quarterback was responsible for all three Clemson scores, passing for two and running for one. The Eagles avoided the shutout with a safety in the last 10 seconds.

In Morgantown, the Gamecocks spoiled West Virginia's homecoming with a 34–13 victory. South Carolina played a complete game, perhaps their best one of the year, in dominating the Mountaineers. With only a 13–7 halftime lead, the Gamecocks enjoyed

South Carolina head football coach Rex Enright (center, wearing a suit), a greatly admired gentleman of the game, and his South Carolina Gamecocks celebrate a big win versus West Virginia in 1951 (*The Garnet and Black*. Students of the University of South Carolina. Columbia, South Carolina, 1952).

an explosive second half. It was the start of a three-game slide for West Virginia that concluded with a 32–12 loss at Pittsburgh and a 54–7 pasting by Maryland in Byrd Stadium. A special season for West Virginia ended badly.

As many Southern Conference schools were performing at an average to below average level, Maryland reeled off commanding victories. On October 27, they traveled to Baton Rouge, whipping LSU 27–0. The Tigers were a sound squad that finished the season 7-3-1, including a win over number nine ranked Alabama. The victory was followed by an equally impressive performance against Missouri in College Park. The Missouri Tigers copied LSU's performance, failing to score, in a 35–0 defeat. To the most casual observer, it was clear that Jim Tatum was coaching a club steamrolling its competition.

These Terrapin victories were followed by a 40–21 win over Navy at Baltimore's Municipal Stadium. The Old Liners were not done mowing down opponents. They had two games remaining in the season, both at home. State arrived on November 17 and suffered a 53–0 drubbing. The following week, West Virginia could do little better, falling 54–7.

What attracted the most attention was the way that Maryland dominated the competition. Its games in the second half of the season were not close, often over by halftime. The Terrapins were redefining football in the Southern Conference, because this type of dominance had not been seen by any club in years. The national media, however, was slow to embrace Maryland, in part because the Terrapins played in the Southern Conference, a league that did not often produce sustained excellence in football. They were accustomed to Big Ten schools and SEC institutions dominating the football landscape. But the beating that Tatum's squad was unleashing gradually wore down resistance. After their win against the Mountaineers, the undefeated Terps were ranked third behind undefeated Tennessee at number one and an unbeaten Michigan State at two.

On November 17, Baylor was much too strong for the Deacons who were overpowered 42–0. Baylor's outstanding squad finished the season 8-2-1, which included a narrow defeat to Georgia Tech in the Orange Bowl. It had been a banner year for the Bears and was a not unexpected low point for the Deacons.

The Gamecocks, on the same Saturday, suffered a heartbreaking loss at Scott Stadium 28–27, to a good Virginia squad. South Carolina led 20–7 at the end of the third quarter before allowing Virginia to score three touchdowns in the fourth quarter. Having unexpectedly dropped a game to George Washington earlier in the year, this was an opportunity for the Gamecocks to gain an upset victory, but, again, South Carolina could not find a way to win.

The surprise of the day was Duke's one-point loss to William & Mary in Williamsburg 14–13. Fumbles and interceptions were costly for Duke, which could not match the enthusiasm of Marvin Bass' Indians. Duke lost a fumble and threw an interception late in the game allowing William & Mary to preserve their victory. For much of the season, Duke had a habit of playing from behind, and this time they were unable to perform. The victory was the most satisfying win of the year for the Indians, while it was a "let down" game for Duke.

Clemson eased by Furman in Greenville 34–14 on November 17 at Sirrine Stadium. Furman was better than in previous years, but they were no match for the Tigers on a chilly afternoon. The contest was Furman's last game of the year in a season that featured wins against a collection of weak teams: Presbyterian, The Citadel, and Newberry.

The Gamecocks headed home and retooled to end their year on a high note, defeating Wake Forest 21–6 on November 24 in Columbia. The Deacons turned the ball over 10 times while the Gamecocks played a solid game. Steve Wadiak had a fine performance, capping a career that was marked by accolades from sportswriters around the South. Four months later, Wadiak was tragically killed in an automobile accident.

On the same weekend, Clemson battled its sister school, Auburn, at Memorial Stadium. Auburn was in the midst of a terrible losing stretch, having been crushed by Ole Miss and Georgia before heading to Clemson. The Tigers had no problem whipping Auburn 34–0, concluding their regular season with only two losses. It was legendary coach Ralph "Shug" Jordan's first year, his nadir in a career at Auburn that would last until his retirement in 1975.

Maryland finished the season undefeated. Its defense relinquished a mere 62 points over the year, while the offense posted a whopping 353 points. Other than North

Maryland president Curly Byrd (right) discusses with William Cole, chair of Maryland's Board of Regents, the construction of Maryland Stadium in 1950. The stadium became the centerpiece of Maryland football success (courtesy University Archives, AlbUM, University of Maryland).

Carolina, no one had been close or even challenged the Terrapins. They were far superior than their Southern Conference foes, setting a new standard for excellence. Tatum had Maryland stepping on the national stage, further signifying that the Southern Conference was an antiquated collection of schools, most of whom could not compete or even approach Maryland's level.

The Big Four completed a very poor season, having defeated no team of great consequence. Collectively, they finished the year 8–17–1, when excluding the games played amongst the four. It was pitiful, although on a positive note they had played a collection of exciting and interesting games.

Snavely in Trouble

The end of the 1951 football season forced UNC to consider Carl Snavely's future. His squad finished with a very disappointing 2–8 record, having posted a 3–5–2 record the previous year. Throughout the season, the defense had played fairly well, holding Maryland to two touchdowns, for example, but the offense sputtered, mustering only 28 points in its last four contests, games against Tennessee, Virginia, Notre Dame, and Duke. Part of the problem was a difficult schedule, but it was also fundamental.

A meeting of prominent North Carolina coaches who helped lay the foundation for the Atlantic Coast Conference in the late 1940s: (from left) Clyde "Peahead" Walker (Wake Forest), Wallace Wade (Duke), Beattie Feathers (State), and Carl Snavely (North Carolina) (courtesy North Carolina Collection Photographic Archives, Wilson Library, University of North Carolina at Chapel Hill).

Snavely had had Charlie "Choo Choo" Justice carrying the football from 1946 through 1949, and he had led the Tar Heels to unparalleled success. Wearing number 22, Justice was the perfect back for the single-wing offense. He ran with recklessness and starred at both tailback and quarterback. He even punted for the Tar Heels. Many have forgotten that Justice was a talented passer, making him a modern-styled player, dangerous with his legs and his arm. The Asheville, NC, native was nationally praised in 1948 and 1949, leading the Tar Heels to heights they had never achieved and finishing second in the Heisman voting both years.[18] His sparkling play led to him being drafted by the Washington Redskins.

Justice spoiled Tar Heel fans, who now expected Snavely to produce teams of the same quality. North Carolina had reached the number one ranking in 1948, something never done before or since. The bar was raised to the point where Snavely could not maintain it, especially after the World War II veterans graduated. Players like Charlie Justice, who refined his game in the Navy, were not matriculating at Chapel Hill.

With two games remaining in UNC's season, against Notre Dame and Duke, it looked like Snavely was finished. UNC officials admitted that alumni pressure was playing an important role in Snavely's fate.[19] Before the season, a great deal of hoopla surrounded the upcoming Tar Heel season. That led to the highest rate of season ticket sales in North Carolina history. Fans anticipated that Snavely would return the Tar Heels to success and convinced themselves that the previous year was an aberration. After all, he always had been successful. Snavely was a fine man who refused to place blame on an anemic running game regardless of who was in the backfield. Instead, Snavely blamed inexperience in the face of a relentless schedule.[20] He was correct. The team was inexperienced, and players had not matured as he had hoped. The chance of winning the last two contests was small, considering that news outlets around the South were reporting that Snavely would be fired at the end of the season. Chauncey Durden, the sports columnist for the *Richmond Times-Dispatch*, led the charge, writing that the Tar Heel loss to Virginia had "finished" Snavely's career at North Carolina.[21] Athletic director Bob Fetzer strongly denied that the loss had ended Snavely's career, instead stressing that no discussion of Snavely's tenure had taken place and even charged that he had alumni and fan support.[22] That was simply untrue.

Complicating Snavely's situation were recent reports concerning the amount of money North Carolina spent on athletics. The victory total was seemingly meager considering athletic expenditures. The two victories had cost an astonishing amount of money. With negative news mounting, Snavely, who was on a yearly contract, found himself under relentless attack.[23]

Prior to the Notre Dame contest at Kenan Stadium, Coach Frank Leahy of the Irish endorsed Snavely, speaking about short memories and Snavely's historic prowess on the sidelines. Frank Leahy owed Snavely, because the North Carolina coach was one of the people who recommended Leahy for the head position at Boston College. That was the job that propelled Leahy to Notre Dame and greatness.[24] Leahy's opinion mattered, but it was the won-loss record that impressed the boosters and alumni.

Having placed itself in the position of a voice for purifying college athletics, going back to President Graham, Chapel Hill's leadership now found itself in a quandary. Coach Carl Snavely was a good man, but he was losing games. Many alumni, fans, and sportswriters were ready to fire Snavely, with some hoping to hire Maryland's Jim Tatum, a brash personality fully devoted to winning games. UNC fans were envious that one of their own had brought gridiron glory to College Park, including a very special 1951 season. The calls for Jim Tatum grew in intensity with each North Carolina loss, but was the administration willing to part ways with a fine man with a long record of success who only now was experiencing losing seasons? What did that say about winning in college athletics? Was it more important for Snavely to continue to produce good citizens for North Carolina and the country or did winning trump everything?

Some UNC alumni were dead set against firing Snavely and hiring Tatum. Some simply wanted UNC to play an easier schedule, dropping games with the likes of Notre Dame and Georgia. Most likely, that would have greatly boosted the Tar Heel win record. To others, Tatum was seen as a great risk, because he was viewed as interested in winning at all costs without much concern for ethics and being the opposite of university leadership from Frank Porter Graham to Bob House to Gordon Gray. Fairly or unfairly, he had a reputation as a rough-hewn man, not much concerned with the university's academic mission.[25] But Tatum's name was not the only one in circulation. Washington and Lee's George Barclay was a possibility. Barclay had starred for UNC in the 1930s during Snavely's first run as coach. At Washington and Lee, he had taken the Generals to the 1951 Gator Bowl, an unthinkable achievement in previous years. Virginia's Art Guepe was enjoying outstanding success at Virginia, a school previously lacking a winning football tradition. It was unlikely that Guepe would leave Virginia for rival North Carolina. Jake Penland of *The State* offered a keen grasp of the problem confronting North Carolina. "On the one hand the school poses as a friend of the de-emphasis program. On the other hand there is dark talk that since Snavely has not produced a winner in the last two years, he is not wanted any longer."[26] Essentially, Penland argued that UNC could not have it both ways. "North Carolina would de-emphasize athletics on the one hand, and throw out the head coach on the other—because he is not winning enough ball games at the moment."[27]

Two days before the Notre Dame game, Dick Herbert provided a thoughtful summary of the Tar Heel predicament. "If he is discharged, then the school's position as the leader in the move for de-emphasis will be untenable. If the coach is retained, then the school risks the wrath of many influential alumni whose loyalty to the institution sometimes is in direct ratio to the number of victories achieved on the football field."[28]

On November 17, the Tar Heels lost a hard-fought battle to Notre Dame 12–7, before a crowd of 45,000, a good portion of which had come to see the Irish. It was a moral victory when Snavely needed legitimate wins. The loss was followed by a 19–7 defeat at the hands of Duke, allowing Bill Murray to enjoy a first-year victory over North Carolina. Although losing, Snavely's Tar Heels had continued to fight hard. Despite the many calls for his head, Snavely, the Gray Fox, was retained for the 1952 campaign.

Gordon Gray on the Record

Prior to the December conference meeting, Gordon Gray offered a public statement to Herbert O'Keef as to his opinions on college athletics and the position intercollegiate sports, in particular football, enjoyed at UNC and State College. Even considering the heat surrounding Carl Snavely's job, Gray attacked the narrative of de-emphasis which had been widely argued among sportswriters as well as the general public. Gray, hoping to sweep back the tide with a broom, stressed that UNC and State were focused on "re-emphasis of the basic values to be had in team sports. Troubles arise when these are obscured and forgotten in an overwhelming desire to have winning teams at any cost."[29] Stressing the importance of maintaining high academic standards and entrance requirements as well as citizenship, Gray explained that the UNC system agreed with Harvard, Yale, and Princeton that athletic grants-in-aid be controlled by the university itself and not an affiliate alumni or booster organization or anything outside of proper university organization. It was not by chance that he mentioned three Ivy League schools by name. They were part of the de-emphasis movement, with Yale having announced the end of spring practice one month earlier. Scholarship requirements, however, were most important to Gray. Like most other presidents, he favored no distinction between athletes and non-athletes as to their qualifications for entrance into the university. Once enrolled, students who received scholarships for extra-curricular activities were to be held to a higher standard.[30] Furthermore, he again stressed his opposition to off-season practice, a trend that was objected to by almost all presidents of conference member schools.

Gray emphasized that the focus on reorienting athletics to its proper relationship with academics was not stimulated by the scandals of 1951, but that rang hollow.[31] It was true that the presidents were moving forward with gaining a tighter control of the reins prior to the scandals, but the corruption that had been made public was an impetus for quick action. No leader wished to endure what had happened at CCNY, West Point, or William & Mary, their conference partner. Gray viewed the future of sports at UNC and State as more like the Ivy League than the Southeastern Conference. Like so many other administrators, he did not understand the rabid fan bases that were at North Carolina and many other schools. Most fans and alumni did not want to hear Ivy League comparisons. They wanted to beat Georgia and Maryland.

Maryland Complicates Bowl Policy

As the 1951 season progressed, it became apparent that undefeated Maryland was likely to be offered a very prominent bowl bid. Consequently, the temperature on the September 28 decision to ban Southern Conference members from bowls increased substantially, with a flood of articles appearing on sports pages around the Southeast. Most sportswriters condemned the decision when it was made, but the stakes were now much higher. Would the conference ban an undefeated Maryland club from a bowl contest? The *Durham Morning Herald*'s Jack Horner had told Jim Tatum, a friend, that the leadership at State and UNC had no problem with bowl participation, but both had to follow suit with Gordon Gray's tough stance.[32] Most likely, this information was conveyed to Curly Byrd, but Horner was off the mark. Neither Harrelson nor House had much tolerance for bowl games.

Horner, as others had done, charged that UNC and Duke, the leaders of the bowl ban policy, were hypocrites, having accepted six bowl invitations between them, the latest being a bowl appearance by the Tar Heels in 1950. Now that Maryland was fielding strong teams, Duke and UNC, he argued, wished to deprive them of the prestige associated with a bowl berth.[33] Horner and others understood that Maryland could leave the Southern Conference, which might be the impetus for creating a new league. A Maryland departure did not bode well for the Southern Conference. The stakes were very high.

The *Washington Post*'s Morris Siegel reported that Maryland's 27–0 victory over LSU in Baton Rouge on October 27 had made a Sugar Bowl invitation almost inevitable.

Sugar Bowl officials met with Curly Byrd in Baton Rouge to discuss the January 1 game. "Byrd ... told them that Maryland is completely receptive to playing in the Sugar Bowl and he doesn't think the conference will try to stop them."[34] Perhaps Byrd was providing some bluster, but he had not attended the meeting that led to the banning of bowl games, and the vote to suspend participation was resolute.

Siegel was well versed in the Southern Conference. Although closely associated with Washington, D.C., he was not a native of D.C. He was a Georgian, having been born and raised in Atlanta. He worked at the *Atlanta Constitution* and the *Richmond Times-Dispatch* before heading north to the *Washington Post* after World War II. Siegel worked at all the major newspapers in D.C., including 19 years with the *Washington Star*.[35] A good deal of his sports information came from his numerous contacts, many honed at D.C. parties and restaurants.

One of Siegel's colleagues was Shirley Povich, a prolific sportswriter, penning thousands of columns in a career that comprised much of the 20th century. A native of Bar Harbor, Maine, Povich was one of the most popular sportswriters in America. Thousands from coast to coast read his syndicated column, *This Morning*, which was a staple at the breakfast table.

Shirley Povich was horrified that Maryland risked being barred from bowl participation. "It will be a crying shame if the Southern Conference, with a sudden seizure of purity, denies to Maryland University the crowning glory of its proudest football season."[36] Povich complimented Curly Byrd's efforts to transform the university, advising that he should not be taken lightly. Povich believed that the Southern Conference was contradictory in allowing spring practice, which took students away from their studies, but banning bowl games, in part because of the practices leading up to the games. As Povich noted, Maryland stood to receive $125,000 for taking the field in New Orleans against the Tennessee Volunteers. That was no small sum of money. Byrd was not going to be denied a chance for his beloved Terps to gain national recognition from a major bowl game.

Coach Jim Tatum, never short for words, vigorously defended college football and the right for schools to determine if they wished to participate in bowl games. Speaking to a sportswriter's weekly meeting at Toots Shor's Restaurant, he praised the sport's contribution to school spirit and the "self-sacrifice" that the sport demanded.[37] In the Manhattan restaurant and bar, Tatum strongly attacked all the recent criticism of football, blaming some of it on the coaches as well as the media. The Maryland coach confidently stated that the Terrapins would ask for conference approval to play in the bowl game; however, Maryland, he suggested, could go its own way if permission was denied.[38] Obviously, this led to questions about Maryland's future affiliation with the Southern Conference. Rarely mincing words, Tatum remarked, "I know what I'd do, but I can't talk for our president. Virginia withdrew years ago. I wonder if it has hurt them much?"[39]

Harold Wimmer of the *Roanoke Times* agreed with Shirley Povich. Congratulating the Terrapins on an outstanding season and explaining that Jim Tatum essentially had accepted a Sugar Bowl bid, he wrote, "Tatum ... had the hard-luck of having his best team just when the tag of over-emphasis is being placed on football."[40] Soup, as Wimmer was known, joked that ending spring practice and banning bowl games would do nothing to decrease corruption in football. Furthermore, Wimmer wrote that basketball teams were allowed to play in tournaments and college presidents had approved the construction of large football stadiums, both in opposition to purifying collegiate sports.[41] The hypocrisy was not going to decrease corruption in football.

It is easy to see the criticisms, but as these sportswriters and Jim Tatum were complaining, Duke's president Edens offered a succinct view of where the majority of the Southern Conference presidents stood. Answering the *News and Observer*'s Herbert O'Keef's query about bowl games and collegiate sports, Edens wrote:

> A sane program of intercollegiate athletics is a constructive influence in the life of a university. However, since athletes are students first, I believe that all athletic activities should be coordinated as to be consistent with a sound academic curriculum. Any practice which tends to commercialize athletics or cheapen the academic offerings of an educational institution, thwarts the purpose of an athletic program and destroys its values. It is therefore the responsibility of university authorities to keep such a program on a sound basis. The recent actions of the Presidents in the Southern Conference were a step in that direction.[42]

Edens emphasized that the presidents believed that bowl games and other practices "cheapened" the university's academic endeavors. For all the criticism that these presidents faced, and it was a barrage, their overriding concern was for academics to be the focus of the university experience, not athletics. Commercialism was growing, especially with television beginning to broadcast games, and these Southern Conference presidents had sounded the alarm. Whether they could do anything to stop it was another issue, indeed.

By the end of the season, Sugar Bowl and Cotton Bowl representatives were eager to host the powerful Terrapins. Both courted Curly Byrd, but the Terps, prior to their last game against State, chose the Sugar Bowl, because it matched Maryland against the formidable University of Tennessee squad coached by the legendary Robert Neyland in his 20th season, one of Tatum's idols. Tennessee completed an undefeated campaign having played only one close ballgame, an 11-point victory over archrival Vanderbilt. The Volunteers shut out five of their 10 opponents, and their record featured a 26–0 thrashing of Duke and a 27–0 beating of a faltering North Carolina. Having compiled a one loss season the year before, Tennessee football was a very hot commodity. Sugar Bowl officials were anxious to host both undefeated teams, making the game a strong draw in person and on television. On November 16, Maryland released an official statement accepting the Sugar Bowl bid. The statement read, "In conformity with the usual procedure by Southern Conference members in considering Bowl bids, [Maryland] has accepted an invitation," to play in the Sugar Bowl.[43] Understanding that this was going to do much more than raise a few eyebrows and acting preemptively, Byrd wrote, "The University is not violating any regulation, and is acting within the rules of the Southern Conference and on the basis of custom and procedure over many years."[44] No mention was made of the September vote in Chapel Hill.

The Sugar Bowl would not have risked inviting Maryland if they were not certain that the Terps would accept the bid, regardless of the Southern Conference's actions. Byrd may have been willing to pull Maryland out of the Southern Conference and perhaps form a new mid–Atlantic conference, as had been broadly discussed, because Byrd could in no way be certain that his fellow conference members would approve Maryland's participation. At least in terms of football, Maryland was at its pinnacle and was highly desired by other schools wishing to form a conference. One must remember that Byrd was an exceptional politician, very confident in his ability to prevail in disagreements. His leadership at Maryland had demonstrated this on numerous occasions.

Jim Tatum expected conference members to allow Maryland to play. Perceiving some wiggle room, he said that the presidents in September had only made a recommendation for a change. He maintained that any bowl decisions voted on in December would only apply beginning in September 1952.[45] This was not what was understood to be the case in September, and the conference by-laws mandated Maryland poll the members about participating in a bowl.

As soon as Maryland accepted the Sugar Bowl bid, there was consternation within the Southern Conference. Commissioner Wallace Wade was "surprised" that Maryland had agreed to play in the Sugar Bowl without gaining conference consent.[46] West Virginia's president Irvin Stewart commented that he was unaware of a Sugar Bowl bid or an acceptance.[47] They had every right to be surprised, because Maryland had not polled conference members as required by the conference's by-laws.

The State's Jake Penland spoke with South Carolina's Jim Penney, chair of the school's athletic committee, about Maryland's acceptance of the bowl bid. Penney simply said, "Since the standing rule requires consent of the conference, the conference would be within its rights to decline permission to play in a bowl. In view of the fact that 13 college presidents at their Chapel Hill meeting this fall voted to instruct their representatives to refuse permission to play in a bowl this year, it is highly probable permission will be refused."[48] A South Carolina graduate, Penland later noted that the vote in Chapel Hill was an "emphatic" statement.

Penney, who later was a major figure in the founding of the ACC, was never one to pull punches when discussing athletics and academics. He was outspoken when expressing his concerns about the status of athletics on college campuses. Speaking before the Rotary Club in Columbia, for example, and considering the West Point and William & Mary scandals, Penney condemned the lack of "intestinal fortitude" at universities to stand up to alumni and boosters to defend the academic mission of the university. Penney was certain that universities needed to control athletics and clear the institutions of those who did not understand that academics were most important. Reiterating what some others had said, the South Carolina biologist supported the hiring of coaches mimic the hiring of faculty, with tenure and similar pay.[49] Penney said that a professor at a college in the West had once said, "We've got the best football team in the country. Too bad we don't have a school to match it."[50]

In what became a national story, Bill Rives of the *Dallas News* wasted no time in attacking Maryland's bowl decision. Rives was appalled that Maryland had accepted an invitation without its conference's approval and done so at a time when collegiate sports, especially football, were under a microscope. The Sugar Bowl, Rives contended, was an accomplice in all of this, aiding the corruption.[51] Rives proclaimed, "The spectacle of a school refusing to act honorably and ethically, because it is prestige-mad or greedy, or both, will sicken some of the men who are charged with the conduct of college athletics."[52]

As bowl questions swirled around the Southeast, Maryland Governor Theodore McKeldin, in a letter to Judge William Cole, Jr., Maryland's chairman of the board of regents, ordered a study to determine if Maryland was operating its athletic program properly. The timing of this request was suspicious and smacked at an attempt to undermine Maryland's gridiron accomplishments. It was a "fishing expedition" no doubt, but Maryland had to take it seriously.

As Maryland was defending itself from charges, Clemson accepted a bid to play in the Gator Bowl against the University of Miami on January 1 in Jacksonville, Florida. Even before their victory over Auburn, rumors spread that the Gator Bowl wanted Clemson. This was a rematch from the previous year when Clemson defeated Miami in the Orange Bowl. The Hurricanes completed a good season, having only lost to Tulane, Pittsburgh, and a strong Kentucky side. Miami's success may have been assisted by a remarkable home slate that had the Hurricanes playing all but two games on their home field, Burdine Stadium.[53] More to the point, Clemson joined Maryland in accepting a bowl invitation, knowing that Southern Conference presidents opposed bowl participation.

Clemson had not casually accepted the bowl invitation. The bid was discussed by the athletic council, and President Poole raised the issue with each member of the board of trustees.[54] All supported accepting the invitation. Lee Milford declared, "Our acceptance of this Bowl Bid, which has not met the usual approval of the Southern Conference, is not intended in any way to be a defiance of the action of the Southern Conference."[55] Milford's statement does not ring true. Clemson's acceptance of the Gator Bowl bid, having been rejected by their Southern Conference colleagues, was a direct challenge to the Southern Conference and was a "defiant" act.

The *Greenville News*, unsurprisingly, fully supported Clemson's participation in the Gator Bowl. Scoop Latimer wrote glowingly of Clemson's administration, from its president to Frank Howard, emphasizing that the university was blameless and had only operated and made decisions in the most honorable of ways.[56] Latimer quoted Lee Milford's statement discounting the defiance of Clemson's actions.[57] Surely, Milford, the Clemson team's physician, understood that Clemson's actions would be viewed as a direct assault on the integrity of the Southern Conference. It could not be seen otherwise.

There was far more sympathy for Maryland's bowl acceptance than Clemson's. The Tigers were not a powerful team. They had lost to Pacific and been spanked by South Carolina. Dick Herbert believed that Clemson accepted the bid to goad the conference, because they had favored bowl participation at the September meeting. Herbert wrote, "Clemson appears to be in a position where the $60,000 check it will get from the Gator Bowl is its only justification for making it almost mandatory for the Southern Conference to throw it out of the league. It's unlikely Clemson has such love for post-season football it is making itself a martyr to glorify it."[58] Herbert took a further step and advocated expelling Maryland and Clemson from the Southern Conference. The *News and Observer* writer suggested that the bowl crisis be an impetus for realigning the league, even if Maryland and Clemson were expelled.[59]

The *News and Observer*'s editorial page saw only two options for the conference. The league needed, "to assert its authority or to quit any pretense of being a responsible regulatory body."[60] The editors admitted that the wisdom of banning bowls was debatable, but the issue at hand, in their opinion, was that the two schools had ignored conference by-laws and authority.

Chauncey Durden had many problems with the bowl ban and how it was instituted but had many more problems with the actions from Clemson and Maryland. In a stinging column on November 28, he condemned both schools and questioned why Wallace Wade was not playing a large role in the crisis. Durden charged that individual schools could not be larger than the conference, expressing that presidential authority must be respected for the league to function. Although many questioned presidential sports acumen, Durden, embraced the concept of presidential control. The *Times-Dispatch* writer stressed that

> it is now or never for the Southern Conference to assert itself, flex its muscles and then let both Maryland and Clemson have it, meaning dismissal from the conference and an immediate five-year schedule boycott in all sports against those two schools. Unless such drastic action is taken, the Southern Conference may as well close shop. And, since the Maryland and Clemson cases have exposed the weakness of the commissioner's office, the conference at its meeting here on December 14–15 should give Commissioner Wade something to near dictatorial powers to enforce its by-laws and rules.[61]

The editorial board roundly endorsed Durden's opinions.[62]

With Clemson and Maryland accepting bowl invitations, a severe conference crisis was at hand. The editorial page in the *Roanoke Times* condemned both schools for their actions, especially Clemson. They charged Clemson with not having even taken the time to poll the other institutions, instead accepting a bowl invitation fully aware that the Southern Conference had banned participation. The editorial called Clemson's behavior "a flagrant and deliberate act of defiance of the Conference."[63] Clemson and Maryland, the editorial argued, left the Southern Conference with no option other than to strongly condemn the actions of both schools. "Maryland and Clemson must be called on the carpet ... and both schools must be summarily expelled from membership or suspended until such time as they make proper apology and promise to abide by Conference regulations in the future."[64] The editors charged the two schools with thinking that they were more significant than the Southern Conference and found no justification for their actions. It was a stinging rebuke.

On November 25, Lee Milford notified Wallace Wade in a terse telegram that Clemson would play in the Gator Bowl.[65] They accepted the invitation without having polled Southern Conference members. Belatedly, the Southern Conference members were polled by Commissioner Wade as to whether they would sanction Clemson's participation in the Gator Bowl. Milford's request to poll Southern Conference members, made on November 25, asked "permission to accept an invitation to play in the Gator Bowl ... according to NCAA Rules."[66] Milford was attempting to draw a distinction between NCAA rules, which allowed for bowl participation, and the decision of the Southern Conference presidents in September, as well as the by-laws of the conference itself. Thirteen schools voted to prohibit the Tigers from playing while four voted to allow their participation.[67] Commissioner Wallace Wade, with a sense of fatalism, reported the results to Clemson on December 5 with no commentary, preferring to simply state the results of the poll.

Milford reasoned that Clemson may have violated a technicality but had not violated the presidential decree of September, as it had not been approved by the conference as a whole. The college's physician diagnosed mistakes he believed the presidents had made over the bowl matter and condemned their newfound interest in athletics. Milford believed that the presidents had acted too "hastily" and had created a retroactive policy. He chafed at embroiling other institutions who were not very much concerned with bowls. Milford even believed that presidential action had been influenced by "papers up east."[68]

Pointedly, Milford was very unhappy with Duke and UNC, at one point saying, "It was really pathetic to see some of the weak, young presidents who had gotten caught in the North Carolina–Duke web. You would be surprised to know how far the Bowman-Gray Fund influences some of the North Carolina members."[69] He may have been referring to Wake Forest and the money they had assembled for the new campus.

What was being missed in all the discussion of bowls and in Clemson's and Maryland's defense of their positions was that the conference, by its by-laws, had every right to prohibit bowl participation. The policy allowed for bowl participation only with the consent of conference members. This meant that the presidential bowl statement in September was a moot point. The meeting of presidents simply had confirmed their views and how they would vote, while raising the stakes for any school that accepted a bid. Clemson and Maryland were fully aware of this. Neither school expected the conference to voice its approval when polled. Both schools simply decided that they did not like the rules and were not going to abide by them.

Geary Eppley at Maryland had the misfortune to be recovering from surgery when the issue of bowl games became the central focus of the Southern Conference in early December. Swede, as he was known, was convinced, however, that bowl games were not a great evil and that their good far outweighed their bad. As a former great athlete at Maryland, he was more receptive to the role of sports in academic institutions. In a letter to a friend at UCLA, Eppley suggested that bowl games were far less intrusive on students than many sports that held post-season tournaments, such as basketball. School was not in session when the bowl games were played, for example. He believed that bowls were key to student and alumni morale, a position with which some presidents agreed. Students wanted to compete on a national level and the competition the games generated was good for the schools and for the country. A veteran of World Wars I and II, Eppley argued that Americans wanted to win and that was the real reason for the excitement over bowl competitions. Commercialism of the games did not concern him much, because he believed that the NCAA was working on this problem and would keep it in check. Even the financial incentive for playing games, he believed, was not much of a factor, because schools could not budget based on the chances of participating in a bowl game. Essentially, Eppley thought that bowls were not a significant contributor to corruption in college athletics. He predicted, nevertheless, that the upcoming Southern Conference meeting would be contentious, and that the bowl game ban might hold fast.[70]

Eppley did not like that bowl bids were extended three weeks before the end of the football season, stripping away some of the excitement from final games. Bowl mania, he correctly argued, became the focus of fans and media alike. It detracted from key games and some significant rivalries that remained on schedules, harming some of the enthusiasm for the game.

Two days prior to Eppley's letter, Curly Byrd was the guest speaker at the Durham Quarterback Club's meeting at the Washington Duke Hotel on December 10, the week of the Southern Conference meeting. It was a good opportunity for Byrd, because he could speak to multiple newspapers and interact with the Big Four schools simultaneously. Introducing Byrd, a man with an enormous aura, was Billy Carmichael, the controller at North Carolina. A good friend of Byrd's, Carmichael was a skillful politician, known for his ability to wrest money from legislative clutches and compel private donors to contribute to the North Carolina system. A former North Carolina basketball player and a major figure in the university's administration, Carmichael made a point to try and bait Byrd, a man he had known for many years, into talking about how Maryland proposed to present its side of the bowl argument at the upcoming conference meeting. In referring to the Southern Conference gathering where bowl game participation was to be in the forefront, Carmichael ended his introduction of Byrd saying, "I promise you the Southern Conference meeting will be rough."[71] That was a sentiment about which all in the room could agree. During the introduction, Carmichael passed a sugar bowl over to Byrd and the Maryland president responded saying, "North Carolina has now relented, we see, and should be willing for somebody else to get a little bit of it."[72] Byrd, of course, was referring to the two Sugar Bowl appearances that North Carolina made in 1947 and 1949, both losses and both approved by the Southern Conference.

Rising to address the gathering, Byrd expressed his belief that collegiate athletics were on a better footing in 1951 than at any time in his life, a bold statement considering the year's scandals. Agreeing with the sentiments of almost all Southern Conference presidents, Byrd maintained that college presidents had the authority to control and better college athletics.[73] Ultimately, Byrd was reiterating his opinion that college athletics were a great good for universities and the broader community.

Byrd passionately defended college football and Maryland. "There isn't a whole lot wrong with the game of football. I will defy anyone to tell me one single thing that is a detriment to the men in it."[74] He took the opportunity to laud Jim Tatum, as well, the recently named Southern Conference Coach of the Year.[75] He probably did not have to say much about Tatum, because the Terrapin leader had spent December talking to groups in Kinston, High Point, and Winston-Salem extolling his Terps and their right to play in the Sugar Bowl.[76]

Meanwhile, Frank Howard, perhaps trying to redirect some of the pressure on his program, released his plan for solving the problems of college athletics, particularly football. Recruiting, he believed, was the essential problem facing football, but it could be successfully addressed. The two-platoon system as well as spring practice and bowls, he argued, were not the problems. Instead, he provided six points for improvement. One was to have athletic scholarships controlled by the conference office without any contact between coaches and high school players. Coaches would provide a list of those players they wanted, and the conference would relay this information to the high school student who would select the school of their choice. Next, if a player accepted "outside aid" from anyone, his time as a collegiate athlete would end, but he could remain a student. This was designed to rid schools of alumni influence. Perhaps most surprising, Howard recommended that coaches be signed to 10-year contracts in line with the salaries of professors and deans. To address academic standards, players would complete a standardized test, the same around the country. Furthermore, those on scholarship would be required to pass all hours that they have taken, trying to ensure that athletes graduated.[77]

Without question, Howard produced an interesting plan that had elements of success, while also trying to draw attention away from Clemson's bowl bid acceptance. It would be very hard to get institutions aboard with a plan like this, but it was a recommendation to improve the conditions of college football. It was hard to argue that spring practices were not a factor in abuse, but he was correct to focus on recruiting, a practice well known for its corruption. Nevertheless, the scandals of 1951 had shown that collegiate athletics' concerns went well beyond simply recruiting.

December 1951 Meeting

On the eve of the conference's December meeting in Richmond, there was much speculation about what would happen to Clemson and Maryland as well as the greater conference. Smith Barrier, like so many others, did not know what to expect. Barrier wrote that there was no conference procedure for expelling a member and referred to Iowa being temporarily banned from the Big Ten in 1930 due to corruption in its athletic department.[78] The Iowa example was not a perfect analogy for this situation, but it was the best that Barrier could find.

One of the finest sportswriters in the country, particularly regarding basketball, was Smith Barrier. Barrier was a Tar Heel native, originally from Concord, North Carolina. After graduating from North Carolina in 1938, he returned to his hometown to begin a journalism career, starting with the *Concord Daily Tribune*. Barrier's star shone brightly and in 1941, he moved to the second largest city in the state, Greensboro, to begin work at the *Greensboro Daily News*.

Barrier's move to Greensboro corresponded with the emergence of basketball greatness under Everett Case at State College. He closely covered the Wolfpack through their remarkable run of success in the Southern Conference. By 1951, Barrier was a household name throughout North Carolina, writing a column that was a must-read for countless people. But Barrier was not limited to basketball. If truth be told, he was one of the finest golf writers in the country, not only covering the Greater Greensboro Open, but extensively writing about amateur golf in the Carolinas as well as the professional game. In some ways, Barrier made the *Daily News* as much of a golfing paper as the *Charlotte Observer*.

The *News and Observer*'s Dick Herbert was hearing that Maryland and Clemson were on the verge of expulsion. The schools in Virginia and North Carolina appeared to be in favor of expulsion, but the current Southern Conference constitution did not speak to how many votes were needed to expel a conference member. If a two-thirds majority were needed, something that the new constitution being voted on at the meeting demanded, there were probably enough votes to keep the two schools in conference.[79] Essentially no one, even the schools themselves, knew what to expect from the upcoming meeting.

Harold Williamson, writing in the *Roanoke Times*, believed that the conference could not do much of anything about Clemson and Maryland, in part because so many conference schools had played in bowls in previous years. Williamson was critical of the conference for making half efforts in its desire to control college athletics. If it were serious, he explained, the conference would abandon playing on future schedules any teams who participated in bowl games. Furthermore, he suggested allowing Clemson and Maryland to play in their 1951 bowls but prohibiting participation the following year.[80]

With the bowl crisis causing instability in the conference, Williamson offered a lengthy analysis of his desires for the future of the Southern Conference. He saw no need for the conference authorities to drastically reduce the present emphasis on college athletics and hoped that the conference leaders at the upcoming meeting would not go "berserk" when offering reforms. He stressed that William & Mary had moved quickly and properly to address their scandal and that Virginia schools did a good job of policing their athletics. Nevertheless, there were areas that needed to be addressed, particularly the number of football and basketball players on teams, the number of games played, and scholarships.[81]

He suggested that the football season be limited to nine games and basketball limited to 20. Furthermore, both squads, he urged, should be reduced in size. He could see no reason to have more than 10 basketball players, while he wished football squads to be capped at 33. Single-platoon football was the only option under this plan. These suggestions were good for the student-athlete as well as athletic costs, but they had little hope of becoming policy, especially with the great variation around the country. The University of Tennessee and others regularly had a roster of over 100 for football, for example. Praising the right of colleges to establish their own policies in the main, he saw no reason for the conference to interfere with the granting of scholarships but hoped that the limit on the size of squads and the length of seasons would greatly reduce the number of scholarships. Even with that reduction in place, Williamson believed a freshman had the right to play in his first year if he was good enough to make the varsity team.[82] The conference had banned freshmen for the 1951 season.

Jack Horner of the *Durham Sun* was direct, titling his column "Duke and Carolina Ought to be Ashamed."[83] Stating that Duke and UNC "ought to go stand in the corner," Horner emphasized that both institutions had played in bowl games and had judged them to be prestigious when their squads played in them.[84] Like others, one of his great concerns was that Maryland would leave the Southern Conference if prohibited from bowl competition. Basically, Horner was deeply offended by the hypocrisy of Duke and North Carolina, something that other sportswriters emphasized.

Chauncey Durden believed that by simply accepting bowl bids, Clemson and Maryland demonstrated the catastrophic weakness of the Southern Conference. "Here is an unwieldy conference with many member schools totally lacking in athletic compatibility and aims. It is a conference whose present constitution does not contain concrete action to be taken against transgressor members. In brief, it is a conference whose many weaknesses considerably outweigh its strength."[85] Durden was right.

The contrast between the Southeastern Conference and the Southern Conference was further brought into focus in December. When polling SEC coaches, nine of whom responded, the *Atlanta Constitution* learned that all nine favored bowl game participation. All but one coach favored freshman participation. Four coaches supported no limits on football scholarships with these four being Bobby Dodd of Georgia Tech, Ralph Jordan of Auburn, Johnny Vaught from Mississippi, and Bear Bryant from Kentucky.[86] The two-platoon rule, opposed by Bobby Dodd previously, was resoundingly embraced as well as allowing substitutions anytime the clock was stopped.[87] There was almost no de-emphasis element in the SEC, except at Vanderbilt, and football was fully embraced with very few restrictions. The comparisons between the SEC and the Southern Conference were striking, but the membership in the Southern Conference contrasted greatly with that of the SEC.

Meeting on the same weekend as the Southern Conference, the SEC in New Orleans defeated a Vanderbilt proposal to ban bowl games and spring practice. Even in this era, the Commodores resembled a Southern Conference institution rather than a Southeastern Conference university. The conference did prohibit freshman from participation for the 1952 season, but it was a league of large state universities, with teams not heavily dependent on freshman participation. The basketball tournament, however, was eliminated with the regular season winner being proclaimed the conference champion.[88]

With Kentucky's league dominance, the Wildcats went 14–0 in conference games the previous year; there was little interest in basketball outside of the Bluegrass State.

The John Marshall Hotel in downtown Richmond was the scene of the Southern Conference's greatly anticipated December meetings. Considering the impending debate about bowl games, perhaps it was appropriate that the conference was meeting in a hotel named for one of America's most famous jurists. The conference's executive committee, consisting of President Max Farrington, Vice President Forrest Clonts, Secretary-Treasurer D.S. McAlister, Geary Eppley, and Commissioner Wallace Wade, met at 3 p.m. on December 13. Easing into the agenda, the first matters dealt with basketball player eligibility. Some schools already had played basketball games without submitting paperwork demonstrating the roster's eligibility. The lack of action could result in teams having to forfeit games, according to conference policy. Continuing the theme of eligibility, the committee endorsed the long-held position that if a player participated in an all-star game, such as the Senior Bowl, they forfeited their eligibility.[89] Amateurism continued to be a focus of the conference members, most of whom saw it as the line that had to be held. The executive committee did not discuss the bowl disagreement, even though their meeting lasted for three and a half hours.

Before their official meeting where the fates of Maryland and Clemson would be decided, the presidents convened and discussed bowl participation.[90] There is no doubt that the meeting was contentious, but no detailed record of it exists. At the official gathering, Byrd presented a prepared statement outlining Maryland's position. This lengthy and legalistic document, which avoided the word bowl in its title, was written by Maryland's attorneys with input from Byrd, Eppley, and perhaps Tatum. This was elevating the dispute to a new level, although some language in the statement was intended to soften the legal aspects of the argument.

Byrd began by stating that Maryland had accepted the Sugar Bowl bid and was in full compliance with the Southern Conference's by-laws as well as the conference's traditional procedures. The decision was final, and the contract had been signed. Byrd argued that the conference's by-laws never intended to ban schools from participation in bowl games. He said, "The By-Laws provide that 'no post-season football game may be permitted, except by the consent of the Conference.'"[91] This part of the by-laws, Byrd said, was never intended to deny schools the opportunity to play in bowls. Instead, the provision was in place to protect schools from outside coercion to play in various post-season contests such as "benefit" games under pressure from alumni and others. Byrd was separating post-season games or exhibitions from bowls. The approval of bowl participation, therefore, was a formality within the conference and the statute was not intended to stop bowl participation.[92] Byrd explained that never had a school been prevented from playing in a bowl and that even North Carolina in 1949 had accepted a bid to the Sugar Bowl without having polled the conference. He was right. Usually a vote, albeit a formality, was taken at the December conference meeting or members earlier were polled to endorse a bowl bid accepted by a member. The by-laws, he stressed, even provided, in two places, financial information about post-season payouts to cover the cost of the booking office and determine the funds going into the conference's coffers.

Byrd's argument was weakened; however, when toward the end of his remarks he broached the topic of the vote taken at the September 28 meeting. This was the area where Maryland was on shaky ground. Praising Gordon Gray's good intentions as honorable and directed toward the best interests of athletics, he stated that the presidents had voted to "recommend" to the conference that it establish a policy to ban bowl participation.[93] Furthermore, after a request from Wallace Wade, the presidents expressed "an intent to vote" against bowl participation at the end of the 1951 season. The presidents, Byrd contended, did not eliminate bowl participation, something that could only be done by the conference itself. This was the crux of the argument. Byrd questioned whether the presidents meeting to establish policy between normal conference gatherings was proper and sound policy, although in the past he had not opposed the meetings called by Gordon Gray. The conference, he argued, should only be ruled by its by-laws, while votes on conference policy should be conducted through faculty representatives unless the presidents wished to minutely manage athletics.[94]

Byrd concluded by stressing Maryland's loyalty to the Southern Conference and its desire to keep high standards in place for college sports. Banning bowl games, he stated, was not the method for doing this. Energies needed to be directed toward other more pressing problems such as the recruitment of athletes and how athletics was treated on college campuses.[95] Byrd spoke for 25 minutes, outlining Maryland's position, knowing that he did not have the votes to carry the day.

Maryland's problem was that in September everyone, in practice, associated with the conference understood the presidents' vote to be binding. The presidents believed that to be the case as well as sportswriters and fans. Curly Byrd was correct about the language that was used on September 28, but almost everyone understood that bowls were off the table. That was the reason Wallace Wade polled the schools to determine how they would vote when bowl games came to the forefront at the end of the season. Wade understood that a majority of presidents prohibiting bowl participation would cause an enormous problem. Maryland was providing a new interpretation of the Chapel Hill meeting.

Chauncey Durden, in attendance, said that Byrd had not sat down when Hollis Edens called for a vote on Maryland's participation in the Sugar Bowl. There was no discussion on Byrd's arguments.[96] The result was 14 against and three in favor. Maryland's allies were Clemson and South Carolina. Most likely, the Tigers and the Gamecocks had discussed their alliance prior to the meeting.

Dick Herbert added that Clemson's Lee Milford proposed banning all post-season competition for all Southern Conference sports, including basketball. The motion did not advance for want of a second, but Milford wanted his proposal to be in the conference minutes.[97] It was a sign of the growing crisis within the league.

A detailed record of what was discussed among the conference members is not available, but Gray, who was late to the meeting because his plane was delayed by snow, and Edens were destined to win this battle. Press reports indicated that the meeting was heated. The *Greenville News* reported that there was a "fierce word battle" conducted between officials from Clemson, Maryland, and North Carolina.[98] Clemson and Maryland representatives were "bitter" about what had transpired with an unnamed figure saying that the probation was the "most high-handed act in conference history."[99] Considering the facts of the case, the paper was much too zealously supporting its local school.

It was 10 p.m. before the final gavel was struck and the sentencing of Maryland and Clemson complete. It had taken 13 hours of meetings, but Clemson and Maryland football were excluded from playing conference schools the following year. They were not expelled from the conference, but they were on probation.

Clemson and Maryland had a handful of allies who opposed their probation. South Carolina, The Citadel, and Furman supported their Palmetto brethren. The grouping was odd and a bit forced, because the presidents of The Citadel and Furman were strongly opposed to bowl games.[100] Both schools, however, needed the revenue that was generated by playing games against the two largest schools in the state. They realized that the financial stability of their programs was directly related to the interests of Clemson and South Carolina.

Gray and Edens stood by their positions, even though it hurt them in terms of public sentiment. Hollis Edens proposed the motion to censure Clemson and Maryland. Dick Herbert wrote that many in the public did not appreciate that punishing the Tigers and the Terps was favored by most conference members, and that it was not simply a Duke and UNC desire.[101] Nevertheless, the public perception was that UNC and Duke had conspired to punish Clemson and Maryland for competing in bowl games. They had exerted their power over the league, many believed.

Smith Barrier knew that the Southern Conference was in real danger of fragmentation with this controversial decision. He wrote, perhaps a bit unfairly, "It was just a case of the college presidents not being able to 'save face' without some sort of anti-bowl action."[102] Barrier remarked that the outcome of the meeting had triggered athletic directors and coaches to find games to replace their contests with Maryland or Clemson. State had quick decisions to make, because they were scheduled to open their season in Raleigh with Maryland before traveling to face Clemson. They had to replace their first two games of the season. Fortunately for State's Roy Clogston, Florida State officials attended the Richmond meeting, hoping to pick up some games with Southern Conference teams, ultimately with the goal of joining the league. Clogston agreed to open State's season in Raleigh against Florida State. Jim Weaver at Wake was looking for a school to replace Clemson on its schedule while UNC faced the same issue with Maryland.[103]

Both State and Wake were concerned that the probation threatened their bottom line, because they depended upon these revenue games. Roy Clogston was not sure what State would do financially, because the games against Maryland and Clemson were big money games. Jim Weaver regretted that Wake Forest was going to lose $20,000 by not playing Clemson. These were significant problems for athletic programs that had modest budgets.[104]

Always an astute observer, Smith Barrier stressed that 1951 had been an extremely eventful year for the Southern Conference. The conference had punished its own, had a commissioner for the first time, opposed the NCAA's Sanity Code, and welcomed a larger role for presidents.[105] In addition, the conference stated that it would not accept any bowl money that was paid to Maryland and Clemson for their participation in bowls. That would amount to about a $9,000 loss.[106] Max Farrington had had a busy year and now was wondering about the conference's future.

Some Maryland supporters demanded that Maryland withdraw from the Southern Conference immediately, but that was unlikely. Byrd never broached the subject of withdrawal and preferred to commit the Terps to the league, at least in all public venues. In addition, there was no alternative in 1951, except the establishment of a new athletic conference.

Clemson was irate over the punishment, more so than the leadership at Maryland, and many thought that the Tigers would leave the league. Its president, Frank Poole, and its faculty chairman of athletics, Lee Milford, believed that Clemson was punished for honesty. Poole emphasized that he "was not sorry" for accepting the bowl invitation.[107] R.H. Fike, a member of Clemson's Athletic Council for over 25 years, favored withdrawing from the Southern Conference. "You can't tell what that bunch is going to do," Fike argued.[108] Fike was ready to pull out of the Southern Conference while Poole called the conference's actions "unfriendly" and stated that the "punitive action was not just and fair."[109] When asked by reporters whether he would follow the same policy again, he stressed that he would do so and was not sorry.[110] Extremely angry and upset by the conference rule, the Clemson president was determined to meet with the board of trustees and the athletic council about what had happened.

Like some other observers, Carter "Scoop" Latimer of the *Greenville News* suggested that the conference members might have punished themselves more severely than Clemson or Maryland. In particular, Maryland games were money games that promised strong dividends for schools that played them. That money was going elsewhere. Furman, for example, enjoyed the money they earned from playing Clemson. Now, the Purple Hurricanes would have to look elsewhere to find revenue, most likely not comparable to what they were receiving.

Frank Howard was very unhappy and seemed to open the door for Clemson to move to the Southeastern Conference. An anonymous attendee at the conference joked in response to Howard's comments, "If Clemson were in the Southeastern Conference and playing a Southeastern Conference schedule, it would never be plagued by bowl troubles."[111] Dick Herbert believed that a move to the SEC was "highly unlikely" because they appeared comfortable with 12 teams. The University of Miami, for years, he explained, had tried to enter the SEC without any luck.[112] Most likely, Howard's words were only a bit of bluster. Howard told Scoop Latimer that as far as he understood, Clemson was not considering conference withdrawal.[113]

The Clemson coach took some solace from his friends at Wake Forest. The two schools, very much different, had been on good terms for years, in part because of the close friendship between Frank Howard and Peahead Walker. About Wake, Howard said, "Wake Forest voted for the resolution, but was a victim of circumstances. When I left the Richmond meeting they were just as friendly with us as they had always been, and, as far as we are concerned we'll play them again when the opportunity presents itself."[114] It is unclear what he meant by "circumstances" but Wake's position was similar to that of other schools in the league. They had no interest in making long-term enemies, especially when the gate receipts were strong when they played the Tar Heels and the Blue Devils. Nevertheless, President Tribble was a devout supporter of limiting the scope of college athletics, especially football.

The majority of the Southern Conference's membership, however, was not too concerned about a potential Clemson departure. The University of Virginia was seen as a likely new member whether Clemson or Maryland left. To some in the league, that was a better option, especially for many of the Virginia schools. Supporters for containing collegiate athletics viewed Virginia as a strong ally.

Even having been placed on probation, Clemson and Maryland were mildly treated by the conference. There was no motion to expel them from the league. There were no attempts to fine them. Their voting rights were not suspended. The outrage, especially from Clemson, did not match the penalty. Clemson would have little problem assembling a new schedule and neither would Maryland. The Tigers, for example, only needed to replace three games.

Clemson president Frank Poole, far right, front row, enjoys a football game with South Carolina governor Jimmy Byrnes, third from right, and their wives in the early 1950s. A former football player at Clemson, Poole was an avid supporter of Tiger football and the game in general (Courtesy Clemson University Photographs, Special Collections and Archives, University Archives, Clemson University).

Although many griped about the outcome at Richmond, the conference remained as one. The meeting demonstrated significant differences in how athletics were perceived and governed and again showed that the variety of schools in the league inevitably caused concerns. But the conference had not split.

Harold Wimmer, not paying much attention to the SEC, believed that bowl games might have breathed their last. With the Eastern Conference, the Big Seven, and the Southern Conference refusing to play in bowls, he believed that the NCAA would move to ban bowls regardless of how enthusiastic the SEC was to play in these post-season contests. He was concerned that big annual regular season games against rivals might be attacked by do-gooders as well. Like other sportswriters, he could not see how banning bowls reduced corruption in college athletics.[115]

Unable to play conference foes, Maryland and Clemson began replacing schools on their schedules. Before the weekend was over, Clemson was trying to schedule a date with Virginia. Washington and Lee's schedule became considerably weaker, because it replaced Maryland at College Park with George Washington and Clemson with N.C. State. West Virginia eased their docket, substituting VMI for Maryland. Clemson's schedule for 1952 had games with Furman, Wake Forest, State, and possibly South

Carolina erased from its schedule. Maryland's schedule remained stout with games against LSU, Alabama, Georgia, and Navy.[116]

The editorial page of the *Roanoke Times*, like most editorial pages, applauded the conference members for sanctioning Maryland and Clemson, expressing that the conference had not gone far enough. There was an unmistakable distinction between editorial page opinions and those of sportswriters. The *Times*, in particular, was harsh on Clemson, condemning them for ignoring the poll of the conference members and agreeing to accept a bowl bid regardless. Maryland was guilty as well, but there was a sense that their desire for bowl glory was more legitimate. The editorial board charged that Maryland and Clemson were acting as victims when they received what they deserved, with some believing that they should have been expelled from the league. Although the Tigers and Terps had decided to play in the bowls, the editorial declared, "The Terps and the Tigers will take the field with considerable tarnish on their colors. Both have shown unmistakably that they rate a bowl bid higher than they do their Conference obligations, and that is not at all to their credit."[117]

One day later, the editorial page fired another salvo across Clemson's bow. Saying that Clemson authorities had suggested that they might leave the conference, the editorial staff at the *Roanoke Times* said good riddance. They argued that a conference member could not be allowed to ignore the rules as Clemson had done. If Clemson decided to withdraw, "nobody should and we hope nobody will try to dissuade them from following their inclinations."[118] Seemingly uninterested in the question of bowl games, the editors focused on the importance of abiding by rules. "One of the things that is seriously wrong with this country today is defiance of constituted authority and the unwillingness to abide by the rules. Clemson athletic authorities should set a better example to the students than to follow such a course as they are apparently contemplating."[119] To the *Roanoke Times*, Clemson's desire to override the Southern Conference's authority was symptomatic of a wider flaw in American culture and deserved punishment.

Contrary to the editorial pages, Morris Siegel of the *Washington Post* vociferously condemned the Southern Conference for its actions while applauding the clarity and openness of Maryland's leadership. Stressing the hypocrisy of the probation, Siegel remarked that nothing of this nature had been done to William & Mary, a school that had acted fraudulently and attempted to cover it up.[120] Siegel noted that the conference took no action when North Carolina allowed Charlie Justice to play, even though Justice had signed a contract with the Philadelphia Eagles prior to matriculating in Chapel Hill.[121] Siegel added that the conference took no significant action about corruption within basketball, even in light of the massive basketball scandals that rocked the sport over the previous couple of years.[122] All of this was correct.

Perhaps most concerning for the league's future was the sense that conference members had harmed other member institutions. Geary Eppley was very disappointed in the bowl ban, stating to conference colleagues, "We have always managed to iron out our problems without hurting one another and there should be no difference now."[123] Pleas like this from Eppley fell on deaf ears, even though he was greatly respected by his fellow league leaders and had served as president of the Southern Conference. It was one thing for Jim Tatum to speak loudly about his concerns, it was another for Swede Eppley to do so.

As if the 1952 ban was not enough, Maryland was deeply disappointed that George Washington University and West Virginia had voted against the Terps. Maryland had sponsored both schools for Southern Conference membership and had enthusiastically scheduled the schools regularly. Maryland expected WVU and GW to provide some support for Maryland and certainly not to vote in favor of banning them from Southern Conference football participation in 1952. Morris Siegel argued that it was certain that Maryland would not be scheduling West Virginia and George Washington too often after the 1952 season.[124]

Siegel's colleague, Shirley Povich, did not shy from condemning the Southern Conference for its actions either. Pointing out the hypocrisy, Povich declared, "North Carolina State and NCU [UNC], which developed a sudden case of righteousness in voting against Maryland and Clemson are blithely sending their basketball teams to Peoria, Ill., and New York City, home of the fixers. Carolina State is playing Bradley U. and N.C.U. is meeting Manhattan College in Madison Square Garden."[125] Peoria and Madison Square Garden had been centers of the basketball fixing scandals, yet there were no issues with State and North Carolina playing games at those sites.

Almost universally, South Carolinians wished to preserve the Clemson–South Carolina contest, Big Thursday. There was no state law mandating the two schools play, something that most at Richmond believed was the case. Clemson and South Carolina officials thought the game would be played, but it was far from certain. There was sympathy for allowing rivalry games like this one to be immune from the sanctions, but there was a great deal to hash out before South Carolina could appear on Clemson's schedule.

The decision to place Clemson and Maryland on probation elicited a torrent of objections from fans. Letters condemning the decisions championed by Hollis Edens and Gordon Gray filled their mailboxes. For example, one critic charged that integrity and honesty formed the foundation of education yet Hollis Edens and other Southern Conference presidents "had performed a dirty, double-dealing trick" against Maryland and Clemson.[126] Charging universities as doing little more than teaching communism, the author applauded the coaches for teaching sportsmanship.[127] Other critics provided similar comments such as calling their action "the dirtiest thing I have ever seen."[128]

One of the few letters of support came from the *News and Observer's* Herbert O'Keef, a Duke University graduate from the class of 1930. O'Keef, in a private letter, complimented Edens for supporting academics in a wave of commercialized football. The editor explained, "You did the game a big favor by your action. Continuation of your policies, I believe, will mean that we will have football for many years…. I was afraid the game would get so big it would collapse of its own weight."[129] Although a minority opinion, O'Keef's judgment was correct. The game was becoming unmanageable. Edens needed the tonic provided by O'Keef, because the criticism was constant and powerful.

Having been placed on probation, Clemson's internal discussions showed that they were irate with the league. In a special meeting held on December 27, 1951, President Poole presented an extensive statement to the board of trustees and the athletic council remarking that the probation "seems to be the result of blundering and dictatorial methods by certain college presidents."[130] After discussing the March and September meetings of the presidents, Poole explained that Clemson had polled the Southern Conference schools about participating in the Gator Bowl. A "substantial majority" of conference members voted against Clemson's participation. Poole provided no dates or specific numbers. The president charged, "Those who were in haste to condemn bowl games, spring practice, and the two-platoon system showed bad manners and dictatorial methods."[131] He criticized the league for not taking actions against basketball and not prohibiting neutral site games. All the while, Poole drew attention to athletic disturbances involving football coaches under pressure at State and UNC and the William & Mary scandal, noting that nothing of the sort had happened at Clemson.

Poole's chief venom was projected toward North Carolina and Duke. Clemson's leader argued that the two were the top schools since the conference was formed, and that conference rules were never adjusted to create financial equality amongst the schools. Instead, UNC and Duke had had the best athletes and the best funding to go along. Essentially, they were charged with hypocrisy and gaming the league for their own benefit. Poole carefully avoided placing all blame on Gordon Gray, but his statement ended with the challenge of waiting to see what UNC and Duke would do to improve the moral and ethical experiences for college athletes.[132]

A few days after the meeting, Byrd wrote Bernie Moore, the SEC commissioner, to provide his personal thoughts about the Southern Conference meeting. Like Byrd, Moore had been a football coach earlier in his career, leading Louisiana State to great success. Byrd explained that the Southern Conference presidents did not disagree with Maryland's position on bowl participation but told him that they "had to save face."[133] Indeed, Byrd was appreciative of the suspension for 1952, viewing it as a positive development for Terp football.[134]

Maryland and Clemson Go Bowling

Ignoring the Southern Conference bluster and bursting with pride, Maryland's Terrapin Club and other friends of the university awarded Jim Tatum a new green Cadillac for his outstanding season. The players received sterling silver tie clips.[135] Tatum, fortuitously, had made it known that he intended to drive from College Park to New Orleans for the Sugar Bowl, and the shiny new Cadillac was perfect for Tatum's journey.

Maryland was the underdog to the well-established Volunteer team. The previous year, Tennessee had lost only one game and had capped the season with a victory over Texas in the Cotton Bowl. Their 1951 season did not have a blot and the Volunteers were sporting a 20-game winning streak, with most of their victories almost uncompetitive. Tennessee had the long tradition of excellence on their side as well as one of the most famous coaches in football, while the Terps were a fresh face on the national stage. The only common opponent for the two schools was North Carolina. Maryland had squeaked by the Tar Heels by seven while Tennessee had hammered North Carolina 27–0. For some, this was convincing evidence that the Volunteers would be Sugar Bowl champions.

Maryland strode into New Orleans without even a twinge of regret. The entire athletic department was provided all-expense paid trips to the bowl game. Prior to the bowl, Curly Byrd publicly defended bowl games and Coach Tatum did the same. The Terps prepared feverishly for the biggest game in Maryland history. Maryland needed this test on a national stage to see if they were equal to the best teams to help justify the direction they had trod over the last several years. With a brand-new stadium in College Park, a coach picked by Byrd to take Maryland to the promised land, and a roster of excellent players, the Terps had what was necessary to win. They lacked Tennessee's tradition, but tradition did not win games.

With few Maryland fans thinking about Southern Conference probation, New Year's Day arrived. Most of the predictions were badly wrong as the Maryland Terrapins blasted the Tennessee Volunteers 28–13. The game was not as close as the score indicated. The Terps took a 14-point lead on the backs of Jack Scarbath, Ed Fullerton, and Big Mo and never looked back. They led 21–6 at halftime. Meanwhile, the Volunteers had difficulty moving the ball against a very stout Maryland defense anchored by the great Bob Ward. Ward controlled the offensive and defensive lines, and left Maryland as one of their greatest players. The Volunteers finished the contest with 156 total yards compared to Maryland's 351. Most of the prognosticators had posted Tennessee as a heavy favorite and had misjudged the power of Tatum's team, especially his stout defense. Tatum had designed the defense to stop Tennessee's rushing attack and that is what they did with six down linemen.

Sunny Jim's defense was the star of the day, controlling the line of scrimmage and stopping Tennessee's great back Hank Lauricella. Neyland was still running the single wing and Lauricella was a fantastic runner, passer, and punter, a dominant player in that offense. In 1951, he was a first team All-American and runner-up for the Heisman Trophy.

Instead of Lauricella, it was Big Mo Modzelewski who carried the day, earning the MVP award for a tremendous performance, gaining 153 yards rushing. Modzelewski was unstoppable as the Terps ran at Tennessee behind All-American Bob Ward at center. The Terps rushed for 289 yards against 81 yards for the Volunteers. Lauricella finished the game with one rushing yard.

Jim Tatum had taken Maryland to the promised land. The victory appeared to validate the bowl position championed by Byrd and Tatum. Maryland had defeated General Neyland's powerhouse and placed the Terrapins in football nirvana, somewhere the team nor the school had ever been. In addition, Tatum defeated Neyland, the coach he admired and emulated. The game was so discouraging for Neyland that he did not meet with the press after the final whistle.

The night before the game, Coach Tatum roomed with Jack Scarbath, drilling his star quarterback on tactics throughout the night. Tatum's meticulous coaching worked. Perhaps most important in the victory was that Tatum ran a different defense during the game than he had run all season. Tatum was boresighted on gaining a statement victory, and he got it.

In the Gator Bowl with Governor Jimmy Byrnes in attendance, the Clemson Tigers ran onto the field behind the Confederate flag which was paraded around the field like the Tigers did at their home games. Although the always dangerous Billy Hair, at times, was explosive, Clemson could not score in a 14–0 Gator Bowl loss to Miami. Although the Tigers had more possessions in the contest, Miami intercepted Hair four times to seal the game. Clad in orange jerseys on a sunny Florida day in Jacksonville, Miami simply was too much for the Tigers. It was a disappointing end to Clemson's season, especially considering all the fuss that erupted over their actions accepting the bowl bid. The pay day, which they did not have to share with the conference, made for a comforting salve, but winning would have strengthened their position on bowl game participation.

Unsurprisingly, Harold Wimmer congratulated the Terps, stressing that there was no harm in these games. Maryland pocketed about $119,000 for their efforts and did not have to share a penny of it. Wimmer was not concerned about the bowl payouts but the "do-gooders" he often criticized were. Wimmer saw the money involved in these games as part of the capitalist system. Americans wanted these games and were willing to pay for them.[136] In some ways it was seen as the antithesis of communism.

Frank Howard, never short of words, after the Gator Bowl loss chose to speak at a banquet with several hundred football fans in attendance. Challenging the de-emphasis group, the Clemson coach stated, "I see all of you heathens out there are enjoying yourself after watching that game today. Actually, you don't look like such bad folks—everybody having a good time. If that's what bowl games do for folks, I'm for the bowl games 100 percent. Yessir. I'm for overemphasizing football if it means that good a time."[137] Always the country showman, Howard knew how to appeal to his supporters.

New Coach at State

As the bowl debate dominated headlines and discussions, State was looking for a new coach to replace Beattie Feathers. Feathers, the longest serving head football coach in State's history at that time, completed a disappointing 3–7 campaign. In eight years, the Big Chief posted a 37–38–3 record, not bad for State, especially considering his slim resources, especially the small number of players on his squads. In particular, 1951 was a bad year. Feathers' team suffered its worst loss in his tenure versus a strong Maryland team and lost to all three of the Big Four opponents, the first time that had happened under his leadership. Feathers had enjoyed two good seasons, going 7–2 in 1944 and 8–3 in 1946, but later records were not strong enough. The losses were not all Feathers' fault, because State put very little money into football, and Riddick Stadium was an aged, poor facility that was destined to be used into the mid–1960s. His teams were undermanned and not as talented as others. When he appeared before the faculty athletic committee to plead his case, he blamed the lack of victories on the school's academic standards and the required afternoon classes and labs.[138] He was not fully incorrect in his assessment. It was another indication of how academics and athletics mixed like oil and water.

Wake Forest's gridiron success under Peahead Walker, and its strong showing in 1951 with similar resources to State's, made many fans believe consistent winning could come to Raleigh if a change were made. Nevertheless, it was hard to say goodbye to the popular Beattie Feathers, one of the greatest players in Tennessee's history.[139]

Complicating matters was a botched firing and search. Feathers had two more years on his contract and was not told of his dismissal. H.A. Fisher announced Feathers' firing before he informed the Big Chief about the changes. Immediately, there was increased sympathy for Feathers and indignation for how the athletic program handled the issue. Soon, news emerged that Feathers was released from his duties because of administrative and faculty displeasure with two assistants, Al Rotella and Dick Peacock. Furthermore, State dismissed Feathers while being unsure of who had interest in the job. Many State fans wanted Jim Tatum; however, Tatum, interested in returning to North Carolina, had no interest in trying to create a winning team at a school that provided few resources for success. Several names were considered for the position such as VMI's Tom Nugent and George Barclay of Washington and Lee. Nugent was one of the originators of the I-formation and quickly had brought victories to the Keydets. Nugent even visited State's campus and appeared to be a promising candidate.[140] Nugent was not offered the position and later coached at Florida State and Maryland. He would have been a very good choice for the Wolfpack.

Many other names were tossed about, but the Pack decided on Horace "The Horse" Hendrickson. An Ohio native who prepped at Pennsylvania's Kiski School, Hendrickson entered Duke in 1930 where he became a three-sport letterman in football, baseball, and basketball.[141] Hendrickson, a history major, had outstanding mentors at Duke, having been coached in football by Wallace Wade and basketball by Eddie Cameron. On the gridiron, Hendrickson gained the nickname the Galloping Horse, because he played all positions in the Duke backfield, and was an outstanding player at all of them. Eventually, he was a letterman in football, basketball, and baseball. After college, Hendrickson's first head coaching position was at Elon where he led the football, basketball, and baseball teams. He even served as athletic director in the small Elon department. State hoped the Elon connection was a good omen, with Wake Forest having won a lot of games after hiring Peahead Walker from the Fighting Christians in 1937. Hendrickson excelled as a football coach, winning two North State Conference championships before moving on to be an assistant at Pennsylvania under head coach George Munger. By 1949, he was back in the Tar Heel state coaching the freshman football, basketball, and baseball squads at Duke. In 1951, Beattie Feathers, hoping for a spark, added Hendrickson to his staff as a backfield coach. Roy Clogston, State's athletic director, promoted Hendrickson to the top position.[142] Feathers landed as an assistant coach at Texas Tech under fellow Tennessee alumni Dewitt Weaver. With his competitive fire and outstanding experience, the decision to hire Hendrickson was welcomed by sportswriters and State fans.

Most fans and sportswriters recognized that 1951 was a transformational year for the Southern Conference. The national scandals as well as the bowl ban and issues concerning athletic de-emphasis generated ill will among league members, forcing many to question the future of the league. It was becoming apparent that the 17-team Southern Conference was unworkable.

5

The Everett Case Invitational
Southern Conference Basketball, 1951–1952

Beginning in the 1946–1947 Southern Conference season, the league was ruled by Everett Case's Wolfpack. Everett Case never played basketball in high school or college, but no one understood the game better than State's leader. The Anderson, Indiana, native elevated Southern Conference basketball to a level fans had never dreamed possible, turned State into a national power, and created ACC basketball. Case graduated the University of Wisconsin in 1923 with a B.S. in physical education. Eleven years later, he obtained a master's degree from the University of Southern California. Before arriving in Raleigh, he was a coaching legend in Indiana high school basketball, winning four state championships at Frankfurt High School, making the Hot Dogs the dominant force in Indiana basketball. At the high school level, he finished his coaching career with an astounding 726–75 record.

Case was one of the pioneers of fast-break basketball and scientifically analyzing the game, long before that was an accepted practice.[1] He was an early convert to film, studying opponents and his own teams to identify weaknesses and methods to exploit them. In addition, the Indiana coach understood how to market basketball to the community, by engaging with businesses and turning games into events that could not be missed. He loved pep bands and appreciated how music affected how teams played.[2] Famously, he installed a fake noise meter in Reynolds Coliseum to encourage the State fans to cheer feverishly for their team. There always was a bit of a showman in Case.

Although scoring was a centerpiece of Case's team, it was the defense that won him championships. Case pressed on defense. It was common for his players to pick up their opponents as soon as the ball was in-bounded. "Getting in their shorts" was a mantra for Wolfpack teams.

After service in the Navy during World War II, Case was hired as the head coach at State College to lead a program with little distinction in a region that had limited interest in the sport. When Case arrived on the Hillsborough Street campus, few were excited about Wolfpack basketball. Since State's first team in 1910, coached by Piggy Hargrove, mediocrity had been the norm. A few seasons with winning records were posted, but there was by no means a strong winning tradition. Famed basketball promoter Chuck Taylor was asked by State officials to recommend a coach to build a power. Taylor did not hesitate suggesting Everett Case as the best candidate. Case was wooed to Raleigh in part because of the construction of Reynolds Coliseum. Construction had begun in 1941 but was suspended because of World War II. The coliseum helped woo the Hoosier to

Raleigh, because he understood that the showplace being erected in Raleigh would give him a significant advantage.

When Case arrived at State in 1946, basketball held limited popularity in North Carolina and in most of the South. Many had never seen a college basketball game and basketball goals were a rarity. Case recruited heavily in Indiana and brought an exciting brand of basketball to the Southern Conference. Almost singlehandedly, State's head coach turned North Carolina into a hotbed of basketball that warranted national attention. It was a significant plank in the development of a New South North Carolina that was sometimes slowly and begrudgingly leaving behind its antebellum history. The mostly urban, northern game was becoming an obsession for one of the leading states of the New South.

One of the chief reasons that Case came to Raleigh was the potential held in the unfinished Reynolds Coliseum. The concept of building a palace for basketball, far exceeding anything else in the South, was enticing for the Indiana native. Initially, it was intended to be a 9,000-seat facility, about the same size as Duke's arena. Although football remained king in the South, State chose not to raze the old and worn-out Riddick Stadium, believing that they did not have the ability to field great teams in football. State was the agricultural college and had a limited number of programs of study, sometimes discouraging players from attending. Basketball was cheaper. Furthermore, the leadership in Raleigh would support a coliseum as an economic engine for the city. When Mary Babcock Reynolds contributed $100,000 to the building in honor of her uncle, William Neal Reynolds, it seemed that only the war could slow down the project.³

Everett Case (pictured here in the late 1940s) reversed the fortunes of Wolfpack basketball and in the process transformed the Southern Conference from a weak basketball league to one of the best and most dynamic leagues in the country (courtesy Department of Communication Services Records, Special Collections Research Center, NC State University Libraries).

Construction began in World War II, but the war hindered completion of the building and when Case came to Raleigh it was not completed. When Reynolds opened in 1949, the construction crew had not affixed all the seats and some fans sat on the floor and on steps. It did not matter. For most North Carolinians and southerners, the coliseum was the largest arena any of them had seen. Except for Duke and West Virginia, Southern Conference schools played in small arenas, some holding only about 1500 fans. With its flags flying above the entrance, with thousands of fans passing through the turnstiles, Reynolds was an intimidating structure.

Case came to Raleigh on a $5,000 per year contract. The bachelor was an immediate success, making State basketball games must-see events. Case employed a style of basketball not yet seen in North Carolina. He played a high-pressure game, focusing on smothering defense and the ability to transition from defensive pressure to a fast break offense. Using the entire court, spreading the floor, and keeping the tempo quick were all hallmarks of Case's teams. In a matter of a year, Case was the toast of Raleigh, dominating his Big Four rivals and taking the program to levels never imagined.

State's coach was a driven man, obsessed with studying basketball and winning at almost any cost. Players such as Vic Bubas, later an assistant under Case, were fully devoted to him. He, however, realized that NCAA and conference rules sometimes needed stretching to their limits to build a powerful program. This was nothing new in college athletics.

In a very short period Case was a legend. In 1950 he took the Pack to a third place NCAA tournament finish, an unthinkable achievement prior to his arrival. Furthermore, he had never lost in the Southern Conference Tournament. His success was so impressive that the *Saturday Evening Post* published an extensive feature on Case and

Pictured on its opening day in 1949, Reynolds Coliseum was a large and impressive venue for Wolfpack basketball, the Dixie Classic, and the Southern Conference Tournament. It became a centerpiece of Southern Conference and later ACC basketball (University Archives Photographic Collection, Campus Facilities and Views, Special Collections Research Center, NC State University Libraries).

the Wolfpack in March 1951. Like everyone else, the *Post* marveled that Case had made Raleigh, a relatively sleepy southern city, one of the centers for college basketball, and Reynolds one of the great basketball venues in the country.[4]

Changes at Duke and Maryland

In Durham, Harold "Hal" Bradley was a surprise selection for head basketball coach in the fall of 1950. Months before he was hired, Bradley sent a letter to Eddie Cameron explaining that he was eager to coach in the South and asked the Duke athletic director to let him know when an opening arose in the Southern Conference.[5] Basketball Coach Gerry Gerrard was desperately ill in the fall of 1950, ultimately succumbing to cancer at age 47 in January 1951. Bradley had no connections to Duke or southern basketball, but Cameron saw something in this quiet and dignified coach, who was extremely likable. Duke's athletic director believed that Hal Bradley had the abilities to challenge Everett Case. Bradley graduated Hartwick College in Oneonta, New York, later leading Hartwick to three very successful seasons, before moving to Duke. The intensely modest Bradley was a fine selection but was a surprise pick.

Although his players knew nothing about him, Bradley inherited a good team led by two sport sensation Dick Groat. The Wilkinsburg, Pennsylvania, native was a skilled athlete and a dominant player on the hardwood and the diamond. Although later best known for his career with the Pittsburgh Pirates where he was part of a World Series championship in 1960, Groat, at Duke, was a smooth shooting six-foot guard who could dominate games. Although Bradley was coming into the coaching position with little time for preparation, he had one of the best players in the country in his starting five. Among the Southern Conference press, Groat, almost unanimously, was considered the best basketball player in conference history and among the best athletes to ever play in the league.

It was good for Groat and the rest of the Blue Devils that Bradley, aged 38, installed a fast break brand of basketball, like Case. Imitating State's head man, Bradley brought a strong, pressing defense to Duke basketball.[6] It did not take long for the Blue Devils to subscribe to Bradley's coaching philosophy.

In College Park, a fresh face was on the sidelines as well. Jim Tatum found Bud Millikan coaching high school basketball in Iowa. Everett Case had gone from high school coaching in Indiana to the college ranks, and Bud Millikan followed that path. Although he was coaching high school, Millikan had pedigree. He was a talented high school guard playing for Maryville High School in Maryville, Missouri. Most significantly, he played and coached under Henry Iba at Oklahoma A&M. As a student, he was an outstanding guard and even served as a president of the student body. He learned his lessons well under Iba and moved from a high school position in Newton, Iowa, to College Park.

Hiring Millikan was not easy, however. After verbally agreeing to the job, Southwest Missouri State announced that they had secured Millikan as their coach. He did not want to leave the Midwest, but Tatum was a bulldog in almost all things and was not going to be denied. He offered Millikan associate professor rank and a much better salary to come to College Park. Millikan could not reject Maryland's offer.[7]

Maryland did not have much basketball tradition when the new coach arrived, and his hiring caused no fanfare and only received minor coverage, usually about a paragraph in the local newspapers. Millikan, a mere 30 years old, was a hard-nosed coach and like his mentor, Henry Iba, focused the team on smothering defense. With strict discipline and demanding practices, Millikan created an exacting type of play that strikingly contrasted with the brand of basketball in the Big Four.

Southern Conference Basketball

The 1951–1952 Southern Conference basketball season was to many observers another coronation for the NC State Wolfpack, but West Virginia and Duke were determined to have their say. Conference members were tired of the Southern Conference being run by Everett Case, and this was a year when there was a good shot to replace the Wolfpack at the top of the league. The biggest question was whether any of the other conference schools had advanced enough to take down the Wolfpack on their home court during the tournament. Dick Herbert, who had the distinction of closely covering the Wolfpack, said, "One of the safest things in athletics is a prediction that State's Wolfpack will be the strongest outfit in the Southern Conference."[8]

Red Brown had assembled an outstanding West Virginia squad which featured six-foot, nine-inch Mark Workman at center. The Logan, West Virginia, native was the team's leading scorer, as he was the previous year, and a prolific rebounder. No one in the league had an answer for him during his senior year. Although suffering a surprise overtime loss at George Washington on December 11, the Mountaineers reeled off 12 consecutive victories, including wins over Duke, Maryland, and NYU. Brown's squad, in a statement game, destroyed NYU by 25 points at Madison Square Garden. By early January 1952, some began arguing that the Mountaineers could replace State as the champions of the Southern Conference Tournament. It was a great misfortune for fans and players that State was not on West Virginia's regular season schedule.

The Wolfpack's fine core from the previous year had graduated, but they had a strong, but young, team led by Bobby Speight and Mel Thompson, both of whom were emerging as great Southern Conference players in their junior years. Thompson, a transfer from Memphis State, was not available until January due to transfer rules. The glue of the team, often a bit in the shadow of Speight and Thompson, was Lee Terrill, a senior guard. The South Orange, New Jersey, native was a first-rate ball handler, perhaps the best ball handler in the league.

As mentioned, Duke was led by the great Dick Groat, one of the finest athletes in college athletic history, regardless of sport. The All-American, who had come to Duke to only play baseball, headed into his senior year as the most feared player in the conference. Wearing number 10, Groat commanded games from his guard position. Bernie Janicki and Rudy D'Emilio were good players who complemented the talented guard, but Groat was special.

Wake Forest had an extremely inexperienced team, and little was expected from the Deacons. Coach Murray Greason, a Wake graduate, in his 19th year leading the Deacons, completed a 16–14 record in the 1950–1951 season and a 10th-place conference finish.

North Carolina was a tall squad, but the Tar Heels, under Tom Scott, were coming off a weak season, finishing 12–15 the previous year and missing the Southern

Conference Tournament with a ninth-place finish. The squad did not have a star and found themselves depending on freshman Al Lifson from Elizabeth, New Jersey. There was little enthusiasm for basketball in Chapel Hill, with few attending games.

On December 6, State beat Wake Forest 65–62 in Gore Gymnasium. It was a tight game with the Deacons often rallying, refusing to fold. What seemed simply like another State victory was much more than that. The game was the emergence of Dickie Hemric, a promising player for the Deacons who scored 20 points and dominated the glass. It presaged a number of great State and Wake battles to come.

In December, Duke was upset by Furman's impressive duo of Frank Selvy and Nield Gordon in a 73–72 defeat. Selvy scored 36 points, stealing the thunder from Groat, who could only muster 15. Furman had lost badly to State and UNC, before gaining the victory at the Shelby Memorial Community Center in Shelby, North Carolina. It was, no doubt, one of the oddest locations for a Duke game, but it was a model facility for the community, and it was packed for the contest. After the game, Coach Lyles Alley praised Selvy's offense and defense, remarking, "I wouldn't trade him for Groat nor any other player in the conference."[9] Sharp observers already could see that Selvy was a once in a generation player for the Purple Hurricanes.

Although a sophomore, Frank Selvy, a Corbin, Kentucky, native that Adolph Rupp allowed to get away, had reversed Furman's fortunes. The previous year, they won only three games, but in the new season, they were a threat to anyone in the league. Selvy was a talented shooter, good with both hands.

Furman desperately needed the victory, because they suffered a horrendous start to the season. State, unsurprisingly, dispatched them in Raleigh 89–53. That spanking was followed by 100–57 loss to North Carolina at Woodside Gym, a facility constructed by Woodside Mills for their workers. This unusual venue was chosen by necessity, because the court at Textile Hall, the scheduled site, was too slippery. Only about two hours before the game, it was moved to the 1,700-seat gym.[10] It was a six-point game at half, but once Frank Selvy fouled out, the Tar Heels rolled. Vince Grimaldi paced the Tar Heels, or White Phantoms as the *Greenville News* still called them, with 24.

Furman was Duke's only loss until December 22, when they traveled to face the powerful Mountaineers in Morgantown. Duke was ripped, 95–74, in a telling game that demonstrated that West Virginia was a conference favorite.[11] The victory margin was even more remarkable because star center Mark Workman, in foul trouble during the third quarter, only played one minute in the fourth period before fouling out.

West Virginia needed the big win, because early in the year it did not look like the Mountaineers would command the league, especially after they lost, in overtime, an 83–81 decision at George Washington. Red Brown righted the ship and posted a series of impressive victories that included a January 3 win over New York University, 100–74, in Madison Square Garden.

The Southern Conference prohibited the season from starting until December 1, but the unofficial start of the season was the Dixie Classic Tournament, now in its third year. Case and *News and Observer* writer Dick Herbert developed the Dixie Classic Basketball Tournament in 1949. The goal was to feature the best squads from around the country against the Big Four, to attract attention to basketball in the state and make a considerable amount of money for each school and the community.[12] The Dixie Classic, played after Christmas, was an immediate success, becoming a highlight of the calendar. It attracted national attention to the Big Four, the Southern Conference, Raleigh, and Reynolds Coliseum. The tournament also served to separate the Big Four from most of the other Southern Conference schools, positioning them as leaders in Southern Conference basketball. It was another indication of conference division.

In 1951, Southern California, Navy, Columbia, and Cornell were the featured teams playing against the Big Four. Although twice beaten, State was the favorite to win another Dixie Classic, even though Navy was unbeaten. State whipped Navy in the first round, while North Carolina slipped by Southern California 49–45, setting up a Wolfpack versus Tar Heels game for Friday. Wake Forest played well in a 58–51 defeat to a much better Cornell squad that had only lost to New York University in the early season. Surprisingly, Duke could only post 58 points in a 10-point loss to the Columbia Lions. Dick Groat scored 21, but the rest of the Blue Devils did little.

In the Friday games, the Wolfpack played a low-scoring and tough game against North Carolina, winning 58–51. Case had the Tar Heels' number, having never lost to them. The victory placed the Wolfpack in the championship game, a place they knew very well. Their opponent was Cornell who defeated Columbia in an Ivy League affair. It took overtime, however, for the Big Red to squeak by the Lions, 66–64.

In the loser's bracket, Wake Forest could not stop Dick Groat who set a Dixie Classic record by scoring 35 points in a 79–74 Blue Devil victory. Groat received most of the attention for a blistering performance, but keen observers saw the emergence of a new star for Wake Forest. Freshman Dickie Hemric had scored 33 points in his first game against a stronger Duke team. It was a coming-out party for the little-known player.

The championship game was a thrilling contest in which the well-coached Big Red gave the Wolfpack all they could handle. State won 51–49, but if the game had lasted an additional minute, Cornell might have emerged victorious. The Wolfpack were paced by 16 points from Mel Thompson. Case's tournament wizardry had struck again.

In the other games, the Tar Heels defeated Columbia 61–60, giving them two wins in the tournament. Howard Deasy of the Bronx scored one of two free throws to give the Tar Heels the victory in the final seconds. Their neighbors in Durham lost badly to Southern California 87–69. Dick Groat could not find his form, scoring only 15 points. The Deacons finished in last place with a humiliating 79–44 defeat against Navy. Murray Greason's Wake Forest club was young, but this was a surprisingly poor performance.

Always an astute basketball observer, Dick Herbert judged that State was lacking some of its "scoring power" from earlier Case teams.[13] Tom Scott's Tar Heels played much better than expected and looked stronger than they had in years. Herbert judged Duke's performance to be disappointing, but he had seen something from Wake's Dickie Hemric, boldly judging that he "had possibilities of becoming an All-American."[14]

By early January, State was undefeated in league play but had dropped games to Texas Tech, Manhattan, Fordham, Louisville, and Villanova. With the loss of Sam Ranzino, Paul Horvath, and Vic Bubas, stalwarts on State's squad from the previous year, this was not an overpowering team, but they were good. For much of the season, Case tinkered with the lineup, looking for the power that so many of his former teams had possessed but never quite finding it. He simply did not have the dominant team of a year before and many believed he was one year away from fielding a dominant squad again.

On Saturday January 5, Duke and State collided in Durham in a much-anticipated game. Could Dick Groat put the Blue Devils on his shoulders and lead them to victory? The game looked like another close State victory in the waning seconds when Duke's Bernie Janicki fired a shot from close to half-court that swished through the net tying the Wolfpack 64–64, with seven seconds remaining. In the first overtime, Duke held the ball seeking a last shot to win. Dick Groat missed with 15 seconds on the clock, leaving Mel Thompson a chance to win the laurels. Thompson missed as well, sending the game into a second overtime. With little scoring in the second overtime, the score stood 70–70 when Duke's Rudy D'Emilio missed a set shot with 15 seconds on the clock. It was the second time Duke had tried to ice the ball, hoping to win on a final shot. It was a mistake to give Case's cagers a second chance. Paul Brandenburg from Staten Island, New York, sank the winning bucket, giving State a 72–70 win. To that point, it was perhaps the best State-Duke game in history, featuring plenty of stars, and enormous tension. No team led by more than six points, and the lead changed 16 times.

State did not lose a conference game until February 5, suffering a 70–61 loss to William & Mary in Blow Gym, their home for basketball since 1925. It was a surprising upset, but the Indians had a solid team and would finish eighth in the conference with a 10–6 record.

Before this game, all of State's losses were out of conference, and some of them perplexing. The Wolfpack, for example, lost on their home floor to Bowling Green, 72–67, on January 29. The Falcons were not a bad team, but it appears that State allowed its previous game, a close win over North Carolina, to linger. State, however good they were, remained a work in progress. They lost back-to-back games in mid–January, first a 73–68 defeat at the hands of the Louisville Cardinals in Raleigh. This was followed by an 86–71 loss to Villanova at the Palestra. State rebounded and gained partial revenge, dropping the Wildcats at Reynolds 71–69, a couple of weeks later, but State could not control games as they had in past seasons.

By February, West Virginia was manhandling most of the conference competition in games that were not very close. Mark Workman, at center, was a fantastic player, averaging 23 points and 17 rebounds per game for the season.[15] Unfortunately for the Mountaineers, they experienced a significant blow when Jim Sottile, the team's second leading scorer and an invaluable leader, suffered a broken collar bone in a January 26 game against Bethany. Sottile was as important to the team as Workman, but the two of them combined made West Virginia a very dangerous team. Sottile's injury was a cruel blow for Mountaineer hopes.

Using all his talents, Red Brown kept the Mountaineers on track, winning 10 of the final 12 games. Ironically, both losses came against Penn State. The Nittany Lions were a good team, but in both defeats Penn State exploited the loss of Sottile to focus their defense on stopping Workman. Otherwise, they licked North Carolina, Wake Forest, Clemson (twice), and other conference foes.

Brown and his charges enjoyed a great advantage when playing in the West Virginia University Field House, later renamed Stansbury Hall.[16] When it opened in 1929, the Field House, seating 6,000, was an impressive venue. With two tiers of seating and fans jammed within inches of the court, some of whom were football players, it was a very tough place to play. It is no surprise that the Mountaineers enjoyed a remarkable home winning record.

In the Palmetto State, South Carolina and Clemson were enjoying some rare, good years. The Gamecocks, coached by Frank Johnson, were humming in mid-season. The team was led by Dwane Morrison, an Owensboro, Kentucky, native who played two years at Campbellsville Junior College before transferring to Columbia. In his senior season, the slick shooting guard averaged almost 20 points per game on what was otherwise an average to below average squad. Morrison was by far the best player on the team.[17]

Late in the season, the Gamecocks were in position to make the Southern Conference Tournament, in which only the top eight squads participated. All these dreams were shattered in the final two weeks of the season when South Carolina dropped its final four games, all conference contests. Playing at home, South Carolina lost to Wake Forest and Duke, followed by another defeat to the Deacons in Gore Gym and an end of the year loss to Clemson. Those four games meant that South Carolina completed the year in ninth place. It was a disappointing end for a season that included a seven-game winning streak and victories over North Carolina, Clemson, and George Washington.

In the Upstate, Banks McFadden, Clemson's head man, was surprising the league, leading the Tigers to a strong season, one of their best. McFadden was a Clemson hero, one of the school's greatest athletes, who had starred in basketball, football, and track as an undergraduate in the 1930s. Not much was expected from the Tigers, who completed the previous year with a 11–7 record. In a league with star talent, Clemson's season was a team effort. The Tigers featured no dominant player, but a number of good ballers. Clemson was helped by not having State on its schedule, always a welcome relief. In the first four games of the season, Clemson was 2–2, having defeated Georgia twice and dropped games to Tennessee and Florida. In an oddity, Clemson's first three victories were against Georgia. They played the Bulldogs three times. After losing to South Carolina 71–65 on January 15, the Tigers scored eight consecutive victories, including a one-point win over Frank Selvy led Furman in Greenville's Textile Hall.

Even by the end of the year, with Clemson sporting a somewhat gaudy 17–6 record and a fourth seed, it was difficult to determine how good the Tigers were. Three of their victories were against a bad Georgia team that finished the year 3–22. At the end of the year, they lost twice to West Virginia in games that were not very close. Without a player able to take over a game and will the team to victory, Clemson was hamstrung.

In College Park, Bud Millikan's hire was showing promise. With their proximity to Philadelphia and New York, it was surprising that Maryland had a long history of poor and mediocre basketball teams. The Terrapin schedule avoided State and did not feature games against Clemson or South Carolina, but Millikan was trying to create a culture of winning. It was an inconsistent season, without an established, great player. Lightly regarded Gene Shue was a sophomore during the season, but the point guard showed flashes of great skill. In games, it was hard not to see that Shue's performances were special. He was a tough, tireless player who never took a step back from anyone. Few schools wanted Shue out of high school, and Bud Millikan may not have been aware of what he had when the Baltimore native came aboard, without a scholarship. LaSalle and Georgetown, for example, turned their backs on him before he decided to join the Terps.[18]

As the season progressed, it was apparent that West Virginia, State, and Duke had separated themselves from the rest of the league, but Furman was not far behind. Like the other top teams, Furman had a star. Frank Selvy, the greatest player in Furman history, was a six-foot, three-inch sophomore forward and guard who could find his shot, regardless of the competition. Establishing himself among the best in the league, Selvy finished the season averaging 24.6 points per game.[19]

Mid-season, the Tigers set a hot pace winning eight consecutive games from January 26 to February 19. Many of the games were tight finishes. They included a one-point victory over Furman, a two-point victory at Davidson, and a one-point win at home over Wake Forest. The best wins of the streak occurred against Furman and a very good George Washington team. Clemson defeated the Colonials 80–65, in their dark and cramped Fike Field House.

What helped Clemson throughout the year was a strong home court advantage. Basketball never had a zealous following at Clemson, but the dimensions of the field house provided the Tigers with as much of a home court advantage as possible. Fike Field House sat about 4,000 at maximum capacity, but it was known as a dark facility with fans inches from the court.

With West Virginia's dominant performance, the end of the season did not have tremendous drama. The Mountaineers did not play a tight conference game in the last month of the season, winning their final nine contests by an average of 21.7 points. It was the type of domination that State had enjoyed for several years.

As West Virginia was rolling, State was playing at a high level as well when they faced Duke on February 12 in Reynolds. Dick Groat scored 21 points in a stunning 71–58 Blue Devil victory. Incredibly, it was the first time that Everett Case had dropped a conference game at home, and was only Duke's third victory against the Wolfpack since Case arrived in Raleigh. In addition, it was the first time in Case's tenure that State was not in first place in league play.

Jack Horner of the *Herald-Sun* believed that Duke's victory was positive for the league. Horner argued that it was not good for the Big Four to see one team exercise a stranglehold over their chief rivals.[20] North Carolina had yet to beat Everett Case and Wake Forest had scored only two wins against State since his arrival from Indiana.

With the victory in Raleigh, Duke had won eight consecutive games and, with Dick Groat at the helm and a strong core of complementary players such as Bernie Janicki and Rudy D'Emilio, they had a solid chance to unseat the Wolfpack as conference champions. Hal Bradley did not let the big win distract his team. They remained sharp for the rest of the season, beating Maryland on February 18 in a low scoring contest, 56–51. The win over Millikan's defensive focused Terps was followed by away victories versus Wake, South Carolina, and Davidson.

On Friday, February 29, Duke hosted North Carolina in its regular season finale. After a shaky start to the year, the Blue Devils were riding a 12-game winning streak, having not dropped a game since a double overtime loss to State on January 5. Dick Groat won his last game played at Duke, scoring 48 points, a Duke record, as the Blue Devils crushed North Carolina 94–64. Groat's 31 second half points devastated the Tar Heels, who had no answer. Furthermore, the raucous crowd screamed their approval throughout the contest, but especially when Groat was substituted with 10 seconds remaining. Everyone knew that they had seen the end of a special basketball career.

Writing in the *Durham Sun*, Hugo Germino described the end of the game in this manner:

> Dick was removed from the game with 15 seconds or so remaining. The 7,000 fans rose [to] their feet and gave him the greatest and longest ovation ever accorded to an athlete in Duke Gym. He sat on the bench next to his coach, Hal Bradley, and sobbed, like a baby. It was his way of pouring out thanks from his heart to the crowd who came to honor him. After the game was over, Groat made his way to the public address system and, still choking with emotion, he thanked the fans for their fine support this season. "We'll do our best to win the Southern Conference championship for you," he cried.[21]

North Carolina's controller, Billy Carmichael, may have summed up Groat's career the best. "With the sincerity of my soul, I say that I have never seen a finer basketball player than Duke's great Dick Groat."[22]

The Tournament: The Everett Case Invitational?

The opening round of the Southern Conference Tournament had a special guest. Richard Crozier founded the first basketball team in the state at Wake Forest and coached them to a win over Trinity (Duke) in the first game played in North Carolina. The game had grown immeasurably in the intervening years and Crozier remarked, "At least they still call it basketball."[23]

State entered the tournament having finished a surprising second in the regular season, their first time out of first place since Case was hired. They were bested by a fine West Virginia team that only dropped one conference game. Even though the Mountaineers won the regular season, everyone knew that defeating State in a tournament that Case had controlled since he moved to Raleigh was a very tall task. West Virginia and State had not played during the season, and fans greatly anticipated a matchup in the final. There was a sense that the Mountaineers were the only squad who could challenge State in Raleigh. Wake's athletic director, Jim Weaver, however, believed that the final would pit State versus Duke, with the Wolfpack securing another championship.[24] There was excitement for this potential game when Governor Kerr Scott conducted the ceremonial tip-off opening the tournament.

Appearing in their first Southern Conference Tournament game, Furman received the honor of playing the Wolfpack. The Baptists from South Carolina earlier in the year were crushed by State 89–53, but that had been the first game of a long season. The Purple Hurricanes were a much better team than the one that lost in Raleigh on December 1, but strangely they had not played a conference game in three weeks.[25]

Furman played furiously in a closely fought game in which State, at times, looked like they were destined to lose their opening round contest. At halftime, the teams were tied at 41, causing concern to permeate the Wolfpack faithful. Frank Selvy accounted for 21 in a scintillating half of shooting. Playing on their home court, the Pack squeaked out a 73–68 win. Selvy scored 27 points and Nield Gordon commanded the backboards. Bobby Speight dropped in 28 to lead all Pack scorers. Although Furman lost, the season had been much better than previous years, and Furman supporters believed that the best was yet to come.

In other quarter-final games on March 6, Duke barely defeated Maryland in a low scoring affair, 51–48. Groat was essential, contributing 21 points, but the game was in doubt in the final minutes when the score was tied 48–48. It was Groat who put the Blue Devils in front 50–48 which was followed by a Rudy d'Emilio free throw to seal the game. The Terps were the best defensive team in the league, and they had Gene Shue, but Groat, who attracted enormous attention from opposing team defenses, gave Duke an extra burst. Maryland's defense dictated the game and frustrated the Blue Devils, but they were unable to score in the last five minutes, even with many chances to win the game. Duke was exceedingly fortunate to win.

Before the tournament, Everett Case warned everyone about George Washington's club, remarking that they could be the "surprise team of the tournament."[26] He rightly called the Colonials "rugged and aggressive."[27] Reflecting Case's words, George Washington dispatched Clemson 78–65, providing an opening round mild surprise, considering that the Tigers had beaten the Colonials earlier in the year, 80–65, in Fike Field House. It was a disappointing conclusion to one of Clemson's best basketball teams. The Colonials ended Banks McFadden's finest opportunity to do damage in the conference tournament. George Washington's reward was a semifinal game against the Wolfpack.

To no one's surprise, West Virginia's Mark Workman was outstanding, scoring 31 points to send William & Mary back to Williamsburg, 77–64. Workman was grand, but he had help from Eddie Becker who contributed 16 points. The Mountaineers had done what was needed. They had defeated an inferior squad without too much trouble.

The semi-final matched West Virginia and Duke in a battle between two powerful clubs, with the Mountaineers fielding the best team in school history. The Mountaineers started quickly, but Workman was in foul trouble throughout the first half, having to ride the pine. With Workman plagued by fouls, playing only 18 minutes in the entire game, it was apparent that the Mountaineers were in a struggle. At halftime, Workman already had four fouls, but even with this challenge West Virginia led 51–44. Although leading, the Mountaineer fans knew that victory would be a tall order if Workman, who ended the game with only 11 points, could not play his usual game. The end of the game was high drama and very controversial. Surprisingly, neither Dick Groat nor Mark Workman were in the game, Groat having fouled out with less than two minutes remaining. Substitute Dick Johnson scored at the buzzer to give Duke a 90–88 victory, but it was more complicated. Mountaineer fans were furious that the basket was allowed, believing time had expired. They also complained that the shot was only possible because of a foul on the play. Mountaineer supporters said that Jim Coalter was manhandled by two Duke players when he lost the rebound that landed in Dick Johnson's hands.[28] It was a devastating loss for West Virginia, but it kept Duke's winning streak alive.

The game was one of the best in tournament history, and it was a shame that it ended on a controversial no call. Compounding suspicion that the officials favored Duke was that Workman was in foul trouble for much of the contest. Seemingly understanding that many fans thought that the Mountaineers had been cheated, Red Brown and his West Virginia players earned great accolades for how they handled the defeat. Brown did not scream and holler. He did not attack the officials at the scoring table when they ruled that Dick Johnson's shot had beaten the buzzer. He congratulated Duke on their victory and treated the crushing loss in an admirable fashion. Bob Quincy, echoing every sportswriter, praised Red Brown's actions in this fashion. "He was mannerly, courteous, friendly, and always smiling. He accepted his defeat graciously, and was one of the first in the Duke dressing room to congratulate the jubilant Blue Devils."[29] Brown said, "I could have sulked and barred the door. There's really no point in going out of one's way to be an ass."[30] At least in the moment, Red Brown had reminded everyone of the true meaning of competition and sportsmanship.

The second semifinal featured State versus George Washington, but it did not have the drama of the earlier game. The contest was close until the fourth period, when the Wolfpack put the game out of reach, playing at a very high level. The Wolfpack won 76–64, setting up the championship match against Duke and one of the greatest college basketball players of the era.

On March 8, State and Duke clashed for the title. It was the third straight year that the two squads had met in the championship tilt. In 1950, State beat Duke by 20, and the following year the Wolfpack scored a close 67–63 victory. Was the third time the charm for the Blue Devils?

It was not. The more complete State squad carried the day defeating the Blue Devils 77–68, in spite of Dick Groat's 27 points. Duke led 38–35 at halftime, but Case's deep bench was the story of the game, especially with five Wolfpack players fouling out of the final. With so many good players on the Wolfpack bench and substitutes playing at a high level, there was no discernable decline in State's performance. Hal Bradley's short bench could not keep the pace, after three Blue Devils fouled out.

Although State lost nine regular season games, they once again put it together to take the tournament. The victory snapped Duke's impressive 15-game winning streak which, ironically, began after Duke lost to State in overtime earlier in the year. With the victory, Case had won 18 straight conference tournament games, having never tasted a tournament defeat since arriving on the Raleigh campus. It was a remarkable run.

With six straight tournament wins, it felt as if the Pack were invincible. The year demonstrated, however, that the league had very fine players who could lead their teams to greatness. Frank Selvy, Gene Shue, Mel Thompson, Jim Sottile, and Dickie Hemric were young, emerging stars of the game, feared players who could take over a contest. Players like Dick Groat, Mark Workman, and Lee Terrill would be missed, but the league had never been healthier. The conference was full of talent, and the bigger programs were slowly closing in on Case's dominance. The season and the tournament had been exciting, but it was only the foundation for a truly special year in 1953.

Saturday night after the championship game, many gathered at Roy Clogston's home for a Southern Conference party. Clogston was the well-liked athletic director at State College. The party complemented the overwhelmingly popular tournament, which was a special event that highlighted friendships and rivalries and the joy of good competition.[31] While enjoying the hospitality of the Clogstons, few were thinking that there would be only one more Southern Conference season in a 17-team league. The greatest season and tournament would be the last one.

6

Conference Struggles and Ineffective Reforms in 1952

With the bowl game ban continuing to receive the attention of sportswriters, Curly Byrd began a charm offensive combined with lobbying to return to the conference's good graces. His opinion on bowls had not changed, but Byrd must have understood that his school's athletic future was tied to some of the Southern Conference schools. Unlike Clemson, Maryland, the higher profile institution, chose to take a proactive stance. In January 1952, still enjoying the great victory over Tennessee, Curly Byrd wrote to each of the presidents of the Southern Conference's colleges asking for them, when convenient, to provide a brief explanation about why they opposed bowl games.[1] Byrd maintained that there was no ulterior motive in his request. He wanted clarity. Nonetheless, Maryland's president wished to be viewed as cooperative, while gaining momentum for bowl game acceptance as well.

Over a couple of weeks, almost every Southern Conference president responded, some in brief but others in great detail. South Carolina's Norman Smith sent a short response telling Byrd that as an old football coach he already knew all the reasons for opposing bowl games. Smith provided the standard justifications such as extending the football season, taking players from their studies, etc. He underscored his remarks explaining that providing explanations like these was like "bringing coals to Newcastle."[2] Perhaps the old admiral had a little bit of humor in him after all.

Washington and Lee, George Washington, Richmond, William & Mary, and The Citadel were unapologetic in their bowl game opposition. None of these schools, however, carried the weight of a North Carolina or a Duke when it came to Southern Conference politics, but Byrd was eager to see how Duke would respond to his request, since Duke was one of the principal leaders in the bowl ban movement. Wishing not to engage Byrd, Hollis Edens responded by sending a note that did not address Byrd's questions. Instead, Edens suggested that bowl games be on the agenda when the presidents next met.[3]

Davidson's president, the Rev. John Cunningham, a man who significantly enlarged and modernized his school, was exceedingly clear about his opposition to bowl games, perhaps more than any of the other presidents representing small colleges. Cunningham's opinions, like those held by presidents of other small institutions, emphasized that bowls interfered with academic performance by lengthening the season by one month. The Presbyterian minister termed the bowl games something akin to a "public spectacle" that became financial equations for universities, a condition that he believed needed to be removed from colleges.[4] Positions like these only served to encourage Maryland to consider a split from the conference.

Although fielding competitive teams and representing a flagship state university, West Virginia president Irvin Stewart was equally opposed to bowl games, comparing them with "a livestock show, a beauty contest, a mardi gras or some similar spectacle designed to bring outsiders into hotels and shoppers into stores."[5] Writing with clarity and energy, Stewart saw no reason why a college should be part of such an endeavor. His lengthy letter criticized bowl games for causing successful seasons to be viewed as failures and for putting much too much pressure on coaches and recruiting while increasing the costs of paying coaches. He well understood that eliminating bowl games would not by itself clean up college athletics, because recruitment and illegal subsidies were the most serious problems. But he believed that bowl games were indelibly linked to scandalous recruitment practices and illegal subsidies, by placing too much emphasis on college athletics. He was convinced that prohibiting bowl participation was a first step at addressing legitimate concerns about college athletics.[6]

VMI's superintendent Richard J. Marshall, a VMI graduate, reinforced much of what Stewart said, adding that he did not think that the level of play in bowl games was achievable without students spending an inordinate amount of time detached from academics to reach a level that was essentially beyond amateurism.[7] A veteran of both world wars, Marshall viewed the games as stepping beyond the bounds of amateurism, although he admitted they could do some good things in regard to public relations.

Harold Tribble, consistent from the start, was succinct and clear about his opposition to bowl games, explaining that it was very simple to him. Wake Forest's president said that bowl games "contribute definitely to the trend toward commercialization of college athletics."[8] Tribble wanted sports to be viewed as "general student activities" while ensuring academic primacy. Tribble even argued, as others had, that December 1 should serve as the end of the college football season.[9]

Furman's president John Plyler delayed his response until mid–February, because he was serving on the Athletic Committee for the American Council of Education. Like almost all others, Plyler, a Furman alumnus and Harvard trained attorney, was worried about the pressures of winning, because this drove many of the problems with college athletics. Similar to Irvin Stewart's positions, Plyler saw bowl games as part of the entertainment business and believed that colleges did not need to be involved in that industry. Agreeing with Harold Tribble, Furman's president opposed lengthening the season by one month, because it detracted from academics.[10]

Clemson's Frank Poole wanted to get the results of Byrd's survey and was assembling information as well to use against some conference members.[11] Poole, clearly disappointed and even angry at the opinions of the other conference presidents, did not think bowl games, the two-platoon system, or spring practices were harmful to college athletes.[12] Each of these positions mirrored views held in the Southeastern Conference far more than those held in the Southern Conference.

When corresponding with Frank Poole, Byrd was far from fair in his judgment of the responses that he received from the presidents. In a short note to Poole, he called the responses "childish" and even incorrectly stated that the presidents were "not too anxious to put their reasons on paper."[13] The views of the presidents were far from childish, because they expressed deeply held opinions that academics needed to dominate university life. Byrd did mention that Gordon Gray and Hollis Edens preferred placing the bowl game on the agenda at the next meeting of the presidents, most likely a better option than submitting letters of justification to Byrd.

Byrd's skewed view of the responses resonated warmly with Poole, a welcoming audience. Clemson's president wrote, "I am certain that you did not expect a sensible reply" and that his respect for the presidents had "hit rock bottom."[14] Poole had not decided to attend the next meeting in Chapel Hill on March 8, but he believed that Byrd and Poole should attend. The relationship between these two allies was deepening throughout the early months of 1952.

Presidents Meet

Gordon Gray called another meeting of the Presidents' Group for March 8 in the faculty lounge of Morehead Planetarium. The agenda was focused on whether the Presidents' Group should continue to function, a ticklish question considering what had transpired in 1951. The floor was open to any other issues that presidents wished to raise.[15] Almost all presidents believed that the meeting would revisit the bowl issue, even if no changes were made to the policy.

In anticipation of the meeting, Gray had decided to relinquish his role leading the group. Managing athletics had very little appeal for him, and his workload was considerable. There was much on Gray's plate, because even as president he remained involved in service to the Truman administration as director of the Psychological Strategy Board, a role that interested him far more, even more than his duties leading the UNC system. Gray, as well, recognized that he was an anvil in the discussions about college athletics and perhaps a hindrance to reform.

The zeal for united efforts at reform languished during the March meeting. The new president of William & Mary, Admiral Alvin Chandler, charged that recruiting and subsidizing athletics were the two biggest problems, yet they received meager attention from presidents.[16] The editors of the *Richmond Times-Dispatch* chided the presidents for failing to ban off-season practice, as was done in the Ivy League, and for reconsidering their ban on freshman eligibility. The paper wanted action on the American Council of Education recommendations and a clear rejection of the opinions of coaches like Jim Tatum who was quoted saying, "We need more emphasis, more teams, more pressure on the boy to win under the rules of the game."[17]

Some were annoyed by Chandler's aggressiveness in the meeting, especially due to his brief period in academics. An unnamed Southern Conference athletic director told Chauncey Durden, "It strikes me that Admiral Chandler would be wiser if he sat in on a few meetings as a listener before he became the supreme judge of the conference."[18]

Curly Byrd continued his campaign to reestablish Maryland's place in the league. Speaking to the other league leaders, Byrd admitted that Maryland acted improperly and that its punishment was deserved. The Maryland president pledged Maryland's commitment to the Southern Conference and even defended Hollis Edens and Gordon Gray for their actions on bowls.[19] Byrd's mea culpa was not celebrated by the other presidents, who realized that Byrd had gotten what he wanted. Maryland had played in the Sugar Bowl and continued to have a good football schedule for the 1952 season, a national slate better than anything in the Southern Conference. They even had pocketed the bowl game earnings, not sharing them with any members.

There was much more behind Byrd's comments and actions. Always a clever politician, he realized that Maryland's future lay with schools like Duke and North Carolina, both of which fielded significant athletic programs and held academic reputations that Maryland desired. Creating permanent enemies was useless if a new conference arrangement was in the offing. Byrd needed the most prominent schools to ally with him. Beyond differences on bowl games, Byrd usually agreed with Edens and Gray about college athletics and their role in the university. There was more common terrain between these leaders than many in the public perceived.

This was supported by an invitation extended to Gordon Gray, Hollis Edens, Norman Smith, Frank Poole, and Colgate Darden to have dinner with Curly Byrd on Thursday, May 8, 1952, at 6 p.m. The purpose of the meeting, held on the evening of a lunch with the presidents of all Southern Conference institutions, was to discuss "our specific future in intercollegiate athletics."[20] Wake Forest and State College were not a part of these discussions, although State's interests probably were understood to be represented by Gordon Gray. Bob House, for example, was not on the invitation list either. Urging to keep the invitation private, Byrd did not offer a specific course of action, instead saying, "perhaps a far-reaching decision may be reached as a result of such a dinner meeting or it may be that it would seem more advantageous to continue our present status."[21] The letter made it apparent that several people had been discussing the future of athletics, specifically the Southern Conference's future, and that Byrd desired to bring these discussion together in a common platform.

Curly Byrd's invitation may have been influenced by a casual meeting held during the January 1952 NCAA Convention at the Netherland Plaza Hotel in Cincinnati. Eddie Cameron met with Rex Enright, Jim Tatum, and Chuck Erickson to discuss their status in the Southern Conference, especially as to scheduling issues.[22] According to Eddie Cameron, "They decided to go back and talk with their faculty chairmen and presidents about these problems and the possibility of forming a new conference."[23] This meeting may have helped move the process forward, but Byrd knew that the presidents needed to be supportive of a new league for secession to happen.

South Carolina's Norman Smith was unable to attend, but he explained to Byrd that university representatives would be present. The dinner hosted by Byrd at the King Carter Hotel at the corner of Eighth and Broad was a significant step. Clemson's president Poole missed the supper as well, but strongly encouraged the talks among like-minded institutions. Poole wanted schools to play more equal competition and noted that some of the smaller conference schools were in economic difficulty and should choose to find a better "competitive atmosphere."[24] Poole's presence was not necessary, considering that Maryland and Clemson had similar sentiments about athletics.

Southern Conference Meets Again

In May 1952, the Southern Conference met for the first time since the bitter bowl controversy which came to a head in late 1951. No one expected major fireworks, but conference leadership was determined to use the meeting to continue their de-emphasis program. An important backdrop to the meeting was the release of a special report from the American Council on Education (ACE), analyzing college athletics and offering suggestions for reform.[25] A committee of prominent academic leadership, including Furman's president John Plyler, the only representative from the Southern Conference, crafted the document. Its chairman was President John A. Hannah of Michigan State.

To outside observers, Hannah was a believer in athletic reform, but to those who knew him, Hannah was a supporter of big-time collegiate sports. As president of Michigan State, Hannah had fought for the school's membership into the Big Ten, something that seemed implausible 10 years prior to their joining the league in 1950. Hannah was a significant athletic booster, seeing athletic prowess as a complement to his campaign to elevate Michigan State to the level of a major, national university. He was not an ally of any of the national figures who favored de-emphasis efforts.[26]

The council provided nothing shocking in the report but offered some basic recommendations to clean up and police college athletics. The committee suggested that admission standards be the same for athletes and non-athletes and students participating in athletics be enrolled in a degree program, making progress towards completion. Budgeting of athletic programs should not differ from the budgeting of all other university elements. They recommended that freshmen be banned from varsity participation, and that all scholarship money be distributed by university-wide policies designed for all students. Scholarships were to be awarded based on financial need or academic performance, although athletic achievement could be a component, but not the main element in awards.[27] Essentially, all academic aid was to be distributed to athletes in the same manner and along the same lines as non-athletes.

Most interesting, the committee recommended the suspension of all post-season contests, including bowl games, urging that seasons should conform to tight parameters. Football would operate between September 1 and the first Saturday in December. Basketball would last from November 1 to March 15. Baseball was limited from February 1 to the end of the spring academic term. The committee hoped to prohibit all university tryouts, a common practice, and prevent universities from paying traveling expenses for recruits. All recruiting costs were to be in line with what was done for non-athletes.[28]

Some of these recommendations, regardless of the distinguished body that compiled them, were dead upon arrival. The recommendations were too late for most schools with big athletic programs. The incentives to disregard the ACE report were strong and growing each year. Bowl games were paying schools over $100,000 for participation, and television was bringing the games into the homes of millions of Americans. Television was eager to broadcast more games. Alumni and boosters were deeply involved in athletic programs. Simply put, there was no way to obtain anything like universal support for the proposals. Perhaps that was one of the reasons why John Hannah had no qualms about placing his name on this document. Michigan State football was not about to retreat from big-time college athletics.

The ACE report was thoughtful, but corruption already was deeply ingrained in the sport. Long after his playing days, Big Mo Modzelewski, for example, commented that when he was being recruited out of high school, Tennessee offered him $5,000 in cash to play for the Volunteers.[29] That was $1,000 less than his father made in a year. A South Carolina recruiter drove a new convertible to his home stating that it could be his, if he signed with the Gamecocks.[30] It makes one wonder if Jim Tatum and Maryland offered something special to obtain Modzelewski's services in their backfield.

To people like Gordon Gray, Hollis Edens, and even Colgate Darden, the ACE recommendations were a compass that could help direct presidents toward the control and minimization of corruption in collegiate athletics. Southern Conference members chose to send the American Council on Education's recommendations to committee to determine if the conference should accept all its proposals, an unlikely outcome.

The conference meeting was met with yawns, but Dick Herbert believed that there was new clarity, with presidents and faculty now leading the way regarding conference policy.[31] This had a calming effect over its proceedings. The football season was limited to 10 games and the basketball season was capped at 22 games, with little discussion. The biggest surprise was that freshmen were allowed to participate in varsity athletics.

Post-season football, whether on the agenda or not, was a significant backdrop. Trying to find some bit of common ground, Max Farrington was interested in playing a league championship game by dividing the Southern Conference into a nine-team southern division and an eight-team northern division, as already was done in Southern Conference baseball. The championship would be played on the same weekend as the famed Army-Navy battle.[32] Farrington's proposal, which showed great vision, was tapped for discussion by conference athletic directors in May. Farrington had suggested a plan that years later would be standard and even adopted by the ACC.

President Plyler of Furman chaired a special committee appointed by Grey to examine off-season practices and the ability of conference members to conform to ACE recommendations. Furthermore, the committee was tasked with studying Max Farrington's suggestion to split the conference into a northern and a southern division, with the champion of each playing a conference championship football game at the end of the football season. They even were asked to take on a study of recruiting and how sports were subsidized.[33] These were herculean tasks for one committee to undertake. Curly Byrd, Alvin Chandler, Hollis Edens, and Bob House agreed to serve as committee members.

With Gordon Gray stepping down as the leader of the presidents, Walter Newman of Virginia Tech was elected to guide the college presidents, who were scheduled to hold their next meeting at Clemson on December 11.[34] As a well-respected and sound leader, Newman was a good choice to replace Gray. Born in Woodstock, Virginia, in 1895, Newman earned an undergraduate degree from Hampden-Sydney, a master's from Virginia Tech, and a Ph.D. from Penn State. Newman devoted a large portion of his career to the development of agriculture in Virginia, solid preparation for leading Tech. In the 1930s, he became Virginia's director of the National Youth Administration, a New Deal initiative that was popular in Virginia. In that role, he focused on training young people, most without jobs or much hope in their lives. His training program was an enormous success that was copied around the country.[35] Assuming the presidency in 1947, as the school's 10th leader, Newman transformed Virginia Tech not just in the sciences but through notable emphasis on the liberal arts. A significant building program enlarged and modernized the campus. He was making Virginia Tech into a modern, comprehensive university, a challenge considering the educational politics within Virginia. These efforts were surprising to some, because Newman's professional life was devoted to agricultural advancement.

Newman was not new to athletics, serving as Southern Conference president in 1949. Nevertheless, he was coming aboard at a time of great stress and held views of athletics that differed from those proclaimed by Curly Byrd and Frank Poole. Newman was more in synch with Gray, Edens, and Tribble.

With little of great consequence coming out of the meeting, the Southern Conference presidents, again, received criticism from pro and anti-reform elements. Clemson's Frank Howard, speaking before Clemson alumni in Charleston, South Carolina, on May 21, attacked Southern Conference presidents for their ignorance of athletics. "The more

I see of college presidents the less sense I think some of them have. Of course, we happen to have a good president at Clemson because he understands football."[36] Howard condemned the banning of tryouts, saying that Clemson deserved to see the quality of the player before they gave him a scholarship. He complained that spring practices were set at only 20 sessions, alleging that Clemson was a poor school that could not recruit talented players.[37] Although some of his statements were meant to excite his supporters who adored him, Howard had minimal interest in athletic reform. His words were indicative of the tens of thousands of fans and alumni who wanted big-time athletics.

Maryland's Future

Before the end of the season, with Maryland enjoying another fine year, President Byrd sent a letter to all Southern Conference presidents suggesting a change to the Southern Conference by-laws that would allow bowl participation. After his goodwill campaign, Byrd now wanted to know if a change was possible. Essentially, he asked for wording that allowed the individual institution to decide if it would play in one of the NCAA sanctioned bowl games. The Maryland president needed to know if bowl reform was possible, in anticipation of the December meeting at Clemson. Byrd made a strong case, even including a quote from George Stoddard, the president of the University of Illinois, that effusively praised the Rose Bowl. Byrd offered a personal plea, writing, "It will help me, as the administrative officer of this University, tremendously if your answer is favorable."[38]

South Carolina's new president, Donald Russell, quickly offered his full support for bowl participation. Russell wanted "clear-cut progress" for a change in policy that allowed conference members to play in bowls. The former State Department official, immensely popular on the Columbia campus, explained that he did not wish to prevent Maryland from participating in a bowl game.[39] Russell supported the right of schools to participate in bowls and wished that the Gamecocks would be able to play for bowl titles. Outside of Clemson, this was the clearest statement of support for bowls that Byrd had received since the bowl issue arose.

Hollis Edens' response was opposite of the one from Donald Russell. The tension was palpable when he tersely stated that he would not offer his opinion in the correspondence. Unrealistically, considering Maryland's football success, Edens wrote that he had "hoped that the subject would not come up at the December meeting and that we could turn our attention to other problems of the conference."[40] In this and many other correspondences, the strain between Edens and Byrd was unmistakable.

The end of the 1952 season was disappointing for the Terrapins, making the bowl participation issue a moot point. Two straight losses to Mississippi and Alabama blighted an undefeated season. Even with Maryland's bowl hopes off the table, Morris Siegel believed that there was a 50 percent chance that Maryland would bolt from the Southern Conference to join a new league or play as an independent.

Agreeing with Siegel, Shirley Povich believed there was a good likelihood of Maryland's conference withdrawal. He maintained that if Maryland had beaten the Crimson Tide, the Terps would have accepted an Orange Bowl bid and withdrawn from the Southern Conference. Povich thought that not having the bowl bid made it easier for Maryland to step away from the Southern Conference to an undetermined future.[41]

Regardless of Povich's opinion, Maryland had proved its worth, and, with a leader like Byrd, would be a hot commodity on the market for conference affiliation.

Although Maryland football was in a strong position, some believed it was a matter of time before Sunny Jim returned to his alma mater in Chapel Hill. Tatum's wife was known to desire a move farther South to be closer to family in South Carolina. Tatum and Byrd wanted to win and had won big at Maryland, but Byrd was a hard man under which to serve, because he believed he knew as much about football as anyone else. Byrd correctly judged that Tatum was his own worst enemy by spending too much time speaking to reporters and offering comments that required more tact. Tatum had a habit of creating headaches for his president. The two men had dominating personalities and exceptionally grand egos, often finding themselves in conflict. As long as Gordon Gray served as president of the North Carolina system, Tatum had no hope of landing a job in Chapel Hill or Raleigh.

Speaking at the Washington Touchdown Club on November 24, for example, President Byrd blamed poor coaching for Maryland's two defeats. Such direct criticism for a coach who had just had a 22-game winning streak was unusual. Nevertheless, about Tatum, Byrd was unusually direct. He is "talking too much. I've been trying to shut him up for three years without success."[42]

The following day, Byrd walked back those remarks a wee bit, expressing his support for Tatum but maintaining that the coaching was not good at the end of the season. Byrd made a point of speaking positively about the two men's relationship. To further emphasize his support for his coach, Byrd planned to provide Tatum with a new contract when he returned to College Park.

With Tatum's success, the question of Maryland leaving the conference continued to simmer. The board of regents had not discussed Maryland's relationship with the conference at its November meeting, and Byrd maintained that the regents had never discussed anything like it.[43] Edward F. Holter, the chairman of the board's committee on athletics, was examining Maryland's athletics, but a final report would not be available until January or February.[44] Board chairman William P. Cole, later the namesake for Maryland's coliseum, was asked if Maryland should remain in the league. Speaking volumes, Cole flatly stated, "I wouldn't care to give my opinion on that."[45] Cole knew a great deal about speaking to the media, having served as a Maryland congressman and as chairman of the board of regents since 1931.

Byrd kept the fires of change lit when speaking at the Dundalk YMCA in Dundalk, Maryland, on November 28, offering words of impending change. The Maryland president was not specific about starting a new conference or reorganizing the Southern Conference, but he was clear that things could not go on as they were.[46] Byrd spoke about Virginia's desire to join a league but was vague about substantial changes to the Southern Conference. These comments, before junior football players, were couched in glowing remarks about the importance of football. Sermonizing, Byrd said, "Football is a game which stresses the will to win, the meaning of self-sacrifice for the good of the whole, and those are the qualities with which we develop our nation's leaders."[47] Associating football and sports with the Cold War, Byrd explained, "It is significant that the greatest drive being made by Russia for its youth is in the field of competitive athletics."[48] Reforming the conference to strengthen football, therefore, was a national imperative, if the United States were to maintain an advantage over the Soviet Union in the Cold War. Although Byrd did not state it directly, he believed that college athletics was a critical element in winning the Cold War. Playing sports, especially football, was a patriotic duty.

A New Eastern Conference?

At some point in 1952—the document does not provide a date—Duke and North Carolina received an extensive proposal from an unnamed source to form a new athletic conference. Believing that a split within the Southern Conference was likely and noting the growing interests in organizing conferences around schools with similar academic and athletic interests, the proposal suggested that the new league include Duke, North Carolina, Notre Dame, Penn State, Pittsburgh, the U.S. Military Academy, and the U.S. Naval Academy. The proposal wished to start with these schools but expand to include Pennsylvania, Syracuse, Georgia Tech, and Virginia. An added element was that this league would include high profile institutions from various regions of the country, most of whom played more national schedules.

There is no recorded response from Duke or North Carolina, but there were good reasons for both universities to reject this proposal. Travel expenses as part of the overall athletic budgets were a consistent issue for both. Duke and UNC desired a closer-knit conference. There would be numerous questions about whether North Carolina could leave the Southern Conference without State. Would these institutions agree to leave behind their long and entrenched rivalries which made athletics for both schools a large draw? Would North Carolinians care about games versus Syracuse and Pittsburgh? Lastly, the close relationship between many of the colleges within the Southern Conference would be tossed aside, something that some administrators did not wish to see. In some ways, it was easier for Duke to explore the possibilities of the new league than North Carolina, but it was unlikely for Hollis Edens to lead Duke in a contrary direction. He and Gordon Gray were like minds on all the most significant athletic issues.

The biggest surprise in the proposal was the omission of Maryland. Maryland was gaining in academic prestige, and its athletic programs were in line with the other institutions. The bowl question may have been the matter that kept the Terrapins outside of this proposal.

December Southern Conference Meeting

Even with the ACE report on many minds, Southern Conference fragmentation was seen as the most likely outcome of the Southern Conference meeting held at Clemson. Naturally, the meeting's location was likely to fuel controversy. Clemson had completed its football season out of conference and had performed rather poorly. Many at Clemson believed that they were sabotaged by the conference and Poole offered no salve to ease the wound. This was contrary to Byrd, who had been clever to repair rifts. Max Farrington wished to preserve the Southern Conference at almost any cost, but Byrd was willing to consider new conference affiliations. To keen conference observers, something big was destined to happen, whether at Clemson or at Sedgefield in May 1953.

Meanwhile, some schools had made headlines by formulating significant changes to their athletic operations. New York University, in the city where the basketball scandal was most prevalent, made over 100 scholarships formerly reserved for athletes open to the student body. Vanderbilt chose to adopt the ACE recommendations as the foundational component of their athletic operations, something the Southeastern Conference was considering, among other proposals.[49] The Commodores were acting unilaterally, thus indicating the gravitas of the reforms that were recommended.

Prior to the meeting, Jake Penland, expecting a new conference to form, provided a blueprint for establishing a new league. Outlining the well-known Southern Conference's problems, Penland emphasized that athletic leadership at the larger schools was eager to see change that produced a clear conference champion and provided more balanced competition between like-minded schools. He predicted a separation of the bigger schools, followed by their association with one of the bowl games. He compared the Southern Conference to a "bad tooth" that needed extraction.[50]

Although Dick Herbert did not predict a new conference coming out of the Clemson meeting, he reported that new conference arrangements had been discussed. One was a simple split of the larger schools from the smaller league institutions. A second concept would create a new eight-team conference that included "Pitt (the leader of the group), Penn, Navy, West Virginia, Maryland, Virginia, Duke, and Carolina. Pitt has been looking for conference membership for a very long time and had hoped to join the Big Ten. Penn doesn't like the Ivy League's de-emphasis. Navy can get along without a conference but is said to be ready to give serious consideration to the plan."[51] There may have been conversations about establishing this league, but this never became a serious proposal.

The Southern Conference had been fortunate in that neither Maryland nor Clemson was in a position to accept a bowl bid. Maryland's two losses at the end of the year and Clemson's losing season meant that the bowl controversy was not on top of the agenda. It could be avoided or postponed, opening the door for other pressing concerns.

Preliminary conference meetings were held on December 11, but Curly Byrd, Gordon Gray and Hollis Edens, among others, were not in attendance. It was surmised that without these figures present, the conference would continue to limp forward without any radical changes. Prepared to write big stories and sell papers, reporters were deeply frustrated that the predicted fireworks did not occur. Without the biggest names in attendance and without key discussions at the preliminary meetings, there was no chance for anything but more minor policy tinkering when President Newman struck the gavel to begin the meeting.

The conference representatives agreed with the presidents that all scholarships were to be precise in their description, and each institution was accountable for documenting all details for scholarships and enforcing their application.[52] This type of reform was not controversial. It was viewed as proper procedure.

Freshman and junior varsity teams, as they did in almost every meeting, received considerable debate, this time led by Richmond's George Modlin. As usual, smaller schools were eager to allow freshman participation so they could better field full and competitive football teams. They needed bodies. Nothing was decided, except all agreed that more study on the overall freshman experience was needed.[53] Freshman eligibility had received more study than almost any athletic issue, yet there remained no firm commitments.

Modlin suggested that the conference examine a reduction of practice time and schedules. No motion was made to accept this suggestion, most likely because it would put the Southern Conference at a notable disadvantage to out-of-conference competition.

It was difficult to pass reform efforts that put teams at a competitive disadvantage to other schools, especially those in the neighboring SEC.

With urging from Lee Milford, the conference dropped its rule that football squads be limited to 40 players. In the 1952 season, teams could field more than 40 players for non-conference games but had to abide by the limit for conference contests. The rule was designed to make competition across the conference more even and to limit increasing athletic costs.[54] It had accomplished neither and had placed the conference at a competitive disadvantage with other leagues, especially the SEC. The ending of the 40-player rule was an acknowledgment that the conference had no problem allowing some schools a competitive advantage.

This was an important change, because it meant that smaller Southern Conference schools would play conference opponents with far more players. It was a recognition that the more competitive schools would enjoy a considerable numerical advantage. There was no way for a school like Davidson or Washington and Lee to compete with the number of athletes available to a school like Maryland or North Carolina.

Recruiting competition and its deleterious effects on college athletics reached the forefront of discussion. Duke led the way, proposing that an athlete be ineligible for collegiate athletics at any school once the athlete had signed an agreement to accept scholarship money. After a very heated discussion about recruiting and its problems, the Duke proposal was rejected as being too binding.[55] Nothing much came of these debates and recruitment remained unchanged.

Bowl games were not discussed, and conference realignment remained off the table. The biggest issues were ignored. Of course, this did not mean that they were not in the minds of participants.[56] More to the point, the conference needed a bit of calm.

It had been a lackluster meeting when the final gavel sounded. Part of this was due to the absence of Curly Byrd and Gordon Gray. It felt that the conference was treading water and trying to avoid controversial issues, especially after what they had endured the previous year. Sportswriters from Maryland to Georgia were disappointed that their travels to Clemson had been unnecessary. There were discussions about the future of the conference, but these were held in small, intimate groups, not before the greater conference. An unnamed Clemson official believed that if a new conference was not formed by May then it might not happen. He predicted that the negotiations for a new league would be done prior to the next conference gathering scheduled for Greensboro.[57] He was right.

Virginia Separates

In December 1952, Gus Tebell notified William & Mary that they had no plans to play the Indians in the 1953 football season and perhaps not in the next three years. Virginia was not interested in playing all the Virginia schools each year and had indicated this a year earlier at a meeting in Richmond. Tebell maintained that there were three games in the state that were natural rivalries that should continue to be played annually. They were Richmond and William & Mary, Virginia Military versus Virginia Tech and Virginia versus Washington and Lee. Otherwise, the Big Six should play only one or two games amongst each other yearly, although they could continue to play each other in full in other sports.[58]

When William & Mary learned that Virginia was not scheduling them, Chancellor Alvin Chandler, in a fit of overreaction, announced that the Indians would not play the Cavaliers in any sport during the 1952 season. Chandler argued that if Virginia refused to play William & Mary in football then he saw no reason to schedule the Charlottesville school in other sports. As of the end of the 1952 season, the Cavaliers had faced William & Mary only 13 times since 1909, with the Indians having scored only one victory.[59] This was hardly an ancient series that was filled with bragging rights for alumni and boosters. The two teams had played in the previous three years, but the series had many gaps. Understandably, William & Mary was very sensitive to any slight, considering the athletic scandals that wracked the campus the previous year, and the school needed the Cavaliers more than Virginia needed William & Mary. Nevertheless, the Indians had not scored a touchdown against the Cavaliers from 1940 to 1952. On November 29, Virginia took home a Big Six title with a 20–13 victory over William & Mary, punctuating the end of the series.

By announcing this alteration to Virginia's upcoming football schedules, Tebell was positioning the Cavaliers away from many of its smaller in-state brethren and toward larger universities with more resources and broader name recognition. This was an indication that Tebell had conference affiliation on his mind, and a closer affiliation with schools more attuned to Virginia's interests. It was also a recognition that Virginia wished to play games that provided more revenue, and contests with small Virginia colleges were not lucrative. Tebell's thinking is even clearer when one considers that the changes he was conducting would make future athletic scheduling increasingly difficult for Virginia unless the school joined a conference. Virginia's athletic director was positioning the Cavaliers for a significant adjustment to its athletic future that was only months away.

The year ended with little substantial change in the Southern Conference. Most of the issues continued to emphasize the gap that existed between large and small conference schools and the inability to conduct reform. If anything, the year's events on and off the court and gridiron reinforced the need for a new conference that served the interests of the larger and more ambitious athletic programs.

7

A Reduced League
Southern Conference Football, 1952

After the bowl confrontation of the previous year and the sentencing of Clemson and Maryland to Southern Conference probation, the 1952 season was destined to be unique. Two of the 17 teams, both of whom had fielded strong squads for several years, were ineligible for the conference championship. Many schools had altered schedules and were trying to find ways to make up for revenues lost when profitable games with Maryland and Clemson were replaced with lesser contests. There was additional pressure, because Maryland was predicted to have a dominant team that would compete for another major bowl bid and a national title.

On September 1, 1952, some of the Southern Conference's schools embarked on fall practice. The schedule for opening games was inconsistent, with some Southern Conference institutions playing on September 13, others on September 20, while a few did not get underway until September 27. This wide variation was another conference problem and caused more difficulties in scheduling opponents.

For North Carolina, the pressure was mounting on Carl Snavely. Although he had led the Tar Heels for eight straight years, his last season was a poor two-win campaign, when hopes were high for a powerful team. Snavely had survived, but he was on shaky ground. The schedule was a problem, with North Carolina playing too many powerful teams. In addition, Snavely did not have the benefit of the excellent players who came to Chapel Hill on the GI Bill after World War II. The gray fox ran a good program, but he was criticized for being out of date and not adopting the split-T until most other schools had done so. There were some good players on his team, but the Tar Heels lacked the spark and the intensity of previous years and did not have the talent found in Knoxville, Athens, or Durham.

As often was the case, Duke was picked as the class of the Big Four and almost everyone pegged them to take the conference championship. There was a sense that Duke was ready to look like the Blue Devil squads of Wallace Wade's pre-war era. The Blue Devils were loaded with fine players like reserve quarterback Jerry Barger, tackle Ed "Country" Meadows, and quarterback Worth "a million" Lutz. Meadows, an Oxford, NC, native, was a ferocious player who would leave Duke after his junior year.[1] Center Lou Tepe, captain of the squad, anchored an experienced offensive line that could unleash their powerful backfield. Duke had won five games the previous year, but they were filled with experienced players and had a fine coach in Bill Murray. Their most difficult games were out of conference contests with Southern Methodist, Georgia Tech, and Tennessee. It was likely that Duke could make an undefeated run within conference play, but they were going to need some good fortune to win the three out-of-conference games. The Tech contest was destined to be one of the biggest national games of the 1952 season, bringing substantial attention to the Southern Conference.

No one was sure what to expect from State and Wake. State had a new coach, Horace Hendrickson, and was installing the split-T, but they had very few returning players and lacked quality at most positions. Tough games with Maryland and Clemson were replaced with games against George Washington and Davidson, much easier foes. Horse Hendrickson made clear that expectations should be modest, saying, "I like to win, but this can't be the season for that. This is the year we will have to start building, the one where we lay the foundation for a revitalized football program here at State College."[2] Rarely has a coach been more honest about an upcoming season and the condition of the program. The Wolfpack were dependent on Kearny, NJ, native Alex Webster to run, pass, and punt, but he did not have a strong line in front of him. Webster was by far the best player on the Wolfpack roster, and everyone knew it, especially the opposition.

Meanwhile, Wake Forest, with a squad roughly the same size as State's, needed to locate a consistent quarterback. Tom Rogers's team played above their heads in 1951 and were coming off two consecutive Big Four championships. As usual, there were more questions than answers on the Deacon sideline, because the school was small and did not have the resources of many of its rivals. Rogers knew that Bob Bartholomew was a good player, but he had yet to see how dominant he would be at tackle. The Deacons would not have to wait to be tested. The year began with a very tough game in Waco, Texas, against a powerful Baylor team that had whipped Wake Forest in 1951. It was a collision between the two most influential Southern Baptist colleges in the country.

Often, Clemson was charged with scheduling a number of weak teams and only playing about two or three good clubs per year, but the 1952 season was going to be a challenge, even for a talented Tiger team that featured the stellar play of Billy Hair, the Orange Bowl MVP. There was talk locally that Hair could compete for the Heisman Trophy. The schedule included Maryland and Kentucky, both bowl champions the previous year, as well as Florida and Villanova. Maryland and Kentucky were at the top or close to the pinnacle of college football success, but all four teams were certain to challenge Clemson. Even Frank Howard was concerned about how his team would handle a tougher schedule than in past years.

In Columbia, no one knew what to expect from the Gamecocks, as often was the case under Rex Enright, but there was cautious optimism. South Carolina had sound quarterbacking with Johnny Gramling and a good running game featuring Hootie Johnson at fullback. There were questions on the offensive line, and there was almost certainty that Enright would lose a game that he should not and a win a game that he should not.

The class of the conference was Maryland, even though they could not compete for a Southern Conference title. The Terps had an arduous schedule in front of them, but they had won the 1952 Sugar Bowl against Tennessee and completed an undefeated season when few thought that was possible. With modern Byrd Stadium and quality football on the field, Maryland was an exciting place to be, but the Terrapins were not a huge draw in the Washington area, something that bothered Jim Tatum. They had yet to deliver numerous years of powerful football and the DC area was not fully engaged in Terrapin football. Tatum was confident that this Terrapin team would be the best in his career. With a dominant running game, a stifling defense, and a skilled quarterback, Tatum had every reason to be optimistic. He had never fielded a team with so much quality.

The fearsome Bob Ward, an All-American on defense and offense, had graduated but some of the stars from the previous year's team remained. Tackle Dick "Little Mo" Modzelewski, a hulking and ferocious player, a giant by 1950s standards, was feared by opponents. Little Mo was far bigger than his brother Big Mo and a beast on the gridiron. He dominated line play and required double-teaming. His skill was awarded with the 1952 Outland Trophy.[3] Combined with Jack Scarbath pitching, running, and throwing the ball, Maryland had two of the best players in the country, players who opponents struggled to contain.

The Maryland schedule was daunting, much harder than their traditional Southern Conference slates. There was only one light game on the docket, a contest with Boston University in Boston. Otherwise, they faced Missouri, Auburn, Clemson, Georgia, Navy, LSU, Mississippi, and Alabama. The schedule probably was the toughest one in the country.

The Season Begins

In Waco on September 20, the Wake Forest football team ran onto the field during the opening prayer. Next, they lined up for kickoff when the Baylor fans were to sing a hymn, awkwardly standing on the field, as the hymn echoed through the stadium. Perhaps at that moment godly intervention decreed that Baylor would squeak out a 17–14 victory on a late fourth quarter field goal with 18 seconds remaining. The Deacons had played well and led twice but could not hold on to the tie on a sweltering Texas afternoon. Rogers and the Deacons were deeply disappointed, but they had almost beaten a much better team on their home field and that, they hoped, was a good omen for the upcoming season.

In the Palmetto State, Clemson and South Carolina opened the season with easy wins. Clemson smashed Presbyterian College 53–13, while South Carolina crushed Wofford 33–0. These games gave fans almost no indication of the quality of teams in Columbia or in Clemson, but playing in-state foes like these was traditional for both schools.

Duke beat a badly overmatched Washington and Lee team 34–0. The contest was a tune-up in anticipation of the game against SMU. The Generals, even without coach George Barclay, played hard, but talent and depth were not strong suits at the small Lexington school. Duke, meanwhile, played a bland game before a surprisingly small crowd of only about 16,000.

In the Old Dominion, Virginia Tech was showing improvement. Tech defeated Davidson 27–14 at Davidson. It was a reversal from the previous year's opener when Tech lost to the Wildcats. Although Davidson was weak, it was a sign that Frank Moseley was moving VPI in the right direction.

One of the biggest surprises of the day was Maryland only scoring 13 points in a 13–10 victory over Missouri. Maryland registered all its points on two touchdowns in the fourth quarter, the last one coming with a bit more than a minute remaining in the game. Although the Terrapins enjoyed a 12-game winning streak, they looked a shadow of the team that defeated Tennessee the previous January. There was concern in College Park that the Terps were not as hungry nor as sharp as the previous year's squad.

The following week, the Terps ventured to Birmingham, Alabama, to play the Auburn Tigers at Legion Field. Maryland was heavily favored, but quarterback Vince Dooley, later the famed Georgia head coach, led Auburn to a 7–6 advantage that held until late in the fourth quarter. Again, heroics were needed, and quarterback Jack Scarbath led the Terps to a touchdown that sealed a 13–7 victory over the Tigers. Maryland had started the season on the road but had narrowly avoided defeat in the first two weeks of the season. Perhaps Maryland was not as strong as pundits believed.

The biggest news in the first couple of weeks of the season was Furman's shocking victory against West Virginia, 22–14 in Morgantown. The Purple Hurricanes took advantage of a fumble happy Mountaineer squad that lost the ball four times. Furman had rushed out to two straight victories in the first two weeks of the season, the first being a 47–6 beating of Newberry College. No one expected the men from Greenville, SC, to defeat the Mountaineers, but Furman dominated the game, stifling the Mountaineers who scored all their points in the fourth quarter.

Fans at Michie Stadium saw a depleted Army squad, still badly shaken by the cheating scandal, surprisingly smash the Gamecocks 28–7. The game, the first between South Carolina and Army, was predicted to be very close, especially considering the poor showing the previous year when scandal had ravaged West Point. Army returned the opening kickoff 84 yards for a touchdown, setting the tone for the game. South Carolina contributed to the Cadet victory by losing three fumbles. The usual rumblings reemerged in Columbia about Rex Enright's ability to turn the Gamecocks into a consistently winning club.

Villanova traveled to Clemson on September 27, where they scored a 14–7 upset over the Tigers on their homecoming weekend. In a closely fought defensive battle, Villanova's punishing back, Gene Filipski, a transfer from Army, made much of the difference. Part of the reason for Clemson's poor offensive showing may have been Billy Hair's shoulder injury suffered in the Presbyterian victory. An overflow crowd had high hopes that Frank Howard would win a lot of games in the 1952 season, but this was a disappointing defeat that was a sign of a disappointing season to come.

The Villanova loss was followed by Maryland's 28–0 thumping of Clemson in College Park in what many had termed the Probation Bowl. Tatum's team finally played in a fashion that had been predicted throughout the pre-season. Jack Scarbath dominated the game which finally had the Terps scoring points. Maryland's defense kept Clemson from crossing mid-field until the last three minutes of the game. Clemson's fine back, Billy Hair, was held to negative two yards rushing. It appeared that the Terps had righted the ship, while the Tigers were listing badly.

The Tar Heels began their season on September 27, ill-advisedly hosting the Texas Longhorns in Kenan Stadium. The overmatched Tar Heels could not move the football against a stout Texas defense that controlled the game. Texas easily won 28–7, but the score could have been much worse. Ed Price's Longhorns were a strong squad that finished the season with nine wins and a 16–0 Cotton Bowl victory over Tennessee. This was another signal that North Carolina could not hope for much success with a national schedule that featured teams that were beyond its abilities. Freshman quarterback Marshall Newman led UNC to its only score of the game late in the fourth quarter. Otherwise, it was a disappointing performance, especially not being competitive.

Horace Hendrickson's comments before the season rang true in State's first game of the season. The underdog George Washington Colonials, with a first-year head coach, dominated the opener before a very disappointed State crowd of 7,500 at Riddick Stadium. The Colonials whipped State 39–0 in a game where State's offense could barely move the football. At least the fans were entertained by a "fine" halftime performance from the "snappy" Rockingham High School Band.[4] No one expected such a humiliating loss in the first game of the season, and some wondered if firing Beattie Feathers had been the right move. Few believed that Feathers' teams would have opened the year in such a horrible fashion.

On September 27, Wake Forest played their second road game of the season, traveling to Williamsburg to take on the Indians of William & Mary. In a close and exciting contest that included two William & Mary comebacks, the Deacons, behind quarterback Sonny George, edged the Indians 28–21 at Cary Field. Wake's defense stopped William & Mary at midfield late in the game to preserve their victory. The Indians were short-handed, but there remained a lot of talent in Williamsburg from previous years of success, and they were a tough out.

In the best game of the weekend, Bill Murray took his promising team to the Cotton Bowl in Dallas to face what was predicted to be a good SMU squad. Absorbing Texas culture, the Duke players arrived at the game on Friday evening wearing cowboy hats purchased on a Dallas street.[5] In a thrilling tilt, Duke's Worth Lutz was truly "worth a million" when he connected with Howard Pitt to score a touchdown with five seconds remaining to take a 14–7 victory back to Durham. Duke's win was significant news for another reason. It was the first time a team from North Carolina had won a football game in Texas.[6] Duke conceded a lot of yardage to SMU, but the Blue Devil defense stood tall when the Mustangs came close to scoring.

Although the start of the Southern Conference season was exciting, Commissioner Wallace Wade, at the end of September, provided some criticism about the commercialism of college football. Speaking in Charleston, South Carolina, before the Charleston Touchdown Club, Wade emphasized that college football was moving in the wrong direction. "The pressure to win has taken football out of the hands of the players and put it into the hands of the promotions. Football was designed to be an educational program for young men and not entertainment for overzealous alumni."[7] Wade stressed that coaches had to win to make more money and college football was being used to make money to fund other athletic programs. Essentially, commercialization of the game was removing it from its original design. Of course, Wade was instrumental in elevating football to a religion among fans and had been a full participant in this endeavor in the 1920s at Alabama. It was somewhat ironic that Wade's success at Alabama and Duke had created rabid alumni fan bases that were focused on winning.

In October, Boston College, after defeating Richmond 14–7 in its opener, travelled to Bowman-Gray Stadium in Winston-Salem to play Wake Forest. It was the first time that BC had ventured to the Tar Heel State to play a football game, although Wake had played the Eagles eight previous times in the Hub City. Athletic director Jim Weaver was well known for having the Deacons play money games away from campus, using the strategy to balance the books for the athletic department.

Over 11,000 fans saw the Deacons come from behind to salvage a 7–7 tie between fairly equal squads. Wake Forest had its chances to take a big lead in the first period but failed to take advantage of scoring opportunities. A fourth quarter touchdown from Wake's Joe Koch tied the score, but the Deacons needed a last-minute interception from Larry Spencer at the Deacon six-yard line to preserve the tie.

With a 2–0 record, Duke now faced the Tennessee Volunteers in game that had grown into a highly anticipated southern rivalry. Duke Stadium, later named for Wallace Wade, was the site of the 1952 game, the 16th in the series. On a glorious October afternoon, the Blue Devils pounded Tennessee. Although Duke won by only a 7–0 final score, the Methodists dominated from the opening kickoff. The Volunteers could muster only two first downs and a total of 34 yards. Although the final score did not illustrate the scope of Duke's victory, it had been a long time since the Volunteers had been so roundly bested on the field. Coach Neyland never had lost a game like it. In honor of the victory, Duke's Bill Murray was named United Press Coach of the Week, an honor fully deserved.

In Chapel Hill, football quickly fell to insignificance when four North Carolina students, including fullback Hal "Bull" Davidson, contracted polio. The Chapel Hill campus became a ghost town while fear and apprehension wracked students and parents. Ultimately, a fifth student contracted polio. North Carolina's administration immediately canceled the Tar Heels' upcoming games with Georgia and State. Athletic director Chuck Erickson canceled the South Carolina versus North Carolina jayvee game as well. Texas officials were alerted to the outbreak and the University of Tennessee changed hotels, preferring to stay at the University Lodge and not in Chapel Hill as scheduled.[8]

With Georgia only having three home games and now only two with North Carolina's cancellation, Coach Wally Butts quickly asked State College if they would be interested in heading down to Athens to play Georgia. The problem was that State was scheduled to face Davidson, and the Wildcats were not very interested in changing their schedule to accommodate Georgia and State. There was talk that State would play a doubleheader on October 4, but Davidson relented and rescheduled their game with the Wolfpack, allowing State to board a train for Athens for a 2 p.m. ballgame. There was added incentive for State to schedule the game, because if the UNC contest was not played, the Wolfpack would lose one of its money games for the year. This way, State was assured that a money game with 40,000 screaming Bulldog fans would help support the athletic department's bottom line. Not many expected much out of the Wolfpack who had played Georgia three times since 1933, having lost all the games without scoring a point.[9] Although the Wolfpack squad was thrilled to play Georgia, they only had one day to prepare for the game. In a rare act of cooperation and goodwill between the two athletic programs, North Carolina's staff provided State with their scouting report on Georgia.[10]

At Sanford Stadium, State paid dearly for its cash. The Wolfpack were hammered 49–0. It could have been much worse, because the unbeaten Bulldogs held a 35–0 halftime advantage and played reserves for the remainder of the game. The defeat was the worst one for State since losing to Duke in 1943 by a 75–0 score. Georgia accumulated 567 total yards, while the Wolfpack were limited to a pitiful 93.[11]

With a good win over West Virginia on its resume, Furman faced longtime rival South Carolina in Greenville. Johnny Gramling led the Gamecocks to a convincing 27–7 victory, dashing Purple Hurricane hopes. All the Gamecock scoring occurred in the first half with Gramling throwing for all four touchdowns.

Meanwhile, Virginia Tech, which had started with three straight victories, was soundly defeated by rival Virginia 42–0 at Victory Stadium in Roanoke, Virginia. The Cavaliers surged to a big lead by halftime and were never pressed in the contest. Tech still had a long way to go to be a consistently competitive club, but the number 16 ranked Cavaliers impressed everyone with their outstanding start to the season.

The following week, few were surprised that Duke pasted South Carolina 33–7, even though the game was in Columbia. It was an impressive Duke performance, with the Blue Devils clearly superior. Their defense stymied the Gamecocks all day. Although Duke was playing a tough schedule, they continued to perform at a very high level. It was a good victory for the Blue Devils who did not have the services of an injured Jack Kistler. The punishing fullback who led Duke in rushing did not travel to Columbia because of an injury suffered against Tennessee.

While the Gamecocks were being whipped by Duke, an enterprising burglar broke into the South Carolina locker room, stealing most of the players' valuables. The Gamecock players, badly disheartened by the defeat, were even more disturbed by the burglary.[12] It was the type of punishment that Rex Enright's players did not deserve.

Back home in Riddick Stadium, the Wolfpack surprised many by topping Davidson 28–6. Finally, the Pack scored points, behind the hard running of Alex Webster. Bill Dole's Wildcats had limited success offensively and defensively, even though they were playing after an open date. Hendrickson and his Wolfpack enjoyed the rare victory, but Duke lay on the horizon.

Wake Forest, again playing away from home, this time at Franklin Field in Philadelphia, were outclassed by Villanova 20–0. The best player on the field was Gene Filipski, one of the West Point players expelled from the academy in the 1951 cheating scandal. Like against Clemson, Filipski was unstoppable, but the Wildcat defense kept the Deacon offense in check all afternoon as well.

Having smashed State the previous week, Georgia now faced, on October 11, a far superior opponent. Maryland traveled to Athens and took the Bulldogs to the woodshed in an impressive and complete game. The Terps dominated Georgia, posting a final score of 37–0. The Bulldogs had a good team in 1952, finishing with seven wins, but they were not on the same level as Maryland. After a checkered start, no one doubted Maryland's offensive power anymore.

With Art Guepe at the helm, Virginia continued to run roughshod over the Southern Conference, stomping George Washington 50–0 in Charlottesville. Having earlier beaten Virginia Tech, the game was another indication of Virginia's competitiveness in the Southern Conference. Art Guepe's Cavaliers had been excellent, but many waited for the Duke-Virginia clash to determine Virginia's quality.

Farther South, Clemson's struggles continued with their visit to Gainesville, Florida. The Gators never trailed in a 54–14 whipping of Clemson, before 25,000 at Florida Field. The Tigers were turnover prone all day, giving Florida several short fields. Billy Hair played well, but the rout allowed Florida to play all 56 players on their team. After the game, the normally chatty Frank Howard had few comments, saying, "When you get beat that bad, you had best keep quiet."[13] Frank Howard's season on probation, playing a more strenuous schedule, quickly had soured. Instead of bowl consideration, Clemson simply was trying to win games in 1952.

After a two-week hiatus, North Carolina football was allowed to return to its regular schedule of practices. Fortunately for the university and for Chapel Hill, this outbreak did not reach epidemic proportions, as polio did on some occasions. Nonetheless, two players were stricken with polio, Bull Davidson and a jayvee player from Winston-Salem, Sam Sanders. Having been released from the hospital, Davidson returned to the sidelines for North Carolina's practice, which, no doubt, gave a lift to his teammates.[14]

Bowl Game Disputes, Again

As the Tar Heels were readying to play the Deacons, President Gordon Gray waded into the bowl debate again. Speaking to a group of alumni at the King Cotton Hotel in Greensboro, Gray softened his stance on bowl participation, indicating that he believed that bowl participation should be determined by the opinions of the individual schools, instead of a conference-wide policy. Gray emphasized that he remained opposed to bowl participation personally and for the Tar Heels and the Wolfpack.[15]

Gray provided an interview, after his remarks in Greensboro, to fully clarify his personal and professional beliefs about bowl games and the role of the conference in governing bowl game participation. The North Carolina president conceded, "If a majority of the conference wishes to remove the ban on postseason football games, I will not vote against the proposal nor will I try to impose a minority view on the remainder of the conference."[16] He added that he was unsure whether he would vote to remove the ban, explaining that an abstention might be his vote.[17]

Immediately, sportswriters and observers began wondering if the Southern Conference ban on bowl games could be immediately lifted, allowing participation at the end of the 1952 season. Gray remarked that he would not lead the way for this, but he was open to discuss the bowl participation question.[18] Obviously feeling pressure that would not relent, Gray admitted that he had considered the ban many times, questioning if it should be regulated by the Southern Conference or controlled by the "conscience" of each member school.[19] Remarkably, the North Carolina president softened his view of bowl games, but not the problems of college football, saying, "I do not think that bowl games are a major evil, they just contribute to our problems."[20]

Gray's comments now placed considerable pressure on Hollis Edens, his chief ally in the bowl controversy. Had Gray discussed this matter with Edens prior to his comments? Was Edens in agreement with this change? Edens chose to stay out of the bowl fracas, simply stating that Duke would follow all conference rules concerning bowls.[21]

Wilton Garrison of the *Charlotte Observer* commented that the conference should repeal their bowl ban immediately. Calling it a "stupid rule," Garrison's hope was for each school to determine its bowl policy, keeping the Southern Conference out of the matter.[22] It was surprising to see Gordon Gray's view dovetailing with sportswriters who cared little for presidential interference in college sports.

Even with Gordon Gray's change of heart, the bowl ban maintained strong support, even with the outstanding seasons being enjoyed by Duke and Maryland. There was a clear majority of conference presidents who were not interested in bowl participation. For example, State's John Harrelson argued that all bowl games be abolished. On the other hand, Clemson's Frank Poole was interested in there being even more bowl games.[23] Clemson and Maryland, being on probation, were unable to launch an action to overturn the bowl ban, but they could work behind the scenes to cultivate change. They faced a good deal of opposition from Wake Forest and other schools that argued that it would take several years to see if the bowl ban helped reduce the heavy emphasis on big-time football.[24]

Football Returns

The Tar Heels, however, would not have to worry about bowl participation. On October 18, North Carolina lost to rival Wake Forest 9–7. The North Carolina defense had been a "bend but don't break" organization for the entire game, until Sonny George kicked an 18-yard field goal on first down with a little over a minute remaining to provide the Deacons the victory. The game was a defensive battle that reversed the result of the Baylor loss that occurred on a late field goal. As usual, North Carolina struggled to secure the football, fumbling 11 times and losing six of them. One must remember that fumbling was much more common in this era of collegiate football, but that was a large number even by the era's standards.

The game at Riddick Stadium was not quite as close as the one in Chapel Hill. Duke demolished State 57–0, removing all the shine from the Wolfpack's victory a week earlier. The halftime score was 43–0. At no time did the Wolfpack challenge the Blue Devils, who won their fifth straight game in convincing fashion. Duke scored a touchdown on its first six possessions, with receiver Piney Woods, one of the great names in collegiate sports, starring. The Blue Devils looked imposing, albeit against a weak club, and now faced an undefeated Virginia.

On October 18, Virginia smashed VMI 33–14 at City Field in Richmond, clearing the table for the big game against the Blue Devils. A crowd of over 23,000, enhanced by the Tobacco Festival, watched the Cavaliers roar back from a 7–6 deficit to defeat the Keydets. It was the first time all season that Virginia's defense had given up points, and it was in front of the largest crowd to ever watch a football game in the capital city. In this contest, it was the diminutive Eddie Knowles with a 56-yard punt return who inspired the Cavaliers.

It was another highly anticipated Big Thursday contest for South Carolina and Clemson, especially because the Gamecocks afforded the Tigers a Southern Conference game. Neither squad had exhibited much prowess on the gridiron, but the contest always proved exciting, regardless of records. Even with mediocre squads, Rex Enright often found a way to defeat or play very closely better Clemson teams. Over the years, the game featured its share of drunken brawls and a great deal of animosity exhibited on and off the field. Good behavior had been a dicey option from year to year.

A sell-out crowd saw the Gamecocks score a first quarter touchdown and take a 6–0 lead. Surprisingly, that one score held up the entire afternoon with South Carolina gaining a victory in the 50th game between the two rivals. It was a defensive battle with the Gamecocks not allowing Clemson star Billy Hair to score. With Johnny Gramling missing most of the game with an injury, the Gamecock offense could not do very much. In a game that usually produced thrills, the 1952 matchup had very little drama, although by all accounts the Gamecocks deserved the victory.

The Virginia-Duke contest on October 25 featured two undefeated and top-10 ranked teams. The Blue Devil offense was too much for the Cavaliers, and Duke commanded the game leading to a 21–7 victory in Scott Stadium. Durham native Worth Lutz was unstoppable and the difference in the game, but both sides of the ball played at a high level. From the first period, the game was never in doubt, in part because Duke had a great deal of experience in pivotal contests like this one. It was Virginia's first home loss since 1949, a remarkable run considering the many years of Cavalier futility. The defeat ended a 10-game Cavalier win streak as well. Art Guepe was winning games at a level never experienced in Charlottesville, but he had yet to reach the elite status where Duke often resided. Nevertheless, the game had drawn the largest crowd to ever watch a game at Scott Stadium. Over 34,000 fans surely influenced observers to the excitement that could be had if Virginia joined the Southern Conference. Duke's victory set up a huge game the following week at home against Georgia Tech. The Yellow Jackets were on a 20-game winning streak.

North Carolina had little hope of beating Notre Dame and lost to the Irish by a 34–14 score at Notre Dame Stadium. It was another dominating Notre Dame performance under Frank Leahy, and another indication that the Tar Heel schedule was too difficult for the team's talent. Snavely had not forgotten how to coach. Simply put, he did not have the quality of players to engage a national schedule that included the likes of Texas and Notre Dame.

Meanwhile, on homecoming weekend, before a tiny crowd at Riddick Stadium, State defeated winless Florida State 13–7. State's Teddy Kilyk returned an interception 76 yards to score the deciding touchdown. Although the Seminole squad was not strong, the Wolfpack showed fortitude by recovering from the terrible loss to Duke the previous week. It was a victory that Hendrickson badly needed.

Virginia Joining the Southern Conference?

As Virginia was hosting its largest crowd to see a football game in Charlottesville, athletic director Gus Tebell had conference affiliation on his mind. Virginia remained an independent, but they played a large number of Southern Conference games, often more than several other league members. Recognizing the need to be in a league, Gus Tebell pledged that Virginia was planning to seek readmission to the Southern Conference in December 1952.[25] Tebell further explained that Virginia was ready to rejoin the conference in May until the Southern Conference voted to make freshmen eligible, a policy that Colgate Darden was known to oppose. Virginia, closely aligned with athletic de-emphasis, had established a policy to deny freshman participation.[26]

When George Washington played Virginia earlier in the season, Max Farrington met with Colgate Darden to discuss joining the league. That meeting may have formed a foundation for membership, but Gordon Gray's nuanced position on bowl participation, called a reversal of policy by some, had not been popular with bowl opponents at Virginia.[27] Darden was not keen to play bowl games and remained concerned about the growing commercialization of sports. He made it clear in 1952 that Virginia would not participate in a bowl, regardless of their record. Freshman eligibility policy and bowl game controversy made Darden unsure of what direction they should take, but remaining independent was not the easiest of options and Gus Tebell knew it.

The Season Resumes

As the cool air of late autumn blew into Durham, Duke was undefeated and had fielded an exceptional defense all season. A sell-out homecoming crowd at Duke Stadium greatly anticipated making a national statement with a victory against Bobby Dodd's Yellow Jackets, hailed as one of the finest squads in the land. Duke ran onto the field wearing all blue while Georgia Tech donned their traditional gold pants and white jerseys. From the opening kickoff, it was apparent that Georgia Tech was the better squad. They gained a 14–0 lead in the first quarter and were dominant on the offensive and defensive lines. The Jackets blocked two Worth Lutz punts and intercepted three passes. Duke played better in the second half, but the game was in hand with Tech winning 28–7. Bobby Dodd commented that it was Tech's best game of the year, and it was. To local observers, the Yellow Jackets looked to be one of the finest teams, if not the best team, in southern football history. Hugo Germino put it bluntly. "We were beaten, period. Georgia Tech out-charged, out-blocked, out-tackled, out-ran, out-played, and out-classed Duke."[28]

There was no shame in the Blue Devil defeat. Duke lost to a Tech squad that finished the season 12–0 and won the national championship. Arguably, it was Tech's finest football team in their distinguished gridiron history. Their defense was sensational, shutting out four opponents and only allowing Florida to score in double digits. Having locked horns with Duke about bowl games, Jim Tatum took the opportunity to show footage of the Tech-Duke game on his television show in Washington.[29] Big Jim never missed an opportunity to take a swipe at Duke, his most significant conference competition.

Unfortunately, this was the last Georgia Tech-Duke contest in a series that had been eventful on and off the field. Tech was suspending the series, because they wanted a larger gate receipt from games, more than Duke could provide in Durham or coming to Atlanta. It was another sign of big-time college athletics.

As Duke suffered its first loss, Maryland added another victory to its 18-game winning streak. Unsurprisingly, the Terps whipped Boston University 34–7. The outclassed Terriers never had a chance. The most entertaining part of Maryland's weekend came moments before the contest when Jim Tatum, full of gusto, challenged Biggie Munn's Michigan State to a game to be played anytime and anywhere. The Spartans, playing their final year as an independent, were having a fabulous undefeated season. As was often the case, Tatum let his competitive juices get the best of him. Following standard procedure, President Byrd cooled emotions, saying that Tatum had enough to do winning the games remaining on his current schedule and that there were no plans to play Michigan State.[30]

At Shield-Watkins Field in Knoxville, the Volunteers spanked the reeling Tar Heels 41–14. The hapless Tar Heels were dominated in every facet of the game. Turnovers gave Tennessee several short fields that allowed for quick scores. Snavely's charges were fading fast as the season was coming to an end.

On November 1, South Carolina scored 21 fourth quarter points to surprise Virginia 21–14, in the Oyster Bowl played at Norfolk's Foreman Field. Like so many stadiums, Foreman Field was another facility that opened in the 1930s and on November 1, 1952, it hosted a sell-out crowd. It was a shocking victory for the underdog Gamecocks who had little hope of winning at the end of the third quarter. Perhaps inspired by all the Oyster Bowl pageantry or a Cavalier hangover, the Gamecocks commanded the final period. Jake Penland wrote, "Gamecocks scored three crazy touchdowns in six and a half crazy minutes to gain an improbable victory."[31] With Johnny Gramling struggling, Dick Balka quarterbacked South Carolina to a touchdown that was followed by two costly Virginia fumbles that led to South Carolina touchdowns.

Clemson bounced back from their defeat to South Carolina, taming Boston College 13–0, behind the fine play of Billy Hair. The Tigers desperately needed a win after a

Maryland head football coach Jim Tatum (center, in suit) enjoys another Maryland victory with his players in 1952 (courtesy University Archives, AlbUM, University of Maryland).

four-week skid. It was a big Clemson victory, considering BC had only lost to a good Villanova team. Although Billy Hair received most of the plaudits, it was the Clemson defense who won the game, holding the Eagles to a measly 50 yards of rushing. It was a good Halloween victory for the Tigers at Braves Field.

The weekend of November 8 did not bring success for Wake Forest, as the Deacons lost to TCU in Fort Worth by a final score of 27–9. The Deacons were beaten in the fourth quarter, as they ran out of steam. This often was the case for the perpetually short-handed squad. The Deacons, however, returned home with a paycheck that would keep the athletic department churning.

State's victory against Washington and Lee came in a highly charged environment. There were fights on the field and leaky gas heaters in the Wolfpack locker room, all seeming to conspire against the men from Raleigh. Even the Washington and Lee band played loudly when State had the ball.[32] This was a good illustration of how college football was played, especially in small settings like Lexington, Virginia. Even with these impediments, the Pack took their opportunities and earned a 25–14 victory.

The previous week, Duke suffered some serious injuries against the Yellow Jackets, but that was not the excuse for the Blue Devil team to soundly lose, 16–6, to a good Navy team in Durham. The Middie defense was stout throughout the day, not allowing the Duke rushing attack to gain momentum. Although Duke was favored in the game,

Navy had only lost to Maryland and Notre Dame before encountering the Blue Devils. In comparison, the Terrapins manhandled Navy, dispatching them 38–7 in College Park. With two straight losses, the bloom was off the rose in Durham, even though the Blue Devils were a good team. Expectations in Durham, however, were much higher than those in the rest of the Big Four.

The Tar Heel story had not changed. They were no competition against Virginia, losing at home 34–7. Surprisingly, this rivalry game was the only time the Cavaliers strayed outside of commonwealth borders during the 1952 season. Suffering many injuries, the Tar Heels did not provide much of a fight. The Cavaliers scored three straight touchdowns running the same play. It was North Carolina's 11th straight loss. Snavely could provide few excuses to satisfy the growing number of Tar Heel fans who believed that North Carolina needed a change on the sidelines. It was this game that, most likely, served as the coup de grace for Snavely in Chapel Hill.

With the crushing defeat, rumors abounded that Snavely either had resigned or was going to be fired. The *News and Observer* reported that North Carolina's Athletic Council had met a week prior to the Duke game and had recommended that Snavely be released.[33] The schedule had worked against the Tar Heels, and the polio outbreak and the season's interruption did nothing to help matters. Even running the split-T for the first time was not working.

Maryland went into the LSU game on October 25 with a tremendous scoring advantage on the season. In the previous two games, they shut out Georgia 37–0, followed by a 38–7 pasting of Navy. With the LSU Tigers coming to College Park, an attempt was made to fix the game. Lou Glickfield, a Maryland student, approached star quarterback Jack Scarbath, Frank Navarro, and Tom Cosgrove to manipulate the 21-point spread. All three were to be compensated for fixing the game's outcome. Instead, the three Terrapin players told Jim Tatum about Glickfield's offer, and Tatum alerted the FBI.[34] Glickfield's actions had no effect on Tatum's men who whipped LSU 34–6. For his efforts, Glickfield was sentenced to 18 months in prison, but it was another example of how college football was susceptible to corruption from gamblers.[35]

Mississippi, on November 15, ended Maryland's amazing 22-game undefeated streak with a 21–14 upset victory in Oxford. The Rebels entered the game sporting a 6–0–2 record with the ties coming at Vanderbilt and at Kentucky. Ole Miss was led by Jimmy Lear who threw for 231 yards and ran for another 44 to keep the powerful Maryland defense on their heels. The Greenwood, Mississippi, native was unstoppable, leading Ole Miss to one of its greatest victories. No one expected the Rebels to post 461 yards against a Maryland defense that was allowing only 156 yards per game entering the contest. Contributing to the victory was a poor performance by Maryland's offensive line, in part responsible for Jack Scarbath completing only one pass during the game.

Shaken by the defeat, Tatum blamed the loss on poor officiating that he argued negated a Terrapin touchdown pass that would have given Maryland a 21–14 lead. He even blamed the defeat on a lack of zeal from his players, because the Southern Conference bowl ban remained in place.[36] The simple fact was that Coach Johnny Vaught, who had been on the same coaching staff at North Carolina with Tatum, had his team much better prepared for the game than Tatum. It was a tough loss for the Terrapins, but they had not played well enough to defeat the inspired Rebels. Perhaps Chauncey Durden said it best. "It was a case of a very good team catching a great, but overconfident team and winning."[37]

Clemson headed to New York to play winless Fordham, hoping to rescue a bad season. Continuing to use the single wing offense, the Tigers posted a 12–0 lead at halftime. But Fordham roared back in the second half scoring two touchdowns as well. The Tigers, playing without the injured Billy Hair, left the Big Apple with a disappointing 12–12 tie. The draw was not due to the loss of Billy Hair, because his replacement, Don King, was sensational. In the first half, the Anderson, SC, freshman ran for 215 yards on 16 carries, scoring two touchdowns. Rarely has a freshman put on such a dominating performance in a half. It was another sign that the Tiger schedule had been tougher in 1952, and that the single wing could not hold up to the powerful split-T offense. This was Clemson's last year playing the single wing.

The Gamecocks stayed home to play in-state rival The Citadel in Charleston. The Bulldogs never entered the end zone in a 35–0 defeat. The Citadel only eked out one yard of total offense in the game that provided South Carolina its fifth victory of the season. It was a depressing homecoming loss for the military academy, but a solid win for the Gamecocks, even considering the weak competition.

Rex Enright's team now prepared for its clash with North Carolina, always a highly anticipated game, even though the series had been dominated by the Tar Heels. Against the men from Columbia, UNC had won 19 games and only suffered four defeats and four ties. The Gamecocks were favored to win, but Flo Worrell, a jayvee freshman from Lexington, North Carolina, thrown into action in the second half, ran roughshod over South Carolina. North Carolina ended its 11-game slide defeating South Carolina in Columbia 27–19. With Carl Snavely's job on the line, it appeared that North Carolina's players fought as hard as they could to ward off what felt like Snavely's impending firing. It was another fumble-ridden game for the Heels, but they cashed in on Gamecock turnovers. For the Gamecocks, it was a disappointing loss, to say the least. It seemed that South Carolina always was the tonic that the Tar Heels needed to save their season. Ignobly, it was UNC's first win since a 21–6 victory over the Gamecocks the previous year in Chapel Hill.

The Big Four title was on the line when Duke and Wake Forest met at 2 p.m. at Groves Stadium in Baptist Hollow. The Deacons had won the last two titles and, surprisingly, had won four straight against the Blue Devils as well. In a closely fought game in which the Deacon offense outplayed Duke, the Blue Devils gained a 14–7 victory, winning the Big Four title, their first since 1945. The Deacons won the statistical battle, but they lost the game.

Football season rarely offered State much to cheer about, and the Wolfpack season continued to spiral downward. State had a tough day, losing 48–6 to a much more powerful Pitt Panther squad in Pittsburgh. It was another miserable year for the Wolfpack who had performed like a bottom dweller Southern Conference team.

In Lexington, Kentucky, a Billy Hair–less Clemson was little competition against the Wildcats. Kentucky beat Clemson 27–14 even though Don King, again Hair's replacement, played another good game. The Tigers simply could not hold up against the stronger Bear Bryant coached Wildcats. Even though this was one of the poorer Bryant coached Kentucky squads, the Tigers could not keep pace.

Needing a win, South Carolina faced an improved West Virginia squad on November 22 in Columbia. The Mountaineers had won five straight heading into the game, while the Gamecocks were coming off a very disappointing loss to the Tar Heels. In a closely fought contest, WVU scored a third quarter touchdown to gain a 13–6 victory. The win was vindication that the Mountaineers were on the right track and emerging as a

Southern Conference football power. This was the last game for the Mountaineers who finished the season 7–2, including a win over number 18 Pittsburgh in the Steel City. On the other hand, some Gamecock fans questioned whether Rex Enright should be retained with another middling season on the books. Enright had a reputation for winning the games he was supposed to win, but expectations in Columbia were for him to take the Gamecocks to a new level of play. Helping him secure his position were a strong record against Clemson and his gentlemanly demeanor.

Meanwhile, Clemson traveled to Alabama to play Auburn. In a defensive battle, Auburn scored a field goal and made it stand for the game. With both teams unable to move the ball, Auburn, quarterbacked by Vince Dooley, won 3–0. The defeat was humiliating for the Tigers, because Auburn was a poor club whose only previous victory was over Wofford College. Auburn ended their season with only these two victories, both coming from Upstate South Carolina schools. The probation year and the tougher schedule had been a disaster for Clemson.

The Southern Conference title was won by Duke with an easy victory over North Carolina, 34–0. Duke finished its conference season undefeated, and that was not a surprise. Without Maryland in league play, the Blue Devils had played the best football in the conference, but they were by no means a club to match national powers. They struggled mightily with Georgia Tech and Navy but feasted on weaker Southern Conference competition.

On November 22, in the battle of the Baptists, Wake Forest pasted Furman 28–0. The most exciting play of the game was a 96-yard kickoff return from Wake Forest's Larry Spencer, one of the best Deacons of the season. The touchdown on the second-half kickoff was the inspiration that the Deacons needed to stop the Purple Hurricanes at Sirrine Stadium. The Deacons snapped Furman's four-game winning streak, but the Greenville school finished a good season at 6–3–1.

On the same day, State's finale against William & Mary punctuated a wretched year for the Pack. In another crushing defeat, William & Mary thumped State 41–6, before a tiny crowd that may have reached 3,000. It was a statement to Wolfpack ineptitude and the William & Mary scandal that no one had much interest in attending the game at Carey Field in Williamsburg. Mercilessly, State had one more game to play. They ended the season with a 54–7 beating at Texas Tech, losing to a weak Red Raider squad that only won three games over the season.

The surprising score of the day was Alabama 27 and Maryland 7. Playing at Ladd Memorial Stadium in Mobile, the Crimson Tide dominated the Terps, running roughshod over the vaunted Maryland defense. Maryland's offense sputtered all afternoon, leading to Jack Scarbath being substituted. Tatum was trying to find a spark that was never there. Although the Tide had lost to Tennessee and Georgia Tech earlier in the year, their defeat of Maryland put the stamp on a successful season. Coach Red Drew, who was under some pressure from Alabama faithful due to a six loss 1951 campaign, ended the season beating a poor Auburn team the following week.

Sportswriters and even Coach Tatum had no good answers for Maryland's late season collapse. Tatum blamed the open date after the Boston University game, saying that it had harmed the team's timing.[38] Tatum complimented Alabama's outstanding play but was at a loss to explain Maryland's collapse. It was hard to explain that a team that relinquished only 37 points in its first seven games, surrendered 48 points in its last two games.[39]

For Tatum and the Terrapins, the defeat meant that there would be no bowl game for them on January 1. Prior to the Mississippi game, most sportswriters were confident that the Terps would receive a bowl invitation, thus placing enormous pressure on the Southern Conference to allow them to play. Maryland was on record maintaining that they had no intention to play in a bowl, if the Southern Conference disapproved. It was easy to make such a statement prior to one of the big bowl games extending an actual invitation to play. The crisis, however, was averted with the losses to the Rebels and the Crimson Tide.

On November 29, South Carolina and Wake Forest met in Winston-Salem. For the Deacons, a second place Southern Conference finish was theirs with a win. The Gamecocks simply hoped to finish the season on a bright note, considering their previous loss to a good Mountaineer team. After a close first period, the Deacons exerted their will, commanding the remainder of the contest at Bowman-Gray Stadium on a chilly afternoon. Taking advantage of Gamecock fumbles and interceptions, Wake Forest scored six touchdowns to easily beat the Gamecocks 39–14. Wake Forest finished the season tied with West Virginia for second in the conference, while the Gamecocks dropped the final three games of the season, completing their year with a 5–5 record.

The Deacon victory was not without drama. Rex Enright accused Wake's Tom Rogers of running up the score when the Gamecocks had no chance of catching the Deacons. He criticized Wake for playing starters too long and even scoring a late touchdown with mostly first-string players.[40] Enright, in a rare moment, urged his players to circle the Wake game in Columbia the following season.

The Cavaliers ended the season on a high note, in a hard-fought 20–13 victory in Williamsburg over William & Mary. A small crowd saw the Cavaliers take the state title. Although Virginia had enjoyed a good season, it remained difficult to determine how good the Cavaliers were. They only lost two games, but most of their victories came against weak teams such as VPI, VMI, Richmond, and Washington and Lee. With defeats to Duke and South Carolina, it was hard to ascertain Virginia's quality.

Carl Snavely's embattled campaign ended in Miami with a resolute victory versus the Hurricanes, 34–7. Having endured attacks from all corners, coach Snavely was treated to a ride on the shoulders of his players after the win. North Carolina ended the year in unlikely fashion, winning two of their last three games. These victories, however, did little to ease the pressure on the gray fox.

Coaching Changes

As customary, the end of the season brought coaching changes, some of which bled into 1953. At the top of the list was the embattled Carl Snavely. Another difficult season, regardless of the Miami game, dug a deep hole for the head man. He had endured three straight losing campaigns and late year losses to superior Duke teams. The 34–0 loss to Duke in their penultimate game of the 1952 campaign was too much to bear. Even his supporters from previous years found it hard to favor retention. Realizing that he was going to be relieved of his duties, on December 2, Snavely requested that he be released from his head coaching responsibilities and reassigned to other duties. The long-term coach expressed a willingness to leave coaching, but in his heart, he did not wish to step away from his football team nor coaching. North Carolina's

Academic Council agreed to his request, providing them with an easy way out of a difficult situation.

There was not a successor in the wings, but most pointed to Jim Tatum. Other names under discussion were Johnny Vaught from Mississippi, clearly a longshot considering his success with the Rebels. Vaught, however, had North Carolina connections. He was an assistant at Chapel Hill from 1936 to 1941. George Barclay of Washington and Lee, a former Tar Heel star, was an intriguing choice because of his success with the Generals and his position as an assistant on Snavely's staff. For those focused on winning and bringing a Tar Heel great back to campus, Tatum was the only option.

Although Snavely's demise was rumored for weeks, North Carolina's athletic administration was caught a bit flat footed when Snavely stepped aside. The search and selection of a new coach was time consuming. Stu Holcomb of Purdue most likely was the leading candidate until he pulled his name from the job search. Repeatedly, Jim Tatum's name was suggested, and there was pressure to pursue the Maryland coach. Simply put, Gordon Gray had no interest in bringing to Chapel Hill a brash and often outspoken coach who had voiced frequently and openly his support for bowl games and big-time football. Gray required a coach with less stature who did not imperil the university's public image. Fielding a winning club was secondary.

When he resigned, Snavely was president of the American Football Coaches Association, a forum where he openly could express his views on college football and coaching. Speaking to attendees at the Scripps-Howard coach of the year banquet in January 1953, he declared that coaches were victims of a misguided system. In frank terms, he offered his opinion of what was wrong with college football in the academic environment. The problem, he argued, had nothing to do with coaches.

> Number one is the desire to win. This is legitimate, of course, and laudable, until it becomes a demand for victory regardless of means or cost—regardless of disparity in size, resources and other factors. Number two is the desire and demand for profits over and above the amount required for football. A college budget which demands revenue from an amateur activity which is presumably part of the educational program is an obvious absurdity. Number three would be the attempt made by so many schools to play opponents out of their class, by reason of resources or recruiting practices. Another cause is the difference in standards—academic standards, entrance standards and, finally, a lack of confidence which our educational institutions should have of the integrity and good faith in one another.[41]

Snavely was bitter about his treatment at UNC, always believing that he had done things honorably and correctly, ultimately being removed due to the mania for winning. Although his attempts to vindicate coaches may have sounded a bit hollow and self-serving, his criticisms of the pressures faced by coaches and their football programs were real.[42]

Soon after Snavely's remarks, the Tar Heels, perhaps seeking a bit of safety, turned to one of their own sons to try and restore prominence on the gridiron. George Barclay starred at North Carolina in the early 1930s as a guard and a linebacker, earning Southern Conference and All-American honors, becoming the first Tar Heel to be named All-American. He captained the 1934 squad that was coached by Carl Snavely. Jim Tatum was one of his teammates. Prior to the UNC position, Barclay led the Washington and Lee Generals in 1950 to an 8–3 record, a 6–0 Southern Conference season, and a Gator Bowl invitation, Washington and Lee's first bowl trip. Although the Generals dropped the Gator Bowl to Wyoming, 20–7, his achievement in Lexington did not go unnoticed. Barclay had led a very small institution to a major bowl game and a Southern Conference championship, levels of success never believed attainable. The following year, Barclay coached the Generals to a 6–4 record and 5–1 in the conference. After debating about his future with the Generals, Barclay decided to resign from Washington and Lee in February and accept an offer from Snavely to join the UNC staff for the 1952 season as an assistant coach. Barclay's hiring was bittersweet, because he was leaving a very successful three-year run at Washington and Lee for an assistant coach position under his mentor who was struggling. Later, ironically, Barclay was replaced by Jim Tatum, his teammate at UNC as well as another player coached by Snavely.

Barclay's hire was intended to modernize the football program, as many Tar Heel fans believed that Snavely was an antique, a man out of date. The game, they argued, had moved beyond the single-wing offense that Snavely had run effectively in the late 40s. The split-T formation was the new rage and Barclay, considered a genius at running it, was viewed as the man who could revitalize North Carolina football. In addition, Barclay's personality, some believed, was a welcome change from the quiet and sometimes dour Snavely. Snavely did not smile very much and, although nationally respected, was a hard man with whom to connect. Barclay had a larger personality and enjoyed being the football hero from his playing days, but he was a tough coach.

Well received by most Tar Heel fans, the transition from Snavely to Barclay was difficult for UNC's administration. In some ways, they had caved in to the section of the fan base that stressed winning over all else. Hiring Barclay confirmed that winning was more important than simply fielding a team of players who did not embarrass the university in the classroom or on the field. Turning to their own alumni, however, was a good strategy for mitigating any of the charges of hypocrisy. By and large, Barclay was a popular hire.

North Carolina's football players, however, had a different opinion. Some of them actively opposed Barclay's hiring, angry at his tough demeanor, and suspicious that he played favorites. He was not popular in his first season as an assistant back at his alma mater. Meeting at the end of season, many players decided to oppose Barclay's selection as coach, believing, correctly, that he was in line to follow Snavely. They made their opinions clear to athletic director Chuck Erickson, but he was not inclined to choose a coach based on the sentiments of players.[43] The UNC administration paid little to no attention to player concerns, selecting Barclay even though a team that he had coached was heavily opposed to him.

Change at Virginia

While North Carolina was struggling to find a replacement for Carl Snavely, Virginia, fans were crestfallen to learn that their remarkably successful coach, Art Guepe, had accepted a position with the Vanderbilt Commodores. Guepe was the toast of Charlottesville, and it almost was inconceivable that he would leave. He had performed the unthinkable at Virginia, leading it to great heights, even with financial constraints which created a numerical challenge for his squad. He was 49–17–2 since coming aboard in 1946. What was more important was that his teams were improving almost each year. Vanderbilt offered more opportunity, with access to many more scholarships, although 10 fewer than its SEC colleagues. Vanderbilt, it appeared, was more serious about winning in the SEC and, in hiring Guepe, they brought aboard one of the best active coaches in the country. Guepe was taking a step into a powerful league and would not have the luxury of playing some of the weaker clubs in the commonwealth on which Virginia had feasted. Vanderbilt was paying him $12,500 on a five-year contract with $110,000 worth of scholarship money under his authority.[44] The Nashville position, therefore, held great appeal.

Colgate Darden was attacked by many alumni for not keeping Guepe at Virginia. Guepe was offered a modest raise and a five-year contract, but Darden had no intention of matching Vanderbilt's offer, a figure he believed Virginia was incapable of paying. Darden thought that a substantial increase in Guepe's salary was a sign that athletics were becoming more important than academics. Gus Tebell knew that the salary was attractive, and in a private letter to Darden he admitted that the salary increase was significant, but Guepe left because of the "present status of our athletic policy. The insecurity of not knowing what might happen was uppermost in his mind when he made the decision."[45]

The Gooch Report, Darden's position on bowl games, Virginia's independence, and the tense relationship between athletics and academics contributed to Guepe's uncertainty about the future of Cavalier athletics. He was unsure about Virginia's commitment to athletics, and Vanderbilt, by paying him a substantial salary and providing resources, made their position apparent.

Ned McDonald, Guepe's line coach, who had served at Virginia since 1946, was elevated to the head coaching position without anyone else seriously considered. Part of this was simply financial. McDonald was hired under a three-year contract at $8,000 per year, exceedingly low pay for 1952.[46] The Texas graduate, who played under Dana Bible, had large shoes to fill, and he knew it. McDonald had never served as a head coach, but he was taking the helm of a winning program that a year earlier posted an 8–2 record and finished the season ranked 20th in the country.

The 1952 season was odd. Maryland and Clemson completed disappointing seasons. The Terps lost their last two games, knocking them out of bowl contention. Clemson's season was disastrous, completing the year with a 2–6–1 record. Their only victories were against Boston College and Presbyterian College. Duke was the class of the conference, only having their season marred by consecutive losses to Georgia Tech and Navy. West Virginia tied Wake Forest with a 5–1 conference mark, while State, North Carolina, and South Carolina had not enjoyed good seasons.

The year showed once again that the variety of schedules was a problem. George Washington, for example, finished fourth in the league, but their victories came against weak sides. They beat a terrible State team, Washington and Lee, VPI, Bucknell, Davidson, and Richmond. They were mauled in their toughest games, losing 50–0 to Virginia and 24–0 to West Virginia. William & Mary further illustrated the point. The Indians ended the year third in the conference, having only scored victories against VMI, Richmond, Virginia Tech, and State. This type of scheduling variability, which allowed for schools to avoid significant opponents, rankled conference leaders like Eddie Cameron and Rex Enright. They wanted change.

8

The Last Was the Best

Southern Conference Basketball, 1952–1953

In every sports season, football lingers into early January, clinging to headlines as basketball gradually gains the upper hand. It was no different in 1953. As the new year dawned and with the January 1 bowl games on his mind, Earle Hellen of the *Greensboro Record* lambasted the Southern Conference's boycott of bowl game participation. Believing that the conference needed bowls and the bowls needed the conference, Hellen asked if the Southern Conference presidents had enjoyed the New Year's Day bowl games, because many Americans had. Calling the September 1951 meeting in Chapel Hill "hasty," most likely a very polite term, Hellen wrote that it would have been grand to see Duke in the Orange Bowl against Alabama instead of a terribly outclassed Syracuse team that lost to the Tide by a final score of 61–6. In addition, Maryland could have played Georgia Tech in the Sugar Bowl instead of Mississippi facing the Yellow Jackets. Arguing that the Southeastern Conference was growing rich off the bowls, Hellen believed that it was time for the "near-sighted" Southern Conference presidents to "wise-up."[1] When writing his column, he could not have guessed that in a few months a new league derived from the Southern Conference would be signing a bowl agreement, having abandoned its previous position.

Although complaints about bowls and the extended search for a new football coach at North Carolina continued to gain attention, most fans turned their focus towards Southern Conference basketball. By January, it was apparent that the league was stocked with the finest talent in its history and the games were being played at a new peak of competitiveness.

To no one's surprise, the Wolfpack looked positioned to take another league championship. State started the season in strong form, winning their first three games over Furman, Washington, and Lee, and Davidson. The first hiccup was a December 9 game against Wake Forest at attractive, but small, Gore Gymnasium. Wake entered the game having scored a 91–86 win over Duke in Durham. In a precursor to the season's outcome, the Deacons defeated State in a thrilling 51–50 game which featured tough defensive play. After the tilt, Deacon head coach Murray Greason received a television set and a refrigerator from alumni in recognition of his 20 years leading Wake Forest basketball.[2]

Although it was only the fourth game of the season, it placed State on notice that this season was to be different within the Southern Conference. The game's outcome hinted that other programs such as Wake Forest and Duke finally might have reached a competitive level with Everett Case's team. State, nonetheless, returned to winning, only dropping a game to St. John's in New York on December 23.

8. The Last Was the Best

Closing out December, the Wolfpack scored victories over Princeton and a strong Holy Cross squad in the Dixie Classic, which placed them in the championship game versus Brigham Young. State had little difficulty winning their fourth straight Dixie Classic title with a convincing 75–59 victory over the Cougars. Case's tournament magic had struck again, and the two earlier losses did nothing to diminish the expectation that the Wolfpack would win another Southern Conference championship.

Six-foot, three-inch Mel Thompson and six-foot, eight-inch Raleigh native Bobby Speight were formidable players with a deep bench to support them. Wearing number 80, Speight was an imposing force at forward and one of the most feared players in the league. Mel Thompson, part of Case's Indiana pipeline, was a hard-nosed competitor who never took a step backward on the court. The duo was hard to contain and were complemented by many other players who had received playing time the previous year. State's early season success, even with the blemish against Wake Forest, indicated that the Wolfpack remained a dangerous team.

West Virginia no longer had its powerful center, Mark Workman, but a good amount of talent remained. The previous year's semifinal tournament loss to Duke had left Mountaineer fans eager to show their mettle. With Jim Sottile returning to the starting lineup, West Virginia had another fine shot at taking the conference championship.

George Washington was a wildcard, but some observers expected a lot out of them. Joe Holup, their freshman center, immediately impressed, and was destined to star for the Colonials. A native of Swoyersville, Pennsylvania, Holup quickly became the dominant player for GW, averaging almost 20 points per game in his first season. Fans throughout the Southern Conference were eager to see Holup in a gym near them.

At the beginning of the season, sportswriters were unsure what to expect from Wake Forest, but by mid-season, it was Dickie Hemric and the Deacons leading the Southern Conference race. Pundits believed that Wake Forest had a chance to be a good club, but most thought that their short bench would be their demise, and others pointed out that they had failed to qualify for the Southern Conference tournament the previous two years. Wake Forest, however, had a special player. The six-foot, six-inch Hemric had matured into a prolific scorer and rebounder. Jack Horner called him "legalized murder" under the bucket, one of the best centers in the country.[3] The Jonesville, North Carolina, native had wanted to attend State but Everett Case, almost always a keen judge of talent, thought Hemric was not good enough for his Wolfpack. Murray Greason saw something in Hemric that others could not see, but Hemric was not a star when he arrived at Wake Forest. He had a lot to learn. It is worth wondering how far the Wolfpack would have gone, if Hemric had been on their team. The additional firepower and rebounding would have made State a favorite to win a national championship.

Hemric led the show, but he had considerable help from Jack Williams and Maurice George, both forwards. Williams, a Johnson City, Illinois, native, was so skilled that teams could not simply focus on Hemric. A talented player, Williams could beat a team as well. On January 20, 1953, the Deacons, undefeated in conference play, took on Frank McGuire's Tar Heels in Woollen Gymnasium. The Tar Heels beat the Deacons 72–68 in a thrilling contest and earned the number one position in the league, a surprise to most observers. The game was a battle of two surprising clubs that had done little the previous year to attract much attention. The difference was that Frank McGuire had been hired by the Tar Heels and Bones McKinney was now the Deacon assistant. These two hires radically changed the fates of their clubs and the history of the Southern Conference and the future ACC.

The Wolfpack's success continued after the Dixie Classic with victories over Cincinnati, Davidson, Duke, William & Mary, and George Washington. On January 24, State faced North Carolina for the 16th time, with Everett Case leading the Wolfpack. Case had never lost to the Tar Heels, winning 15 straight contests, an impressive feat in this always heated rivalry. Case had made up for State's gridiron futility against North Carolina.

Frank McGuire

Frank McGuire was the new man in the league and was determined not to take a back seat to Everett Case. In August 1952, McGuire was hired to restore winning to a downtrodden North Carolina program that brought little energy and few fans to Woollen Gymnasium. UNC finished the previous season 12–15, failing to qualify for the Southern Conference Tournament. Tar Heel coach Tom Scott was fired as much for losing games as for his bland personality. Scott quickly was hired as head coach of the Phillips Oilers in Oklahoma.[4] Many coaches were considered for the North Carolina position, including Lenoir-Rhyne's Jim "Pappy" Hamilton, one of the favorites. The Pittsburg, Kansas, native had finished his collegiate career at North Carolina and was emerging as a sensational coach for the Bears. The fact that Frank McGuire's St. John's had defeated State and Kentucky in the previous year's NCAA tournament was more than enough to offer the Irishman the job.

Born in 1913, the son of an Irish American New York policeman who died when he was two, it was unlikely that McGuire ever would make his way to the University of North Carolina or later the University of South Carolina. Growing up in Greenwich Village, McGuire attended St. Francis Xavier High School before studying at St. John's University. After graduating St. John's, McGuire returned to St. Francis Xavier where he coached basketball and taught history. Ultimately, St. John's brought him aboard. He built a powerhouse for the Redmen, and his squad was runner-up in the national championship game in 1952. UNC's Billy Carmichael was McGuire's great advocate, convinced that the Irishman could do the job. Remarkably, McGuire also coached the St. John's baseball team to the 1949 College World Series, demonstrating his coaching acumen.

When North Carolina approached McGuire about the job, he already was familiar with Chapel Hill and the university. McGuire was stationed at UNC during World War II as part of the Navy's V-5 program. He spent some of his time coaching high school basketball on a part-time basis in the Chapel Hill area.[5] McGuire liked the region, even though he understood that basketball in the Tar Heel State was behind the game as played in northeastern cities.

After winning 103 games at St. John's, he came south to North Carolina with a great assistant, previously McGuire's head coach at St. Johns, James Andrew "Buck" Freeman. Freeman was the secret ingredient for much of McGuire's success. Freeman had starred at St. John's in the 1920s and took over the coaching position upon graduation. He turned St. John's into a dominant basketball program, winning 85 percent of his games while crushing the opposition in the New York region. His greatest fame came as coach of the Wonder Five from 1927 to 1931. These St. John's squads won 86 games, simply an unheard-of run of success. Freeman was a tactical and strategic genius, usually the man who prepped games. Unfortunately, alcohol was a problem for Freeman. He was persona non grata in New York when McGuire asked his mentor to head south to Chapel Hill and a new beginning.

Basketball was far behind football in interest on the Chapel Hill campus. McGuire inherited a struggling team, understanding that much was to be done. Later, the New Yorker said, "There was little or no interest in college basketball there. Everybody was a football fan."[6] This was true, but it was changing, especially at Duke, Wake Forest, and Maryland. Everett Case's dominance was forcing other schools to develop strong programs.

The smooth-talking, well-dressed, and impeccably groomed McGuire was a dream recruiter, who was not shy about bending the NCAA rules to bring the best New York players to Chapel Hill. He knew all the important basketball coaches in New York City and had strong relationships with many of them. His St. John's squads were almost exclusively New York City players, and high school coaches knew that their boys would win under the tough-talking Irishman. McGuire's connections to New York became extremely important when the point shaving scandals ravaged CCNY, Long Island University and other New York powerhouses. New York high school players were eager to look elsewhere to play ball, as those schools were tainted by point shaving and were in the process of de-emphasizing their basketball programs. McGuire's connections with private Catholic schools in New York would be critical to his success in Chapel Hill.

Frank McGuire, pictured in 1951, was hired by North Carolina to challenge Everett Case and the Wolfpack's dominance on the hardcourt. It was a challenge he was happy to undertake (courtesy North Carolina Collection Photographic Archives, Wilson Library, University of North Carolina at Chapel Hill).

Bones McKinney

In the same year that McGuire arrived in Chapel Hill, Murray Greason hired Bones McKinney as his assistant at Wake Forest. Greason knew he was getting a showman, full of energy, a devoted Christian, and an experienced player and coach when he hired

McKinney. The Wake Forest coach understood that there always was a bit of showmanship in a good preacher or teacher.

Horace "Bones" McKinney, a star at Durham High School, joined Greason in 1952. The Deacons struggled in the previous season, but Greason had a core of good players who could use the coaching of a former professional player, especially a coach who knew how to instruct big men. His basketball pedigree was without peer. McKinney attended Durham High School where he was the star of a team that won 69 straight games. At State, he was a dominant player before World War II when army service intervened. After the war, McKinney starred at UNC, the only star basketball player to have played at both schools. Bones took his playing skills to the fledgling professional ranks, although there was little money to be made. He spent six years in the league and was an All-Pro with the Washington Capitols under the famed Red Auerbach. He retired from basketball in 1952 when the Washington Capitols with whom he was a player/coach folded. Tired of the life of a professional player in a dodgy league, he came to Wake Forest to begin seminary education.

Wake Forest did not have a lot of resources in 1952 and offered Bones a paltry annual salary of $750 as an assistant. It was not much money for a Pepsi swilling father of four children who was trying to make ends meet with a paper route. Although the money was sparse, basketball was again in the young coach's life. The affable and pleasant Murray Greason was the perfect complement to McKinney, who was outspoken and fiery, much unlike Greason's down-home, folksy demeanor. It did not take long to see that McKinney was the spark that Greason needed. Having Dickie Hemric on the squad did not hurt. The equally tall McKinney took Hemric under his wing and molded a good player into one of the best players in Southern Conference history.

It was a picture of opposites when Greason and McKinney sat on the Wake Forest bench. No one in basketball history contorted his body as much or made as many gestures as McKinney. Few could take their eyes off the tall, lanky seminary student who sometimes was more entertaining to watch than the game. Greason, a man who loved his hunting dogs, had been leading the Deacons for 20 years, and he was a rather quiet and unassuming man, who liked to fish and hunt. Unlike McKinney, Greason sat quietly on the bench, often with his arms crossed. They made an excellent pairing.[7]

The Season Heats Up

The day after George Barclay was named head football coach, UNC finally ended its run of futility against Everett Case, defeating State at Reynolds Coliseum 70–69. McGuire had shown that State was not invincible on their home court. North Carolina's Jerry Vayda, a Bayonne, New Jersey, native, hit the winning shot with 26 seconds left in the game, but the Tar Heels led most of the tight game from the start. The raucous crowd appeared to will State to victory when they took a 67–64 lead with 2:20 remaining, but it was not to be.[8] It was a surprising loss for the Wolfpack, but State remained a powerful team, the favorite to win the conference championship. On the other hand, it was the coming-out party for Frank McGuire. He had beaten Case in their first head-to-head match on Case's home floor. McGuire may not have known it, but the defeat occurred while Case was wearing his lucky brown suit that had brought him many victories against the Tar Heels.[9] The spell was broken.

The victory over State was the high-water mark of the season for the Tar Heels. Little was expected of them at the beginning of the year, especially not a victory at Reynolds Coliseum. They began the season with rather easy wins over The Citadel, Washington and Lee, Richmond, and Clemson, before dropping a December 29 matchup against a strong Holy Cross team that finished the year 20–6.

McGuire brought great enthusiasm to Tar Heel basketball, guiding North Carolina to the lead in the Southern Conference and having notched wins against State and Wake. The New York coach was a sensation in Chapel Hill. McGuire's team remained young, but the Tar Heels were playing with enthusiasm and confidence. That, combined with Buck Freeman's strategic and tactical expertise, made for success.[10]

Surprisingly, State lost its second consecutive game, this time against Villanova in Philadelphia. Case's squads rarely lost two games in a row, but State was much too good of a team to lose consecutive home games, especially in front of their rabid fans. They followed their defeats to UNC and Villanova by avenging a previous loss to Wake Forest, winning 99–80. The Wolfpack were led by substitute Bobby Goss, a Raleigh High School product—many of Case's stars were from Indiana—who poured in 24 points. A foul-plagued Wake Forest squad, with a very short bench, as the Deacons rarely went beyond six men, could not keep pace with the Wolfpack, although Dickie Hemric scored his usual 24 points. The game was an indication that Wake's Achilles heel was its short bench.

The season only got more interesting on February 3 when an extremely young Richmond Spider squad surprisingly defeated North Carolina in double overtime 87–82. The outcome in Richmond, at Benedictine High School Gymnasium, was even more startling because Richmond only played six players: one sophomore and five freshmen.[11] Perhaps the loss was not as startling as it seemed at first light, because Richmond beat UNC in the middle of a nine-game winning streak that included a victory over a very strong Maryland team at Ritchie Gym in College Park. Richmond's Warren Mills, the leading scorer in the game, was emerging as a fine player who would later be a great star for the Spiders.

The Tar Heel defeat was followed by North Carolina losses to Duke and NYU. The Duke game in Chapel Hill was a hard-fought and high-scoring game with the Blue Devils securing a 95–89 victory. Perhaps the victory over State in Raleigh had caused a bit of overconfidence to seep into the North Carolina team. The Tar Heels dropped three in a row and were replaced by State as the conference leader.

For much of the early season, it looked like Duke would miss the Southern Conference Tournament for only the second time since World War II. Beginning on December 20, Duke hit the skids, losing consecutively to Temple, George Washington, Brigham Young, and Pennsylvania. Most concerning was a December 20 game against George Washington in which Duke surrendered 113 points to the Colonials. But the Blue Devils rallied and won seven straight games from late January into early February. It was hard to keep up with the blistering conference pace set by State, UNC, and Wake, but Bradley's players were doing their best. This included an eighth straight win, this time against Wake Forest in Gore Gym, avenging a Deacon victory at Duke early in the season. Dickie Hemric was unstoppable and poured in 44 points in a 101–99 overtime loss. Hemric fouled out in the second half without a chance to score over 50 points, something he surely would have done. With Hemric out of the game, Duke had an opening, and it was their star guard Rudy D'Emilio who scored the winning layup. Although it had been apparent all season, the game reinforced the belief that Wake was beatable without the dominant Hemric scoring and sweeping the glass. Philadelphia native Rudy D'Emilio had become an indispensable player for the Blue Devils, the sparkplug for the club.

As the Southern Conference season reached a fever pitch, more fuel was added to the excitement as Furman's Frank Selvy was attempting to become the nation's leading scorer. Selvy had taken the lead after posting 66 points against Mercer.[12] Hemric remained at his heels, but Selvy was scoring at a record-breaking clip while creating headlines for Furman basketball. He was assisted by the fine play of Nield Gordon, a transfer from Wingate Junior College, who averaged more than 20 points per game. Selvy and Gordon proved a tough combination for opposing squads.

With the Big Four trading haymakers, Deacon athletic director Jim Weaver was concerned about the growing intensity of basketball games, especially the upcoming Wake Forest–North Carolina game. He was not alone in expressing concern about fan behavior. His campus and Chapel Hill were approaching a feverish level prior to the game. Everyone around the tiny campus was ready for the Deacons to gain revenge for their earlier loss to the Tar Heels. Wake's Gore Gym was a bandbox with fans almost on the court and the Deacon football team positioned behind the opposing team's bench. Furthermore, McGuire had installed a new tactic of fouling players who were in position of scoring an easy bucket. This meant Deacon players could be pushed into the crowd. This was not a popular tactic and held the chance to be explosive in small facilities like Gore.[13]

Weaver had good reason to be worried. The intensity of basketball games had grown yearly with the increased level of conference play. With squads trying mightily to unseat State's dominance, they had resolutely increased their talent level and developed better game strategies. The outcome was a great deal of pushing and shoving as well as trash talk during conference games. In the Wake-Duke game, for example, Hemric was hit so hard by a Duke player that he was knocked out for a few moments and suffered a bloody nose. At South Carolina, the fans, angry at calls going against the Gamecocks, threw pennies and paper airplanes at the officials during a game with North Carolina.[14]

This type of fan behavior had been increasing in intensity for years. As early as 1951, basketball games had become so rough that Wallace Wade sent telegrams to each conference school asking athletic directors to announce publicly that fans must behave properly toward visiting teams.[15] With State being on the forefront, because of their conference dominance, Roy Clogston would appeal to the crowd at Reynolds. He even had Coach Case speak to crowds at games to tame them a bit.[16] With a highly competitive regular season in 1953, Wallace Wade, athletic directors, and coaches understood that the excitement about Southern Conference basketball was a double-edged sword.

Meanwhile, Duke won its ninth straight game, dropping State 84–82 in a thrilling Valentine's Day matchup at Reynolds Coliseum. Duke gained revenge from losing to State in Durham, the last game that the Blue Devils lost. This time it was forward Bill Reigel, who only played one season at Duke, leading the way with 29 points. Mel Thompson scored 30 for State, but they needed Speight to contribute more than 17 in this very tight game. Duke had kept the lead for much of the game, as the Wolfpack struggled to gain command. After the final buzzer, Coach Hal Bradley justifiably was carried off the court on the shoulders of his Blue Devil players.

In some ways, the game was a turning point for State's dominance in the Southern Conference. For the first time since Coach Case came to Raleigh, the Wolfpack had lost to all the Big Four opponents in one season. In this case, the three defeats, amazingly, occurred by a total of only four points. This included dropping games at Reynolds, where State had constructed an impregnable advantage. Earle Hellen commented, "In a little over two weeks the top eight teams in the Southern Conference assemble here for the annual tournament and this time there won't be the big fear of the Wolfpack."[17] Hellen was right. Everyone knew that the Pack could be beaten, but it would take a Herculean effort in the tournament that State owned.

On the same evening, North Carolina moved back into first place in the conference with a 94–69 victory over a weak Citadel club in Charleston. The Bulldogs suffered through a tough season, winless in conference play, and finished the year with only four victories.

Wake Forest kept pace by taking down Clemson 87–56 with Dickie Hemric capturing 22 rebounds, the same number as the entire Tiger squad. It was going to be a blistering finish to the season for the Big Four.

On Tuesday, February 17, UNC and Wake Forest met for the rematch in Gore Gymnasium. In a game wholly unlike the earlier contest, Wake smashed the Tar Heels 89–63, knocking them out of the top spot in the conference and placing great pressure on North Carolina to make the tournament. Dickie Hemric dropped in 30 points, doubling his tally from the first game, and tabbed 17 rebounds. The Deacon victory placed State again in first place as musical chairs continued in the conference top spot.

As the Tar Heels were losing, State scored 108 points in a victory over a woeful Washington and Lee squad. State dominated the game and posted its third 100 plus game of the year while bettering their record to 21–5 on the season. The Generals, playing in rival VMI's gym, could muster only 69 points. With their victories, State and Wake qualified for the conference tournament.

In the Old Line State, Maryland, was playing good basketball. With star Gene Shue commanding games, the Terps sported a 13–6 record, but their schedule was not particularly strong. Maryland split their games with North Carolina and had lost to a good George Washington team, but they did not play Duke, State, or Wake, three of the best teams in the league. Nonetheless, the defensive-focused Terps were a hard team to defeat.

On Thursday night, February 19, in a surprising turn of events, Duke's winning streak was ended by a depleted William & Mary squad in Williamsburg. The final score in overtime was 85–82. Even with Rudy D'Emilio not playing with a dislocated toe, the loss was hard to explain. It was William & Mary's fifth league win of the season, and it came without the Indians scoring a field goal in overtime. All their points came from free throws. With the loss, Duke had a 9–4 conference record and stood seventh in the standings. With three games remaining, it looked like Duke's tournament hopes were in jeopardy, even with their impressive nine-game winning streak. The Blue Devils needed to win out to ensure their conference tournament bid.

On February 21, Furman dropped fading South Carolina 105–68 at Textile Hall in Greenville. It was revenge for a surprising loss at the hands of South Carolina a month earlier in Carolina Field House. The Gamecocks completed the season 10–13 and offered little competition for Furman. It was looking more and more like tournament attendees would get a chance to see Frank Selvy put on a scoring show at Reynolds.

On the same day, State made a strong claim to first place in the conference by gaining revenge against a previous loss in Reynolds to North Carolina. This time the

Wolfpack did not need its biggest stars in the fourth period. Bobby Speight and Mel Thompson were in foul trouble and on the bench in the final period as State scored a resounding 87–66 victory in Woollen Gymnasium. Case and the Pack gained the number one seed in the Southern Conference Tournament and made it very clear that a new order had yet to be established.

The game was a hard-fought contest with a good deal of pushing and shoving. Case remarked, "Our boys wanted to win that one so badly they could taste it. Maybe I'm wrong but I don't think Carolina wanted to battle us Saturday night. And did you notice our students? When we lost to Carolina, our student president went over to Chapel Hill to get a block of student tickets. He got 400, and every one of them was filled with noise, wasn't it?"[18]

Meanwhile, Duke cruised to an easy 98–68 victory over a listless Gamecock squad with nothing to play for. Rudy D'Emilio, again, did not play, but he was never needed against Frank Johnson's poor South Carolina team. Bradley's squad, like most good teams, was quick to distance themselves from the previous defeat in Williamsburg.

On Monday, February 23, the Deacons, playing their final regular season game, clinched second place in the conference with a 88–62 win over South Carolina at Gore Gym. It was Dickie Hemric again. Hemric scored 33 points and grabbed a staggering 33 rebounds. Although Hemric's scoring received most of the attention, careful observers of the season were deeply impressed by his rebounding prowess. McKinney's addition to Murray Greason's staff had propelled Hemric to a scoring and rebounding force, making him the best big man in the league.

By February 25, the eight qualifiers for the Southern Conference were known. Maryland's victory over George Washington meant that the Colonials were left out of the tournament. This was the Terps' first win over George Washington in nine consecutive contests, but the Colonials and no one else had an answer for Gene Shue, the finest player in Maryland basketball history to this point. Shue was not as well known in North Carolina and South Carolina, but those in Virginia who had seen him play knew he was an excellent player.

With North Carolina only having Duke left on its schedule, McGuire took some time to chat about the season and the surprising success the Tar Heels had enjoyed. McGuire did not hesitate to compliment Everett Case for revolutionizing basketball in the Southern Conference. "Case is responsible for this Southern Conference rise. The league wasn't anywhere near this good when I was down here in the Navy in 1944 and 1945. Case brought good basketball down here to stay, and the conference has improved because the other teams have been forced to try to keep up with Case—and State."[19]

McGuire was right. With Case at State, some league schools had separated themselves from the remainder of the conference. The Big Four as well as Maryland were making a statement that their brand of basketball was different from that found at most of the Virginia schools and in South Carolina, save Furman. Maryland, Duke, North Carolina, Wake Forest, and State had good head coaches and outstanding assistants. They had the athletes who could play a fast-paced and exciting brand of basketball. Although playing a much more deliberate game, Maryland was at their level as well. These staffs had located superb talent and, in the process, had turned 1953 into the best Southern Conference basketball season in history. It was not perceived, however, that the level of play at the top of the conference was another reason for the conference to fracture, but it was. Everett Case's success had forged conference division, because there were schools that simply could not or would not take up the challenge that Case had leveled.

Dick Herbert may have said it best in his February 17 column. "The bottom part of the league is woefully weak, and perhaps something should be done about it. The Citadel, for instance, doesn't care anything about qualifying for the tournament. It makes no effort to have an outstanding team."[20] The contrast between the top and the bottom of the conference was extraordinary. Herbert remarked that it might take a minimum of a 70 percent winning rate to qualify for the tournament, while "the bottom five teams in the conference standings have won a total of five conference games."[21] The Southern Conference was two different leagues playing in one conference.

The Duke–North Carolina game on February 27 was for the Big Five Title—Davidson was still included in basketball—and tournament seeding. A Duke victory would give them the Big Five Championship, an honor that State had controlled for six years. In addition, the losing team would find themselves in eighth place in the tournament seeding, which meant a date with Case's Wolfpack in the first round. That was considered a death sentence. Duke had little reason to be concerned, because they destroyed the Tar Heels 83–58, securing themselves a sixth seed and dropping North Carolina to the seventh or eighth seed. The game was a tale of two halves with the score tied at intermission. The second half was all Duke.

In the Palmetto State, Frank Selvy again led Furman to an impressive victory as Furman whipped Clemson 95–70 at Textile Hall, a 5,000-seat facility in downtown Greenville. Clemson finished the year with a 6–8 conference record and an 8–10 total record, returning to its norm after a better previous year.

Furman, by far, was the best team in South Carolina and one of the top teams in the league. They completed the year with a six-game winning streak. Furman was 21–6 and 10–3 in conference play, but they had not played the type of schedule that the Big Four had played. Furman had lost to State in the first game of the year, but the rest of the schedule featured teams with poor records. They did not play Maryland, Duke, North Carolina, West Virginia, or Wake Forest, for example. But Selvy was a treat and held great fascination for the fans intending on attending the conference tournament.

The 1953 Southern Conference Tournament: The Championship

Wake Forest and Maryland completed the conference season with equal 12–3 records, and thus were tied for second place. The Deacons ended the season with an overall 14–5 record while Maryland was 14–7. In a drawing made at the Sir Walter in Raleigh, Wake Forest secured the second seed, placing Maryland in third. Wake Forest probably deserved the seed more than Maryland, because the Deacons played a tougher schedule, but it was a shame that these two excellent squads had to have the seeding settled in this manner.

The opening game was the four seed West Virginia versus Furman and scoring machine Frank Selvy, who finished the season averaging 29.5 points per game. At 4 p.m. on Thursday, Maryland was to play the blazing hot Blue Devils. At 7:30 Wake Forest was slated to combat Richmond while the nightcap was North Carolina versus State College. State had a right to be upset playing in the 9:30 time slot, because they were the number one seed.

Tournament excitement was at its peak, but the betting money was on State to repeat as conference champions. Case had dominated the tournament, and the Wolfpack was a better club than the previous year. Hal Bradley's Blue Devils were on a blistering pace, but all the Big Four had a chance to win the tournament, unlike in previous years. Duke was playing well, but they did not have a Dick Groat–like player. Wake Forest had Hemric, an exceptional player who could win a game by himself. Other teams had a legitimate star that could carry them to victory. Furman's Frank Selvy could will his team to success, and Gene Shue at Maryland could play with anyone. The league well understood that State's Thompson and Speight could put a team on their shoulders when needed. West Virginia's Jim Sottile could do the same thing. Richmond seemed a bit too inexperienced to do too much damage, but they had enjoyed a fine year.

Scoring was one of the main themes of the 1952–1953 season. The league was filled with players of the highest quality who lit up the scoreboard. Never had the quality of competition been this high. Before World War II, few could have dreamed that Southern Conference basketball would have talented players like Frank Selvy, Gene Shue, and Bobby Speight.

The tournament was a sellout, and Willis Casey, State's swim coach, was overworked managing ticket sales at the Reynolds Coliseum box office.[22] Fans were thrilled for the opportunity to see two of the hottest scorers in the game. Frank Selvy finished the season averaging 29.3 per game and Dickie Hemric with 25.1. Both players were named to the All–Southern Conference squad. Bobby Speight, West Virginia's Jim Sottile, and George Washington's Joe Holup, who had a tremendous first year, were the other additions on the first team. Gene Shue, Maryland's finest player, was a glaring omission which may have added fuel to his conference performance.

Frank Selvy–led Furman was the highest scoring team in the country and did not disappoint in the tournament's first game. West Virginia Mountaineer fans were present in large numbers at Reynolds, hoping to see their team gain revenge for their heartbreaking loss in the previous year's tournament. The Mountaineers purchased their full allotment of tickets, 300.[23] Star center Nield Gordon set the tournament single-game scoring record with 37 points and Selvy scored 34, but it was all in a losing effort. Gordon broke the record of 36 points set by William & Mary's Chet Giermak in a 1949 semifinal game against George Washington. West Virginia star Jim Sottile of Bristol, Pennsylvania, poured in 29 points to help edge Furman 91–87. The 91 points was the most points scored by any team in Southern Conference Tournament history, yet it was barely enough to defeat Selvy's and Gordon's scoring efforts. Unfortunately for Furman, Gordon, a Wingate transfer, had played his last game for Furman. Although Selvy had another year, Furman would miss the outstanding complementary play that Gordon provided.

Even though Maryland was the third seed, their 74–65 victory over Duke was a small surprise. The Blue Devils played at a torrid rate, but they struggled from the floor against the hot-shooting Terps. In the first half, the Blue Devils were 5 of 34 from the field, scoring only one field goal in the first period. They did a little better for the game but finished with a miserable 22 percent from the floor. Gene Shue was unstoppable, pacing Maryland to victory.

The evening games went according to form. Wake Forest beat Richmond 85–70 in a game that was blown open in the second half. The Tar Heels were badly beaten by a much superior State squad in the late game 86–54. Frank McGuire's team had been much better than expected, but they had faded at the end of the season. There was not much drama in either contest, but fans knew that a Wake Forest–State matchup was brewing.

Having tied for second in the league, the Maryland–Wake Forest semifinal was another thrilling contest. It was a gut-wrenching game for both teams, because neither squad was able to exert their will over the other. There were 22 lead changes in this possession-focused game. Gene Shue was unstoppable as usual and posted 40 points, making him the leading scorer in tournament history. Terrapin strategy was to play a man-to-man defense that sagged a bit to cover Hemric like a blanket. Even with the tight defense, Hemric scored 23 points and grabbed 21 rebounds. Maryland's focus on the Deacon big man allowed Larry Williams to score 26 points for the Deacons. The game was tied as it entered the fourth period, but Maryland could not score a point in the final three minutes, allowing Williams and Hemric to put Wake on top 61–59. In the last three minutes, Wake's pressure defense made all the difference, not allowing the Terps to freeze the game. Gene Shue almost won the game by himself, because no other Maryland player scored in double figures. Unfortunately for Shue, he missed the game's last shot, Wake Forest rebounded and won, sending them to the finals for the first time since 1946. The remarkable Gene Shue scored 73 points in two games, almost breaking Dick Groat's all-time scoring record of 78 points, which was achieved over three games.

It was a conference embarrassment for Shue not to have been voted first team all-conference. He missed the honor by two votes. Bud Millikan, the Maryland coach, heaped praises on Shue, comparing him to Dick Groat, at that time the most heralded player in conference history. Shue had performed at the highest level on the conference's biggest stage.

Having lost in the semifinal by two points the prior year without the services of Jim Sottile, West Virginia was eager to take on the Wolfpack and advance to the finals. The Mountaineers started with tremendous spirit, eventually building a 17-point lead before settling for a 46–39 halftime advantage. They held a 15-point lead on three occasions. The game shifted when Sottile fouled out with 6:06 remaining in the third period, on a controversial call. Sottile had scored 11 points at that point, but he was captain of the team and had averaged 19 points per game. This was a devastating loss for the Mountaineer five and the senior was badly missed on the court. Mountaineer center Pete White fouled out with 5:49 left in the game, another major blow. Playing on their home floor, State rallied for the win, 85 80. State fans poured onto the court chanting "Poor Wake Forest" in anticipation of Saturday's final.[24] Case believed that this was State's greatest comeback, and he may have been right. West Virginia had five players in double figures and still did not win. There was a sense that the Mountaineers, who had come up short in 1952 and 1953, were snake bit.

The finals were held on Saturday at 8 p.m. in Reynolds Coliseum between the Wolfpack and the Deacons, two old rivals who knew each other well. Many had predicted a State-Wake matchup and the excitement for a rubber game between the two was felt throughout the Tar Heel State. Although there was a sense that the best two clubs had made the finals, State had most of the momentum. They had won six straight Southern Conference titles, and Everett Case was a genius coaching in the tournament. The Deacons were hoping to win their first Southern Conference title, having only made the finals once since joining the league in 1936. State had a much deeper squad compared to the Deacons, who only played six players. Fatigue was a concern for Wake Forest as well as foul trouble. Wake could not afford for Hemric or Williams to be out of the game, while State had a deep bench, with several substitutes having the ability to make the difference for the Pack. Of course, playing in Raleigh on their home floor was another significant advantage for State.

As March 8 dawned, most people believed that State's deep bench as well as Case's magic would be the deciding factors in the championship game. Although Murray Greason was well liked by North Carolina basketball fans, many thought of him as the bridesmaid who never was the bride. From the tip-off, the ballgame, as expected, was extremely close with many ties. Wake Forest gradually gained a small lead, but the home court advantage and State's fine team helped keep the Wolfpack close. The second half was nip and tuck to the end, with no team gaining a significant edge. Concern resonated among the Wake Forest faithful when Al DePorter, one of the team's linchpins, who finished the game with 14 points, fouled out in the third period. He had been critical to helping the Deacons stay tight with State. Eventually, Ray Lipstas and Maurice George, with a little over one minute left in the game, were lost for the Deacons for a total of three players eliminated from the contest, placing even more pressure on the perilously thin Wake team. It looked as if the Wolfpack had the title in their grasp when they established a five-point lead with 5:31 left to play. Wake's Billy Lyles scored two buckets to help bring the Deacons even. The game was tied at 65 with 4:18 to go. It was anyone's contest. By way of free throws, the Deacons grabbed the lead 68–65 with 2:07 remaining.

Jack Horner described the game's final two minutes this way. "Those last two minutes were loaded with dynamite. It was wild and wooly with the Wolfpack pressing the stalling Deacons all over the floor."[25] Only the most confident of Deacon fans believed that Wake could outlast the Pack.

Late in the game, State's Bobby Speight went to the free throw line, hitting both to make it a one-point 68–67 Deacon advantage. Williams scored one of two free throws to give Wake a slim 69–67 lead. The free throw contest continued with State's Bernie Yurin scoring only one of his two free throws making it 69–68. With everyone scoring only one of two free throw shots, Wake's Billy Lyles and Jack Williams did the same giving the Deacons a 71–68 lead. The last seconds of the game were high drama and frantic. Wake's Lowell Davis fouled State's Bernie Yurin, who dropped in both free throws for State with 26 seconds remaining. The score stood 71–70, Wake Forest. Little-used Deacon John DeVos was fouled and missed both free throws, leaving the door open for State to snatch victory in the final 10 seconds. State got the rebound from the second miss, but Hemric intercepted a pass. Yurin stole the ball from Hemric, but it was too late for the Pack. The buzzer sounded. Speight's last shot, which rimmed out, came after the final horn. In ecstasy, Deacon fans stormed the court. Twenty years of frustration had ended for Murray Greason, and Case's Southern Conference dominance was broken. The Wolfpack were human. State's run of championships had ended, and Wake Forest was the first team in the league to beat Case's Wolfpack twice in one season. It was a momentous moment for Southern Conference basketball, but perhaps more of a moment for basketball in North Carolina and for the game in the new league that was only a couple of months from its founding.

Dick Pierce of the *Charlotte Observer* summed up the game in this manner. "The battle, and it was that all the way, will certainly go into the archives as one of the hottest in history. Both teams managed the same number of field goals, 20, while Murray Greason's Baptists were accurate on 31 line attempts to the Wolfpack's 30."[26]

After the game, Greason was plenty emotional but modest as usual. Even though his relationship with Wake Forest was decades in the making, Greason described the victory as "the greatest thrill of my athletic career. Yes, even a bigger thrill than catching an eight-pound bass."[27] The outdoorsman gave a lot of credit to guard Al DePorter who played one of the best games of his career before fouling out in the third period. DePorter, from Patterson, New Jersey, scored 14. After years of small budgets and searching the reeds for players who others did not want, he had his championship.

The victory was intensely meaningful for Greason. He had grown up next to the campus, and, as a student at Wake had lettered all four years in basketball, baseball, and football. He was a campus legend, famous for his athletic achievements, especially a 72-yard touchdown run against North Carolina in 1924. Greason returned to Wake Forest in 1933 as an assistant football coach, and in the same year, he was assigned the duties to lead the Deacon basketball team. The title was a crowning achievement.

Bones McKinney's role as an assistant was key to victory and that is not a slight to Murray Greason. McKinney brought animation and energy to the sidelines that complemented Greason's calm demeanor. Furthermore, the former Durham High School star knew how to play basketball at the highest level. He was the proper tutor for Hemric and Williams, heavily responsible for turning them into outstanding players. McKinney always provided good quotes for reporters, and after the game, he did not disappoint. The animated McKinney told reporters about the close win, "just say we had it all the way."[28] Knowing basketball like he did, Bones followed the comment with a remark that is always true in sports. "We were pretty lucky, though."[29]

Murray Greason (standing, far right), Bones McKinney (standing, third from right), and the Wake Forest basketball team celebrate their 1953 Southern Conference Championship, giving Everett Case his first conference tournament loss (courtesy Wake Forest Historical Museum, Wake Forest, NC).

McKinney was right to some degree. Hemric, Williams, and Billy Lyles played every minute of the game. Lyles played all 120 minutes of the three games. State's deep bench and press certainly had an effect, but the Deacons were able to gut out the victory.

McKinney almost jinxed the Deacons with his comments to sportswriters before the game. He was quoted saying, "We're gonna beat State. We've got it tonight."[30] If Murray Greason had heard Bones, it is certain he would have cringed in fear. After the game, the seminary student reminded reporters about his prediction and added, "the good Lord meant for us to win."[31]

Everett Case was gracious in defeat, complimenting the Deacons. "Tonight proves what I have said about this Wake Forest ball club. It's a great team."[32] Case was concerned about winning the tournament in 1953 with so many fine clubs in the Southern Conference. It was a shame that the Wolfpack season ended without Speight and his talented teammates having the opportunity to play in the NCAA tournament. If able to participate, there was an outstanding chance that they would have made a very deep tournament run.

The tournament provided a little bit of justice for Gene Shue, who was omitted from the All-Southern Conference First Team. Although his team did not play in the final, Shue, deservedly, won the most outstanding player award for his record-breaking play in two games. The junior forward hit 33 against Duke and 40 against Wake. It was a remarkable two games for a player who worked as a janitor in Maryland's Richie Gym.

Murray Greason had led the Deacons to a 10–19 campaign the previous year, but 1953 brought him the Gerry Gerard Award as the Southern Conference coach of the year. With only six players playing significant minutes, Greason had done yeoman work. The 20-year veteran finally had gained the top slot for the small college, bringing the Southern Conference trophy to Baptist Hollow.

Jake Penland offered glowing praise for an outstanding tournament. Always a colorful writer, Penland wrote, "This was the most nerve-wrecking session of what has been the most ulcer-producing tournament in conference history."[33] He was right. If the last big event for the conference was the basketball tournament, truly it was a classic. The last season for the 17-team league had been the best season.

As the 1953 campaign was put to bed, sportswriters regarded it as the best season and tournament of all. No one was able to hold on to first place, and Duke, North Carolina, State, and Wake had never been as competitive. The tournament did not disappoint either. It was thrilling, drawing more fans than any tournament in conference history and offering heart-stopping action played by the best athletes in the conference's history. It was a season for the ages, one that signaled that a new league of the top teams was required.

9

The Atlantic Coast Conference Is Born

With basketball over for the year and baseball season underway, attention was turned to critical conference business. The formation of a new conference, although slow in its development, having been discussed by sportswriters and fans for years, moved quickly and covertly to fruition in the spring of 1953. As late as the end of February, there was no public indication that a new conference was being considered, but a break was brewing.

In February, Walter Newman wrote to Southern Conference presidents that he had heard that bowl games and freshman participation would be issues raised at the May meeting, knowing that those topics often dominated conversation. The Virginia Tech president believed that the presidents needed another meeting prior to the formal conference gathering to gain clarity on those issues.[1] This was due, in part, to Virginia Tech's proposal to ban all freshmen from intercollegiate competition, including the suspension of freshman or junior varsity squads. The conference had allowed freshmen to participate in athletics for the prior two years, but clarity on the rule was needed prior to the start of fall sports.[2]

Virginia Tech had some supporters for its proposal, but there were too many institutions that believed a suspension of all freshman athletics went too far. Harold Tribble was a Tech ally, but Clemson, State, and most of the other schools were not willing to ban freshmen. Hollis Edens maintained that Duke would oppose "vigorously" any proposal to allow freshman participation, a long-standing Duke position.[3]

The bowl question required a more nuanced approach. Edens was surprised that sportswriters had not relinquished their opposition to the presidents and their bowl policy. The issue continued to attract attention and damage the presidents' reputations in the eyes of many fans. Edens was willing to reconsider the bowl question if some basic principles were approved. These included allowing only one team, chosen by the conference, to play in a bowl game. In addition, Edens opposed allowing a team to play in a bowl game two consecutive years.[4] Perhaps Gordon Gray's moderation on a conference-wide policy banning bowl games was influencing his colleague in Durham.

After hearing from most of the presidents, Newman determined that a meeting of the presidents was needed. To put it bluntly, the presidents would lose all standing with the public if they ran from the bowl question. Newman scheduled the gathering for May 7 at 2 p.m. at the Sedgefield Inn.[5] By the time of the meeting, the Southern Conference would be fracturing.

The Sedgefield Inn at Sedgefield Country Club in Greensboro, North Carolina, was the site for the conference meeting. Greensboro was a thriving city, a center for the textile industry and the second largest city in the state, only trailing Charlotte. In some ways, it was one of the centers of the New South, a city where the Woolworth sit-ins would change the course of history for the South and the country.

In the 1920s, the Southern Real Estate Company, seeing Greensboro's potential, envisioned a new and better Pinehurst, featuring two 18-hole golf courses and even a polo ground. A grand Tudor style clubhouse was completed, and the famed golf course designer Donald Ross constructed one of the two planned golf courses, but the original plan for establishing a business community to complement the residential area faltered after the stock market collapse of 1929. The Depression ended the hopes of establishing a Pinehurst-like attraction, but Sedgefield, an unincorporated community, still attracted many of Greensboro's elites.[6] By the early 1950s, it was a well-established golf club community, hosting the Greater Greensboro Open, one of the earliest professional golf tournaments, founded in 1938.[7] Sedgefield was an excellent choice for a conference meeting because Greensboro had the advantage of being a significant southern city but not the home of one of the Southern Conference schools. The city featured Woman's College of the University of North Carolina (later the University of North Carolina Greensboro), Guilford College, Negro Agricultural and Technical College of North Carolina (later North Carolina Agricultural and Technical University), and Greensboro College. It was a city with a prominent educational heritage, but it was neutral terrain.

This was the first time that the Southern Conference had met in Greensboro since 1944, and the first conference meeting at Sedgefield Country Club. Most attendees were excited to play the golf course before the meeting, ready to have some fun wagering and to simply enjoy themselves. Golf was a mainstay at all conference gatherings with as much conference business settled on the links as in the conference rooms.

Sedgefield Country Club in Greensboro was the site of the Atlantic Coast Conference's founding in 1953 (author's photograph).

Southern Conference president Max Farrington left Washington to visit Wallace Wade on Wednesday before the conference, with his golf clubs packed. On Thursday, Wade and Farrington traveled the short distance from Durham to Greensboro for the meeting at Sedgefield.[8] The two men had been kept in the dark about any talk of a split, and neither expected secession.

Before the meeting, most writers, like Earle Hellen, did not predict the formation of a new league. Hellen believed that there would not be a conference split and that nothing would change bowl opposition, even though the Orange Bowl allegedly wanted a tie with the league.[9]

Dick Herbert directly confronted the question of a conference fracture, commenting that there had been discussions about a split so that each conference team could play one another. He did not predict secession, but he noted that some of the small schools were not averse to division. He used Davidson as an example. The Wildcats were prohibiting freshman participation in varsity athletics starting in September 1953. That would mean that they would have about 28 football players for the season.[10] By comparison, SMU, although not an opponent, often had as many as 150 football players on their team. The same was true at powerhouses like Tennessee. Maryland regularly maintained a team approaching almost 100 players.

Roy "Legs" Hawley was the first athletic director to arrive in Greensboro. Hawley, a tremendous advocate for West Virginia University, immediately informed the press that the Mountaineer sports program was the equal of the largest schools in the Southern Conference, fielding 12 athletic teams. What Hawley faced was representing a university whose profile was very low in comparison to the schools in more highly populated states. What also worked against West Virginia was that its chief rivals were Pittsburgh and Penn State.[11] Although it was developing rivalries with Southern Conference schools, these did not have the gravitas of many current rivalries in the league. Hawley understood that a big part of his job was promoting West Virginia athletics to all who would listen. He had no indication that his publicity duties were destined to quickly accelerate in a matter of hours.

With national and international news captivated by questions surrounding new leadership in the Soviet Union after Stalin's death, Southern Conference meetings began on May 7. Within hours of the conference's first gathering, there were abundant rumors of a potential split, perhaps a few more than usual. The Associated Press reported that a division was soon on the horizon, predicting that some university officials would be burning the "midnight oil" with, perhaps, an announcement being made on May 8.[12] Six Southern Conference presidents met for three hours on May 7 discussing Maryland's proposal for bowl participation and Virginia Tech's suggestion to suspend freshman teams, leaving freshmen unable to participate in athletics. Tech's proposal had no hope of approval. The presidents did agree to one change, however. Irvin Stewart, president of West Virginia, succeeded Virginia Tech's Walter S. Newman as chair of the presidents committee.[13] His leadership term would start with a conference having seven fewer members.

Even Chauncey Durden of the *Richmond Times-Dispatch*, a paper where he had covered sports since 1939, did not anticipate a break at the Greensboro meeting. He believed it was destined to happen but did not know when. Durden reported, "There has been considerable undercover work, though it may not be the appropriate word for it, work carried on leading to division in the conference ranks."[14] The Richmond scribe explained that division had gained steam after the December 1952 meeting at Clemson, and that substantial behind the scenes machinations had been accomplished. With Orange Bowl officials attending the conference meeting, Durden believed that something about splitting was afoot but when it would happen was unknown.[15]

The *Washington Post*'s Herman Blackman reported that Chuck Erickson, North Carolina's athletic director, had visited College Park in late April to confer with Maryland officials about forming a new league. Writing after the new league was founded, Blackman believed that the split came about because "Maryland had the idea, Carolina had the friends."[16] Byrd was the indispensable man, Blackman argued, but he implied that the seceding schools would not have left the Southern Conference had North Carolina not favored a split.

Irwin Smallwood, a North Carolina graduate and former editor at *The Daily Tar Heel*, reported that schools desiring a new league had held a meeting in Chapel Hill on Wednesday, May 6, to begin finalizing the separation.[17] Smallwood's information as well as rumors of additional meetings in the spring rings true. Unfortunately, the records of these negotiations do not exist.

Throughout the afternoon and evening of the 7th, there were many informal gatherings where separation was the only issue discussed. The first formal meeting of the conspirators involved in creating a new conference was held at 9:30 p.m. on May 7, 1953, at the Sedgefield Inn. The prediction of the midnight oil had been accurate. In Room 230, South Carolina's Jim Penney was tapped as temporary chairman while Oliver Cornwell served as the temporary secretary. These were old and trusted hands in the athletic community. The seven seceding schools were represented by coaches, athletic directors, faculty, and presidents. Lee Milford and Frank Howard represented Clemson. Duke's Eddie Cameron and Charles Jordan were in attendance. State was represented by H.A. Fisher and Roy Clogston. Maryland had Geary Eppley and Jim Tatum present. There was a large contingent from North Carolina, featuring Bob House, A.W. Hobbs, Chuck Erickson and Oliver Cornwell. South Carolina brought Jim Penney and Rex Enright. Wake Forest's Harold Tribble was present as well as Forrest Clonts and Jim Weaver.[18]

Tribble and House were the only chief executives in attendance, while no basketball or baseball coaches attended, although basketball was the conference's chief money maker and was rapidly gaining a rabid following that would exceed football. The list of attendees was more confirmation that football coaches, some of whom doubled as athletic directors, were an essential driving force for the new conference.

After much discussion as to the purpose of the meeting, a motion was made. "In view of the increasing problems in intercollegiate athletics it is the opinion of the group present that the formation of a smaller conference is desirable."[19] Furthermore, they recommended that the seven institutions proceed through "proper channels" to gain approval to join the conference. As soon as approval was achieved, a meeting of the new league members was to be held. Mathematician H.A. Fisher of State, a Cabarrus County, North Carolina, native, made the motion to form the new league, and it was seconded by Lee Milford of Clemson. The roll call vote was unanimously approved.[20]

Their statement did little to highlight the many factors that had led the seven schools to this point. Not all had jumped enthusiastically into the new conference arrangement. Duke was very hesitant and most likely was the last of the seven to agree to the new conference formation, according to Dick Herbert.[21] Duke had enjoyed a long series of competitive football games with Tennessee, Georgia Tech, Army, Navy, and other prominent teams. It was concerned that its football scheduling as well as its stature as a football power would be harmed if it had to play a full schedule of games within the conference.[22] Its broader national footprint could be damaged by a small, closely knit conference that lacked the grand stage to which it was accustomed.

North Carolina, a champion for the new league, and State, an institution with limited gridiron influence in 1953, only agreed to join if five conditions were met. Driven by Gordon Gray, the five stipulations stated that each conference member had to play each other member in football as rapidly as possible. A prohibition on freshman participation in varsity athletics, a highly controversial topic as we have seen, was required. Both schools requested that "adequate standards" be forged for athletes to be admitted to conference schools. The seceding institutions were encouraged to play all conference members in all sports. Lastly, but of great significance, UNC and State wished for bowl participation to be allowed under the condition that individual institutions did not make money from the games. Funds were to be distributed to schools in a fashion to be determined.[23]

Gray's reversal on bowls was a surprising change that did not reflect his personal belief that bowls were counterproductive to the educational experience. Although he had changed course for the good of the new league, it was doubtful that Gray would allow North Carolina or State to appear in a bowl game. He was fortunate in that he never had to make that decision during his time leading the North Carolina system.

According to Smith Barrier, State had been part of the secession group only because Gordon Gray and State officials made a commitment to becoming more competitive in football. State's lack of football success was a yoke around its neck. The Raleigh school had sent officials to study Jim Tatum's Maryland operation and the school had committed to improving and enlarging Riddick Stadium from 20,000 to 30,000 seats. Because of the lack of revenue from the smaller Riddick, State often played its rivalry game with UNC in Chapel Hill. State gained as much as $36,000 by making the trip to North Carolina's campus.[24]

If there was a surprise member, it was Wake Forest. It did not have the enrollment of the other schools, and traditionally it was financially lean. It was never going to match the enrollments at the large state universities, but the Deacons had won a lot of football games under Peahead Walker and were continuing to win under Tom Rogers. Their monumental Southern Conference Tournament championship two months earlier was another sign of their strength. Wake was competitive with the other schools leaving the league. In addition, it led the seceding schools in optimism, with a new campus being constructed and financial security in place. Lastly, it did not hurt that Gordon Gray was involved with Wake Forest for many years in efforts to develop Winston-Salem.

The next step for the seceding institutions was to develop a strategy for presenting this action to the collective Southern Conference members the next day at the scheduled 10 a.m. meeting. Understanding the delicate nature of the topic and hoping to secede from the Southern Conference on good terms, Charles Jordan of Duke with a second from Wake's Clonts moved they should make a motion for the "president of the Southern Conference [to] declare a recess and that the recessed group go into executive session."[25] The motion passed unanimously.

Even late into the evening, Max Farrington was unprepared for what was about to happen. He was devoted to the Colonials and had performed well leading the conference through a difficult period. Membership in the conference had been good for George

Washington, but he was about to receive news that would destabilize the Southern Conference and George Washington's athletic future.

A strong committee composed of Clonts, Jordan, and Eppley, men with many years of outstanding service to athletics, was chosen to meet the Southern Conference president prior to the 10:00 a.m. gathering to alert him to the secession. Anticipating problems, another committee consisting of old hands, Fisher, Cameron, and Penney, was created to discuss with an appointed Southern Conference committee five issues. They were the commissioner's office, the booking office, the conference name, financial matters, and the Southern Conference's attitudes toward the new conference members. Lastly, the seven schools agreed to meet at Raleigh's Sir Walter Hotel on June 12, 1953, to finalize the foundation of the conference, including the all-important selection of a new name.[26]

The following morning, the committee met with Farrington over breakfast to present their plans for leaving the Southern Conference. Records of the meeting do not exist, but it appears certain that the George Washington athletic director was caught unaware of the finality of the decision and initially retained some hope of holding the organization together.

When the conference gathered for their morning meeting on May 8, the die was cast. As had been agreed, Farrington called the Southern Conference into executive session, dismissing all who were not representing a member institution. South Carolina's biologist, James Penney, pronounced the following:

> As most of you well know for some time there has been under consideration the possibility of the forming of a new and smaller playing conference. This idea was crystalized at a meeting last night at which Clemson College, Duke University, University of North Carolina, University of South Carolina, Wake Forest College, North Carolina State College, and the University of Maryland decided they should notify the Southern Conference that they propose to organize a new intercollegiate athletic conference. This action was taken with mixed feelings, as all of us have formed many personal and institutional friendships through the years. It is our belief that this action will be the best for all concerned.[27]

Penney requested a special Southern Conference committee be established to negotiate with the Penney Committee formed the previous evening.

Farrington asked that the seven members leave the session so that the remaining members could discuss freely their course of action. The seceding representatives retired to the ninth hole at Sedgwick to talk about the future. Not fully shocked by the secession, but surprised by the timing, the Southern Conference, holding their meeting at 11:05, quickly formed a committee of Washington and Lee's Cap'n Dick Smith, Davidson's John Cunningham, Virginia Tech's Walter Newman, The Citadel's David McAlister and Commissioner Wallace Wade. Immediately, this group began discussions with the new conference's committee, debating conditions of separation and the future. The remaining conference members hoped to avoid a split and pledged to make "every effort" to hold the conference together and resolve scheduling issues. If division were inevitable, they agreed to establish good relations with the new league.[28]

The remaining members hoped differences could be repaired and invited Jim Penney, Eddie Cameron, and A.W. Fisher to join them to answer some questions. Striking a tone of finality, Penney said that he had nothing to add to the statement of separation that he earlier had read. Cameron focused his remarks on scheduling problems, especially in basketball where there was enormous variation in schedule strength.[29] With football front and center in the split, Fisher remarked that football needed to carry more of the financial load.[30] He was hinting at the need for higher gate receipts that could not be had with the smaller schools in the Southern Conference.

None of the three men directly addressed the multitude of reasons for leaving the Southern Conference. No one wanted to embarrass other institutions, and it was obvious that the seceding schools had no intention of remaining in the league.

Meetings between the committee of Penney, Cameron, and Fisher and D.S. McAlister's Southern Conference committee occurred throughout the day, discussing everything from playing in two divisions in one league, to conference assets, to the booking office, to the commissioner's role.[31] By 5:30 p.m., the foundation for an agreed upon departure from the league was established. The conference resolved that "the remaining ten colleges and universities [were] to retain all assets of the Southern Conference and to assume all liabilities."[32] The conference's assets totaled about $150,000. The seven members of the new conference would "receive all services of the Commissioner's office and the Booking Office through the basketball season of 1953–1954."[33] Wallace Wade was caught in a very difficult position, because he was now the commissioner for two conferences until his contract expired on January 1, 1955. He was also conflicted because of his deep affection for the Southern Conference and an outstanding legacy on the gridiron leading Duke. Wade may have wondered what he had gotten himself into when he stepped down as coach to accept the commissioner position only two and a half years earlier.

All these negotiations were bittersweet. The split separated friends and institutions, some of whom had relationships going back decades. Adding to the anxiety were sportswriters waiting for an official announcement, hanging around Sedgefield Inn smoking cigarettes. Earlier in the day around noon, Wallace Wade left the meeting room to speak to the gathered reporters. Trying to alleviate some of the hard feelings, Wade said, "This is a perfect setup for you fellows. Nobody has told you anything, yet you know everything. You, therefore, can write anything you like."[34]

The last action of the 17-member Southern Conference was to appoint two members from the Southern Conference and two members from the new league to draft a press release. Max Farrington and D.S. McAlister represented the Southern Conference while Charles Jordan and Oliver Cornwell were tapped from the seceders. The news release was the first for the new league.

At 8:30 p.m. on May 8, the newly separated seven schools met for the first time in room 230 as a new league. The difficult business of organization now lay clearly in front of the men. The split had been, in the main, painless, but hard work was ahead of them. Unanimously, they decided to adopt the rules of the Southern Conference through the 1953–1954 season, a wise decision because there was no need to quickly draft new by-laws. Requiring some kind of recognizable executive, Fisher moved that Clonts, Eppley, and Jordan "serve as a temporary executive committee, with Clonts as chairman until the June meeting."[35] This was a statement of the high regard in which he was held by the fellow members, because the faculty member of the smallest school in the new league was tapped for this important leadership role. There was an enormous amount to consider prior to convening in Raleigh. They placed on their June agenda key issues such as finances, organization, and their relationship with the NCAA. The naming of the new conference was of critical importance as well as the difficult question of adding an eighth member. Scheduling for the first couple of years was destined to cause significant problems and needed full discussion as well. As had often occurred in the Southern Conference, the athletic directors proposed holding a meeting before the June meeting in Raleigh. Chuck Erickson, Jim Tatum, and Eddie Cameron began organizing it.

Lastly, each institution was charged with providing official notification that their governing authorities approved the change in conference affiliation. Although agreement had been reached by each school's representatives, boards had to approve these actions. That would take time, but it was necessary.

It is remarkable how effectively the seceding institutions kept their negotiations secret. Commissioner Wade knew nothing of the split, and he was well connected at Duke and with all the seceding schools. West Virginia's president Irvin Stewart and their athletic director, the ever-popular Legs Hawley, were not a part of any new conference discussions. The secession "caught them by surprise" and neither had any clear understanding of the direction that West Virginia, a league member for a mere three years, would go.[36] The Mountaineers and their remaining Southern Conference brethren had to scramble to right their ship.

The remaining Southern Conference members called a meeting to be held in Roanoke, Virginia, on June 26 and 27 to discuss their future. Their conference executive committee was named and included Max Farrington of George Washington, Sally Miles of VPI, Col. Kenneth S. Purdie of VMI, Dr. R.C. McDaniel of the University of Richmond, and Col. David S. McAlister of The Citadel.[37] It was surprising that no one from West Virginia, the premier sports program remaining in the conference, was selected for the committee. That was a mistake.

With news of the split spreading rapidly, some colleges around the South believed that the Southern Conference was a good destination for their programs. Officials at East Carolina College, now East Carolina University, saw an opportunity to withdraw from the North State Conference and join the Southern Conference.[38] East Carolina was making great strides as a college and was attempting to accelerate the development of its football program which had matured beyond most of its competition in the North State. The former East Carolina Teachers College was well positioned to leave behind schools such as Atlantic Christian College and Guilford College for a more prominent league. No one was certain, however, if the Southern Conference wanted to expand immediately after losing seven schools. There was more talk about Virginia schools pulling away from the remaining Southern Conference schools than expansion.

Trying to play both sides, Florida State courted the new league as well as the Southern Conference. Max Farrington confirmed Florida State's interest but spoke more positively of the chances of East Carolina joining the league.[39] Tallahassee was a very long way from the Virginia schools and George Washington. No one was interested in stomaching the expense of traveling to the Florida panhandle even though the Seminoles were a good fit for either conference.

The most pressing question among fans and journalists was the issue of the eighth member. It absorbed enormous attention, because it held the possibility of further weakening the Southern Conference. Virginia Tech's Sally Miles, known as Mr. VPI for his career at the institution, seeing his school left behind but hoping it would be the eighth member, was deeply hurt by the conference split. Miles was an old Southern Conference leader who had been president of the conference in 1932. Upon learning of the secession, with disappointment in his voice, Miles commented, "I've been with these folks for 31 years and haven't missed a single meeting and I just hate to see the conference break up."[40] "This is the saddest day I have known in a long while."[41]

Miles was close friends with Milford, Clonts, Cornwell, and Penney, but it was Milford to whom he appealed for help. A few weeks after the split, Sally Miles asked Lee Milford about VPI's chances for joining the league. A longtime pal of Miles, Milford was fully in favor of VPI, but he could not promise their election to the league. While in Greensboro in May, Milford spoke to Hobbs, Clonts, and Fisher about VPI, concluding that "the four of us seemed to be in accord about inviting V.P.I."[42] Jim Penney needed to see what direction came from South Carolina's Athletic Council. "I was never able to get anything definite from Maryland or Duke."[43]

Virginia Tech leaders had feared this situation. Shelley Rolfe of the *Richmond Times-Dispatch,* before the Greensboro meeting, explained that Tech leaders disliked being left out of discussions about conference division. Frank Moseley, Virginia Tech's athletic director, pointed out that it was difficult to attract schools to play in Blacksburg and even Victory Stadium in Roanoke, the home for the Thanksgiving VPI–VMI clash, was not a strong enough enticement. A reduced Southern Conference would make it even more difficult for Tech to attract large schools for home games. Furthermore, the Blacksburg institution simply did not have the athletic facilities that most of the other more significant athletic departments did.[44]

Like Virginia Tech's Sally Miles, West Virginia's Legs Hawley was truly disappointed that they were omitted from the new group. Although the Mountaineers had been very successful on the hardwood and less so on the football field, Hawley fully believed that West Virginia was too large a school and had too large an athletic program to be tossed aside.[45] Hawley was correct, when arguing that West Virginia possessed an athletic program on par with and exceeding some of those who were entering the new conference alignment.

West Virginia had an important friend in State College's Roy Clogston, who wrote Hawley three days after the conference split, urging him to be present in Raleigh when the new league met in June. "I have politicked with Clemson, Wake Forest, and State regarding your entry into our new Conference. I personally feel that you can make it. Every one in the Conference thinks a lot of you personally and also of your fine President. The only thing they held against the University of West Virginia is your geographical location, and if you can give them some sales talk on this matter, I am sure you can be the eighth member of our new Conference."[46] Clogston had support for favoring West Virginia over the Cavaliers, recognizing that many faculty members "don't care much for Virginia."[47] The State athletic director may have been more sympathetic with West Virginia because it was a school that had to fight for everything it got, much like State. Clogston well understood that State had "not seriously [been] considered at first" but was allowed to join the new conference's party "The leading universities in this movement are Maryland and the University of South Carolina," he judged.[48]

Virginia supporters and officials, like so many others, were surprised about the rapid split of the Southern Conference. Although Gus Tebell was on record favoring joining the new conference if Virginia were invited, membership was far from a sure thing. Some who favored the continued independence of Virginia athletics said that "the Cavaliers would find the competition too tough in this new league," especially if a round robin was established.[49] A strong undercurrent to these arguments was the desire of many to continue playing other Virginia schools such as Virginia Tech, William &

Mary, and Richmond. To those who wanted to continue all these rivalries, membership in the Southern Conference was the best option.

Tebell's attraction to the new league was in part due to his familiarity with schools in the new conference. A native of St. Charles, Illinois, who had starred in football and basketball at Wisconsin, Tebell had substantial connections to the Tar Heel state. He coached State's football squad from 1925 to 1929, compiling a record of 21–25–1, not bad for a school that placed little emphasis on its football program. By 1934, he was at Virginia where he coached football, baseball, and basketball. His basketball record was the best. Tebell recorded 240 wins, third most in Cavalier history. There is little doubt that Tebell's familiarity with the schools in the new conference, as well as his regular contact with UNC through the Virginia rivalry, influenced him to support Virginia's membership in the new league. Tebell, in addition, was a realist and could see that some of the schools that Virginia saw as their peers had forged this new league. It was important for Virginia to be a part of it.

Even with the unrest, joy, and anxiety, the question of Virginia's future was consistently present. A popular figure in Charlottesville, Tebell, who also served on the Charlottesville City Council, urged the school to seriously examine joining the new league, but he understood that Colgate Darden and the Board of Visitors would have the final word. Virginia was an independent since 1935, and some wanted to keep their independence. Charlottesville's *Daily Progress* reported on May 19, 1953, that UVA had been part of discussions to create a conference that included Army, Navy, Pennsylvania, Maryland, and Pittsburgh. These discussions, if successful, would have created a powerful football league, far in excess of Virginia's football tradition. Nevertheless, when Maryland joined the new league and Pennsylvania began a de-emphasis agenda, any hope for an eastern conference like the one proposed faded.[50]

In that context, Virginia was far from certain if it wanted to dance with the seceding schools. With mixed messages coming out of Charlottesville, the *Daily Progress* reported that the Big Four and Maryland "harbored a feeling that Virginia has taken a 'high and mighty' attitude toward its own athletic policy."[51] Even though Tebell and Darden were generally liked, there was a fair amount of truth to this allegation. The *Daily Progress* did not believe that Virginia held this condescension towards the other schools; however, the paper charged, "When it comes to athletic decisions, the University acts slowly. This has often irked the Southern Conference members. Many resent Virginia's attitude of superiority."[52] The newspaper, though, rightly judged that the Cavaliers needed the new conference, or they faced potential decline, especially as scheduling for football would become more problematic outside of an established league.[53]

Reactions to the New Conference

Campus newspapers, an important component of college life, generally praised the establishment of the new conference. Cautiously optimistic, *The Technician* at State College said, "Some people seem to think the new conference will give the Pack even less chance of having a winning [football] team."[54] Others thought that State's teams, often underdogs to their more powerful neighbors such as Duke, would improve with the new stronger conference. The cautious outlook was not surprising considering that the

Wolfpack had struggled on the gridiron for several years and had only enjoyed accolades on the hardcourt.

At North Carolina, *The Daily Tar Heel* offered a different interpretation. The editorial staff was very happy with the new league, but their optimism had nothing much to do with what the change meant for competition on the field or the court. Instead, the staff believed that it was a positive step for de-emphasizing athletics and restoring sanity to college sports. The paper hoped that "athletes will gain their proper niche in college life" under the new conference.[55]

A very confident Duke, accustomed to victories on the field and court and wealthy by comparison to its Southern Conference brethren, responded very differently. Eddie Cameron explained to *The Chronicle*, "Duke will bitterly oppose the plan to require scheduled football games with each other conference member each year. Duke would favor five games with circuit [conference] members, but a compromise six-game loop schedule may have to be arranged, if plans for an eight-team conference materialize."[56] This was a clear statement that Duke's ambitions were to remain a national power and not to be confined by the formation of a new conference. Cameron believed that the conference would be a great benefit to smaller sports and even commented that baseball and basketball scheduling would be rather easier than football.[57] It is important that Cameron, a very careful man, used the word "bitterly" to describe how Duke would fight against a full league football schedule. Football was king at Duke in this era.

At Wake Forest, optimism was in the air. An editorial in the *Old Gold and Black* commented that the college's membership in the new league "should be looked upon as an opportunity which this college has not had in twenty years."[58] The paper was harkening back to when Wake Forest joined the Southern Conference in 1936, a positive step for the small college that was punching way above its weight on the field and the court. As a small institution, Wake needed to be a part of a larger league for its athletic program to flourish, therefore; it was no great surprise to see enthusiasm among the Deacon faithful.

In Columbia, no tears were shed over the demise of the old Southern Conference. The campus newspaper, *The Gamecock*, believed that the new league was a good step forward and quoted Rex Enright to that effect. Like almost everyone else, the paper's sportswriter, Johnny Ray, predicted that Virginia would be added to the conference as its eighth member. As usual, *The Gamecock* took a swipe at their rival Clemson, suggesting that the Tigers would have a much more difficult time having to play teams like Duke, UNC, and Virginia on a consistent basis.[59] For several years, Gamecock supporters had charged Clemson with racking up wins against lesser competition.

Clemson's *The Tiger* was happy with the split, but not effusive with enthusiasm. The new conference, they argued, was good for Clemson, but their school needed improvements to its basketball and football facilities, the paper argued. The college's funding, the editors noted, was not as great as most of the seceding schools.[60] Chronic underfunding was a problem that plagued their sister school in Columbia as well.

Maryland's *The Diamondback* did not offer much commentary. Instead, on the newspaper mast in large print, it declared, "Terps Quit Southern Conference."[61] Not much more was necessary.

Some schools left out of the new league were happy with the split. For years, Davidson College had placed far fewer resources into athletics than most of the other Southern Conference schools and in football had fallen well behind the Big Four. Wildcat basketball and baseball were hurting badly as well, basically not competitive in the league. In the May 8, 1953, edition of the *Davidsonian*, the sports editor endorsed the Wildcats playing schools more in line with them. John Handley, the sports editor, very much hoped that a split was in the mix and that it would provide the Wildcats with a conference in which they would be much more competitive.[62]

After the new conference was created, *The Davidsonian* excitedly endorsed the new, smaller Southern Conference. Football Coach Bill Dole, who had only led the Wildcats for one year, commented that Davidson was about the primacy of academics and not athletics and that the conference split was very good for the Wildcats. It was a small attack on the North Carolina schools that had turned their backs on Davidson, crafting a Big Four to replace the Big Five. Furthermore, he noted that Davidson was not focused on winning championships. Dole summarized his feelings explaining that "this league split is obviously just the right thing for which Davidsonians have been hoping for a long time. It gives the opportunity to form the type of league that we have always wanted with athletic scholarships set at a minimum among all the schools left in the conference."[63] While extolling Wildcat virtue, Dole was ignoring the athletic ambitions of conference mates West Virginia and Virginia Tech.

At William & Mary, the feeling was not so optimistic. The unruly size of the Southern Conference was always a problem, but athletic director and football coach Jack Freeman believed that a split was unnecessary for the larger schools to obtain what they wanted, although he did not elaborate. It was apparent that the Indians were deemphasizing football, and that William & Mary's athletic fate was undetermined. This action simply added to the instability. Freeman, a three-sport letterman at William & Mary in the 1940s, was concerned about travel costs to schools like Furman and The Citadel and was unsure if the Virginia schools would draw closer together with institutions like West Virginia and George Washington.[64] Freeman expressed the sentiments of many who realized that the creation of the new conference left enormous questions about the future of the Southern Conference and what the athletic life of each institution would be. William & Mary had more to concern itself with, considering the desire of many faculty members to stoutly limit the role of college athletics at the school.

The *Hatchet* at George Washington University was not disappointed in the division. Jim Rudin wrote that the Southern Conference had followed a "sane and sensible path free from extremes."[65] Rudin, taking a somewhat accurate jab at the Terrapins, was proud that the remaining Southern Conference schools had not followed the "blind and ruthless ambition of a Maryland" and had avoided going the way of Georgetown's suspension of football.[66] Bob Alden of the *Hatchet* wrote that Southern Conference president Max Farrington was optimistic about GW's future. Farrington, with a brave face, believed that the conference was on a stronger footing, especially regarding football. Nevertheless, Alden, like most observers, realized that GW faced an uncertain sports future.[67]

Richmond students thought secession could foretell a new era for Spider athletics. The campus newspaper, the *Collegian*, commented that Richmond could be a leader in the new Southern Conference and spoke optimistically of the city hosting the conference basketball tournament. "Several members of the University athletic staff agreed that Richmond has benefited by the withdrawal of the big-time schools," Lucien Hall wrote.[68] The paper reported that Max Farrington supported Richmond as the site for the basketball tournament, if a location that fit the tournament's needs could be identified.[69]

With five Virginia schools remaining in the Southern Conference, Richmond had a strong argument for hosting the tournament. Richmond leaders, however, would be disappointed. The 1954 tournament, in which Richmond was a runner-up to champion George Washington, was held at the West Virginia Field House which seated 6,000. It was a far cry from modern Reynolds Coliseum in Raleigh with its capacity of 12,400.

By contrast, there was much less enthusiasm at Virginia Tech. The student newspaper, *The Virginia Tech*, commented, "Tech's coaching staff is dumbfounded."[70] Tech was recruiting better players with Frank Moseley leading the football team, but now the split had endangered his efforts. The better teams were in the new league, and "VPI is in a league of little athletic colleges."[71] Moseley told Tech students that the change was a challenge, because the Blacksburg school and West Virginia were the only two schools remaining in the Southern Conference with more than 1,200 students.[72] Indeed, they had almost nothing in common with Davidson, Furman, or even Virginia schools like Washington and Lee. Although he did not comment about it to the student paper, Moseley and the Tech administration were concerned about the financial future of their athletic program, playing schools that were not going to provide substantial gate receipts.

Sportswriters uniformly favored the formation of the new league although admitting that a fair amount of uncertainty remained. Questions abounded about a future eighth member, with the discussion often exceeding the many other issues that faced the establishment of the new conference. Virginia, Virginia Tech, and West Virginia were the most discussed and appropriate institutions. There were rumblings about Georgia, Florida, or Pennsylvania joining the seven seceding schools. At one point, Kentucky of the Southeastern Conference spoke with the new league about admittance.[73] A seven-member conference was awkward for many reasons, but the founders were concerned about rapidly adopting more schools that would create the same travel and scheduling problems that plagued the Southern Conference. Other issues such as scheduling and traditional rivalries that might be lost contributed to the anxiety about the future.

The always opinionated and highly entertaining Jake Penland of *The State* called the formation of the new conference an "intelligent move" but cautioned that South Carolina and Clemson were "not on par with some of the North Carolina schools and Maryland in football, and will have to grow stronger or else slip into the roles of weak sisters."[74] He was confident that the Gamecocks would continue to schedule The Citadel or Furman, keeping some of the traditional opponents in place. Expansion was clearly the next issue, with Penland believing that Virginia would be invited to join, although admitting that Virginia Tech had its supporters. West Virginia, in his view, was simply too remote. He noted that everyone liked West Virginia's AD Legs Hawley, a very popular figure throughout the South, but that "Morgantown is a somewhat drab, hard-to-get-to town. We recall making one trip, starting by plane, catching an ancient train out of Washington and completing the tiresome trip by rickety bus. The big, chartered planes cannot land at Morgantown."[75] Morgantown's remoteness would be its undoing.

Importantly, Penland thought the new arrangement was good for the remaining Southern Conference as well, but he did not say anything about how schools like Virginia Tech or West Virginia would feel about playing The Citadel and Furman instead of Maryland and North Carolina. He was right about how the remaining schools fit together better, but the Southern Conference remained with very unequal members.

Penland even suggested that the conference might have an opportunity to align itself with a bowl, possibly the Gator Bowl in Jacksonville, Florida.[76]

Dick Herbert expressed concern about the loss of the Southern Conference Basketball Tournament, an event that was one of the top highlights of the sports calendar. Herbert, most likely, was still thinking about the thrilling Wake Forest victory over State, which had ended the Wolfpack's impressive six-year run of dominance in the conference tournament. To survive, the new league would need the revenue from a basketball tournament. Herbert wondered if the new conference would establish a tournament. Would the regular season champion serve as conference champion? How would the conference be financed if a tournament were not held?[77] Herbert had little reason to be concerned, because Everett Case and other basketball coaches were eager to organize better schedules than those in the Southern Conference as well as a tournament with the champion claiming the conference title.[78]

Earle Hellen, a bit unfairly, argued that the league was formed by the athletic representatives, and that there was a noticeable abdication of duty by the college presidents. Only seven presidents were present for the presidents' meeting, one having suffered a flight delay, and Curly Byrd, one of the ringleaders, was in Europe. Hellen argued that the new conference came from the will of Jim Tatum, Rex Enright, and Frank Howard along with Jim Penney and Lee Milford, not the presidents.[79]

Hellen was correct in pointing out that the athletic people had pulled the trigger. But the groundwork was laid by presidential leadership, especially those eager for presidents to take a more forceful voice in college athletics. The new league would not have been formed without the presidential leadership that had originated two years earlier via Gordon Gray, Hollis Edens, Curly Byrd, and others. Presidential meetings and conference gatherings, combined with athletic performance on the field and court, had brought the seven schools to this junction.

With bowl participation having gained so many headlines in previous years, Dick Herbert spoke of rumors that the new conference would sign an agreement for its football champion to appear in the Orange Bowl or the Sugar Bowl. If bowl participation was allowed, it would provide a new method for financing the conference rather than depending on basketball tournament revenue.[80] It was a logical question considering that Orange Bowl officials attended the meeting at Sedgefield, entertaining their friends in Room 327.[81]

Nevertheless, Herbert was optimistic about the new league, especially considering the cumbersome nature of the Southern Conference. He "hoped the new conference will have a central office which has the power to make interpretations on many matters and whose job it is to keep the members up to date on the rules and regulations."[82] In part, this was due to the problems which plagued the Southern Conference. Even as late as May, the conference had flubbed the selection of teams for the Southern Conference baseball tournament, causing sportswriters and fans to be supremely annoyed.

Hugo Germino of the *Durham Sun* effusively praised the split, calling the future "happy days."[83] He believed this was "the finest move possible for all concerned—even the 10 schools left behind."[84] He must not have discussed the matter with Legs Hawley or Sally Miles.

Harold Wimmer offered a different perspective, because he closely covered Virginia Tech, one of the schools omitted from the new league. His response was cautious, emphasizing that athletic departments were more than simply football programs.

Wimmer talked to Tech's Frank Moseley about the league and the Tech head man indicated that the Blacksburg school wanted membership. He was hurt that VPI was left at the altar. Mosely maintained that VPI needed a good football team, but the goal was not to field big-time football. In a traditional manner, Mosely argued that Tech was a fine school where "good athletes were good students."[85] Nonetheless, Mosely's trajectory was to win and to win big at Virginia Tech. He had played on a Rose Bowl winning team at Alabama and wanted to bring victories to Blacksburg.

The new conference caused other schools in the Eastern U.S. to reassess their athletic associations. It was reported, "Villanova, Boston College, and Holy Cross are said to be in favor of a new Eastern League including Army, Navy, Pennsylvania, Penn State, and Pittsburgh."[86] The problem in the Northeast was that the Ivy League was not a fully organized conference until 1954, and did not sponsor competition until 1956. Northern schools were members of the Eastern College Athletic Conference, an unwieldy sports organization with 98 institutions, clearly out of date with the trends in conference association. Some type of new league was very much needed, and it appeared that the seceding schools had offered a blueprint.[87] These moves were being proposed too late, especially as professional football slowly gained the upper hand in northern, urban markets.

The mastermind behind forming a new eastern conference was Villanova's athletic director Ambrose "Bud" Dudley. The Philadelphia-raised Dudley was as much a promoter as he was athletic administrator. Seeing the formation of the ACC and concerned about the future position of college football in the northeast, Dudley recognized opportunity. Grouping Villanova with other major northeast universities, he believed, would drastically reduce travel costs and create strong rivalries that would draw large numbers of fans.[88] Dudley was on the right track, but many of the schools, like Villanova, Boston College, and Holy Cross, did not have appropriate football facilities in place to craft a new league. Villanova, for example, played at Philadelphia's Municipal Stadium for many home games. It was a cavernous facility, built in 1926, that offered little in the way of home field advantage. It could seat 102,000 and had a track that surrounded the football field, further distancing fans from the action. Although Dudley was a great promoter, he never achieved his ambition of forming a northeastern league.

New League and New Directions

The new conference meant opportunity for some cities, especially Greensboro and Charlotte, both neutral territories. The Queen City, however, was the first to take advantage of the new league. The *Charlotte Observer*'s Wilton Garrison wasted no time in urging Charlotte officials to respond to this economic and athletic opportunity by making improvements to the city's Memorial Stadium. Charlotte had hosted Southern Conference games in the past and was scheduled to have South Carolina play Wake Forest in November 1953. Garrison, a Washington and Lee graduate who would serve 20 years as a sports editor at the *Charlotte Observer*, thought that Charlotte would be a great location for a future Clemson-Duke or a Clemson–North Carolina contest.[89]

In the summer, Charlotte voters approved a bond to fund the construction of a 10,000-seat coliseum to serve the city. One of the incentives was the opportunity to host ACC basketball games and perhaps even the ACC or Southern Conference tournaments.

The new conference and the excitement created by the Dixie Classic as well as the end of season tournaments were seen as financial opportunities. The domed Charlotte Coliseum, strikingly modern in the 1950s, opened in 1955 on Independence Boulevard.[90]

With the new conference at hand but still worried about the role of athletics on college campuses, Gordon Gray wasted no time in attempting to persuade presidents and chancellors to take an active role in the new league. He sent a memo to each of the seven urging them to not only attend meetings but to actively involve themselves in the development of the conference. Gray noted that he had heard that "certain of the coaches and others" desired for the presidents to recede into the background after the initial organization.[91] Gray issued this alert as a warning to the other presidents that vigilance was key to controlling the growing commercialization and professionalization of intercollegiate athletics. Gray envisioned the new league's formation as an avenue to maintaining and restoring integrity in college sports.

Gray had allies, one of which was Harold Tribble at Wake Forest. In late May, Tribble told Edens that he fully agreed with Gray that presidents needed to be involved in the formation and operation of the new conference. He was deeply disappointed, however, that the Bowman Gray School of Medicine graduation interfered with his attendance at the first organizational meeting in Raleigh on June 14. Gray and Tribble had joined hands in their united opposition to bowls; the Wake Forest president in his letter was uncompromising on his opposition to bowl games but was willing to accept a championship game outside of the bowl system. In some ways, he was envisioning the conference championship games of today, without the money and fanfare, something very unlikely to occur. The Wake Forest president understood that his position on bowls was not attacking the "basic problem" of "subsidy and recruiting."[92]

Naming and Organizing the New Conference

Prior to the June meeting, the conference's name was the subject of much discussion and frivolity among sports fans. Almost countless names were tossed about. Jim Tatum joked that the conference should be called the T–Formation Conference, because no one in the new conference played the single wing.[93] Frank Howard, one of the last to hold on to the single wing, may have wanted to say something about Tatum's suggestion. Some wanted to call the league the Mid–South or the Rebel Conference, while others supported the Colonial Conference.[94] Smith Barrier preferred Mid–South as the name, but he enjoyed tossing around lots of ideas from his readers and friends. Barrier's brother suggested the Rebel Yell Conference.[95] Some liked Great South and others preferred Dixie, although there already was a Dixie Conference.[96] It was Eddie Cameron who proposed the name Atlantic Coast Conference. It had a pleasing sound and a progressive feel that was needed in the South during the 1950s. In addition, it offered an easy abbreviation that only had competition from Atlantic Christian College (now Barton University) in Wilson, North Carolina. Atlantic Christian, though, was a small Disciples of Christ institution that played in the North Carolina Athletic Conference, with the likes of Elon and Appalachian State. Most in the state were unfamiliar with the school.

Scheduling opponents had been one of the principal problems among Southern Conference schools and the same issue held potential to derail the new league. As mentioned earlier, Duke's football prominence, far exceeding that of its brethren, save Maryland, meant that the Blue Devils desired to retain more flexibility in scheduling that held the potential to be compromised by playing mandatory dates against conference teams. Charles Jordan, secretary of Duke University and a Duke undergraduate and law graduate, adamantly conveyed these sentiments near the beginning of the June 14 organizational meeting. In a letter to his friend Oliver Cornwell, but blind copied to Edens and Cameron, Jordan was profoundly concerned that the minutes reflect Duke's scheduling position. "Our being a member of the conference is contingent on the accurate incorporation in the minutes of the agreement that member institutions must play five other members of the Conference annually while there is a seven-member Conference and six if and when there is an eight-member Conference and must play every other member of the Conference within a span of three years but not all of them in any given year."[97] Duke's position was in conflict with how others interpreted the direction of the new conference. Most schools believed the new conference would ease scheduling and reduce costs, but Duke had other ideas. Playing only five or six games with conference opponents was not a popular idea at the other colleges, because it would mean that the new conference would have the same problem establishing a conference champion that had plagued the Southern Conference for years. Ultimately, Duke was going to have to decide if it wanted this conference affiliation or its freedom to schedule football games. Both were not in the offering.

Two weeks prior to the June conference meeting scheduled for Raleigh, the athletic directors of the seven seceding schools met at Hope Valley Country Club in Durham on May 26. Like Sedgefield, Hope Valley, home to many Duke administrators and alumni, was another Donald Ross designed course; however, Ross had a hand in planning the community around the course as well. In the luxurious surroundings of the 1926 clubhouse, the athletic directors discussed the addition of an eighth member. West Virginia appeared to be the choice as the eighth member, because Virginia had been aloof,

Duke athletic director Eddie Cameron, pictured in the late 1930s or early 1940s on the field at Duke Stadium, later Wallace Wade Stadium, was the cornerstone of Duke athletics, serving as a coach and an administrator for 47 years (courtesy Sports Information Office: Photographic Negatives Collection, David M. Rubenstein Rare Book and Manuscript Library, Duke University).

not showing its hand. As the *Daily Progress* had explained, Virginia's glacial movement had rubbed conference members the wrong way. It was rumored that Legs Hawley was so popular that he would be able to overcome West Virginia's distance and isolation by his magnetism.[98] There was a reason to believe this, because Legs, who had spent almost his entire life on the Morgantown campus, was beloved by everyone.

Feeling the pressure mounting on Virginia, Gus Tebell tried to keep Virginia in the forefront, without fully committing the Cavaliers to membership. "Personally I'm in favor of joining this new group. I feel we'll be better off in this conference, or in any other major conference for that matter."[99] Virginia had not received a formal invitation from the new conference, although Tebell emphasized the long football series with North Carolina as well as games with Duke, South Carolina, and Maryland.[100]

On Saturday June 1, Virginia's Athletic Council met to discuss conference membership. Unfortunately, the council "took a 'definite stand'" as to conference membership, without indicating the nature of the stand.[101] Although it was rumored that the council supported membership, it was this type of veiled language that annoyed and frustrated members in the new conference. The *Washington Post* reported that the Board of Visitors would meet on June 12 to discuss joining the league, a move favored by Virginia's new football coach, Ned McDonald.[102] McDonald would have difficulty keeping the Cavaliers on the winning side of the ledger.

The First Conference Meeting

As scheduled, the new conference met at the Sir Walter Hotel, in the middle of Big Four country. Soon after its opening in 1924, the Sir Walter earned a reputation as the meeting place for North Carolina politicians and businessmen when they were in Raleigh. Located on Fayetteville Street, the Sir Walter was a landmark featuring elegant dining, an impressive lobby, and a neon sign on the roof. It was the natural location to begin the serious work of this new North Carolina centric conference, a reality with which Clemson, South Carolina, and Maryland later would struggle.

The meeting in Raleigh, over the same weekend that Ben Hogan won the U.S. Open at Oakmont, was attended by only three presidents, but it was important that Gordon Gray and Curly Byrd were present along with State's John Harrelson and his soon to be heir Carey Bostian. The athletic leaders, faculty athletic representatives, and these three presidents settled a number of issues, but the question of an eighth member remained pressing. Although rumors abounded about Virginia joining the ACC, the gathering in Raleigh settled nothing. In the morning, Jim Penney, feeling the media pressure, said, "I sure would like to see Gus Tebell walk in here right now."[103] Virginia did not send a representative to the meeting, although Gus Tebell had given indications that he was going to attend. Tebell, however, missed the conference meeting to see off his son who was leaving for Korea. At any rate, Virginia did not send a representative to replace Tebell, an act interpreted as in bad form. West Virginia had no one in Raleigh either, certainly a mistake. When asked about the status of Virginia, Jim Penney provided a simple "no comment."[104] It was believed that Virginia's Board of Visitors had voted to join the new conference on Friday, June 12, but there was no confirmation. On the phone, however, Gus Tebell would not commit, saying that the board would decide if Virginia were invited.[105] In fact, the board had made no commitment to reject or join the league. They had only heard a recommendation from Tebell and Virginia's Athletic Council to claim membership.[106]

Although indications pointed to Virginia eventually joining the conference, there was not unanimous support for the Cavaliers. Bob Brooks in the *News and Observer* reported, "At least two of the seven seceders—State and South Carolina—are known to prefer them [Virginia Tech] over Virginia."[107] State may have favored Virginia Tech, because of the similarity between the two schools, but it was hard to see State not agreeing with Chapel Hill on Virginia. Even the University of Georgia and the University of Florida had their names indirectly floated for membership. Both schools, it was alleged, had difficulties within the Southeastern Conference that compelled them to join the ACC. Pennsylvania continued to be a wildcard in the process, with its frosty relationship with the other Ivy League members. Although eight felt like the right number of teams for a conference, there were discussions about expansion beyond that number.[108]

To no one's surprise, expansion was proposed at the Raleigh meeting. North Carolina's A.W. Hobbs moved that Virginia be extended membership in the league with a second, not unexpectedly, from Duke's Charles Jordan. Most likely, Duke and North Carolina had cooperated to bring Virginia's membership to the table. The motion passed and the procedures for inviting Virginia to join were left to Jim Penney and Eddie Cameron.[109] Hobbs made a motion that Virginia Tech and West Virginia be invited, but it was not voted upon, due to the lack of a second.[110] Representatives wanted to vote on the schools individually, not in tandem.

Meeting in May, the athletic directors agreed to a recommendation about football scheduling. Wishing for the league to play all members but conceding to Duke's desires, the conference voted for the following: "Should the Conference remain with seven members, each shall play five others in conference football no later than 1956. Should the Conference become eight, each school shall play at least six other members, beginning not later than 1957. Each school must play each other school at least once each three years."[111] Chuck Erickson moved that this be passed, and Eddie Cameron seconded it without hesitation.[112] Most likely, the two schools had again worked together to make sure this wording, which Duke desired so very much, would be in place.

Basketball scheduling proved to be more difficult, because Maryland had so very few conference teams on its schedule. That being the case, a full slate of basketball games was not to take place until the 1954–1955 season. For the 1953–1954 season, there would be an inconsistent number of conference games, with the number one regular season squad seeded first, and the remaining schools placed by a draw. If the conference had eight members, seeding would be based on regular season finish. The winner of the tournament, to be held at Reynolds Coliseum, would be the NCAA participant, in hopes of continuing the excitement that had been created by the Southern Conference Tournament.[113] In the following season, all schools would play each other twice per year.

Importantly, conference leadership was officially elected. Jim Penney, whose train to Raleigh was delayed by signal problems, was the first president and Forrest Clonts of Wake Forest, missing the meeting because of a vacation, was tapped as vice president. North Carolina's Oliver Cornwell was selected as secretary-treasurer. One of Cornwell's first duties was to send notification of the new conference to the NCAA. These selections were not a surprise considering how effectively they navigated the secession in May.

Realizing that the new conference needed a strong public relations office, the conference moved quickly to establish a public relations committee. Jim Penney announced that Rex Enright was the chair of the five-man body that included Forrest Clonts, Brent Beedin from Clemson, Ted Man from Duke, and Joe Blair of Maryland.[114]

The league decided to hold its next meeting on neutral territory at the King Cotton Hotel in Greensboro on August 7 and 8. Beginning in 1955, the King Cotton was the ACC's home for many years under the leadership of future commissioner Jim Weaver. This was another early indication that North Carolina schools were going to be influential in the league's operations.

Throughout the meeting held in the Roanoke Room, the central matter was never decided. Gus Tebell was not present, and there was no reason to attempt to finalize several policies when the eighth conference member was not decided. Furthermore, Virginia did not send a replacement for Tebell, encouraging some to believe that the Cavaliers simply were not dedicated to joining the new conference like the seceding seven had been. The meeting adjourned early, chiefly because of the questions surrounding an eighth member.

According to Smith Barrier, tranquility did not reign at the June meeting. Unlike the Southern Conference gatherings where sportswriters attended meetings and deliberations, the ACC went into executive session, barring the scribes. Barrier remarked as well that Duke was the source of most controversy. The Blue Devils were the last to join, he believed, and were now impediments to football and basketball scheduling. Barrier remarked that by the watercooler, it was common to call "the Blue Devils names."[115]

There was a level of truth to the Blue Devil intransigence. The last school to provide authorization for membership in the new conference was Duke. Charles Jordan insisted that Duke would not provide membership authorization until the scheduling issue was resolved.[116] Duke, though, had leverage because their football program had a long history of success. With the scheduling arrangement to Duke's liking, Charles Jordan announced that Duke would file its conference membership authorization immediately.[117] It was the last of the seven seceders to officially join the ACC. Duke strong-armed the league before it officially was a member.

Meanwhile, football scheduling had a great deal of urgency, because the season was close on the horizon. Duke was interested in maintaining its "big" games with national powers, but Pennsylvania and Texas had pulled out of future scheduled contests. North Carolina had five conference games scheduled and would have a sixth if Virginia were to join the league. Duke's schedule did not include Maryland or Clemson. Wake Forest excluded Virginia and Maryland from their slate. Some schools could arrange only three conference games. They included State, Clemson, and Maryland. No championship could be awarded in a situation like this, although plenty of schools would wish to line up and claim it.

The Eighth Member?

Some believed that the August 7 and 8 meeting at Sedgefield Country Club would announce Virginia as the eighth member or the Cavaliers would be omitted from consideration. Patience was running thin when Duke football Coach Bill Murray, in Richmond on July 22, remarked that the ACC "needs Virginia 'very badly.'"[118] Murray's comments rankled some members of the conference who were weary of the intransigence and had less enthusiasm for bringing in a school that seemed very aloof from its peers.

Virginia's football coach Ned McDonald, speaking before the Sportsmen's Club at the Hotel Richmond, strongly advocated for Virginia's membership in the ACC. Although he had not coached a down as the head man, McDonald urged that the Cavaliers risked a decline in their football opportunities if they failed to join the league. Rightfully, he feared that Virginia would struggle to secure in-state players if they remained an independent.[119] McDonald did not have the pull of Art Guepe, though.

Unknown to the public, Virginia's Athletic Council rapidly embraced the ACC opportunity. In a meeting on May 30, 1953, Gus Tebell explained to the council that Virginia had played no role in the Southern Conference split but expressed that a "standing invitation" was proctored to Virginia for membership.[120] He outlined a long list of reasons why Virginia needed to become the eighth member. Basically, Tebell and the committee believed that it was a disadvantage for Virginia to stand alone and by joining the new league, they could assist in forming policies and procedures in line with their values and with schools who viewed athletics in a similar manner. Scheduling would be made much easier and the prestige of being associated with other prominent schools was appealing. Another key benefit was the economic prosperity that seemed almost inevitable from a strong eight-team league.[121]

After much discussion about this opportunity, Gaston Moffatt, chair of the committee and professor of romance languages, proposed that the council go on record favoring membership in the ACC. Moffatt's motion was unanimously approved by the council, providing a strong statement in favor of joining the league.[122]

According to Julian Scheer at the *Charlotte News*, and well known within Virginia's administration, Colgate Darden was the problem. Scheer reported that there was consensus at Virginia that they needed to join the ACC, but Darden was not convinced. He remained on the fence even after visiting Duke and UNC to discuss ACC membership.[123] It was up to Gus Tebell to convince Darden that if Virginia did not join the conference and if they refused to increase their financial support for athletes, the Cavaliers would be left behind. There was no bigger proponent for joining the ACC than Tebell.

During the summer, West Virginia appeared to have as much support as Virginia, especially because the Mountaineers were excited about being the eighth member, something that Virginia had not demonstrated. In *The Charlotte Observer*, Dick Pierce summed it up nicely.

> If the Atlantic Coast Conference wants a member of guaranteed loyalty, and one that will certainly be and stay in keeping with whatever athletic level that might eventually evolve, they couldn't go wrong with West Virginia. The Mountaineers are gassed up with high octane material, most of it good for two or three years of service, and it seems a shame to turn Art Lewis and Red Brown loose on the piddling competition left for them in the Southern. George Washington, Richmond, and Furman may give some basketball opposition, and ambitious VPI is coming in football, but will they last now that the spur of keeping up with the departed seven is removed?[124]

Pierce was right in his judgment. There was much more enthusiasm for West Virginia, but Morgantown's location continued to be the one drawback that the Mountaineers could not overcome. Although the city had a population of 22,525 in 1950, its location in the northeast corner of the state was a serious travel problem in the pre-interstate days.

Nevertheless, West Virginia had a great deal going for it, more than Virginia and Virginia Tech. Their basketball program had been strong for many years and football was no slouch either. In 1950, West Virginia hired Art Lewis as its football coach. Pappy, as he was called, reversed several years of mediocre performance, bringing the Mountaineers a 7–2 season in 1952, which included a thrilling victory over the 18th ranked Pittsburgh Panthers, West Virginia's first victory over a ranked opponent. The Mountaineers routed Pittsburgh 16–0 at Pitt Stadium, elevating West Virginia football to a position it had not often achieved. Combined with winning were Lewis's popularity and his reputation as a tireless recruiter.

Basketball coach Red Brown had continued the winning tradition of Coach Lee Paton, who in 1950 died of complications from injuries sustained in an automobile accident. Paton fielded strong clubs and from 1945 to 1950 went 91–26. Red Brown, a native West Virginian, led the Mountaineers to a 15–1 record in conference and a 23–4 overall record in 1952. West Virginia won the regular season Southern Conference Championship but lost a controversial game to Duke 90–88 in the conference tournament semi-finals.

In the summer of 1953, West Virginia had far more to brag about athletically than did Virginia or Virginia Tech. The future was also much brighter for West Virginia with Red Brown and Art Lewis leading their highest profile teams. In comparison, Evan Male led the Cavalier basketball team to a 10–13 record in 1952–1953. The previous year, Virginia had recorded only 11 victories. Although the well-liked Gus Tebell had been the head basketball coach for 21 years, he never coached powerful clubs. West Virginia had a better athletic program than Virginia.

On the gridiron, Virginia was enjoying a golden age under coach Art Guepe. His 1952 squad went 8–2, losing only to Duke and South Carolina on consecutive weekends, but Guepe resigned after the 1952 season to take the head position at Vanderbilt. Although his record in Charlottesville was an outstanding 47–17–2, there was little reason to think his successor, Ned McDonald, could sustain this success. Before Guepe, Virginia never had won consistently on the gridiron. Guepe was a spectacular coach while leading the Cavaliers, but until the 1980s when George Welsh took the helm, his era of success was an aberration.

Although Charlottesville only had 25,969 people in 1950, it was not a remote location. There were good roads that connected it to Richmond and Washington. Likewise, its proximity to Maryland and the North Carolina schools made it more attractive.

Virginia Tech received fewer mentions as a front-runner for the ACC's next member. Blacksburg was almost as remote as Morgantown. With a 1950 population of only 3,358, Blacksburg was a small town in the mountains of southwestern Virginia. Roanoke was the only significant population center nearby, enjoying a population of over 90,000 at mid-century. In December 1951, Virginia Tech president Walter S. Newman admitted, "The school's remoteness ... was an important factor in Tech's disastrous football fortunes."[125] Newman had little interest in elevating the football program to the level of the major powers, commenting that Virginia Tech should be in a position to win "about half the games they play."[126] These were the type of comments that would not have impressed conference leaders such as Curly Byrd and Jim Tatum.

Frank Moseley's football Hokies had been worse than West Virginia and Virginia. Tech had finished the 1952 season with a 5–6 record. This was a great improvement on the two-win 1951 campaign, Moseley's first. These were remarkable improvements on the 0–8 1950 season, when Tech was toothless. These weak records conspired to work against Tech's hopes to join the new league. There was not much on which to base hope for consistently successful football campaigns.

On the hardcourt, Tech had posted a woeful 4–18 record under coach Red Laird. The former Davidson headman only won four games the previous season as well. Perhaps some of those struggles can be forgiven, because Virginia Tech had Laird coaching baseball and basketball simultaneously, a clear indication that the athletic program was not a top priority.

If the judgment were made on future potential, West Virginia was the clear favorite. Tech trailed far behind the Mountaineers and the loss of Art Guepe at Virginia signaled that their winning football seasons most likely would be a distant memory in a few years. The school had an impressive 33,000-seat horseshoe football stadium and a 6,000-seat field house, the third largest in the Southern Conference, demonstrating its commitment to major college athletics. The Mountaineers were regular rivals of Pittsburgh and Penn State, but in a few years of competition there would be strong rivalries with schools in the ACC.

Enhancing their case for membership was West Virginia's charismatic leadership. A Bluefield, West Virginia, native, Legs Hawley starred as an athlete at West Virginia before taking the AD reins in 1935. He was one of the driving forces that built the Mountaineers into a football and basketball power. If the selection of an eighth member was made on athletic success and the popularity of the athletic director, the Mountaineers were a shoo-in.[127]

Unfortunately for West Virginia and Virginia Tech, Hollis Edens and Gordon Gray had a solid and long-term relationship with Virginia's Colgate Darden. It was their plan all along to bring Virginia into the new conference. As mentioned, Darden had attended Southern Conference meetings, and the Charlottesville school was viewed as more prestigious than West Virginia or Virginia Tech.

Nevertheless, by late July, the UVA membership saga was as vague as it ever was. Speaking to the press on July 22, Colgate Darden sounded doubtful, saying, "Right now I can't see how we can do anything the other Virginia institutions don't do."[128] Virginia was being pressured to remain involved with its long-standing rivals such as Washington and Lee, Richmond, and Virginia Military Institute. Under the new football guidelines approved by the ACC in June, it would be unable to play these schools on a yearly basis; however, if the lion's share of them remained in the Southern Conference, Virginia could seek membership there and retain its rivalries in a conference format. The Southern Conference, however, had voted to remain at 10 members, thus forcing Virginia's hand on ACC affiliation, but the Southern Conference was open to Virginia joining the league. Darden did not believe that Virginia would have a decision by the scheduled August 7 and 8 meeting of the ACC. Virginia's Board of Visitors would not meet again until the last Friday in August, making any decision to join the new league before the start of football season seemingly impossible.[129]

What was taking so long for Virginia to make a commitment? It started with Colgate Darden. Although Darden was invited to many Southern Conference gatherings and Virginia played several Southern Conference schools, the former governor was deeply attached to the Commonwealth of Virginia's broader interests. Darden had only been out of the governor's mansion since 1946. His view of the Charlottesville university was focused on how it could serve the entire state, a position he encouraged while serving as president. As historian John S. Watterson wrote, "Darden strongly opposed joining the ACC or even re-affiliating with the Southern Conference."[130] Darden, though, was out of step with many Virginia supporters who viewed conference affiliation as an important addition to the university's athletic program.

With pressure to join the ACC coming from many fronts, Darden was being lobbied by Walter Newman at Tech and Irvin Stewart at West Virginia. At the end of June, Walter Newman visited Charlottesville and spoke about conference matters with Colgate Darden for an hour. Newman hoped that Virginia would stand with West Virginia and Virginia Tech "to take unified action regarding our place in any conference, or outside any conference."[131] Newman concluded that Darden did not wish to join the ACC and was planning to speak with some board members about subscribing to the Southern Conference, as long as West Virginia and Virginia Tech remained members. Unfortunately for West Virginia and Virginia Tech, the attempt to craft a united front never gained traction.

Darden was acting like the governor and not the president of the University of Virginia. The Associated Press asked if Virginia and Virginia Tech would join the conference together. Speculation was widespread that Virginia was having difficulty deciding to join the ACC as the only member institution from Virginia.[132] To help Tech's position, Virginia Tech's football coach, Frank Moseley, campaigned for membership in the new league.[133]

Shelley Rolfe broached the idea as well, noting that Colgate Darden had voiced concern about the athletic fates of other Virginia schools, if UVA joined the ACC. Rolfe rightly believed that Darden and Walter Newman had discussed athletics a few weeks earlier. If that were the case, perhaps Virginia would only join the league if Tech came along as well.[134] These were rumors, but without any clear communication from Virginia and Colgate Darden, the future of the eighth member of the conference remained a mystery.

The Board of Visitors met on September 11 to discuss conference affiliation. Unsurprisingly, the board failed to agree on joining the ACC.[135] Instead, another month of delay was at hand. Nevertheless, it appeared that momentum for joining the league was growing, and the excitement brought on by football could influence Virginia's administrators.

Southern Conference's Future

Having lost seven of its members, the Southern Conference needed to reorganize and move forward. The conference officially met at the grand Hotel Roanoke in Roanoke, Virginia, on June 27, 1953, to chart their future. Meetings began on Thursday and Friday in preparation for the Saturday conference meeting. On Thursday, the basketball committee, which managed the tournament, the chief source for revenue, met to discuss the future. With the financial success of the conference tournament even more important than before, the committee could not make a decision that evening. Richmond, Lynchburg, and Greenville, South Carolina, were considered as potential host cities, but none of these could compete with the loss of Reynolds Coliseum in Raleigh.[136] Of the three, Greenville appeared to be a long shot, especially with Virginia schools now dominating conference membership.

With the split, the Virginia schools began to think that visiting Furman, The Citadel, and Davidson was a hassle. The conference now was centered on Virginia.[137] Although some schools had expressed interest in joining the Southern Conference, the conference voted not to expand their membership. That left institutions such as Florida State, Wofford, East Carolina, Emory and Henry and even Presbyterian College, all of which had shown interest in joining the league, outside of the conference.[138] Wofford College went as far as to send head football coach Conley Snidow to Roanoke to represent the Terriers. Also sending a representative for Saturday was Florida State. The Tallahassee school was eager to join but the travel was cost prohibitive for Virginia schools and George Washington.[139] It was even rumored that The Citadel, Davidson, and Furman would be asked to withdraw from the conference, because they were too far from the remaining five Virginia schools and George Washington, but the by-laws only allowed for expulsion if schools had made egregious violations.[140] With expansion settled, freshman participation rose to the forefront, as it had done for years. Although the Southern Conference football coaches recommended freshman participation on varsity teams, the conference rejected the proposal. Conference leaders believed they had no choice but to ban freshman participation, because opening the door to freshmen was an admission that some schools in their league did not have enough players to compete with major programs. Although that was true, the conference knew it was in the precarious position of slipping behind its peers. Image was important. Lastly, the conference established a committee to study bowl participation, the hot-button topic of previous years.[141]

The Roanoke meeting was filled with anxiety. The largest question facing the league was future stability, and it was tied to West Virginia's fate. The Mountaineers, as we have seen, had a large and successful athletic program and rumors swirled about how long they would remain in the Southern Conference. Would West Virginia return to independent status, with the Southern Conference's big-league image dimming? Although the Mountaineers had pledged their loyalty to the league, everyone knew that they would bolt to the ACC if given the chance.[142] With West Virginia being the linchpin for stability, it seemed destined that the basketball tournament would be played in Morgantown. They had the biggest facility, holding 6,000, a rabid fan base, and they needed placating to remain in the league.

Although the conference had voted to remain with 10 teams, Harold Wimmer thought that the Mountaineers might last less than one more year in the Southern Conference, because they aspired to continue to compete on the level of Pittsburgh and Penn State and not The Citadel or Davidson. West Virginia very much viewed itself, and rightfully so, as a football school.[143] There was real pain in Morgantown, but Wimmer remained hopeful that an invitation to the ACC was coming.

Most Virginia Tech graduates wanted to secede from the Southern Conference, longing for an ACC offer to materialize. Even if they were not invited these alumni were happy to tread the path of an independent, until a good offer was at hand. There was little interest in remaining a part of the Southern Conference. Some believed that Southern Conference membership would harm Tech's athletic aspirations.[144] There was a sense that Tech ran the risk of falling well behind its peer schools, if it kept playing a large number of small private institutions.

As if campaigning for league division had not been enough to harm the Southern Conference, Curly Byrd struck again by stealing the thunder from the Roanoke meeting. Publicly announcing a secret that everyone knew, Byrd declared that he would resign his position as president of the University of Maryland effective January 1, 1955. Byrd was determined to be the next governor of Maryland, although that announcement was yet to be made. The Maryland president, with his powerful Terrapin football team under Jim Tatum, was one of the catalysts for secession and now he had stolen headlines from the remaining 10 in the Southern Conference.

August at Sedgefield

The June meeting in Raleigh was followed by an August 7 meeting at the Sedgefield Inn, site of the secession. As expected, bowl games were the subject of much discussion, but the new conference charted a new course away from the Southern Conference. Now that Gray had softened his stance on bowl participation, a compromise could be reached. In the context of impending bowl acceptance, Bob House urged that no ACC school be forced to participate in bowls, and that schools should not profit from their participation. House added that players should not be paid for playing in bowls.[145]

Geary Eppley followed by presenting a motion allowing ACC members to participate in bowls "according to the criteria established by the NCAA and other limitations set up by the conference."[146] With H.A. Fisher's second, the motion passed. Bowls were now part of the conference.

If bowls were to be allowed, financial compensation needed resolution. The conference approved, "The team participating will receive ½ the team share of the game receipts, that of the remaining ½ twenty five (25%) percent will go to the Conference and seventy five percent (75%) will be divided equally among the other members of the Conference."[147] For the upcoming season, the conference members would determine who represented the ACC in post-season play.[148] This selection would be governed by a conference post season committee comprised of one faculty chair and two athletic directors appointed by the president of the ACC.[149] After the events of September 1951, it was startling that the vote to approve bowl participation, sponsored by Maryland's Swede Eppley and seconded by State's Fisher, was unanimously approved by a voice vote.[150]

It was surprising how quickly league members had changed their views on bowl participation. The January 1953 NCAA meeting may have led some to alter their position on post-season games, because the NCAA committee on extra events had issued a report, unanimously supported by the NCAA member schools, that endorsed bowl games. None of the Southern Conference schools voted in opposition when attending the NCAA meeting.[151] The NCAA vote demonstrated that the Southern Conference's attempts to ban bowl game participation were out of step with national opinion. Now, whether out of sentiment for unity or financial need, the ACC was declaring itself to be fully aboard with bowl games, further distancing the league from the Southern Conference.

The conference members tackled the never-ending saga of freshman participation, agreeing to allow freshman to begin practice on September 5.[152] This proposal from Clemson's Lee Milford only papered over the essential problem of freshman participation in football and all athletics. To most academics, it was a serious question of academics versus athletics, with faculty believing that an athlete needed academic seasoning before playing varsity sports.

No meeting of the new ACC was complete without reexamining the question of an eighth member. Bob House desired that Virginia be reserved the spot as the next member, but he believed that Virginia Tech and West Virginia deserved consideration as well. "Mr Eppley stated that the problem of V.P.I. and West Virginia would have to be discussed with the administrative heads of the respective institutions."[153] The problem referenced by Geary Eppley could have been a number of things, from the location of these schools to concerns about exceeding eight members.

The ACC chose to stand by its decisions made at the June meeting in Raleigh and function with the current seven members until May 1954.[154] It appeared that this final approved motion from Clemson would end the debate about the eighth member until after the conference had operated for one year. The saga for an additional member, however, was far from finished. The more immediate concern for the new conference leaders was allegations of rules violations at State.

Probation for Wolfpack Basketball

Corruption has never been far from college athletics and only three months into its existence, the conference was dealing with allegations against the Wolfpack's highly successful basketball program. Jerry Weber, a six-foot, eleven-inch high school basketball star from Cincinnati, alleged that he and 14 others had attended a tryout at State College. Weber declined to attend State, instead deciding to join with Adolf Rupp and Kentucky. It was rumored that Rupp, wary of Case's success in Raleigh, turned in the Wolfpack to the NCAA. Although Rupp's involvement was unclear, Lennie Rosenbluth, a future great at North Carolina, had been one of the 14 players that Case had on campus for tryouts.[155]

According H.A. Fisher, the no tryout rule was very unpopular and widely abused or tweaked by coaches. Fisher asked Everett Case to pen a formal response to the NCAA allegations. Regarding the recruitment of Lennie Rosenbluth, whom he called "Lennis" in the letter, Case said that Jack Rosenbluth, his father, drove him down to Raleigh using his own money. Case examined Rosenbluth's transcript and told father and son that he did not have the grades to enter State and suggested summer school or pep school. He maintained that there were no workouts and nothing untoward happened.[156]

Case admitted that it was an alumnus who sent the plane ticket to Jerry Weber and others. Weber was one of 12 players who visited State's campus on May 1 and 2. These included Robert Price, Paul Underwood, Rod Hundley, Leonard Califano, John Kovarovic, Ronald Terwilliger, Alvin Serkin, Ronnie Mazelli, John Seival, Jim Mitchell, and Robert Lakatta. The State alumnus contacted each of the players and sent them tickets.[157]

Case admitted that the school had been paying for prospective athletes to visit, at least since 1949, but this was known by all in the athletic department and the administration and was in the budget. After reading Case's comments about a budget for paying travel expenses for prospective athletes, Harrelson said that there was no money to his knowledge in the budget for this. The money was for staff travel and scouting.[158] Harrelson was right to be surprised. There was no such budget; it was an ill-founded tradition at State.

With Wallace Wade inquiring about the allegations, Fisher and the athletic council conducted a thorough investigation into what happened. Travel cards, approved travel documents, were given to coaches to pay for tickets for prospective athletes. The alumnus was to reimburse the athletic department for travel. "Coach Case's claim that prospective athletes stayed over for practice during Alumni Week festivities for certain all-star games in the area from which they came apparently has some validity. However, the committee believes that this procedure violated the spirit of the NCAA regulations."[159] The athletic committee believed that these rules were regularly violated throughout the country, but they did not deny that State had broken rules.

Case's blame was mitigated a little when he explained that his assistant coaches, Carl "Butter" Anderson and Vic Bubas, led the "scrimmage." Using the term scrimmage instead of tryout was an important distinction. Case sat in the stands. The potential State players competed against "college freshmen, varsity, intra-mural, and football players."[160]

Allegations against State hijacked the meeting at Sedgefield, temporarily surpassing the eighth member discussion. The Wolfpack faced charges of "holding try-outs for basketball players, using Athletic Association funds to pay transportation expenses for prospective athletes visiting N.C. State campus" and providing "grants-in-aid or scholarships to athletes that exceeded the amount allowed under N.C.A.A. and Atlantic Coast Conference rules and regulations."[161] Ultimately, State and the ACC concluded that tryouts were held and that athletic association money was used to pay for players to visit the Raleigh campus. The last of the charges could not be proven by the conference or the school. State was placed on one-year probation by the conference, and any player involved in the proven charges was banned from participating in Wolfpack athletics.[162] This included Rosenbluth, who later starred for Frank McGuire at UNC. The Wolfpack had the ignoble distinction of being the first Atlantic Coast Conference member sanctioned by the conference for violating NCAA and ACC regulations.

Gordon Gray was alerted to the situation at State over the summer. He was profoundly concerned that the athletic programs at UNC and State follow NCAA and conference regulations and that violations be harshly condemned, with mechanisms put in place to prevent violations.[163] On July 3, 1953, Gray issued a directive calling for the AD to hold monthly meetings of all coaching staffs to make sure that all conference and NCAA rules were followed. Each system president had to write Gray once a month stating that they were in compliance. The president and the chancellors were charged with attending each athletic department meeting at the beginning of each school year. Consistent focus on conference and NCAA rules was underscored.[164] Gray's zealotry was clear throughout the memo, and considering some of the problems at State, he treated Harrelson a bit like a child, as if he could not keep his house in order. This was unfair, because State was fortunate to have a man of Harrelson's abilities, even though he was in his last year in office.

Smith Barrier, echoing the comments of other sportswriters, pointed out that State was caught doing what many others regularly did, and tryouts were even worse in football than basketball. Barrier suggested that other schools should be a bit wary of what happened to State, considering how prevalent these tryouts were.[165]

The conference, most likely, hit State with more authority than a conference usually would, considering tryouts were very common, because the stakes were high for the new conference. If the NCAA decided to provide additional sanctions, the lucrative conference tournament could come into question and the league's most outstanding basketball program could be in jeopardy. The basketball tournament revenue stream was essential, if the conference was going to be a financial success. Furthermore, the scandal ridden previous years, which included point shaving in basketball, meant that State had to be punished.

The conference did not make public additional allegations that State had provided financial incentives for Ronnie Shavlik to play for the Wolfpack, including travel and even a country club membership. Shavlik was a Denver, Colorado, basketball star that every school wanted. The six-foot, nine-inch player chose the Wolfpack over Kentucky and became a sensation on State's freshman squad. The freshman team was an outstanding group, and Shavlik was quickly the star. There was enormous anticipation for Shavlik to play on the varsity team.

Shavlik denied all allegations, and even provided a written refutation of the charges. Fisher concluded that "Coach Case claims an alumnus in Denver made arrangement to send Shavlik to State College."[166] There were no special payments or gifts provided to Shavlik.

Where had all these charges originated? A conference school had told Wallace Wade about a tryout and referenced a report in the March 15, 1953, *Richmond Times-Dispatch*.[167] Because of State's increasing basketball prominence, some believed that almost all charges went back to Adolf Rupp at Kentucky. Regardless, all of this demonstrated the high stakes world of recruiting that most of the college presidents, academic leaders, and a few coaches loudly condemned. Recruiting was damaging collegiate competition.

Finally, an Eighth Member

With only seven conference members and Virginia frustratingly dragging its feet, Mississippi Southern College (later University of Southern Mississippi) made a direct appeal for conference membership.[168] Until 1952, Mississippi Southern was a member of the Gulf States Conference, a new league formed in 1948.[169] In 1953, the Hattiesburg school was looking for a new conference with more competitive teams to join, but it was almost unknown to ACC schools and much too far away to be considered for membership. No one was interested in taking a long trip to Southern Mississippi for ball games and with the focus being in part on travel costs, the Hattiesburg school had no chance of gaining membership.

Before the conference even had a name, the University of Miami and Florida State had sent feelers about joining the new league.[170] Both schools were independents, with Florida State having left the Dixie Conference in 1950. Like Mississippi Southern, the Florida schools were too far away to warrant consideration and were well behind more traditional opponents located closer to the core of ACC country.

Knowing they were the favorite, Virginia remained noncommittal to the ACC. Although the athletic council had endorsed conference membership, they were compelled, again, to consider the pros and cons of joining the league. A long list of potential negative effects was drafted to contrast with the positive effects that they discussed in May. It is unclear who penned the list of reasons for remaining out of the ACC, but they included an equally long list of justifications. The most important of them argued that Virginia had no significant relationship with Wake Forest, State, Clemson, or Maryland, and that joining the league could have deleterious effects on their long-standing relationships with the other Virginia schools. There was concern about Virginia keeping pace with some of the ACC's athletic programs as well as the league's new position on bowls. Darden had taken a strong stance against bowl participation. There even was apprehension that other sports would suffer with the conference emphasizing football.[171]

The airing of these potential negative consequences did nothing to sway the athletic council from its original opinion. The members took another vote and unanimously reaffirmed their recommendation for the Cavaliers to sign up with the ACC. This was a powerful statement that the Board of Visitors would have difficulty opposing.

The saga of the eighth conference member finally reached its conclusion on October 9, 1953, during the football season. As if there had not been enough debate on the issue, it required a four-hour meeting of Virginia's Board of Visitors. The deliberations were revealing in many ways, especially as to their opinions of other schools as well as conflicting ambitions for Virginia. Alumni chapters in Washington and Maryland were strongly opposed to joining the ACC because of their dislike of the University of Maryland, believing that the Terrapins were corrupt and scandalous in their football obsession. When asked how he felt about playing Maryland, Virginia's Mortimer Caplan, head of the athletic council, humorously remarked, "I don't think we would be contaminated by one game a year."[172] Tebell stressed that Virginia had good relations with Maryland in all the sports in which they played, but added that the view towards Maryland was based on "its ruthless attitude in building a football team."[173] Tebell was optimistic that Maryland would improve its football reputation when the new academic administration came aboard upon the departure of the controversial Curly Byrd.

Some board members had difficulty understanding that Virginia's independence was working against the school. Duke had told Maryland that they would not schedule the Cavaliers until Virginia decided about the ACC. Some on the board wished Virginia to join the Ivy League, something that was impossible, and well out of step with alumni and boosters. They were condescending toward most of the ACC members, viewing Virginia more like New England schools. Those envious of the Ivy League desired more games with Ivy League

Virginia's president Colgate Darden (shown in an early, undated photograph) was wary of the role college athletics, especially football, was playing on college campuses. Darden never warmed to athletic conference affiliation (courtesy University of Virginia Visual Historical Collection, Special Collections, University of Virginia Library).

universities, but the formation of the Ivy and the demand for more money games were going to make that very difficult to achieve. Tebell noted that Virginia had not played North Carolina or Duke in basketball for 10 years, because the Southern Conference required a 14-game schedule, stressing the difficulties that were arising from Cavalier independence.[174] It was hard for an independent to schedule games in money producing sports as well as non-revenue athletics.

The last voice in the meeting was given to Colgate Darden, who argued in opposition to joining the ACC or the Southern Conference. He told the board that he was concerned about alienating Virginia's alumni in Washington and Maryland. His chief worry was that joining the league would cause division between Virginia and its long-time rivals in the state. Lastly, Darden thought that conference membership would work against his policy of attracting more public school boys of modest means to the university and its athletic programs.

During the meeting, Virginia's board, somewhat embarrassingly, discovered that the Southern Conference had a higher academic standard for its athletes than Virginia, mandating students pass 12 hours of work per semester to compete, while Virginia only required nine. They were concerned that this would be bad publicity, unless Virginia changed its academic requirements. Even with this difference, many on the board were certain that Virginia's standards were higher than those in the ACC.[175]

Frank Talbott, a board member involved in athletics and a future rector of the university, cleared the air with an excellent statement outlining the need for Virginia to join the ACC, Darden's opinion withstanding. Talbott said:

> Our athletics are commercialized whether we like it or not. If we remain aloof, we will in time be unable to schedule conference members like North Carolina. Revenues will diminish along with interest in our program.... Nor are we in a position, like Oxford and Cambridge, to ignore athletics and public relations.... The ACC approach is an admission of evils and a plan for their control. Our influence will be great in the ACC. Duke and North Carolina want us there because they respect us and want our weight on their side.[176]

Talbott was correct. The ACC was not a challenge to Virginia's academics; it was an invitation to be with like-minded schools, with perhaps a couple of exceptions. This was a grand opportunity, considering that purists would never find a landing spot in the Ivy League. Talbott correctly judged that the ACC was founded by people who wanted to run athletics the right way, and that Virginia had an opportunity to enact policies that fit its academic and athletic desires.

Objections to Talbott's position were loudly voiced, with concerns that Virginia's membership would be a replaying of its Southern Conference days and ultimately lead to its withdrawal. Some implied and even stated that Virginia followed rules while others did not and that the same would happen in the ACC. There were accusations that some of the Southern Conference schools, none named, would lower their standards or even cheat. A consistent theme in the minutes was that some board members held condescending attitudes toward other universities and colleges in a fashion not replicated by Virginia's athletic administration.

The final tally was far from convincing, with the Board of Visitors voting 6–4 in favor of joining the ACC.[177] Knowing that Virginia would accept, Jim Penney, when hearing of the vote, quickly phoned Colgate Darden at 3 p.m. to extend an official invitation for membership, which Darden accepted.[178] Virginia was a member of the league, but it was unclear when they would be part of league competition, because the conference had ruled months earlier that May 1954 would be the date for any new member to be activated. Now that Virginia was in the ACC, Tebell and others wanted the Cavaliers to participate in the spring semester, pending full conference approval at its December meeting. It was predicted that football scheduling would take until 1955 for the Cavaliers to be fully participating on the gridiron, but there were ways to include Virginia in the spring sports season.[179]

Membership was a major achievement for Gus Tebell, who for months had been lobbying to join the league. Having leaped the final hurdle for membership, Tebell with relief, said, "I consider it [league membership] a definite step forward for us in athletics."[180] It had not been an easy sell, but he was fortunate to have Hunter Faulconer, the president of the alumni association and a millionaire, on his side.[181] Faulconer was a key supporter of athletics, involved in raising financial support for athletic scholarships. The negotiations were divisive at times, but Tebell had won, even though Virginia was suffering through a winless football season. Upon gaining membership, Tebell remarked, "We are delighted. After working for it for so many years, we are very happy that the board of visitors has given its approval."[182]

Chauncey Durden was pleased and relieved that Virginia had joined the league, recognizing that membership should place the Cavaliers as the dominant sports program in the commonwealth.[183] Knowing that Curly Byrd favored the creation of a strong Maryland-Virginia rivalry, Durden expressed confidence that the Maryland president was fully satisfied with Virginia's membership.[184] Maryland needed a team closer to College Park to be perfectly happy with the new league, and now it was in place. Byrd always wanted a rivalry game between Virginia and Maryland. Furthermore, league membership only strengthened the rivalry between Virginia and North Carolina.[185]

Although Colgate Darden was not in favor of membership, he could take solace knowing that the conference did not require the champion to play in a bowl game. The Virginia president retained the right to prohibit Virginia's participation; however, in practice, this would have been extremely difficult.

The students at Virginia were in favor of league membership, and Mebane Turner, a former Cavalier guard, one year removed from the gridiron, who now was the student voice on the board, made impassioned pleas for membership at the board's previous meeting.[186] It seems that allegiance to what was best for the University of Virginia finally outweighed desires to remain with VMI and Richmond.

For the public, Max Farrington was "surprised and disappointed" that Virginia had joined the ACC. He had hoped that the Cavaliers would have remained with the Virginia schools that were in the Southern Conference. Surely, Farrington understood that the attraction of schools within the ACC was too rich for Virginia to accept a Southern Conference offer. Jim Tatum, who had been a leader in the conference's formation, was satisfied that Virginia finally had joined. It meant that there were schools in four states in the new league.[187] To sportswriters and conference officials, Virginia's membership was a welcome relief from the annoying diplomacy of the preceding months.

Ironically, George Washington and Virginia were scheduled to play a football game in Alexandria, Virginia, on October 10. This offered the Colonials an opportunity to punish the Cavaliers for declining the Southern Conference's offer of membership. To the disappointment of the Colonials, the Cavaliers scored their only victory of the season, a narrow 24–20 win. Virginia started the season with a 20–6 loss to Virginia Tech and a 19–0 loss to South Carolina. The 24 points scored on October 10 were the most Virginia would score in a single contest all year. Nevertheless, the Cavaliers were in the ACC.

Darden, though, did not give up on bringing Tech into the ACC. At the end of October, he wrote letters to Hollis Edens and Gordon Gray asking for their assistance on the Virginia Tech situation. Darden stressed to Gray that he had reports that VPI enjoyed "a good deal of support" among league members.[188] Edens' response does not exist, but Gray replied immediately and favorably, frankly asserting that he had no concerns about adding Tech. Gray understood that some had qualms about exceeding eight schools, hinting that that was the basic problem. Gray added that Bob House favored VPI's entry, but he did not know Cary Bostian's view.[189] With Harrelson's retirement, Cary Bostian was State's new chancellor. It was difficult to see Bostian opposing another land grant institution or running counter to Harrelson's favorable view towards Tech's membership.

About Face: A Bowl Contract

In late September, there was growing confidence that the ACC and the Big Seven were coming close to an agreement for their champions to play in the Orange Bowl. Eddie Cameron confirmed that the ACC Bowl Committee, which included Swede Eppley and Chuck Erickson along with Cameron, had been in negotiations with the Big Seven and the Orange Bowl.[190] The conference, perhaps chiefly for financial reasons, was eager to craft a bowl relationship and had spoken to other bowls as well. These were not confirmed, but rumors suggested they were the Sugar and Cotton Bowls.

Gradually, the Orange Bowl became the league's focus and an agreement with the Big Seven was necessary. The Big Seven sent representatives to Duke to discuss finalizing an agreement between the three partners. Meeting on October 12, representatives from the two conferences refused to make any formal announcements and were content to stand by no comment. The Big Seven sent Nebraska's Faculty Representative Earl Fulbrook and Kansas State's Athletic Council Chairman R.I. Throckmorton, along with commissioner Reeves Peters, to finalize a relationship between the three.[191]

On October 18, 1953, the Atlantic Coast Conference announced an agreement with the Big Seven and the Orange Bowl. In two years, five of the conference members had reversed course from opposing bowl games to accepting a contract for the champion to participate in one. Not yet being able to forge an official champion, the ACC members chose to vote on the deserving member to participate in the January 1 contest. Impressively, both schools who played in the game were guaranteed $110,000. In addition, the game was to be broadcast on CBS television.[192]

The Orange Bowl was eager to bring stability to its game and not be forced to select uncompetitive teams. In 1953, for example, Red Drew's Alabama destroyed a far out-classed Syracuse squad 61–6. Orange Bowl officials wanted to secure a much more competitive game, fearing a decline in fan interest. They were hopeful that this agreement helped secure the future of the Orange Bowl.

Commercialism always had been one of the charges against bowl games, and the contract with the Orange Bowl, some believed, helped reduce the commercialization of bowl games. Don Faurot of Missouri and Wallace Wade, both spoke favorably of the agreement, because they believed that colleges could effectively manage their participation in these games. Furthermore, the payout was destined to be a major benefit for the ACC.[193] The conference had few streams of revenue, beyond its basketball tournament, and ACC leaders were eager to put the conference on a strong financial footing.

Bowl Games and the Southern Conference

Meeting in Roanoke in November, the Southern Conference's Special Events Committee was scrambling to reposition itself as a leading athletic league. With West Virginia having an exceptional season and worried leaders hoping to keep the Mountaineers and the Hokies in the fold, a meeting was called for November 16 to discuss the bowl game policy. It was Sally Miles, responding to a report from the special events committee, who changed the conference's position. Instead of a sweeping decree endorsing bowl game participation, Miles proposed a conservative approach, allowing the conference's executive committee to permit bowl participation on January 1, 1954. All approved his proposal except William & Mary.[194] Regarding financial matters, Miles recommended that 25 percent of the game's revenue go to the school, and 75 percent be granted to the conference.[195] This was unanimously approved. The meeting had been long, but the Southern Conference gave West Virginia the opportunity to compete on New Year's Day.

There is little doubt that the ACC's tie with the Orange Bowl, as well the undefeated West Virginia Mountaineers, heavily influenced the Southern Conference's discussions. The league needed bowl money, because conference basketball tournament revenues were destined to decline, and it had to retain its prestige.

Before the meeting, Smith Barrier spoke with Max Farrington about the Southern Conference and the bowl ban at Congressional Country Club in Washington. When asked about bowls, Farrington commented that the leaders of the bowl ban initiative were in the ACC and no longer part of the Southern Conference. This was a jab at the well-known sentiments of Gordon Gray and Hollis Edens.[196]

The ACC in December 1953

The football season was over, but conference business never had an off-season. With golf clubs in tow, participants for the ACC meeting at Sedgefield began arriving on December 3, with the ubiquitous rumors of new members swirling around. Earle Hellen of the *Greensboro Record* said that his paper had it on good authority that the ACC would vote on inviting Virginia Tech and West Virginia for membership. Jim Penney and Forrest Clonts denied that this was on the table, but Clonts suggested that Tech had a better chance of membership than the Mountaineers.[197] No one was sure about expansion.

Meeting in Greensboro on December 4, 1953, Virginia became a full conference member, paying an entry fee of $200 to join the league, a laughably low price by today's standards. Somewhat comically, the conference was operating with a $14 deficit until the Cavaliers paid their bill, pulling the league out of the red.[198] Several of the representatives thought that their financial situation was rather humorous, which it was. The conference members, though, had anticipated some financial strains until the bowl money, predicted to be about $13,000, and the conference basketball tournament money was earned.

Moving to membership, Bob House, seconded by H.A. Fisher, presented a motion to invite Virginia Tech and West Virginia to join the league. Perhaps media outlets were correct in that there had been conversations about conference expansion. Maryland was not keen to expand, and Geary Eppley remarked that he needed to confer with Maryland officials about adding new members. Jim Tatum, supporting Eppley, stated that the establishment of a conference champion would be difficult with additions.[199]

Virginia's Gus Tebell argued vigorously for Virginia Tech's inclusion.[200] Most likely remembering how difficult it was to convince Virginia's Board of Visitors to support conference membership, Tebell saw Virginia Tech as an important addition that would ease some of the opponents to Virginia's membership.

The motion to accept Virginia Tech and West Virginia as members failed, with three votes in favor and five against. Wake's Clonts had reservations about voting on the two schools in a single motion. With the failure of House's motion, Clonts moved that Virginia Tech be invited to join the conference. Fisher, fully behind Tech, like Clonts, seconded the motion. Sally Miles' good friends were hoping to get the Blacksburg school in the ACC. Virginia Tech came up one vote short of approval. Five schools voted for VPI while three were opposed. Six votes were needed for the motion to pass. The no votes were cast by Duke, Maryland, and South Carolina.[201]

West Virginia's membership was voted upon as well. Unfortunately for the Mountaineers, only State, North Carolina, and Wake voted in favor of WVU.[202] Neither Legs Hawley's popularity nor Mountaineer success in athletics mattered.

Obviously, this was a great disappointment to everyone in Morgantown and Blacksburg, but conference members had remained consistent. They wanted a small, tightly-knit league when they left the Southern Conference, and that was what remained at the end of 1953.

House, Clonts and Fisher had shown their stripes as vocal proponents of West Virginia and Virginia Tech joining the league. In a letter after the December meeting, the popular chancellor wrote, "I am uncompromisingly for taking West Virginia and Virginia Tech into the Atlantic Coast Conference, and I stir up the question every chance I get."[203] House charged the alumni of Duke, Clemson, and South Carolina as being the stumbling blocks for these schools. Even more strident, he said, "I simply think it is an insult to the State of Virginia and the State of West Virginia to leave these two institutions out."[204]

In the most anti-climactic news of the day, the league voted to hold its basketball tournament at Reynolds Coliseum. Although State continued to enjoy its home court advantage, there was no other facility that offered anything close to Reynolds. In addition, holding the tournament in Raleigh guaranteed good hotels and good travel connections. For example, the Raleigh-Durham Airport had three runways in 1953. It was decided that the Cavaliers would participate in the first ACC basketball season and tournament. Because they did not have enough games scheduled with league opponents, the Cavaliers were penned into the eighth seed.

During the meeting, Rex Enright spoke to defend athletics, during a discussion about the evils of sports. He suggested to coaches that a key element for ending corruption in athletics was granting of tenure to coaches. This would eliminate some of the pressure to win at all costs, a pervasive part of college athletics.[205] The need to win in order to retain one's job was the fuel for corrupt practices that were damaging college football, Enright argued. Of course, tenure had the luxury of giving almost permanent employment to coaches as well. It was hard to see boosters and alumni interested in providing tenure for coaches. How could they fire a coach, if tenure and academic rank were involved?

The new conference discussed standardizing athletic entry requirements, a topic that had been debated for decades and was consistently pursued by Duke. Nothing came of it, because entry requirements varied greatly among the schools. Wallace Wade agreed to serve as league commissioner until January 1, 1955. Strangely, he remained the commissioner of the Southern Conference as well, most likely making him the only person to simultaneously lead two major athletic conferences in college athletic history.

Obviously happy with the current conference leadership, the triumvirate of Penney, Clonts, and Cornwell were reelected to their posts. This was a wise move, because no one could argue with the outstanding work that these men had done in seceding from the Southern, establishing the ACC, and bringing Virginia into the fold. They had successfully navigated the construction of a new conference and had operated a successful football season.

The pressure of handling conference business was lightened by the arrival of Peahead Walker, who made an appearance on Friday. Walker already had a substantial following in Canada, due to his humor but also his success on the CFL gridiron. Using some former Southern Conference stars, Walker led the Montreal Alouettes to first place in the Canadian Football League posting an 8–6 record, losing in the playoffs to the Grey Cup Champion Hamilton Tiger Cats. Former Wake Forest great Red O'Quinn and Wolfpack standout Alex Webster were important components in Montreal's success.[206]

The summer and fall of 1953 had not been a time of relaxation in preparation for a new year of collegiate sports. In a matter of months, the Atlantic Coast Conference was formed, an eighth member joined, sports seasons were organized, a new study of by-laws initiated, and a public relations office established. The division of the Southern Conference caused celebration and disappointment. Amongst sportswriters there was jubilation. After many years of debate, the conference split had created a tight and competitive league. There was consensus that the division was good for the remaining Southern Conference schools as well. The conference's formation, however, fractured old friendships and old rivalries, while leaving Virginia Tech and West Virginia questioning their athletic futures.

It was remarkable how fast the schools, some still bitter after the 1951 bowl ban, formed the ACC. Maryland, who wanted new league membership, had convinced North Carolina that it was in their best interest to leave the Southern Conference. They needed North Carolina and Duke aboard to establish a strong league. With Chapel Hill in favor, State was destined to follow. Duke would not want to remain adrift of its local rivals, and neither would Wake Forest. South Carolina and Clemson were active participants in founding the conference, ready for their athletic programs to enjoy more distinction. Visionary leaders with impressive political qualities, although sometimes differing on the role of athletics in academic life, brought the ACC into existence.

10

ACC Football

The First Season

Excitement about football in 1953 was not limited to the upcoming season. With the implementation of one-platoon football and the rejection of expensive two-platoon football, the game was going to be very different. Gone were the "specialists" as they were called, players who only played one position on one side of the ball. Fitness to play multiple positions at a high level was restored to the game. Not everyone liked this change, but Bill Murray, the highly respected Duke coach, was one of the outspoken supporters of the one-platoon game. Speaking in Richmond, Murray said that one-platoon football would increase competition, change game strategy, and make the kicking game more important.[1] Critical of the specialization of the two-platoon game, Murray emphasized "efficiency is not, and should not be, the goal of college football. Football is a game played between representatives of two educational institutions and, thank the Lord, we're getting back to principles."[2] He added that the two-platoon system created selfish players who needed to be taught team spirit.[3]

Murray's focus always was on competition and sportsmanship. He was never one to embrace the commercialism and professionalism of the sport. The concept of a team representing a university was supremely important to him, and Murray was a great representative of Duke. He would find the current status of college football unrecognizable.

As the season grew closer, Virginia Tech, out of support for Frank Moseley as well as a desire to signal to the ACC their commitment to football, ripped up the coach's contract and signed a new eight-year deal.[4] Although Moseley's contract did not expire until 1956, Tech was determined to keep their momentum moving forward. Since 1951, VPI was focused on upgrading their athletic program, after many years of losing and mediocrity. Moseley was the essential element of this plan, and, to Moseley's credit, he signed the extension without demanding a pay increase. Virginia Tech's leadership had made the right decision, regardless of its true intent. Moseley was a fine football coach and administrator, who coached football through the 1960 season but remained athletic director at Tech until his retirement in 1978.

Duke and Maryland were predicted to be the class of the conference, especially with the return to single platoon football. Both schools fielded deep and talented teams. Duke and South Carolina were scheduled to have the honor of playing in the first all-ACC football game under the lights in sultry Columbia on September 19. Usually, the Gamecocks did not have much luck when facing the Blue Devils.

As usual, the Blue Devils scheduled stiff competition, facing Tennessee, Purdue, and Army. Unfortunately, in the first season, the two best teams, Maryland and Duke, were not scheduled to play each other. Jim Tatum's split-T men had a small conference schedule but played a daunting non-conference slate that included Georgia, Mississippi, and Alabama.

With a plethora of talented players, the Terrapins had hopes of winning another national championship in Tatum's seventh year. The 1953 version of the Terrapins, eager to rid itself of the depressing conclusion to the previous season, was perhaps the best team Tatum had fielded. Jack Scarbath had graduated, but he was being replaced by senior Bernie Faloney at quarterback, defensive back, and punter. Faloney was a fantastic player, skilled on both sides of the ball. Tatum believed that Faloney was better than Scarbath. A Carnegie, Pennsylvania, native, Faloney seamlessly stepped into Scarbath's slot, without missing a beat. He was complemented by another Pennsylvania native, Stan Jones, a dominant tackle, one of the best players in the country and ultimately a consensus All-American in 1953. After his playing days at Maryland, Jones starred with the Chicago Bears, eventually landing in the Pro Football Hall of Fame as one of the greatest Bears to play the game.[5]

Duke's line had questions, but the Blue Devils were good in 1952 and had a very deep backfield in 1953. Their offense was powerful and could score on anyone in the country. Jerry Barger was a fine quarterback who could play other backfield positions as well. He was one of the best players in the league, although he was second string to Worth Lutz. Furthermore, the return to single platoon play was going to work to the advantage of Duke, especially in the contest against Tennessee.

Rex Enright was beginning his 13th season in Columbia, hoping that quarterback Johnny Gramling would lead South Carolina to great heights. The senior was unlike any Gamecock quarterback before him, playing the position more like a modern quarterback. The Gamecocks needed more success, because there were grumblings that Enright had been there too long and was not the man for the job. Although Enright was successful against Frank Howard, his teams always came up a little short, even during prosperous campaigns.

There was not much excitement at Riddick Stadium in Horace Hendrickson's second year. The Horse led State to a 3–7 overall record and a 2–4 conference record in its last campaign. With more of the weaker teams having been left in the Southern Conference, there was not much likelihood that State could improve on its poor record. The team was very young, relying heavily on a number of sophomores. Al D'Angelo was the team's biggest star, a powerful and talented guard from Pennsylvania. Otherwise, the talent pool in Raleigh was lean, and Wolfpack fans already were excited for basketball season.

The Deacons started practice with Bob Bartholomew as their most talented player. The sophomore was a powerfully built tackle who played football with a ferociousness that excited the fans. Wake, as usual, had fewer players than its chief competitors and many more holes to fill, especially on the line. But most believed that the Deacons would be a middle of the road squad. Working to their advantage was that Wake Forest never played full two-platoon football during the years when it was allowed. Because of a shortage of players, most of its athletes had played both ways. That included starting quarterback Sonny George, who played linebacker on defense and, with Bartholomew, was one of the most important players on the team.

In Chapel Hill, George Barclay's Tar Heels were a mystery. The successful teams of the late 1940s were a distant memory, but there was hope that the first-year coach would begin restoring winning seasons to Chapel Hill. They had underperformed the last two years, and no one knew if Barclay would gain success from a squad that had not done much. Although there was guarded optimism in Chapel Hill, the squad was predicted to be a mediocre team that needed to win its first few games before the schedule grew more difficult. Many thought that a good season would end with five victories and hopefully a close game against Duke.

Having endured a poor outing in 1952, playing a much tougher schedule, Clemson hoped for a better season. Frank Howard abandoned the single wing and adopted the split-T, the last conference squad to make the change. The hope was that sophomore quarterback Don King from Anderson, South Carolina, replacing the graduated Billy Hair, would bring many more victories. By and large, no one was sure what to expect from the Tigers after their disastrous 1952 season.

Regardless of season expectations, the Big Four coaching ranks held interesting relationships. George Barclay and Horace Hendrickson were teammates at Kiski Prep. Now, they were facing one another as rivals at North Carolina and State College, respectively. Bill Murray at Duke and Tom Rogers at Wake experienced similar circumstances. Both men were teammates at Duke, having been coached by Wallace Wade. All four coaches played their collegiate ball at Duke or North Carolina. It was a family affair when these four schools met one another.

On Saturday, September 19, 1953, the first ACC contest took place at Carolina Stadium at the fairgrounds in Columbia, South Carolina. Thankfully, the game was in the evening, avoiding the famous midday Columbia heat. There was great excitement with over 30,000 fans descending on the capital city for the game between Duke and South Carolina. The outcome was closer than the previous year, and South Carolina showed more ability, but Duke won, as they had done the previous years and many times versus the Gamecocks. Duke boarded the train back to Durham with a 20–7 victory, gaining the distinction of winning the first ACC football game. It was a solid showing for the Blue Devils and even in defeat the Gamecocks played well at times. Duke, with star back Red Smith and good line play, were simply too much.

Maryland, the other favorite, opened their campaign with a 20–6 win over Missouri in Columbia, Missouri. Surprisingly, the Tigers kept it close until the fourth quarter when Maryland scored two touchdowns to pull away from Missouri. This was a good win for the Terrapins, but not as satisfying as was expected.

Meanwhile, Wake Forest dropped a 16–14 game to William and Mary before about 20,000 fans in Richmond's City Stadium. It was a poor start for the Deacons, although the Indians fielded some fine individual players who had remained at the school after the scandal of 1951. A controversial William and Mary field goal was the difference, with Wake faithful claiming that the kick never crossed the bar. Nonetheless, the weak and young line was what cost the Deacons in Richmond.

The Clemson Tigers opened their season in a typical fashion, playing an instate opponent. This time it was the Blue Hose of Presbyterian College who drove from Clinton, South Carolina, to play at Memorial Stadium. The game was never in doubt. Clemson was a 33–7 winner over a vastly overmatched Presbyterian squad. Although the Tigers won easily, the contest did not give any indication of Clemson's ability.

Meanwhile, Virginia Tech beat Virginia at Scott Stadium in Charlottesville by the convincing score of 20–6. It was a statement game for VPI, which hoped that it would signal to the ACC that Tech should come into the conference with UVA. Moseley's contract extension and the victory were important steps. With West Virginia the class of the Southern Conference, Hokie and Mountaineer supporters believed they were making a clear case for league membership. For the Cavaliers, the defeat was a reminder that they were not the same program without Art Guepe. Almost overnight, Virginia had descended from the heights and reestablished themselves as a mediocre or worse football program. This was the beginning of a nightmarish football season in Charlottesville.

ACC games continued the following week, with State playing against North Carolina in a series that the Tar Heels had dominated. This was the 43rd meeting between the two sides, but the Tar Heels held the advantage 31–5–6. It was the opener for both squads, but few put much hope on the shoulders of the Wolfpack. The game, again, was in Chapel Hill, an arrangement that State had made for the gate receipts. That alone did not bode well for the Wolfpack. George Barclay enjoyed a good start to the season, beating State 29–7, on a rainy day at Kenan Stadium. The game, however, was in doubt until the fourth quarter when the Tar Heels posted two touchdowns. State played well for much of the contest and enjoyed a strong running game, but the talent at North Carolina was too great for the men from Raleigh.

Meanwhile, in equally rainy Durham, Duke blew open a 0–0 halftime score to beat Wake Forest 19–0. Duke was simply too talented for the Deacons, who struggled to develop an offensive threat for most of the game. Duke's defense was outstanding, holding Wake Forest to less than 100 yards rushing. Duke was undefeated while Wake Forest had only posted 14 points in its first two games, both defeats. For the Deacons, Bob Bartholomew was the shining star, dominating play from his line position, but Duke's talent was simply too much.

In the season's third week, Duke faced Tennessee in a contest that some believed was a good gauge for Duke's quality. In the previous week, Tennessee, a shell of their former teams, was dominated by Mississippi State 26–0. With Coach Neyland retired, many fans questioned whether Harvey Robinson could maintain success in Knoxville. The Volunteers were at home and badly needed a win to remove the bad taste of a devastating loss to the Bulldogs. Duke quarterback Jerry Barger, playing for the injured Worth Lutz, did the Vols no favors, leading the Blue Devils to three scores in 10 minutes resulting in a commanding 21–7 victory that could have been worse for Tennessee. Barger played all but a handful of plays in the game and was the spark for Duke's victory. The outcome was more indication that Bill Murray was Wallace Wade's equal in big contests, but it also indicated that Harvey Robinson, who lasted only two years in Knoxville, was not up to the job.

The biggest conference game of the week was Maryland's visit to Clemson. Jim Tatum's charges shut out the Tigers 20–0, in front of about 200 Tatum fans from his hometown of McColl, South Carolina, who had ventured over to Clemson to see the game. Maryland returned the kickoff for a touchdown and a punt for a touchdown in the victory, but the Terrapins had not exhibited the offensive firepower that fans expected prior to the season. There was a haunting feeling that something was not right in College Park, because the Terps did not have the offensive spark that was predicted.

Wake Forest desperately needed a victory but were facing a talented Villanova squad that had an impressive running game. Playing under an intense sun on October 3 at Bowman Gray Stadium in Winston-Salem, the Deacons upset the Wildcats 18–12.

In the process, the Deacons found a running game with Bruce Hillenbrand. The victory was fueled by Wake's passing attack which picked on Villanova's Gene Filipski. Filipski was a great running back, but he was a liability on defense, and it showed during the game. It was a good win for the Deacons, but they suffered key injuries, including the loss of Sonny George, their starting quarterback.

State's season worsened, with a late game loss to George Washington 20–7. The Wolfpack showed some fire on offense and outplayed the Colonials on the stat sheet, but they could not put more than one touchdown on the scoreboard. Neither team scored in the first half, and the Colonials only had four first downs for the game. But State could not take advantage of its better play and were beaten by a second-string George Washington quarterback. The defeat was tough to swallow for the Wolfpack, especially with few winnable games remaining on the schedule.

In Chapel Hill, North Carolina had no trouble with Washington and Lee, George Barclay's old team. Barclay had coached the Generals to a league championship, but now he had led the Tar Heels to a dominating 39–0 result. The impressive win was due more to Washington and Lee's eight fumbles than anything that North Carolina did. The Generals could not hold on to the ball, and the Tar Heels were given very short fields to drive for scores. After game two, it remained very hard to determine the quality of the North Carolina squad. George Barclay was glad for the victory but did not demonstrate much enthusiasm in a lackluster game against an overmatched team. Having beaten State and Washington and Lee, the jury was very much still out on North Carolina.

South Carolina played two games during a five-day period in late September and early October, both victories. The Gamecocks defeated The Citadel in a Monday contest that was postponed because of Hurricane Florence. On the following Saturday, October 3, they scored a commanding victory against Virginia in Charlottesville 19–0. The win over the Cavaliers snapped Virginia's 63-game streak without a shut-out. The last time the Cavaliers were shut-out was against Pennsylvania in 1946. South Carolina could have won by much more, but Enright played many substitutes throughout the game. It was a poor start to the season for Virginia, and it was going to get worse.

Rex Enright's team followed these victories with a 27–13 win over Furman. The Gamecocks were winning under the direction of quarterback Johnny Gramling, who had been busily rewriting the South Carolina record book since 1951. Gramling was assisted by a sound running game that was not as flashy as Steve Wadiak but did a good job. The year was quickly becoming a special season for the garnet and black.

As usual, the Wake Forest–North Carolina game engendered a good deal of excitement throughout North Carolina. Entering the contest, UNC was untested but undefeated. Wake Forest had beaten a good Villanova squad but suffered injuries that left its backfield perilously thin. Never a deep squad, Wake was destined to have its season derailed by injuries. The Tar Heels scored a late fourth quarter touchdown to edge the Deacons 18–13 in Groves Stadium. Wake Forest controlled the first three quarters, but a tired and thin Deacon team could not prevent UNC from scoring two touchdowns in the fourth quarter to grab the win. The Deacons simply did not have enough players to contend with the deeper Tar Heels who wore down the smaller Wake squad.[6]

Duke followed the Tennessee game with a home contest against Purdue out of the Big Ten. As Duke was enjoying victory in Knoxville, the Boilermakers suffered a 37–7 loss to rival Notre Dame and previously dropped a game to Missouri. The Purdue game was a significant bout, because it was the first time a Big Ten team had traveled to North

Carolina to play a football game.[7] In the 1950s, it was a noteworthy event for a northern team to come South to play football. Even though the Blue Devils gave up five fumbles to Purdue, Duke had enough firepower to pull out a 20–14 win, keeping them undefeated and dropping the Boilermakers to 0–3. Jerry Barger secured the victory, scoring the go-ahead touchdown with only 40 seconds remaining in the game. Although it was an important victory—a North Carolina team and an ACC member had beaten a Big Ten school—the Boilermakers were a weak squad, finishing the year with only two wins, one notably being over a very strong Michigan State team that completed the season with only this single 6–0 loss on their schedule.

The Duke victory created a quarterback controversy. Former Durham High School star Worth Lutz injured his knee against the Deacons, allowing Jerry Barger to star versus Tennessee and Purdue. Barger played like an All-American. Before a homecoming crowd against Purdue, fans were deeply impressed by his ability to rally the Blue Devils.

With its offense now in gear, Maryland reinforced its claim to being the best team in the country, with a resounding 40–13 trouncing of the University of Georgia in College Park. Although the Bulldogs were not very good in 1953, this was a statement win over head coach Wally Butts, who was in his 15th season in Athens. Again, it was Bernie Faloney sparking the Terps. He ran for one touchdown, passed for two more and even returned an interception for a fourth touchdown. Faloney was a rare talent, a scrambling quarterback who almost was equally good at defense as offense. The Bulldogs had no answers.

Davidson, now outside the ACC in the Southern Conference, played State at Riddick Stadium in front of a small crowd on October 10. The Wolfpack were surprised by the Wildcats, who switched from the split-T to the old single wing. After Johnny Gray, Davidson's quarterback, left the game with a knee injury, the Presbyterian school was out of good options. The game ended with State fans elated that they had scored their first victory of the season 27–7, albeit in a game in which they were strongly favored. Unfortunately for the Wolfpack, there was little more to cheer about throughout the season.

Meanwhile, Army and Duke were meeting for the fourth time, with Duke having never beaten the cadets. The matchup was at the Polo Grounds in New York, adding additional energy and excitement to the contest. With Worth Lutz, Jerry Barger, Red Smith, and Ed Meadows on the roster, the undefeated Blue Devils were the favorite, with fans sensing that there was a chance for an undefeated season. In 1953, Army was not playing a punishing schedule, but Red Blaik, in his 13th season, was fielding a solid Army team for the first time since the cheating scandal. The contest was tight throughout, with the fourth quarter being the deciding period. With Army holding a 14–13 lead, Duke ran a double reverse, and the speedy Red Smith carried the ball 73 yards to the Army seven-yard line. The clock stood at 2:50, and Duke had first down and goal to go, with plenty of momentum behind them. The Army line stiffened and on the first three downs, Duke advanced the ball five yards. With fourth and two, Duke attempted a quarterback sneak with their great quarterback Worth Lutz. Lutz followed the center but was stopped inches short of the goal line. Duke could have kicked a field goal on fourth down, but Bill Murray thought Duke did not deserve the win if they could not score a touchdown. Army took over on downs and won the game. The Blue Devils were no longer part of the undefeated ranks and again were stymied by West Point. Army was scheduled to come to Durham in 1954 for only their second time below the

Mason-Dixon Line, but that was little solace for the emotional defeat. Army finished the year with a 7–1–1 record, losing only to Northwestern in Evanston.

In Chapel Hill, Maryland was challenged by a gritty Tar Heel club, but the game was never in jeopardy. George Barclay and Jim Tatum were teammates at UNC in 1934, but in 1953 they were on opposite sides of the field. Maryland was the better team in all aspects of the game and defeated the Tar Heels 26–0, on a sunny afternoon. It was a game dominated by long Maryland drives that wore down UNC's resistance. Maryland remained ranked nationally in the top five and was unquestionably one of the nation's best teams. It was another contest where Tar Heel faithful dreamed of luring Jim Tatum back to Kenan Stadium to bring the Tar Heels the success that Maryland enjoyed.

Analyzing Maryland's victory, Dick Herbert bluntly described Maryland's supremacy. "Tatum has surrounded himself with a group of brawny young men who like to hit hard and can run like antelopes. Time and again Saturday you saw plays on which the strength of the Maryland players was greater than that of the Tar Heels."[8] Herbert's judgment was sound.

In Raleigh, State had hopes of defeating rival Wake Forest, in a game that always seemed to be closely fought. The talented Bruce Hillenbrand, carrying the ball for the Deacons, scored two touchdowns before leaving the game with a dislocated kneecap in the third quarter. The injury was a crippling blow to Wake's season. As usual, State played tough against the Deacons and were inspired in front of their home crowd. Nevertheless, Wake scored a 20–7 triumph, in part due to State mistakes, such as a two-yard punt that gave the Deacons the ball on the State 20.

On Big Thursday, October 22, 1953, the Gamecocks were favored against rival Clemson at the fairgrounds in Columbia. Each year the game was a state-wide celebration which served as an economic engine for the Columbia economy. Before a packed stadium in a game where South Carolina's star quarterback Johnny Gramling was injured in the third quarter, the Gamecocks outplayed Clemson, taking a 14–7 victory. The Gamecock offense was strong throughout, although it was not reflected on the scoreboard. Again, Rex Enright had had his charges ready for the Big Thursday game. Many sportswriters judged that this 1953 Gamecock squad was the best of Enright's time in Columbia.[9]

In a game that usually featured fist fights among fans and a fair share of pushing and shoving on the field, it appeared to the editors of *The State* newspaper that behavior was improving. They complimented fan demeanor, declaring that "rowdies seemed virtually non-existent, with a minimum few feeling no pain, but good natured and well-behaved."[10] The good feelings were only an aberration in this overheated rivalry that featured a good deal of animosity.

North Carolina faced quarterback Zeke Bratkowski and his Georgia Bulldogs in Athens on October 25. Few gave the Tar Heels much of a chance, especially with the prolific passing of Bratkowski, a Danville, Illinois, native, who was tossing the ball around in an era when few passes were thrown in an average game. Against the Tar Heels, he was 18 of 29 in a 27–14 win. Even with Bratkowski's throwing acumen, Georgia was not a good team. Their victory over the Tar Heels was the last of their season, and they finished 3–8. The game made some North Carolina fans begin to wonder if Barclay was the proper coach for the Tar Heels.

On the same day, Duke had no problem with State, smashing the Wolfpack 31–0 in Durham. State was reeling from injuries, and the game was never in question, serving as a good tonic for Duke's disappointing loss one week earlier. State was not close to Duke's level of play.

The following week, the Tar Heels dropped another game, this time to Tennessee. On homecoming in Chapel Hill, North Carolina played the Volunteers evenly, but North Carolina fumbled the ball four times and threw two interceptions to deliver victory to the men from Knoxville. Turnovers were a big problem for UNC. Against Georgia, the Tar Heels had endured seven turnovers. Taking advantage of Tar Heel mistakes, the Volunteers bested the Heels 20–6. It was a disappointing showing for North Carolina, because the Volunteers were not nearly as good as the teams fielded by Robert Neyland.

At Clemson, the injury-riddled Deacons fell to the Tigers 18–0. The depleted Deacons even lost a running back in warm-ups, leaving them with almost no one to carry the football. Clemson took advantage of the severely depleted Deacons to easily win. The game would turn out to be Clemson's biggest win in an otherwise forgettable season.

Duke continued its romp through the ACC, crushing Virginia in the Oyster Bowl, an annual contest designed to raise money for the Shriners. Playing in Norfolk, the Blue Devils used a dominating second half to crush the Cavaliers 48–6. The Cavalier season quickly was disintegrating. They had beaten George Washington, but were bested, and sometimes clobbered, by everyone else. To rub salt in the wound, the previous week Virginia was defeated by its former coach at Vanderbilt, Art Guepe. It was Vanderbilt's first win of the season in a year when they won only three.

As November's cool temperatures invaded the South, it was apparent that Maryland was going to receive the vote for conference champion and consequently conference representation in the Orange Bowl. To all but Terrapin fans, Maryland games were uninteresting, because they were destroying the opposition. In the first six games of the season, they surrendered only 19 points while scoring 188. Missouri had played them the best in the first game of the year, only losing by 14. Otherwise, the margins of victory were staggering.

On October 30, a good Gamecock team tried to blunt the Terrapins, but they fell 24–6 at Byrd Stadium. South Carolina could take some solace in that they scored against a stout Terrapin defense. Even in the loss, Rex Enright believed that South Carolina played their best game of the season, and he probably was right. Maryland, however, was a deep and skilled team with no match in the ACC.

On November 7, Duke battled Navy to a disappointing scoreless tie. Playing on a muddy field at Municipal Stadium in Baltimore, a facility that had been steadily renovated for years, neither team distinguished itself, although Duke had more scoring chances. Bill Murray remarked that it was a shame that the field conditions were so poor, considering how much money had been spent on the stadium. Army and Navy had been the Achilles heel for the Blue Devils in 1953. The Navy tie was very disappointing, especially considering that the Middies had lost games the previous two weeks to Pennsylvania and Notre Dame. With a defeat and a tie on their record, there was no chance that this outstanding Blue Devil squad would gain a bowl bid over the undefeated Terps.

On the same day, Maryland played a lethargic first half, before they accelerated in the second, casting aside a determined George Washington, 27–6. The Colonials played a fine game containing the explosive Terp offense, but like other smaller schools, they tired in the fourth quarter, allowing Maryland to pull away for the victory, in front of a small crowd at Griffith Stadium.

Wake and State continued their difficult seasons. State played Army as well as could be expected but lost by a final score of 27–7 in Michie Stadium at West Point. In another cold contest, the fellows from Raleigh finally wilted in the fourth quarter with Army scoring 14 points. The game, though, remained close until the last quarter and observers interpreted the contest as a moral victory for Hendrickson and his Wolfpack, especially considering that Army had defeated the powerful Blue Devil squad.

Not too far away in Boston's Fenway Park, Wake Forest, like State, played valiantly for three quarters until they were worn down in the last session. Boston College scored three fourth quarter touchdowns to win 20–7. The Eagles dominated with their ground game and were the better team, on a cold and windy afternoon, before a tiny crowd. With injuries hindering the Deacons, especially Hillenbrand continuing to be a spectator, Wake simply was too thin to hold fourth period leads. This was the fourth contest that they lost in the final quarter.

Unlike its rivals, North Carolina headed south to play South Carolina in Columbia. It seemed that almost every year, the Tar Heels could count on beating the Gamecocks, sometimes rescuing their season. Although the Gamecocks were viewed as a passing team under Johnny Gramling's strong arm, it was the running game that they rode to success, defeating the Tar Heels 18–0 on a Homecoming afternoon. The Tar Heels were hampered at quarterback, having to start reserve sophomore Marshall Newman. Newman threw the ball well but struggled with consistency while Gamecock runners, especially halfback Carl Brazell, slashed the Tar Heel defense. Rex Enright, wearing an eye patch due to an infection, had struggled against the Tar Heels in previous seasons, but this was a complete victory and a bit of redemption. North Carolina's initial enthusiasm at its fine start to the new year had faded into a series of tough losses, many of them inspired by costly turnovers, including the loss to the Gamecocks. In this contest, North Carolina continued its turnover problems, fumbling the ball three times in the first eight plays.

Clemson headed to Atlanta to deal with SEC powerhouse Georgia Tech. Surprisingly, Clemson took a 7–0 lead in the first quarter with an 80-yard scoring drive and outplayed the Yellow Jackets initially. But Tech was too strong and subsequently scored a 20–7 victory over a fading group of Tigers. Frank Howard's men had played a series of good games, but they had mostly come up short, falling to 2–4–1 on the season.

The next slate of games was an outstanding opportunity for the ACC, because the three undefeated teams in the nation were involved in ACC games. Undefeated Notre Dame was visiting Chapel Hill, Mississippi was traveling to unbeaten Maryland, and South Carolina was playing a never beaten West Virginia in Morgantown. Saturday, November 14, was destined to be a good test for the ACC and a bellwether of the conference's potential. Bowl games were watching and fans around the country as well.

The Mountaineers were enjoying a great year which was badly needed for the depleted Southern Conference. With their undefeated season, the Morgantown crew left many in the South wanting to see the Mountaineers line up against Duke and Maryland. An emerging star on the West Virginia squad was Sam Huff, the son of a coal miner, who would become one of West Virginia's greatest players. But the team was led by Bob Orders at center, a transfer from West Point, and Fred Wyant, one of the best quarterbacks to don a West Virginia University jersey. Leading the Mountaineers was head coach Pappy Lewis who enjoyed an exceptional relationship with Wyant. Lewis was the right man at the right time and had transformed the Mountaineers into a winner.

After a very successful slate of games, West Virginia had survived a close challenge from Virginia Tech on November 7, coming back from a 7–0 deficit at half to score a 12–7 victory in Bluefield. The game was played in Michell Stadium, another of the many WPA construction projects that opened in the 1930s. It was one of those days when despite a dominant performance on the ground, the Mountaineers could not score many points. With the victory, West Virginia boasted a gaudy 13-game winning streak and appeared destined to receive a Sugar Bowl bid.

The eighth-ranked Mountaineers, playing in front of 31,000 rabid fans in Morgantown, had little but an undefeated season on their mind when they clashed with a good South Carolina team on November 14. In a hard-fought battle, West Virginia was stunned by Rex Enright's Gamecocks 20–14. In one of South Carolina's greatest victories, West Virginia's fate was sealed with an interception by Clyde Bennett on the South Carolina eight-yard line, as West Virginia was driving for a victorious touchdown. The interception capped a stellar year for the St. Matthews, SC, native. For the Gamecocks, the win was one of the best in program history, because the Mountaineers entered the game undefeated with wins over Pittsburgh and Penn State. It had been a glorious season, but the loss also broke a Mountaineer 13-game winning streak, the longest in the nation. The defeat did not affect the Mountaineers' hold on the Southern Conference title, but it did call into question a bid for the Sugar Bowl. Rex Enright's club were impressive, having lost only two games before heading to Morgantown.[11]

On the same weekend, Maryland had good reason to be wary of Mississippi. The Rebels derailed the Terps in 1952 by the score of 21–14 in Oxford. On that day, Ole Miss snapped Maryland's 22-game winning streak behind the coaching of Johnny Vaught and the quarterbacking of Jimmy Lear. Their 1953 squad was traveling to College Park with only one loss on their record, a 13–0 defeat to a good Auburn club in Cliff Hare Stadium, but the All-American Jimmy Lear had graduated, and Maryland wanted revenge.

This much anticipated game did not live up to its predictions. From the first snap, Maryland dominated the contest, exploding for 24 points in the second quarter. Mississippi had no answers, and the Terps throttled the Rebels 38–0. Jim Tatum's crew made an emphatic declaration in defeating the nation's number 11 team so very badly.

Louis Hatter of the *Baltimore Sun* punctuated the victory, writing that it was an "eager, alert Maryland football team, with vengeance riding on every jarring tackle," that won the game.[12] Even Mississippi's Governor Hugh White, in attendance and speaking over the public address system at halftime, apologized for the "great many errors" that the Rebels committed in the first half.[13]

Number one and undefeated Notre Dame arrived at Kenan Stadium eager to continue their dominance over the Tar Heels and in general. The Irish routed UNC 34–14, in an uncompetitive game. Notre Dame rushed for 489 yards, slashing through a porous Tar Heel defense, reinforcing their position as America's top team. The Irish had been ranked first in the country at the beginning of the year and had done nothing to diminish that argument. Many of the 43,000 in the stands came not to watch North Carolina, but to admire the powerful Notre Dame squad led by head coach Frank Leahy in his 11th year at the helm. His charges would finish the year 9–0–1, with only a tie to Iowa as a blemish on their record.

Although the Tar Heels lost, the North Carolina fans did not know they were watching one of Leahy's last games on the sidelines. He resigned in the winter of 1954 and never coached another game. A Notre Dame player and graduate, Leahy was an extraordinary coach at all his stops, completing his head coaching career at Boston College and Notre Dame, with an amazing 107–13–9 record. Even to the most diehard Tar Heel fan, it was a treat to have the chance to watch Leahy coach on the sidelines at Kenan Stadium.

With Maryland and South Carolina winning, the ACC had distinguished itself against strong competition that was at the top of the Southeastern Conference and the Southern Conference. The Terps made it clear that they were one of the best teams in the country, while the Gamecocks defended the new league's honor against the best West Virginia team in the school's history. This was a very good start for the league.

With Wake and Duke not playing, State hoped to gain positive headlines against Pittsburgh. The Wolfpack could not replicate its performance against Army and were mauled by the Panthers 40–6 in Pittsburgh. Playing a very difficult schedule, Pitt only won three games during the season. State could not stop the explosive running of Bobby Grier, an African American star who later broke the color barrier in the Sugar Bowl.[14] Grier gained 198 yards on the ground.

On November 21, Duke traveled to Atlanta, seeking revenge for a bad loss to Georgia Tech in 1952. Tech was licking its wounds from a surprising defeat against Alabama the previous week. Coach Bobby Dodd spent much of the week crying about how poorly his 1953 Tech squad had performed, despite having lost only to Notre Dame and Alabama, both on the road.[15] Almost every school in the country wished their teams played as poorly as the Yellow Jackets. In a sell-out Grant Field, Tech edged Duke 13–10, in a tough game in which Duke had its chances to avenge the previous year's loss. It was Andrews, North Carolina, native Billy Teas who scored on a punt return to lead the Yellow Jackets to victory. The game was Duke's second loss of the season, but it left many Blue Devil fans thinking about how close they were to an undefeated campaign.

The following week, West Virginia, eager to reclaim its position as one of the best in football, travelled to Riddick Stadium to play the Wolfpack at 2 p.m. The Mountaineers arrived in Raleigh keen to get on the football field to purge the bad taste of defeat. In front of a tiny crowd of 5,300—State had only scored 19 points in its previous five games—the Mountaineers ripped the Wolfpack 61–0. Such a convincing win, even over a woeful Wolfpack squad, combined with defeats suffered by other competitors, led to a Sugar Bowl invitation for the Mountaineers. It was some vindication for West Virginia, having been left out of the ACC.

When hired, Horace Hendrickson signed a three-year contract, but after the loss to West Virginia when State did not gain a first down until the third quarter, calls for his firing were being heard all around the Hillsborough Street campus. Very few were attending games at Riddick Stadium, and Wolfpack fans were tired of losing. Even in a year when North Carolina and Wake Forest were not very good, the Wolfpack remained behind them. Almost everyone knew that change was necessary, regardless of the result from their final game at Florida State.

State's athletic administration had been concerned about Hendrickson's potential to win for several months. State officials spoke with Jim Tatum in the spring of 1953 about becoming the Wolfpack head coach, an almost inconceivable dream. In December, H.A. Fisher wanted to know if Tatum was still available and interested in the position. Fisher and the athletic council had determined that Hendrickson was not the man to lead the Wolfpack, but they did not have a replacement in the wings.[16] Fisher was convinced that Tatum had no interest in leading State, and even if he showed a modicum of interest, Gordon Gray would have disapproved the hiring.

The following week, Maryland continued its undefeated campaign, whipping Alabama 21–0, gaining revenge from the previous year's crushing defeat in Mobile. The Terrapin defense was the star of the game, stopping the Tide four times inside the Maryland 10-yard line. The victory most likely would have been much greater if Maryland had not lost Bernie Faloney early in the game to a knee injury. The injury was deeply concerning, because Faloney was a talented player, one of football's top athletes, who finished the year fourth in the Heisman Trophy voting.[17] The victory was bittersweet.

Sporting an undefeated record, Maryland was certain to represent the ACC in the Orange Bowl. With the Fighting Irish forced to settle on a tie with a tough Iowa squad at Notre Dame, the polls now had a reason to promote Maryland to number one, the spot the Irish had held for the entire season. On November 23, 1953, the ACC had its first number one ranked football team in its first season. By any estimation, that was a great achievement for Maryland, the only undefeated team in the country, and the fledgling ACC.

Auburn, Alabama's next opponent, smashed Clemson 45–19 at Memorial Stadium in Clemson. Auburn was optimistic about receiving a bowl bid, having enjoyed a very successful season. The Plainsmen had lost to Georgia Tech, which almost everyone did, and tied Mississippi State. Otherwise, their season was sterling, and one of the best for Auburn in many years. In comparison, Clemson suffered through a tough campaign, ending the year 3–5–1.

Having defeated West Virginia, South Carolina was awarded with the 15th spot in the AP Top-20 poll. The Gamecocks easily thrashed an outmanned Wofford 49–0 in a game that allowed South Carolina to play many second stringers for much of the contest. Only a struggling Wake Forest squad, which lost to Furman 21–19 in another fourth quarter collapse, remained on the schedule. Furman, though, had completed their best season since 1936, posting a 7–2 record. The fourth quarter and a load of injuries, many to key players, were the demise of Wake Forest the entire season. It had been a year to forget.

After weeks of losing, North Carolina was licking its lips seeing a woeful Virginia squad on the schedule. Throughout the season, Virginia had shown little resistance to its opponents and the same took place against North Carolina. The Cavaliers were whipped 33–7 in their final game of the year. It was a wet day and a muddy field, symbolic of Cavalier football fortunes under first-year coach Ned McDonald. Only Duke remained on the North Carolina schedule.

South Carolina and Wake Forest played a Thanksgiving afternoon contest in Charlotte in the final regular season game for both teams. Rex Enright's squad had enjoyed one of its best seasons in school history. The Gamecocks had never won more than seven games in a season and had accomplished that feat only three times. The week before, the Gamecocks had had the opportunity to rest many of their first-string players, and the team was reasonably healthy. Meanwhile, the Deacons were having their worst season since prior to Peahead Walker's hire in 1937. The game was a clash of two teams going in much different directions. The Deacons headed to the Queen City with nothing for which to play, except a paycheck, while South Carolina was ranked 15th, and faced the opportunity to win eight games for the first time.

The horseshoe shaped Memorial Stadium was a WPA built facility that opened in 1936. Only 90 miles from Columbia, Charlotte always had a large number of

South Carolina alumni, and many fans turned out to see the Gamecocks score a record-breaking victory. South Carolina received the ball and marched downfield to a touchdown on their first possession, and it looked like the Deacons were defeated. But in their best game of the year, Wake Forest piled up 19 points going into the fourth period. Even missing most of its best players, it seemed like Wake's young and depleted team had found its game. The final period was the Achilles heel all season, and Deacon anxiety appeared again, with the Gamecocks scoring a fourth period touchdown making the score 19–13. Big Bob Bartholomew played all 60 minutes of the game and was a stalwart for the Deacons, who needed him on the field for every snap. The Gamecocks could not score another point and Wake Forest's season was redeemed. In the biggest upset of the ACC season, the Deacons had stopped the best Gamecock team in history to that point from scoring a record eighth victory. Rex Enright was voted UP ACC Coach of the Year, but that was little solace considering the loss. A wonderful year for the Gamecocks ended on a very sour note. Dick Herbert correctly commented, "It wouldn't have been an official season had not Wake Forest scored one major upset."[18]

If anything, the Wake Forest victory gave North Carolina inspiration to salvage their season with a win over rival Duke. The Blue Devils entered the game with the outstanding Jerry Barger leading the team. Duke did not disappoint, earning a 35–20 victory over their rival in a game that was not close. The Blue Devils controlled the game from the kickoff, and UNC only made it respectable by scoring two touchdowns late in the fourth quarter. North Carolina was one of the best punting teams in the country, but at Duke Stadium, it was a disaster. They executed one good punt out of eight attempts, giving Duke a short field on multiple occasions.

Meanwhile, Florida State put the final nail in State's season, defeating the Pack 23–13. It was another tough year for State, but there was a recognition that with the new conference the Wolfpack must do better. Some level of respectability was the goal and fortunately for State it was around the corner.

The Orange Bowl, 1953

Although Duke and Maryland finished the year undefeated in conference play, it was very clear that the Terps would be named conference champions. In a year of spectacular victories, the Terrapins were crowned national champions, a title they fully deserved. This was an era when the national title was awarded prior to the playing of bowl games. It was a remarkable accomplishment that in the ACC's first football season, a founding member completed the year undefeated and was crowned the best team in America. Although many other ACC squads had not distinguished themselves very much, it did not matter. The ACC was a success, featuring a team that had whipped some of the best schools in football.

Jim Tatum's Terps spent the days before the Orange Bowl at the Flamingo Hotel on Miami Beach, enjoying their status as a touchdown favorite over Oklahoma. The Flamingo was the first grand hotel built in Miami and had been a center for well-heeled guests for decades. It was another example of the commercialism that had gained a powerful footing in college football. Maryland, however, would be one of the last sports teams to stay at the Flamingo, which closed in 1955.

Although the ACC champions were confident, there was one overwhelming

Achilles heel for them. Star quarterback and defensive back Bernie Faloney was doubtful for the game. Faloney was the team's catalyst, but the knee injury he suffered in the Alabama game plagued him and weighed on the team's morale. He reinjured the knee in practice prior to the Orange Bowl, making his participation very doubtful. Tatum turned to junior Charley Boxold to lead Maryland's attack. Although Boxold had considerable experience, he was not of Faloney's caliber. Maryland fans were deeply concerned that Boxold would not hold up against the stiff competition brought by the Oklahoma Sooners.

The game had an added dimension, because Don Faurot, the originator of the split-T offense, had tutored Jim Tatum and Bud Wilkerson, teaching both the offense during World War II. Adding to the game's intrigue was that Wilkerson had taken over the Sooners after Tatum left for Maryland. These two teams were very evenly matched, both playing the same offense and with both coaches knowing each other well.

Wilkerson's Sooners started the season with a seven-point loss to Notre Dame and a tie with Pittsburgh. After those games, Oklahoma went into the bowl game with an 8-1-1 record, which included a dominating performance within the Big Seven. As the season progressed, the Sooners appeared to improve, closing out the regular season with a 42-7 victory over Oklahoma A&M. Their only close conference matchup was a touchdown victory over Colorado. Most of the rest of the league could not score on the Sooners.

The game in Burdine Stadium was close. Oklahoma scored a second quarter touchdown on a 26-yard sprint to the endzone. Maryland threatened; on two occasions they went for a field goal instead of attempting to score on fourth down. Oklahoma's one score held up, however, and the Sooners captured a 7-0 victory. It appeared that without Faloney, Tatum did not have full confidence in his offense. Wilkerson and the Sooners deserved the victory, and Tatum may have been outcoached, but all wondered if Faloney would have made a difference.

Tatum was gracious in defeat and complimented Oklahoma, but he may have lost the game due to the ill-advised decision to place his second string on the field at the start of the second quarter when the Terps held first and goal. He had done this all season, but when Maryland's second team could not score, the questioning began.[19] As usual, Curly Byrd was outspoken, hoping to face Oklahoma as soon as possible so his Terrapins could redeem themselves. Byrd said that he wished to play the Sooners in the Orange Bowl next year and even urged that Maryland do whatever possible to get the Sooners on their schedule for the 1954 season.[20]

The football season was a success by any standard. Although only Maryland, Duke, and South Carolina, to a lesser extent, could claim to have fielded strong teams, the season was a good one. The conference gained national attention with Maryland playing clubs like Mississippi and Alabama, and Duke lining up against Georgia Tech. The Gamecocks had defeated West Virginia in Morgantown, easily the best team in the Southern Conference, demonstrating strength within the ACC. Although the five other squads had struggled, the top of the league was distinguished. The ACC's journey to prominence had begun.

Conclusion

It did not take long for the Atlantic Coast Conference to show its competitive strength at the national level. At the end of the 1953 regular season, Jim Tatum's Maryland Terrapins were crowned national champions. Although they suffered a disappointing loss in the Orange Bowl to Oklahoma, their regular season was extraordinary. The bowl game was viewed as akin to an exhibition game; thus the polling for a national champion in football was conducted prior to the bowl games. Two years later, the smallest school in the conference, Wake Forest, won the College World Series, delivering another national title to the league. Maryland captured a lacrosse championship in the same year. Frank McGuire led North Carolina to the NCAA basketball championship in 1957, giving impetus to the ACC's storied basketball tradition. In 1954, Wake Forest's Arnold Palmer won the ACC golf championship and the U.S. Amateur, spring-boarding him to greatness. By the late 1950s, the league's founding schools had crafted a successful conference that exercised national influence in a fashion impossible under the old Southern Conference's structure.

One of the reasons for the league's success was long-term, strong leadership. Some of the ACC's most important founders remained significant leaders as the conference matured. Eddie Cameron was a league stalwart, remaining at Duke until his retirement in 1972, having spent 47 years in Durham. State's athletic director Roy Clogston served 21 years with the Wolfpack, retiring in 1969. North Carolina's Chuck Erickson was athletic director until 1968, a post he held for 16 years. Gus Tebell, who brought Virginia into the ACC, remained athletic director until 1962. Their colleague Jim Weaver resigned his position as athletic director at Wake Forest to become the ACC's first solo commissioner. Placing the conference on a firm financial and competitive footing, Weaver led the ACC from 1954 to his death in 1970. Meanwhile, Jim Penney, Forrest Clonts, Lee Milford, and Oliver Cornwell remained in leadership roles on their campuses and in the conference until the late 1960s.

Coach and athletic director Frank Howard remained an anchor for the conference, not stepping away from Clemson's sideline until after the 1969 season. Bill Murray captained the Blue Devils through the 1965 campaign, enjoying years of success that included a Cotton Bowl victory in 1960. One of the new conference's most vocal supporters, Jim Tatum, left Maryland for North Carolina in 1956. Tragically, he died in 1959 from an illness related to Rocky Mountain Spotted Fever at only 46 years old, never gaining the opportunity to win big at his alma mater. Rex Enright, another great supporter of the ACC, led the Gamecocks until 1955 when he relinquished coaching duties due to declining health. He remained athletic director, but ill health led to an early death in 1960 at 59 years old.

On the hardcourt, consistent excellence remained a hallmark of the new conference. Everett Case directed State through many successful campaigns until the conclusion of the 1964 season when cancer forced him to abandon his coaching duties. He passed away in 1966. Frank McGuire coached North Carolina until 1961 when he was forced out under a cloud of NCAA infractions and point shaving allegations. Later, he experienced great success coaching the Gamecocks. Murray Greason enjoyed winning years with the Deacons until 1957 when Bones McKinney was promoted to head coach. Greason died tragically in an automobile accident in 1960. McKinney coached the Deacons until 1965. Hal Bradley was very successful at Duke until 1959 when he left Durham to spend eight years leading the Texas Longhorns. When defensive specialist Bud Millikan resigned from Maryland in 1967, he had led the Terrapins to their greatest period of basketball success in their history. This remarkable run of stability and excellence was essential for building the ACC's basketball heritage.

At the executive level, there was more volatility. Harold Tribble remained in office the longest, not retiring from Wake Forest until 1967. He was the dean of the league's college presidents at that time. Differing from the trend, Gordon Gray left North Carolina in 1955 for government service as an assistant secretary of defense. He never liked the academic world, but he enjoyed a distinguished career in government service that did not end until the Carter administration. His ally in so many battles, Hollis Edens, remained at Duke until suddenly resigning in 1960, when a group of trustees and faculty members forced him out of office. Edens deserved better. Curly Byrd, having done so much to advance athletics at Maryland and craft the ACC, resigned from the university in 1954, choosing to run for governor. He failed in his pursuit for the governor's office as well as in campaigns for the Senate and the House. He died in 1970. Like Byrd and Gray, Colgate Darden's tenure ended soon after the conference was established. Darden left Virginia in 1955 to take a role in the Eisenhower administration. Byrd's ally, Frank Poole, served 18 years as Clemson's president, dying in office doing the job he loved in 1958.

From its inception, the league was different from its peers. Of its eight schools, two were private, religious institutions. Three were some of the oldest state universities in the country, and the remainder were land grant schools. Except for Maryland, none of the institutions came close to matching the enrollments of most Big Ten institutions. Likewise, there was more variety of mission, ambition and resources than found in the SEC or Big Ten. Even the intimate nature of the league, spanning only four states, two of them very small, was different.

Although they looked dissimilar, there were similarities. Maryland, Virginia, North Carolina, Duke, and Wake Forest operated medical schools, while all but State and Clemson housed law schools. Duke, North Carolina, Virginia, and Maryland had extensive graduate programs, a common ambition for South Carolina, State, and Clemson. All the schools, except Clemson, were significantly altered by the rush of students from the G.I. Bill. Academically, the schools were a good mix, forming a solid foundation for athletic development.

The ACC's founding was a slow developing process that moved rapidly once a strong base of leadership among seven colleges realized that the 17-team Southern Conference was no longer reflective of their athletic ambitions. The scandals of 1951 influenced Southern Conference presidents, under the leadership of Gordon Gray, to exercise more influence and control over collegiate sports. Many of them were unprepared to handle athletics, but the growing significance of sports in the early 1950s, even with national football attendance declining, meant they had little choice. Presidents found themselves combating commercialism and professionalism, placing them at the forefront of reform. In a matter of months, the presidents piloted the conference into the bowl ban of 1951, fomenting a crisis that led Maryland and Clemson to consider leaving the league. Although the majority stood by the ban, division was clear, and the idea of schools departing the Southern Conference felt very real.

Meanwhile, competition in the league was crafting discord as well. Football scheduling was so varied that a school that played four or five weak teams could win the conference championship. In 1952, for example, VMI had an excellent shot at being league champion, playing a light schedule. Duke, Maryland, Wake Forest, South Carolina, and North Carolina and a few other schools played schedules that were much tougher than those slated by many fellow Southern Conference institutions. It was difficult to crown a legitimate champion.

Some of the league's institutions such as Davidson and Washington and Lee struggled to field even the minimum number of players to compete and certainly could not do so if freshmen were banned from competition. Furthermore, these schools were competing against institutions that were many times their size and rapidly developing into research universities. In an expensive sport like football, university size and access to financial resources played a significant role in dividing the Southern Conference.

Even on the basketball court where costs of participation were much lower, there was a growing separation and radically different schedules leading toward division. Although State had dominated the league since Everett Case stepped on campus, Duke, North Carolina, Wake Forest, and Maryland finally had closed the gap. In the process, they left other schools behind, save for exceptions such as George Washington and Furman. With Reynolds Coliseum hosting the Southern Conference Tournament and the Dixie Classic, and intense competition emerging amongst the Big Four, basketball was becoming an obsession in North Carolina. Regular season clashes amongst the teams were sold-out affairs that fans could not miss. This growing mania for the sport infected Maryland as well. As with football, there was a vast difference between the top of the league and the bottom, which had resigned themselves to not competing with the best.

The founding of the ACC was not strictly a story of professionalism and commercialism defeating academics. It did not conform to such simple explanations that so often are used to explain the development of college sports. The founding demonstrated more nuanced views of athletics and a variety of opinion about their role on college campuses. It is simple to point to coaches like Jim Tatum, Frank Howard, and Everett Case as men not too much concerned with academics or as leaders who chafed under regulations they believed made little sense. Each of these coaches was important to the development of the league, and each had a penchant for seeing little wrong with big-time athletics. Nevertheless, they cared about their players. Often, Frank Howard, who lived a long life, spoke pridefully about his many players who enjoyed distinguished professional careers after graduating Clemson.

The league, however, was peppered by athletic coaches and leaders who did not identify as much with the "hell for leather" approach of a Jim Tatum. Duke's Bill Murray prized sportsmanship and was not keen on the growth of big-time college football. His boss, Eddie Cameron, wanted to preserve the best parts of college athletics and was part of the faction desiring stricter academic guidelines. Rex Enright and Murray Greason were consummate sportsmen who wanted to do what was best for their teams, athletically and academically.

Amongst the presidents, there were disparate views on athletics. The academic purists such as Hollis Edens, Gordon Gray, Colgate Darden, John Harrelson, and Harold Tribble contrasted with the far more athletically liberal ideas of Curly Byrd, Frank Poole, and a newly arrived Donald Russell at South Carolina. The former group saw the formation of the ACC as a way to control the evils of big-time athletics, especially after southern schools and conferences flexed their muscle to end the Sanity Code. With the Sanity Code gone, there was an opportunity for schools to craft policy that fit their needs. These leaders wanted athletes to be treated, as much as possible, the same as non-athletes. They did not like spring practice, wanted to confine the seasons to specific months, disliked post-season games and tournaments, and simply hoped to keep athletics on the level of any other element of university structure that was subordinate to academics.

Curly Byrd and Frank Poole may not have been zealous reformers, but their support of big-time athletics was nuanced as well. Byrd, for example, wanted to win, but he also acquiesced with several of the policies championed by the conference's reformers. Sometimes, Byrd is portrayed as similar to John Hannah at Michigan State, but the documents indicate that he was more moderate on athletic policy than he is often credited for being. It is unmistakable, however, that the Maryland president fully believed that big-time athletics were not a problem in the 1950s. Often his ally, Frank Poole was convinced that Clemson's house was in order and wished to allow athletic administrators to play the lead role. Poole, a former professor and football player, had no wish to see athletics run roughshod over academics, but he was supremely annoyed by the demonization of bowl games, especially considering post-season basketball tournaments and past bowl participation among schools that reversed their policies in 1951.

The conference was formed because supporters of big-time college athletics and reformers had a common interest in leaving the unwieldy Southern Conference. The reform element saw an opportunity to form a conference of like-minded colleges that would craft policies restricting the growth of big-time athletics, while keeping athletics in a controlled and proper relationship with academics. They understood that a small league of only eight institutions made it easier to negotiate policies and implement change. These men appreciated that some reform had to occur at the national level, but they believed their new league could help spur reform. The smaller league even had the benefit of reducing costs and time away from academics.

Those with more direct interests in athletics had no desire to continue playing in a league where the gap between the best and worst teams was gigantic. The Big Ten and the Southeastern Conference did not struggle with a significant number of schools that fielded simply uncompetitive teams. Schedules for football and basketball were more consistent in these leagues, while Southern Conference schedules had enormous variety. Meanwhile, most of the coaches at the seceding schools wanted to play for championships and had desires to compete on a national level. Jim Tatum and Everett Case wanted to win conference and national titles. Even though Bill Murray was viewed as a reformer, he and Eddie Cameron wished Duke to play at a national level. The Southern Conference had several schools that could not dream of reaching that standard of competition.

10. Conclusion

The conference's initial academic leadership was a sign that the intent was for the league to be academically controlled. Jim Penney, Forrest Clonts, and Oliver Cornwell were academics who believed that athletics played an important role on modern college campuses, but none of these figures wished athletics to subvert academics. They were believers that athletics were beneficial to the college experience, but their decision-making processes indicated that they held no interest in removing academic oversight from athletics.

It is interesting that television played no role in the ACC's founding. Although televised games were in their infancy, Southern Conference schools were not much a part of the college sports television wars of the early 1950s. These were dominated by institutions like Notre Dame, Pennsylvania, and Michigan. The league's founders had not yet foreseen how television, especially focused on ACC basketball, would alter the conference's future.

For West Virginia and Virginia Tech, the creation of the ACC without their inclusion profoundly altered the course of their athletic programs and their institutions. For years afterward, these two schools found themselves in a league of small private schools, very different from their campuses. Virginia Tech resigned from the Southern Conference in 1965, becoming an independent. West Virginia remained in the league until 1968, when they, too, chose the independent route. This left both schools in the wilderness in relation to most of their peer institutions. Their exclusion from the ACC greatly altered their athletic journeys.

In 1953, a group of academic and athletic leaders, many from small southern towns and communities, united in a small southern city to create an athletic conference for the benefit of seven institutions. Men from Clemson, Duke, Maryland, North Carolina, North Carolina State, South Carolina, and Wake Forest put aside differences for their common athletic and academic good. With the addition of its eighth member, Virginia, later in the year, the ACC was in position to grow and mature as one of the most important collegiate athletic leagues in the country.

Chapter Notes

Preface

1. There are many outstanding works on college athletics and attempts at reform, especially studies of the 1940s and 1950s. For a unique perspective, see Murray Sperber's *Onward to Glory: The Creation of Modern College Sports* (New York: Henry Holt, 1988); Ronald A. Smith's *Pay for Play: A History of Big-Time College Athletic Reform* (Urbana: University of Illinois Press, 2010); and John R. Thelin's *Games Colleges Play: Scandal and Reform in Intercollegiate Athletics* (Baltimore: Johns Hopkins University Press, 1996). For football, see John Sayle Watterson's *College Football: History, Spectacle, Controversy* (Baltimore: Johns Hopkins University Press, 2000).

2. The most important work on the founding of the Big Ten is Winton U. Solberg's *Creating the Big Ten: Courage, Corruption, and Commercialization* (Urbana: University of Illinois Press, 2018).

3. For the ACC's founding, the most substantial material is found in Bruce Corrie's *The Atlantic Coast Conference 1953–1978: Silver Anniversary* (Durham: Carolina Academic Press, 1978). Some background on the league's founding is in J. Samuel Walker's *ACC Basketball: The Story of the Rivalries, Traditions, and Scandals of the First Two Decades of the Atlantic Coast Conference* (Chapel Hill: University of North Carolina Press, 2011) and Barry Jacobs's *Golden Glory: The First 50 Years of the ACC* (Greensboro: Man Media, 2002).

Introduction

1. Bob Williams, "Bobbin' Along," *Rocky Mount Telegram* (May 10, 1953), D-1.

2. Sometimes in the text, North Carolina State University will be referred to as State College, the name most often used in the early 1950s. State College was commonly used in some rural parts of North Carolina well into the 1980s.

3. For a new discussion of the SEC, see Eric A. Moyen, "Presidents, Football, and Athletic Policy in the Southeastern Conference, 1929–1936," in *The History of American College Football: Institutional Policy, Culture, and Reform*, ed. Christian K. Anderson and Amber C. Fallucca (New York: Routledge, 2021).

Chapter 1

1. For decades, State struggled with finding a name that suited the campus and University of North Carolina leaders.

2. George H. Callcott, *A History of the University of Maryland* (Baltimore: Maryland Historical Society, 1966), 314.

3. Jennings L. Waggoner, Jr., and Robert L. Baxter, Jr., "Higher Education Goes to War: The University of Virginia's Response to World War II," *The Virginia Magazine of History and Biography* 100 (July 1992), 411.

4. V.R. Cardozier, *Colleges and Universities in World War II* (New York: Praeger, 1993), 52–53.

5. *Ibid.*, 53.

6. Bynum Shaw, *The History of Wake Forest College*, vol. IV, 1943–1967 (Winston-Salem: Wake Forest University, 1988), 2.

7. Waggoner, 416.

8. Corrie, 27.

9. Waggoner, 414–417.

10. For an examination of the G.I. Bill's effects on American society and notions of civic duty, see Suzanne Mettler, *Soldiers to Citizens: The G.I. Bill and the Making of the Greatest Generation* (Oxford: Oxford University Press, 2005). Initially, the G.I. Bill brought large numbers of veterans to campus. After they received degrees, there were enrollment declines at many colleges before the numbers increased steadily in the late 1950s.

11. Pamela Grundy, *Learning to Win: Sports, Education and Social Change in Twentieth Century North Carolina* (Chapel Hill: University of North Carolina Press, 1993), 203–205.

12. See Hugh Talmedge Lefler and Albert Ray Newsome, *North Carolina: The History of a Southern State*, 3rd ed. (Chapel Hill: University of North Carolina Press, 1973).

13. David W. Southern, "Beyond Jim Crow Liberalism: Judge Waring's Fight Against Segregation in South Carolina, 1942–52," *The Journal of Negro History* 66 (Autumn 1981), 209.

14. For a good examination of South Carolina in this era, see Walter B. Edgar's *South Carolina: A History* (Columbia: University of South Carolina Press, 1999).

15. Henry H. Lesesne, *A History of the University of South Carolina, 1940–2000* (Columbia:

University of South Carolina Press, 2002), 71–73. State representative and board of trustee member Sol Blatt was the force behind the proposal.

16. See Peter Wallenstein, *Cradle of America: A History of Virginia* (Lawrence: University of Kansas Press, 2014). For a more detailed examination of the liberal challenge to the Byrd Organization, see Peter R. Henriques, "The Byrd Organization Crushes a Liberal Challenge, 1950–1953," *The Virginia Magazine of History and Biography* 87 (January 1979), 3–29.

17. Waggoner, 427.

18. *Ibid.*

19. Robert J. Brugger, *Maryland: A Middle Temperament, 1634–1980* (Baltimore: Johns Hopkins University Press, 1996), 552. Brugger provides a fine general history of postwar Maryland. Ironically, McKeldin defeated Curly Byrd, winning re-election in the 1954 Maryland gubernatorial election.

20. Annie Dankelson, "The Postwar Campus Crunch," *Maryland Today*, https://today.umd.edu/the-postwar-campus-crunch, accessed on November 2, 2021.

21. John R. Thelin, *A History of American Higher Education*, 3rd ed. (Baltimore: Johns Hopkins University Press, 2019), 260.

22. *The Gray Legacy: How a Family Helped Change a City* (Winston-Salem: Wake Forest School of Medicine, n.d.), 10. Gray Sr.'s death was significant news throughout North Carolina and well beyond it.

23. "Inauguration of Gordon Gray as President of the Consolidated University of North Carolina, 1950" (North Carolina Digital Collections) 10–11, http://digital.ncdcr.gov/cdm/ref/collection/p16062coll9/id/403665/, accessed on October 7, 2019. The inauguration program includes a great deal of information about Gray.

24. *The Gray Legacy*, 13.

25. Quoted in Crow, 40.

26. *Ibid.*, 164.

27. "Inauguration of Gordon Gray," 14.

28. For a full discussion of Frank Porter Graham's career at North Carolina, see William A. Link, *Frank Porter Graham: Southern Liberal, Citizen of the World* (Chapel Hill: University of North Carolina Press, 2021).

29. Jeffrey J. Crow, "The Paradox and the Dilemma: Gordon Gray and the J. Robert Oppenheimer Security Clearance Hearing," *The North Carolina Historical Review* 85 (April 2008), 164–166. Also see William A. Link, *William Friday: Power, Purpose, and American Higher Education* (Chapel Hill: University of North Carolina Press, 2013), 74–75.

30. Link, 77.

31. Woman's College became the University of North Carolina at Greensboro, a co-educational institution, in 1963.

32. Crowe, 43.

33. F. Weston Fenhagen and Alice A. Joyce, "The Birth of the Chancellorship," *Carolina Alumni Review* (November–December 1995), 15. Also see Link's *Frank Porter Graham*.

34. *Ibid.*, 16.

35. *Ibid.*, 20.

36. Letter to J.G. Stripe from Gordon Gray, January 22, 1952 (UNC, Chancellors' Records, R.B. House Series, Subseries 7, Faculty Affairs). The letter appeared with Gordon Gray's signature, but it was written by Bob House and is reflective of House's views.

37. *Ibid.*

38. Alice Elizabeth Reagan, *North Carolina State University: A Narrative History* (Raleigh: North Carolina State University Foundation and North Carolina State University Alumni Association), 97–98.

39. In 1954, State granted the first nuclear engineering Ph.D. in the world. It was another sign of its emergence from Chapel Hill's shadow.

40. John N. Popham, "Edens Is Inducted as Duke President," *New York Times* (October 23, 1949), 55.

41. Russell Porter, "Colleges Vote Freedom Code Banning Reds from Faculties," *New York Times* (March 31, 1953), 1.

42. Robert F. Durden, "Donnybrook at Duke: The Gross-Edens Affair of 1960: Part I," *The North Carolina Historical Review* 71 (July 1994), 334–335. Also see Robert Franklin Durden, *The Duke Endowment: Lasting Legacy to the Carolinas: The Duke Endowment, 1924–1994* (Durham: Duke University Press, 1998), 143.

43. Edens resigned the presidency in 1960 after dealing for three years with an administrative controversy not of his making. A small number of board of trustees combined with Dr. Paul Gross, vice president of education, pushed Edens out of office by maintaining that he was not adequate for the position and had lost support of the faculty, charges which were untrue. Edens' removal was unjust and a dark period for Duke.

44. Byrd's nickname can be found spelled Curley or Curly. The latter spelling was used a bit more often than the former and is used in this study.

45. John V. Hinkel, "Career of Curley Byrd, Maryland Coach, is most Unique in U.S. College Athletics," *Washington Post* (November 30, 1930), M23. This was one in a series of articles that Hinkel wrote about prominent coaches in the Washington area.

46. *Ibid.*

47. *Ibid.*

48. For a full discussion of Byrd's tenure at Maryland see Callcott, 314–358.

49. Bayard Webster, "The Fall and Rise of the University of Maryland," *Harper's Magazine* 213 (October 1, 1956), 64.

50. In 2015, Byrd Stadium was renamed Maryland Stadium, due to Byrd's views in favor of segregation.

51. Eugene Olive, "Meet President Tribble," *Biblical Recorder* (August 19, 1950), 1–2.

52. *Ibid.*

53. *The Biblical Recorder*, the most significant

journal for North Carolina Baptists, featured several articles in 1950 expressing approval and excitement about Tribble's selection starting with "Dr. Tribble Wake Forest's New President," *The Biblical Recorder* (June 10, 1950), 6.

54. "At the Inauguration of President Tribble," *Biblical Recorder* (December 9, 1950), 4.

55. James McKissick was so popular that he was buried outside the doors of the original library on the South Carolina campus.

56. Daniel Walker Hollis, *University of South Carolina: College to University*, vol. II (Columbia: University of South Carolina Press, 1956), 341.

57. George D. Terry and Catherine Wilson Horne, eds., *The Bridge Builder: Solomon Blatt Reflects on a Lifetime of Service to South Carolina* (Columbia: McKissick Museum of the University of South Carolina, 1986), 75.

58. Daniel W. Hollis Oral History Interview, February 5, 1987, https://digital.tcl.sc.edu/digital/collection/savage/id/56/rec/8, 13, accessed on December 27, 2019.

59. Guy Friddell, *Colgate Darden: Conversations with Guy Friddell* (Charlottesville: University Press of Virginia, 1978), 21–25.

60. *Ibid.*, 100–101. Also see Virginius Dabney, *Mr. Jefferson's University: A History* (Charlottesville: University Press of Virginia, 1981).

61. Jonathan Walker and Rich Gooch, "The Life of Don Faurot," Harry S. Truman Library, https://library.truman.edu/scpublications/Chariton%20Collector/Fall%201986/The%20Life%20of%20Don%20Faurot.pdf, 10, accessed on December 21, 2019. In 19 seasons at Missouri, Faurot compiled a 101–79–10 record.

62. Mal Mallette, "Jim Tatum of the Tar Heels," *Saturday Evening Post* (November 2, 1957), 90.

63. Bill Connors, "Tatum's 1946 Recruits Launched OU Dynasty," *Oklahoman* (August 18, 1996), https://www.tulsaworld.com/archive/tatum-s-recruits-launched-ou-dynasty/article_f32af08d-429b-5a1d-9a82-f974a02adf95.html, accessed on December 21, 2019. Also see Bob Hersom, "Tatum: OU's Vain Attraction. They Called the Big Guy Coach ... among other things," *Oklahoman* (August 21, 2001), https://oklahoman.com/article/2752360/tatum-ous-vain-attraction-they-called-the-big-guy-coach-among-other-things, accessed on November 20, 2020.

64. Jeff Snook, *Sooner Nation: Oklahoma's Greatest Players Talk about Sooner Football* (Chicago: Triumph Books, 2015), 4.

65. "Jim Tatum to Coach Maryland Grid Team," *The Sun* (January 19, 1947), 1.

66. Tatum hoped that Wilkinson would come with him to Maryland. Nonetheless, Bud Wilkinson and Tatum remained friends until Tatum's untimely death in 1959.

67. Mallette, 91.

68. *Ibid.*, 90.

69. Herbert O'Keef, "Tar Heel of the Week: Eddie Cameron," *News and Observer* (August 24, 1952), IV-3.

70. John Roth, *The Encyclopedia of Duke Basketball* (Durham: Duke University Press, 2006), 124–126.

71. Bill Brill and Ben Cohen, *An Illustrated History of Duke Basketball* (New York: Sports Publishing, 2012), 34–38.

72. Robert Franklin Durden, *The Launching of Duke University, 1924–1949* (Durham: Duke University Press, 1993), 239.

73. For a complete examination of Wallace Wade's career see Lewis Bowling's *Wallace Wade: Championship Years at Alabama and Duke* (Durham: Carolina Academic Press, 2006).

74. Terry, "Sol Blatt," 75.

75. Howard led the Tigers from 1940 until his retirement from football in 1969.

76. Bob Quincy, "UNC's Erickson Worked Behind Scene," *Charlotte Observer* (November 10, 1977), C-1. Also see "Chuck Erickson Dies," *News and Observer* (November 10, 1977), 19.

77. "Meet the Wolfpack: North Carolina State College Football Information, 1951" (Raleigh: North Carolina State University, 1951), 10–11, https://d.lib.ncsu.edu/collections/catalog/ua015_010-008-bx0116-009-001#?c=&m=&s=&cv=9&xywh=-1952%2C0%2C7476%2C2660, accessed on May 28, 2020. Clogston was NC State's AD until 1969. Although retired from State, he spent several years as athletic director at Appalachian State. He died in 1990 in Boone, North Carolina.

78. Dick Herbert, "The Sports Observer," *News and Observer* (July 13, 1970), 13. Also see Elton Case, "Remembering Jim Weaver," *Herald-Sun* (July 12, 1970), C-12.

79. "Surprising Facts on SC Wildlife Brought to Life," *The State Magazine* (March 1, 1953), 57.

80. Bynum Shaw, *A History of Wake Forest College*, vol. IV, 1943–1967 (Winston-Salem: Wake Forest University, 1988), 212.

81. Frank O'Brien, "Dr. Ollie Knows His Business—His Business is UNC Athletics," *News and Observer* (May 18, 1952), II-2.

82. "Clemson's Dr. Milford to Slow Down, Not Stop," *Greenville News* (August 12, 1956), 3. Also see "Clemson Physician Lee W. Milford Dies," *The State* (January 6, 1980), C-14.

83. Corrie, 16–18. Also see "The History of the Southern Conference," https://soconsports.com/sports/2008/6/30/177772.aspx, accessed on June 16, 2020, and John Iamarino, *A Proud Athletic History: 100 Years of the Southern Conference* (Macon: Mercer University Press, 2020).

84. Sanford served as president of the University of Georgia for three years and from 1935 to 1945 led the University System of Georgia.

Chapter 2

1. Letter to Clarence P. Houston from Gordon Gray, January 6, 1951 (UNC, General Administration/Consolidated University: Subgroup

2: Consolidated UNC Campus Files; Series 2: UNC-CH; Subseries 3: Athletic Affairs; General, 1951).

2. Allen L. Sack and Ellen J. Staurowsky, *College Athletes for Hire: The Evolution and Legacy of the NCAA's Amateur Myth* (Westport, CT: Praeger, 1998), 41.

3. Smith, *Pay for Play*, 97–98.

4. Ronald A. Smith, *The Myth of the Amateur: A History of College Athletic Scholarships* (Austin: University of Texas Press, 2021), 104.

5. Smith, *Pay for Play*, 98.

6. *Ibid.*

7. *Ibid.*

8. See Ronald A. Smith, *The Myth of the Amateur: A History of College Athletic Scholarships* (Austin: University of Texas Press, 2021).

9. Wilton Garrison, "Wilton Garrison's Sports Parade," *Charlotte Observer* (December 10, 1950), B-16.

10. Bob Brooks, "Conference Heads Made History at Charlotte," *News and Observer* (December 10, 1950), II-1.

11. Ken Alyta, "Wade Preparing for New Duties," *Charlotte Observer* (December 10, 1950), B-18.

12. Shelley Rolfe, "U.Va. Expected to Apply for Southern Conference Membership," *Richmond Times-Dispatch* (January 15, 1951), 14.

13. *Ibid.*

14. Sandy Grady, "Feared of Uncle Sam's Roundup, Coaches Ride Hard to Corral Beefy Freshmen," *Charlotte News* (February 23, 1951), B-6. Also see Sandy Grady, "Bugle and Polish Schools Can Relax, They Have Little Need to Fear Service Call," *Charlotte News* (February 22, 1951), B-11.

15. Letter to Hollis Edens from Gordon Gray, February 8, 1951 (Duke, President's Office, A. Hollis Edens Papers, Southern Conference).

16. *Ibid.* These invitations are found in almost all the archives of Southern Conference members.

17. *Ibid.*

18. "Proposed Agenda for March 3 Meeting of the Southern Conference Presidents" (CU, Athletic Council Records, Series 26, Athletic Council, 1951, January–May).

19. Letter to Eddie Cameron from Hollis Edens, February 16, 1951 (Duke, President's Office, A. Hollis Edens Papers, Southern Conference).

20. Letter to A.W. Hobbs and Charles E. Jordan from H.A. Fisher, April 14, 1951 (NCSU, Committees, Council on Athletics Records, Correspondence, 1949–1953, Box 12).

21. "The Intercollegiate Scandals and the Southern Conference," *Richmond Times-Dispatch* (March 3, 1951), 8.

22. "Minutes of the Meeting of Presidents, Faculty Chairmen, and Athletic Directors of the Southern Conference Members Held in Chapel Hill, North Carolina Saturday, March 3, 10 A.M." (Duke, President's Office, A. Hollis Edens Papers, Southern Conference).

23. *Ibid.*
24. *Ibid.*
25. *Ibid.*
26. *Ibid.*
27. *Ibid.*

28. Moses Crutchfield, "Wade Urges Fight on Sports Betting," *Greensboro Daily News* (March 3, 1951), 10.

29. *Ibid.*
30. *Ibid.*

31. "Georgetown Drops Out of Football after 60 Years," *New York Times* (March 23, 1951), 28.

32. *Ibid.*

33. Letter to Roy Clogston from J.G. Vann, November 10, 1952 (NCSU, Office of the Chancellor, John William Harrelson Records, Chancellor's' Meetings, Athletic Council, Box 40).

34. "Report to Athletic Council N.C. State College," January 17, 1953 (NCSU, Office of the Chancellor, John William Harrelson Records, Chancellor's' Meetings, Athletics, Box 46).

35. Shelley Rolfe, "Duke Happy about Setup of Conference," *Richmond Times-Dispatch* (May 5, 1951), 15.

36. "Cleaning up College Athletics," *Richmond Times-Dispatch* (May 5, 1951), 10.

37. *Ibid.*

38. Dick Pierce, "Wade Talks to Athletes at Davidson," *Charlotte Observer* (May 8, 1951), Sports-2.

39. Shelley Wolfe, "Virginia's Pritchett Sits in as a Listener at Conference Gathering," *Richmond Times-Dispatch* (May 6, 1951), 5D.

40. "Pulmonary Embolus Causes Death of Norton Pritchett at Charlotte," *Richmond Times-Dispatch* (July 18, 1951), 20.

41. William D. Snider, *Light on the Hill: A History of the University of North Carolina at Chapel Hill* (Chapel Hill: University of North Carolina Press, 1992), 246–247.

42. "The Admission of Negroes" Memo, June 20, 1951 (NCSU, Office of the Chancellor, John William Harrelson Records, Chancellor's' Meetings, Box 37). The archives at N.C. State University possesses many documents about African Americans using the library. It was a particular obsession of some board members.

43. Snider, 248.

44. Albert J. Figone, *Cheating the Spread: Gamblers, Point-Shavers, and Game Fixers in College Football and Basketball* (Urbana: University of Illinois Press, 2012), 24–26. Also see Ronald A. Smith, *Pay for Play*, 111. For a close look at CCNY and the scandals in New York, see Matthew Goodman, *Triumph, Scandal, and a Legendary Basketball Team* (New York: Ballantine, 2019).

45. Humbert S. Nelli, "Adolph Rupp, The Kentucky Wildcats, and the Basketball Scandal of 1951," *The Register of the Kentucky Historical Society* 84 (Winter 1986), 52–57. Also see Smith, *Pay for Play*, 111, 114.

46. Nelli, "Adolph Rupp," 52–57.

47. "Sport: Lifting the Curtain," *Time* (December 3, 1951), 84.

48. "Excerpts from Judge Streit's Comments on College Basketball Fixing Scandal," *New York Times* (November 20, 1951), 26.
49. "Dr. Byrd Doubts Streit is Qualified to Speak on Sports," *Washington Post* (November 25, 1951), C-6.
50. "Tatum Hits Back at Critic Judge," *The Sun* (November 26, 1951), 28.
51. Nelli, 20–21.
52. *Ibid.*, 21.
53. Red Smith, "View of Sport: It was High Time," *New York Herald Tribune* (November 21, 1951), 22.
54. *Ibid.*
55. Blaik's Army teams compiled a 166–48–14 record. Seven of the 48 losses occurred in the 1951 scandal-ridden season.
56. "Blaik Admits too much Grid Pressure Led to Cheating Scandal," *Hartford Courant* (August 9, 1951), 11.
57. *Ibid.*
58. "Beyond West Point," *New York Herald Tribune* (August 10, 1951), 14.
59. "West Point Tragedy," *Christian Science Monitor* (August 7, 1951), 16.
60. *Ibid.*
61. "Is Football Situation in the Big Four Healthy?" *Durham Morning Herald* (September 30, 1951), 13.
62. "Honor of the Corps," *Newsweek* 38 (August 13, 1951), 78.
63. Morris Siegel, "Iron Curtain Surrounds West Point," *Washington Post* (August 7, 1951), 13.
64. Ronald A. Smith, "The William & Mary Athletic Scandal of 1951: Governance and the Battle for Academic and Athletic Integrity," *Journal of Sport History* 34 (Fall 2007), 355–356. Also see Susan H. Godson, et al., *The College of William and Mary: A History*, vol. II, 1888–1993 (Williamsburg: King and Queen Press, 1993).
65. President Harper hired Amos Alonzo Stagg as coach and athletic director, positions he held at Chicago for 41 years.
66. Voyles was not very successful at Auburn, but a later career with the Hamilton Tiger Cats of the CFL was marked by winning the 1953 Grey Cup.
67. The Delta Bowl, played in Memphis, Tennessee, only survived for two years, 1948 and 1949. Oklahoma A&M is known as Oklahoma State University today.
68. Smith, 357–358.
69. *Ibid.*, 361.
70. *Ibid.*
71. "And Now William & Mary," *Roanoke Times* (August 14, 1951), 6.
72. Ronald A. Smith, "The William & Marty Athletic Scandal of 1951," 364. Ruben McCray never coached again. He spent many years working at the Boys' Home of North Carolina. There are several good works examining the William & Mary scandal. See Ronald A. Smith's *Pay for Play: A History of Big-Time College Athletic Reform* (Champagne: University of Illinois Press). Also see John Sayle Watterson, *College Football: History, Spectacle, Controversy* (Baltimore: Johns Hopkins University Press, 2000).
73. "Many at W&M Surprised by Resignation," *Richmond Times Dispatch* (September 14, 1951), 5.
74. "W&M College Faculty Releases Statement Concerning Recent Academic Irregularities; Unanimously Accepts Formal Resolutions," *The Flat Hat* (September 20, 1951), 1.
75. *Ibid.*
76. *Ibid.*, 2.
77. Charles Karmosky, *Daily Press* (September 21, 1951), 10.
78. "Let's have the full Story on W&M," *Richmond Time-Dispatch* (September 10, 1951), 14.
79. *Ibid.*
80. "Next the Board of Visitors" quoted in *Bulletin of the American Association of University Professors* 37 (Autumn 1951), 486.
81. "B.A. in Athletics," *New York Times* (September 21, 1951), 22.
82. Robert Moore, "Bass seems Choice as Indians' Coach," *Roanoke Times* (August 14, 1951), 15. Also see Shelley Rolfe, "W-M Board Meets, Defers any Action in Coaches' Case," *Richmond Times-Dispatch* (August 16, 1951), 1.
83. "Presidents of Member Institutions of the Southern Conference, September 1, 1951" (Duke, President's Office, A. Hollis Edens Papers, Southern Conference).
84. Letter to A. Hollis Edens from C.P. Summerall, September 3, 1951 (Duke, President's Office, A. Hollis Edens Papers, Southern Conference).
85. Letter to A. Hollis Edens from J.R. Cunningham, September 4, 1951 (Duke, President's Office, A. Hollis Edens Papers, Southern Conference).
86. Letter to A. Hollis Edens from J.W. Harrelson, September 4, 1951 (Duke, President's Office, A. Hollis Edens Papers, Southern Conference).
87. Letter to A. Hollis Edens from John E. Pomfret, September 4, 1951 (Duke, President's Office, A. Hollis Edens Papers, Southern Conference).
88. Letter to A. Hollis Edens from R.F. Poole, September 4, 1951 (Duke, President's Office, A. Hollis Edens Papers, Southern Conference).
89. Letter to A. Hollis Edens from Walter S. Newman, September 5, 1951 (Duke, President's Office, A. Hollis Edens Papers, Southern Conference).
90. Letter to A. Hollis Edens from Irvin Stewart, September 6, 1951 (Duke, President's Office, A. Hollis Edens Papers, Southern Conference).
91. Letter to A. Hollis Edens from Curly Byrd, September 11, 1951 (Duke, President's Office, A. Hollis Edens Papers, Southern Conference).

Chapter 3

1. Letter to Gordon Gray from Curly Byrd, June 4, 1951 (UM, Southern Conference, 1951 [1951–1952]).
2. Letter to Hollis Edens from Gordon Gray,

August 17, 1951 (Duke, President's Office, A. Hollis Edens Papers, Southern Conference).

3. "Football is a Farce," *Life* (September 17, 1951), 38.

4. *Ibid.*

5. Letter to Gordon Gray from Curly Byrd, September 27, 1951 (UM, Southern Conference, 1951 [1950–1952]).

6. William Friday, "Minutes of the Chancellor's Meeting of 9/10/51 in Office of Chancellor Harrelson" (NCSU, Office of the Chancellor, John William Harrelson Records, Chancellors' Meetings, Box 35).

7. Bill Friday was the successor to Gray, leading the North Carolina system from 1956 to his retirement in 1986.

8. "Minutes of the Meeting of Presidents, Faculty Chairmen, and Athletic Directors of the Southern Conference Members Held in Chapel Hill, North Carolina, Friday September 28, 1951" (Duke, President's Office, A. Hollis Edens Papers, Southern Conference).

9. *Ibid.*
10. *Ibid.*
11. *Ibid.*
12. *Ibid.*
13. *Ibid.*
14. *Ibid.*
15. *Ibid.*
16. *Ibid.*
17. *Ibid.*
18. *Ibid.*
19. *Ibid.*

20. "SIC Presidents Act to Restrict Sports," *Durham Sun* (September 28, 1951), 11.

21. "Frowning on Bowls," *Evening Telegram* (Rocky Mount, NC) (October 3, 1951), 4.

22. "Prexies on Notice," *News and Observer* (October 2, 1951), 4.

23. Smith Barrier, "Southern Colleges Vote to Abolish Brid Bowl Games," *Greensboro Daily News* (September 29, 1951), 12.

24. *Ibid.*

25. Dick Herbert, "The Sports Observer," *News and Observer* (September 29, 1951), 11.

26. *Ibid.*
27. *Ibid.*

28. Wilton Garrison, "Sports Parade," *Charlotte Observer* (October 6, 1951), 6.

29. Bob Quincy, "Close-Up," *Charlotte News* (October 9, 1951), B-2. A lover of boxing, Quincy had a long and distinguished writing career at the *Charlotte News* and later at the *Charlotte Observer*.

30. Letter to Dr. Smith from Herbert O'Keef, October 17, 1951 (USC, OOP, Norman Smith, 51–52, Box 1, Southern Conference).

31. Letter to Mr. O'Keef from Norman M. Smith, October 19, 1951 (USC, OOP, Norman Smith, 51–52, Box 1, Southern Conference).

32. Letter to Herbert O'Keef from J.W. Harrelson, October 31, 1951 (NCSU, Office of the Chancellor, John William Harrelson Records, Department of Athletics, Box 34).

33. *Ibid.*
34. *Ibid.*
35. *Ibid.*

36. Letter to J.W. Harrelson from H.A. Fisher, October 26, 1951 (NCSU, Office of the Chancellor, John William Harrelson Records, Department of Athletics, Box 34).

37. *Ibid.*

38. Letter to R.B. House from Alfred Engstrom, November 2, 1951 (UNC, Chancellors' Records: R.B. House Series, Subseries 4: Athletic Affairs, Athletics, 1950–1953).

39. Letter to Zane Robbins from Gordon Gray, November 9, 1951 (UNC, General Administration/Consolidated University: Subgroup 2: Consolidated UNC, Campus Files; Series 2: UNC-CH, Subseries 3: Athletic Affairs; General, 1951).

40. "Suggested Joint Statement by Southern Conference Presidents," n.d. (Duke, President's Office, A. Hollis Edens Papers, Southern Conference).

41. *Ibid.*
42. *Ibid.*

43. "No More Bowl Games and No More Long Trips is Chandler Dictum for W&M Gridmen," *Daily Press* (Newport News) (October 19, 1951), 1.

44. "Sanity in Athletics Makes Headway in the State," *Richmond Times-Dispatch* (October 19, 1951), 14.

45. Susan Tyler Hitchcock, *The University of Virginia: A Pictorial History* (Charlottesville: University Press of Virginia and University of Virginia Bookstore, 1999), 119.

46. "Virginia Rejects all Bowls," *Richmond Times-Dispatch* (November 21, 1951), 12.

47. Watterson, 376.
48. *Ibid.*
49. *Ibid.*
50. *Ibid.*, 379.
51. *Ibid.*

52. "Moving in on the Football Racket," *Richmond Times-Dispatch* (October 14, 1951), B-2.

53. *Ibid.*

54. Letter to Henry B. Sell from J.W. Harrelson, October 8, 1951 (NCSU, Office of the Chancellor, John William Harrelson Records, Department of Athletics, Box 34). Sell was editor of *Town and Country* magazine. In the 1950s, Johns Hopkins abandoned athletic scholarships and played schedules of small institutions very close to Baltimore.

Chapter 4

1. Ace Parker was an outstanding athlete who was inducted into the Pro Football Hall of Fame. Ironically, he later coached as an assistant at rival North Carolina, a bit disappointed that he was passed over for the head position at Duke.

2. Smith Barrier, "Wyoming's Bowden Wyatt No. 1 Candidate for Duke Job," *Daily News* (January 19, 1951), 2–1.

3. "Short Sketch," n.d. (Duke, President's

Office, A. Hollis Edens, Duke University Athletics, Football).

4. Bob Quincy, "Wallace Wade was a Great Coach, but He Made it Tough," *Charlotte News* (May 21, 1952), B-4.

5. Dick Herbert, "The Sports Observer," *News and Observer* (March 6, 1951), 13.

6. The archives at Wake Forest contains letters from some Baptist leaders and alumni who were very critical of Peahead Walker's personality and rumored behavior. Nevertheless, the coach was beloved by players and students.

7. Bass later coached the South Carolina Gamecocks for five seasons ending in 1965. Seemingly never in one place for very long, Bass coached in the college ranks as well as in the NFL, the CFL, the WFL, and even the Continental Football League.

8. Robert Moore, "Football Teams of SC Will Open Drills Saturday," *Roanoke Times* (August 26, 1951), 3.

9. Football and basketball game accounts, throughout this book, have been drawn from the newspapers listed in the bibliography, unless otherwise noted. In the main, the most extensive game coverage is found in the *Charlotte Observer*, the *Greensboro Daily News*, the *News and Observer*, the *Richmond Times-Dispatch*, *The State* (Columbia), and *The Sun* (Baltimore).

10. Dick Herbert, "The Sports Observer," *News and Observer* (October 9, 1951), 13.

11. Jake Penland, "In the Press Box," *The State* (September 20, 1951), 21.

12. Hugo Germino, "Do You Agree," *Durham Sun* (October 8, 1951), B-2.

13. Dick Herbert, "The Sportsview," *News and Observer* (October 29, 1951), 13.

14. Sandy Grady, "Duke's Gamble on Lutz Netted Tie," *Charlotte News* (November 5, 1951), B-7.

15. Jake Penland, "In the Press Box," *The State* (October 26, 1951), D-1.

16. Smith Barrier, "At 4:25—Difference was Punting, Big Bill George," *Greensboro Daily News* (November 13, 1951), 14.

17. The Chicago Bears retired Bill George's number 61.

18. In 1948, Justice finished second to SMU's Doak Walker. The following year, he finished second again. This time he came up short to Notre Dame's Leon Hart. Hart was a great end, but he had the benefit of playing for an undefeated Notre Dame. North Carolina football did not have any of the prestige of the Irish.

19. Smith Barrier, "Football Coach Decision off until Dec. 4," *Greensboro Daily News* (November 15, 1951), 24.

20. Irwin Smallwood, No Title, *Greensboro Daily News* (November 15, 1951), 24.

21. Smith Barrier, "Football Coach," 24.

22. "Council Won't Say Whether Snavely in or out," *News and Observer* (November 15, 1951), 15.

23. Smith Barrier, "Football Coach," 24.

24. Smith Barrier, No Title, *Greensboro Daily News* (November 17, 1951), 10.

25. The R.B. House Papers at UNC Chapel Hill possesses several letters from fans and alumni concerning Snavely and Tatum. They run the gamut from those who wanted Tatum at any cost to supporters who wished to retain Snavely.

26. Jake Penland, "In the Pressbox," *The State* (November 21, 1951), B-1.

27. *Ibid.*

28. Dick Herbert, "The Sports Observer," *News and Observer* (November 16, 1951), 19.

29. "Statement Made to Herb O'Keef RE Athletic Situation," December 2, 1951 (UNC, General Administration/Consolidated University: Subgroup 2: Consolidated UNC Campus Files; Series 2: UNC-CH; Subseries 3: Athletic Affairs; General, 1951).

30. *Ibid.*

31. *Ibid.*

32. Letter to Jim Tatum from Jack Horner, November 14, 1951 (UM, Athletics—Misc. (1/2)—1951).

33. *Ibid.*

34. Morris Siegel, "Sugar Bowl Gives Terps 'Heavy Consideration,'" *Washington Post* (October 29, 1951), 12.

35. Gildea, "Veteran Sportswriter Morris Siegel Dies at 78," *Washington Post* (June 3, 1994).

36. Shirley Povich, "The Morning," *Washington Post* (November 12, 1951), 10. For a detailed look at Shirley Povich, see Lee Congdon, *Legendary Sports Writers of the Golden Age: Grantland Rice, Red Smith, Shirley Povich, and W.C. Heinz* (Lanham, MD: Rowman & Littlefield, 2017).

37. Leonard Koppett, "Tatum Says Football Coaches Cause Much of Bad Publicity," *New York Herald Tribune* (November 13, 1951), 28.

38. Joseph M. Sheehan, "Maryland Favorably Inclined Toward Bowl Game Bids," *New York Times* (November 13, 1951), 49.

39. *Ibid.*

40. Harold Wimmer, "Time for Sports," *Roanoke Times* (November 18, 1951), 18.

41. *Ibid.*

42. Letter to Herbert O'Keef from A. Hollis Edens, November 30, 1951 (Duke, President's Office, A. Hollis Edens, Duke University Athletics, Football).

43. Statement on Sugar Bowl, November 16, 1951 (UM, Athletics—Misc. (1/2)—1951).

44. *Ibid.*

45. Louis M. Hatter, "Maryland and Tennessee Accept Sugar Bowl Invitations," *The Sun* (November 17, 1951), 11.

46. "Wade 'Surprised' Maryland did not Consult Conference," *The Sun* (November 17, 1951), 11.

47. *Ibid.*

48. Jake Penland, "In the Press Box," *The State* (November 18, 1951), B-1.

49. "USC Teacher Hits Catering to Athletics," *The State* (August 14, 1951), A-1.

50. *Ibid.*

51. "Maryland Blasted by Dallas Editor," *Roanoke Times* (November 19, 1951), 13.

52. Ibid.
53. Burdine Stadium later would be renamed the Orange Bowl.
54. Memo by Lee Milford, no date (CU, Athletic Council Records, Box 2, Series 26, Athletic Council, 1951, August–December).
55. Ibid.
56. Carter Latimer, "Scoopin' 'em Up," *Greenville News* (November 28, 1951), 18.
57. Ibid.
58. Dick Herbert, "The Sports Observer," *News and Observer* (November 30, 1951), 19.
59. Ibid.
60. "Function or Quit," *News and Observer* (November 30, 1951), 4.
61. Chauncey Durden, "The Sportview," *Richmond Times Dispatch* (November 28, 1951), 23.
62. "Both Clemson and Maryland Should be Fired by the SC," *Richmond Times Dispatch* (November 30, 1951), 18.
63. "Conference Authority Defied," *Roanoke Times* (November 29, 1951), 6.
64. Ibid.
65. Telegram to Wallace Wade from Lee Milford, November 25, 1951 (CU, Athletic Council Records, Box 2, Series 26, Athletic Council, 1951, August–December).
66. Telegram to Wallace Wade from Lee Milford, No Date (CU, Athletic Council Records, Box 2, Series 26, Athletic Council, 1951, August–December). Date of the telegram is confirmed by a letter from Wallace Wade to Lee Milford on November 30, 1951. It is in the same file as the previous document.
67. Letter to Lee Milford from Wallace Wade, December 5, 1951 (UM, Southern Conference September–December, 1951).
68. Letter to A.C. Mann from Lee W. Milford, December 19, 1951 (CU, Athletic Council Records, Box 2, Series 26, Athletic Council, 1951, August–December).
69. Ibid.
70. Letter to Wilbur C. Johns from Geary Eppley, December 12, 1951 (UM, Southern Conference, September–December 1951).
71. Smith Barrier, "Byrd Dodges Bowl Issue, Saves Fire," *Greensboro Daily News* (December 11, 1951), 15. Carmichael Auditorium on the Chapel Hill campus, home of North Carolina basketball for many years, was named in honor of Billy Carmichael.
72. Ibid.
73. Ibid.
74. Dick Herbert, "The Sports Observer," *News and Observer* (December 12, 1951), 15.
75. Ibid.
76. Dick Herbert, "The Sports Observer," *News and Observer* (December 8, 1951), 9.
77. "Frank Howard has Program for Football," *Greensboro Daily News* (December 11, 1951), 15.
78. Smith Barrier, *Greensboro Daily News* (December 14, 1951), 37. In January 1930, the University of Iowa was suspended from Big Ten competition because a university investigation discovered that the athletic program had conducted illegal loans with athletes and used a slush fund to help recruit. Their 1930 football squad only played one Big Ten team during the season. Iowa football went into a steep decline for several years. See Raymond Schmidt, "The 1929 Iowa Football Scandal: Paying Tribute to the Carnegie Report?" *Journal of Sport History* 34 (Fall 2007), 343–351.
79. Dick Herbert, "The Sports Observer," *News and Observer* (December 14, 1951), 21.
80. Harold Williamson, "Time for Sports," *Roanoke Times* (December 9, 1951), 31.
81. Ibid.
82. Ibid.
83. Jack Horner, "Jack Horner's Sports Corner," *Durham Morning Herald* (December 10, 1951), II-2.
84. Ibid.
85. Chauncey Durden, "The Sport View," *Richmond Times-Dispatch* (December 14, 1959), 34.
86. "Coaches Support Grid Activities," *Roanoke Times* (December 13, 1951), 49.
87. Ibid.
88. "Southeastern Conference Refuses to Ban Bowl Games or Spring Practice," *Roanoke Times* (December 15, 1951), 12.
89. Wallace Wade, "Meeting of the Executive Committee of the Southern Conference at the John Marshall Hotel, in Richmond, Virginia, December 13, 1953" (UM, Southern Conference, September–December, 1951).
90. Letter to William P. Cole Jr., from Curly Byrd, December 18, 1951 (UM, Southern Conference 1951 [1951–1952]).
91. "Request of the University of Maryland for Permission of the Southern Conference to Play a Football Game at New Orleans with the University of Tennessee on January 1, 1952" (UM, Southern Conference 1951 [1951–1952]).
92. Ibid.
93. Ibid.
94. Ibid.
95. Ibid.
96. Chauncey Durden, "The Sport View," *Richmond Times-Dispatch* (December 15, 1951), 10.
97. Dick Herbert, "The Sports Observer," *News and Observer* (December 15, 1951), 9.
98. "Schools Told Must Change '52 Schedules," *Greenville News* (December 15, 1951), 1.
99. Ibid.
100. Dick Herbert, "Conference Punished Balking Members and Kept Group Intact," *News and Observer* (December 16, 1951), 26.
101. Dick Herbert, "The Sports Observer," *News and Observer* (December 17, 1951), 13.
102. Smith Barrier, *Greensboro Daily News* (December 16, 1951), 32.
103. Ibid.
104. Dick Herbert, "Bowl-Bound Football Teams Put on Probation for a Year," *News and Observer* (December 15, 1951), 2.

105. Smith Barrier, *Greensboro Daily News* (December 16, 1951), 32.
106. *Ibid.*
107. Robert Moore, "Loop Delays Action on Frosh Participation," *Greensboro Daily News* (December 16, 1951), 29.
108. *Ibid.*
109. Robert Moore, "Clemson Officials say School Got Raw Deal," *Roanoke Times* (December 16, 1951), 32.
110. *Ibid.*
111. Chauncey Durden, "The Sportview," *Richmond Times-Dispatch* (December 16, 1951), IV-1.
112. Dick Herbert, "The Sports Observer," *News and Observer* (December 18, 1951), 13.
113. Carter Latimer, "Scoopin' 'em Up," *Greenville News* (December 16, 1951), Sports-1.
114. *Ibid.*
115. Harold Wimmer, "Time for Sports," *Roanoke Times* (December 16, 1951), 31.
116. "Boycott Brings Grid Scramble," *Roanoke Times* (December 16, 1951), 31.
117. "Terps and Tigers on Probation," *Roanoke Times* (December 18, 1951), 6.
118. "Let 'em Go," *Roanoke Times* (December 19, 1951), 6.
119. *Ibid.*
120. Morris Siegel, "Carolina's Schools Decide to Punish Maryland, and Do It," *Washington Post* (December 16, 1951), C-5.
121. *Ibid.*
122. *Ibid.*
123. *Ibid.*
124. Morris Siegel, "Terps Turning Boycott on W. Virginia, GW," *Washington Post* (December 17, 1953), 12.
125. Shirley Povich, "This Morning with Shirley Povich," *Washington Post* (December 18, 1951), 17.
126. Letter to Hollis Edens from Bert Whittington, December 17, 1951 (Duke, President's Office, A. Hollis Edens, Duke University Athletics, Football).
127. *Ibid.*
128. Letter to A. Hollis Edens from A Foot Ball Fan, December 15, 1951 (Duke, President's Office, A. Hollis Edens, Duke University, Football).
129. Letter to A. Hollis Edens from Herbert O'Keef, December 20, 1951 (Duke, President's Office, A. Hollis Edens, Duke University Athletics, Football).
130. "Minutes of the Meeting of the Board of Trustees of the Clemson Agricultural College held in the Governor's Office, State Capitol, Columbia, South Carolina," December 27, 1951, https//tigerprints.clemson.edu/trustees_minutes/578.
131. *Ibid.*
132. *Ibid.*
133. Letter to Bernie Harris from H.C. Byrd, December 20, 1951 (UM, Athletics—Misc. (1/2)—1951).
134. *Ibid.*
135. "Alumni Present Tatum with Car," *Baltimore Sun* (December 19, 1951), 17.
136. Harold Wimmer, "Time for Sports," *Roanoke Times* (January 3, 1952), 14.
137. "Emphasize Football Sez Sad Tigs' Coach," *Charlotte News* (January 2, 1952), B-4.
138. Minutes of Meeting of Faculty Athletic Committee, November 26, 1951 (NCSU Committees, Council on Athletics Records, 1949–1953, Box 2).
139. Beattie Feathers enjoyed a long coaching career after being fired at State. For many years, he was an assistant football coach at Wake Forest and spent his last years as head baseball coach for the Deacons.
140. "Hendrickson Named to State College Grid Position," *Greensboro Daily News* (December 13, 1951), 4-1.
141. Moses Crutchfield, "Feathers to be Retained as Frosh Coach," *Greensboro Daily News* (December 13, 1951), 4-1. Feathers was retained as freshman football coach before Hendrickson offered him a position on his staff.
142. *North Carolina State College 1952 Football Information* (Raleigh: North Carolina State University, 1952), 12–14. In 1980, Hendrickson was inducted into the Elon Sports Hall of Fame. In 2011, the Horace Hendrickson Football Center at Elon opened, honoring one of Elon's greatest coaches and advocates.

Chapter 5

1. Fast break basketball was pioneered by several coaches, most notably John McLendon at North Carolina College at Durham (today's North Carolina Central University) and Frank Keaney at Rhode Island.
2. Jerry Krause and Ralph Pim, *Lessons from the Legends: Beyond the X's and O's* (Monterey, CA: Coaches Choice, 2006), 66–67. For a full biography of Everett Case see Tim Peeler, *Legends of N.C. State Basketball* (New York: Sports Publishing, 2015) and *NC State Basketball: 100 Years of Innovation* (Raleigh: North Carolina State University Athletics Department, 2010).
3. Krause and Pim, 68.
4. Harry T. Paxton, "Basketball Bug Bites Dixie," *Saturday Evening Post* (March 10, 1951), 31; 111–114. Even the obstructed view seats in Reynolds were close enough to the floor to provide a great game experience.
5. Hugo Germino, "Do You Agree," *Durham Sun* (November 17, 1950), B-2.
6. *Ibid.*
7. Herb Heft, "In-Again, Out-Again Millikan is in Again," *Washington Post* (April 21, 1950), B-4.
8. Dick Herbert, "The Sports Observer," *News and Observer* (December 1, 1951), 11.
9. Van Newman, "Wouldn't Trade Selvy for Dick Groat: Alley," *Columbia Record* (December 12, 1951), B-6.
10. Frank Ballenger, "North Carolina Rolls over Furman, 100 to 57," *Greenville News* (December 4, 1951), 9.

11. Dick Herbert, "The Sports Observer," *News and Observer* (December 12, 1951), 15.

12. J. Samuel Walker, *ACC Basketball: The Story of the Rivalries, Traditions, and Scandals of the First Two Decades of the Atlantic Coast Conference* (Chapel Hill: University of North Carolina Press, 2011), 63–64. For a full examination of the Dixie Classic, see Bethany Bradsher's *The Classic: How Everett Case and His Tournament Brought Big-Time Basketball to the South* (Houston: Whitecaps Media, 2011). Amazingly, all Dixie Classic championships were won by Big Four squads.

13. Dick Herbert, "The Sports Observer," *News and Observer* (December 31, 1951), 9.

14. Ibid.

15. Workman would break almost every significant West Virginia basketball record by the end of the season.

16. Stansbury Hall was razed in 2019. While playing in the arena, West Virginia won 82 percent of their games. It was the Mountaineers' basketball home until West Virginia Coliseum opened in 1970.

17. After his playing days, Morrison was head basketball coach at South Carolina, Mercer, and Georgia Tech.

18. Later, Shue was a five-time NBA All-Star, playing 12 years in the league. After retiring from the court, he coached in the NBA from 1966 to 1989. It was a remarkable career for a player that few wanted out of high school.

19. Like Gene Shue, Frank Selvy enjoyed a distinguished NBA career playing nine years in the league and earning All-NBA twice.

20. Jack Horner, "Sport's Corner," *Herald-Sun* (February 14, 1952), 4–1.

21. Hugo Germino, "Do You Agree," *Durham Sun* (March 1, 1952), 8.

22. Ibid. In his final season at Duke, Groat was an All-American in basketball and baseball. The only other Southern Conference athlete to achieve that distinction was Clemson's Banks McFadden, who earned both honors in football and basketball in 1939.

23. Eddie Allen, "Old Coaches Visit Tourney to See Groat," *Charlotte Observer* (March 7, 1952), 24.

24. Dick Herbert, "The Sports Observer," *News and Observer* (March 3, 1952), 13.

25. Ibid.

26. Ibid.

27. Ibid.

28. Chauncy Durden, "The Sportview," *Times-Dispatch* (March 9, 1952), IV-1. Durden gave the best analysis of the controversial final play of the game.

29. Bob Quincy, "W.Va.'s Brown Won Friends, Influenced People Despite Loss," *Charlotte Observer* (March 11, 1952), 16.

30. Ibid.

31. Dick Herbert, "The Sports Observer," *News and Observer* (March 11, 1952), 11.

Chapter 6

1. Letter to Norman Smith from H.C. Byrd, January 24, 1952 (SC, OOP, N. Smith, Box 3, Departments and Schools: Athletics).

2. Letter to H.C. Byrd from Norman Smith, January 26, 1952 (SC, OOP, N. Smith, Box 3, Departments and Schools: Athletic).

3. Letter to H.C. Byrd from R.F. Poole, February 3, 1952 (UM, Southern Conference Presidents—Letters re. Bowl Games (Folder 1 of 2), 1952.

4. Letter to H.C. Byrd from J.R. Cunningham, February 4, 1952 (UM, Southern Conference Presidents—Letters re. Bowl Games (Folder 1 of 2), 1952).

5. Letter to H.C. Byrd from Irvin Stewart, February 4, 1952 (UM, Southern Conference Presidents—Letters re. Bowl Games (Folder 1 of 2), 1952).

6. Ibid.

7. Letter to H.C. Byrd from R.J. Marshall, February 4, 1952 (UM, Southern Conference Presidents—Letters re. Bowl Games (Folder 1 of 2), 1952).

8. Letter to H.C. Byrd from Harold Tribble, February 5, 1952 (UM, Southern Conference Presidents—Letters re. Bowl Games (Folder 1 of 2), 1952).

9. Ibid.

10. Letter to H.C. Byrd from John Plyler, February 18, 1952 (UM, Southern Conference Presidents—Letters re. Bowl Games (Folder 1 of 2), 1952).

11. Letter to H.C. Byrd from R.F. Poole, January 30, 1952 (UM, Southern Conference Presidents—Letters re. Bowl Games (Folder 1 of 2), 1952).

12. Ibid.

13. Letter to R.F. Poole from H.C. Byrd, February 4, 1952 (UM, Southern Conference Presidents—Letters re. Bowl Games (Folder 1 of 2), 1952).

14. Letter to H.C. Byrd from R.F. Poole, February 9, 1952(UM, Southern Conference Presidents—Letters re. Bowl Games (Folder 1 of 2), 1952).

15. William Friday, "Memorandum to Presidents of the Southern Conference Institutions," February 14, 1952 (Duke, President's Office, A. Hollis Edens Papers, Southern Conference).

16. "The SC Shouldn't Weaken in Cleaning Up Athletics," *Richmond Times-Dispatch* (March 12, 1952), 14.

17. Ibid.

18. Chauncey Durden, "The Sportview," *Richmond Times-Dispatch* (March 12, 1952), 21.

19. Herb Heft, "Byrd Says Terps Deserved Spanking for Going to Bowl," *Washington Post* (March 9, 1952), C-1.

20. Letter to Norman Smith from H.C. Byrd, May 5, 1952 (SC, OOP, N. Smith, 51–52, Box 1, Southern Conference).

21. Ibid.

22. Corrie, 42.

23. Ibid.

24. Letter to H.C. Byrd from R.F. Poole, May 9, 1952 (UM, Southern Conference Presidents, 1952).
25. The American Council of Education, founded in 1918, assisted in coordinating the development of higher education. Discussions of the ACE report are found in many works. See John R. Thelin, *History of American Higher Education* and *Games Colleges Play*.
26. See Beth J. Shapiro's "John Hannah and the Growth of Big-Time College Intercollegiate Athletics at Michigan State University," *Journal of Sport History* 10 (Winter 1983), 26–40.
27. "Report: Special Committee on Athletic Policy of the American Council on Education," February 16, 1952 (SC, OOP Norman Smith, 51–52, Box 1, NCAA). This report was widely distributed to the media and all institutions playing collegiate athletics.
28. *Ibid.*
29. Bill Free, "Fifty Years Ago, Terps Ruled," *The Sun* (November 3, 2001), accessed on April 29, 2021, https://www.baltimoresun.com/news/bs-xpm-2001-11-23-0111230149-story.html.
30. *Ibid.*
31. Dick Herbert, "The Sports Observer," *News and Observer* (May 10, 1952), 11.
32. "Report: Special Committee on Athletic Policy."
33. Letter to Hollis Edens from John Plyler, March 31, 1952 (Duke, President's Office A. Hollis Edens Papers, Southern Conference).
34. Letter to the Presidents of the Southern Conference from Walter Newman, December 2, 1952 (UM, Southern Conference Presidents, 1952).
35. Ronald L. Heinemann, *Depression and New Deal in Virginia: The Enduring Dominion* (Charlottesville: University Press of Virginia, 1983), 96.
36. "Howard Hits Restrictions of College Heads," *The State* (May 22, 1952), B-8.
37. *Ibid.*
38. Letter to Donald Russell from H.C. Byrd, November 7, 1952 (SC, OOP, Russell, 52–53, Box 2, Associations: Southern Conference).
39. Letter to H.C. Byrd from Donald Russell, November 10, 1952 (SC, OOP, Russell, 52–53, Box 2, Associations: Southern Conference). Russell's popularity was so great that he was the only candidate considered for the university's presidency and was unanimously endorsed by administration, faculty, students, and alumni.
40. Letter to H.C. Byrd from Hollis Edens, November 11, 1952 (UM, Southern Conference—Letters to the Presidents re. Bowl Games, Folder 2 of 2, 1952).
41. Shirley Povich, "This Morning," *Washington Post* (November 25, 1952), 24.
42. "Maryland's President Blames Coaches for Football Collapse," *New York Times* (November 25, 1952), 36.
43. Larry Laurent, "Terps Prexy Says He was just Kidding in Remarks," *The Sun* (November 26, 1952), 15.
44. *Ibid.*
45. *Ibid.*
46. Louis M. Hatter, "Byrd Foresees League Change," *The Sun* (November 29, 1952), Sports-15.
47. *Ibid.*
48. *Ibid.*
49. Smith Barrier, *Greensboro Daily News* (November 15, 1952), 2-2.
50. Jake Penland, "In the Press Box," *The State* (December 5, 1952), D-1.
51. Dick Herbert, "The Sports Observer," *News and Observer* (December 12, 1952), 21.
52. "Minutes of the Southern Conference Presidents' Meeting," December 11, 1952 (Duke, President's Office, A. Hollis Edens Papers, Southern Conference).
53. *Ibid.*
54. Carter Latimer, "Scoopin' 'em Up," *Greenville News* (December 14, 1952), Sports-1.
55. "S-C Confab Produces Few Concrete Moves," *The State* (December 13, 1952), B-1.
56. Larry Laurent, "Conference Presidents Shun Bowl, Split Talk," *Washington Post* (December 12, 1952), 37.
57. Jake Penland, "In the Press Box," *The State* (December 14, 1952), B-1.
58. "Rift Results as Cavaliers Drop Rival in Football," *Washington Post* (December 8, 1952), 1.
59. *Ibid.*

Chapter 7

1. Meadows' pro career was highly controversial, especially after he leveled a brutal hit on Detroit's Bobby Layne in 1956, a shot that left Layne with a concussion. Many fans accused Meadows of being a dirty player.
2. Smith Barrier, *Greensboro Daily News* (September 17, 1952), 2-5.
3. After Dick Modzelewski graduated Maryland, he was in the NFL from 1953 to 1989 as a player and then as a coach.
4. "Wolfpack is Victim of 39-0 Grid Upset," *Durham Sun* (September 29, 1952), B-2.
5. Smith Barrier, *Greensboro Daily News* (September 27, 1952), 2–2.
6. Smith Barrier, "Lutz-to-Pitts Passes Good for Triumph," *Greensboro Daily News* (September 27, 1952), 2-2.
7. "Wade Charges Football Now Promotional," *Greensboro Daily News* (September 30, 1952), 2–5.
8. Smith Barrier, "Fullback Hal Davidson Stricken with Disease," *Greensboro Daily News* (October 3, 1952), 4-1.
9. Moses Crutchfield, "Davidson Sets State Contest to Next Week," *Greensboro Daily News* (October 4, 1952), 2–2.
10. Dick Herbert, "The Sports Observer," *News and Observer* (October 4, 1952), 11.
11. Moses Crutchfield, "Wolfpack Humbled by Bulldog Power," *Greensboro Daily News* (October 5, 1952), Sports-1.
12. Bill Rone, "Gamecocks Dealt Double Blow

as They Lose to Duke while Locker Room is Burglarized," *The State* (October 12, 1952), B-1.

13. Brent Breedin, "Howard Says 'No Comment' after Routing," *Greenville News* (October 12, 1952), B-1.

14. Irwin Smallwood, *Greensboro Daily News* (October 16, 1952), 2–8.

15. "Gray Hints Relaxation of Stand on Football," *Greensboro Daily News* (October 15, 1952), 2–1.

16. Smith Barrier, "Gray Opens Door … Will Southern Conference Remove Ban on Bowl Games?" *Greensboro Daily News* (October 16, 1952), 2–8.

17. Ibid.

18. Ibid.

19. Ibid.

20. Ibid.

21. Will Grimsley, "Will Terps, Duke Show in Bowls," *Charlotte Observer* (November 1, 1952), 8.

22. Wilton Garrison, "Sports Parade," *Charlotte Observer* (October 29, 1952), 10.

23. William A. Shirers, "Presidents Hold Firm to Ruling," *Greensboro Daily News* (November 3, 1952), 2–2.

24. Ibid.

25. Smith Barrier, *Greensboro Daily News* (October 26, 1952), Sports-2.

26. Ibid.

27. Ibid.

28. Hugo Germino, "Do You Agree," *Durham Sun* (November 3, 1952), B-2.

29. Smith Barrier, *Greensboro Daily News* (November 16, 1952), Sports-4.

30. Sandy Grady, "Tatum after Sparts, but Byrd says 'No,'" *Charlotte News* (November 4, 1952), B-5.

31. Jake Penland, "Gamecocks Score Stunning Upset over Virginia," *The State* (November 2, 1952), B-1.

32. Smith Barrier, *Greensboro Daily News* (November 10, 1952), 2–2.

33. Dick Herbert, "Snavely Denies he has Resigned at Carolina," *News and Observer* (November 10, 1952), 13.

34. "U.M. Student Accused of Trying to Bribe 3 Grid Starts Gives Up," *Baltimore Sun* (October 30, 1952), 40.

35. "Glickfield Found Guilty in Bribe Case," *Sun* (May 19, 1953), 32.

36. "Tatum Assumes Blame, Says Officials Helped," *Greensboro Daily News* (November 19, 1952), 2–5.

37. Chauncey Durden, "The Sportview," *Richmond Times-Dispatch* (November 19, 1952), 22.

38. Louis M. Hatter, "Tatum Blames Week Layoff," *Sun* (November 24, 1952), 17.

39. Paul Menton, "Navy is Considering Trip to Orange Bowl," *Evening Sun* (November 24, 1952), 35.

40. Van Newman, *The Columbia Record* (December 1, 1952), B-3.

41. Irving Marsh, "Snavely Call Coach Victim, Not Cause, of Football 'Evils,'" *New York Herald Tribune* (January 18, 1953), B-2.

42. Snavely's coaching career did not end after his resignation in Chapel Hill. He was on the job market for only a couple of months when he was hired to coach the Washington University Bears in St. Louis, a far cry from the pressures at North Carolina. He retired from coaching in 1958.

43. Herb Heft, "North Carolina Football Players Campaign against Barclay," *Washington Post* (January 1, 1953), 11.

44. University of Virginia, "Board of Visitors Minutes" (February 13, 1953), http://xtf.lib.virginia.edu/xtf/view?docId=2006_10/uvaGenText/tei/bov_19530213.xml&chunk.id=d3&toc.id=d3&brand=default, accessed on August 10, 2022.

45. Letter to Colgate Darden from Gus Tebell, February 12, 1953 (UVA, Papers of the President, Colgate Darden, Athletics, January–June 1953, Box 3). Art Guepe spent nine seasons at Vanderbilt where he had some success, including a 1955 Gator Bowl victory.

46. Ibid.

Chapter 8

1. Earle Hellen, "Recording Sports," *Greensboro Record* (January 2, 1953), B-2.

2. "Coach Gets Gifts," *News and Observer* (December 10, 1952), 17.

3. Jack Horner, "Sport's Corner," *Herald-Sun* (December 11, 1952), IV-1.

4. Tom Scott later coached basketball at Davidson serving as their athletic director from 1955 to 1974.

5. Gerald Holland, "Dixie's Yankee Hero," *Sports Illustrated* (December 9, 1957), 82.

6. Sam Goldaper, "Frank McGuire, 80, Basketball Coach, Dies," *New York Times* (October 12, 1994), B8.

7. For a detailed examination of Bones McKinney's career see Bethany Bradsher's *Bones McKinney: Basketball's Unforgettable Showman* (Alpena, MI: Whitecaps Media, 2014). Also see Bones McKinney's *Honk Your Horn If You Love Basketball* (Shrewsbury, MA: Garland, 1988).

8. Smith Barrier, "Tar Heels Beat State 70–69; Retain Conference Lead," *Greensboro Daily News* (January 25, 1953), Sports-2.

9. Bob Brooks, "Case's Favorite Suit has Tar Heels Jinxed," *News and Observer* (January 24, 1953), 12.

10. Ken Alyta, "McGuire Revives Carolina Win Spirit," *Greensboro Daily News* (January 29, 1953), B-2.

11. "Spider Frosh Top UNC in Overtime," *Greensboro Record* (February 4, 1953), B-8.

12. In 1954, Selvy scored 100 points against Newberry College, setting the NCAA record for points in one game.

13. Earle Hellen, "Recording Sports," *Greensboro Record* (February 13, 1953), B-2.

14. Smith Barrier, *Greensboro Daily News* (February 15, 1953), Sports-5.

15. Telegram to Roy Clogston from Wallace Wade, February 2, 1951 (NCSU, Athletics Subject Files, 1948–1951, Box 2).

16. Letter to Wallace Wade from Roy Clogston, February 7, 1951 (NCSU, Athletics Subject Files, 1948–1951, Box 2).

17. Earle Hellen, "Amazing Duke Five Spells End of Wolfpack's Big Four Reign," *Greensboro Record* (February 16, 1953), B-4.

18. Smith Barrier, *Greensboro Daily News* (February 23, 1953), 2–2.

19. Irwin Smallwood, *Greensboro Daily News* (February 26, 1953), 2–4.

20. Dick Herbert, "The Sports Observer," *News and Observer* (February 17, 1953), 13.

21. Ibid.

22. After successfully coaching swimming at State, Willis Casey became athletic director from 1969 to 1986.

23. Smith Barrier, *Greensboro Daily News* (March 6, 1953), 4–1.

24. Dick Herbert, "State and Wake Forest Reach Tourney Finals," *News and Observer* (March 7, 1953), 11.

25. Jack Horner, "Pack's Reign Comes to End," *Herald-Sun* (March 8, 1953), II-1.

26. Dick Pierce, "Deacons Win Loop Crown, 71–70," *Charlotte Observer* (March 8, 1953), D-1.

27. Irwin Smallwood, "Greason: Greatest Thrill of Career," *Greensboro Daily News* (March 8, 1953), Sports-1.

28. Ibid., Sports-2.

29. Ibid.

30. Sandy Grady, "Skill Won it, but only Fate Gathered the 'Unlikely' Deacs," *Charlotte News* (March 9, 1953), B-5.

31. Bob Brooks, "Greason Waited Twenty Years to Win Tourney," *News and Observer* (March 8, 1953), II-1.

32. Smith Barrier, *Greensboro Daily News* (March 9, 1953), 2–3.

33. Jake Penland, "Deacs Grab S-C Title," *The State* (March 8, 1953), B-1.

Chapter 9

1. Walter Newman to Southern Conference Presidents, February 19, 1953 (Duke, President's Office, A. Hollis Edens Papers, Southern Conference).

2. Reese Hart, "Frosh Teams Gain Support of Members," *Charlotte Observer* (April 28, 1953), 13.

3. Hollis Edens to Walter Newman, n.d. (Duke, President's Office, A. Hollis Edens Papers, Southern Conference).

4. Ibid.

5. Walter Newman to Southern Conference Presidents, March 27, 1953 (Duke, President's Office, A. Hollis Edens Papers, Southern Conference).

6. Jim Schlosser, "Depression Kept Sedgefield from Intended Course: Sedgefield Never Became What it was supposed to be, Another Pinehurst, but the Course has Developed its own Distinct Charm and Personality after 70 Years," *Greensboro News and Record* (June 27, 1988).

7. Sedgefield and Starmount Country Clubs alternated hosting the Greater Greensboro Open until 1961.

8. Smith Barrier, *Greensboro Daily News* (May 3, 1953), Sports-4.

9. Earl Hellen, "Recording Sports," *Greensboro Record* (May 6, 1953), D-1.

10. Dick Herbert, "The Sports Observer," *News and Observer* (May 6, 1953), 13.

11. Irwin Smallwood, *Greensboro Daily News* (May 7, 1953), 2–9.

12. "Realignment Seen Near as S. Conference Meets," *The Sun* (May 8, 1953), 21.

13. Ibid.

14. Chauncey Durden, "The Sport View," *Richmond Times-Dispatch* (May 8, 1953), 35. Durden had worked at the *Charlotte News* before moving to Richmond.

15. Ibid.

16. Herman Blackman, "Seven Big Schools Glad Over Split," *Washington Post* (May 10, 1953), C-3.

17. Irwin Smallwood, "Split of Conference Appears Imminent—Could Come Today," *Greensboro Daily News* (May 8, 1953), 4–1. Smallwood, young in his career, was emerging as one of the greatest golf writers in the country. Although an average player, he adored the game and was a close friend of Arnold Palmer's.

18. "Following are the Minutes of the Various Meetings Held at Sedgefield INN, Greensboro, North Carolina on May 7 and 8 1953" (WFU, Tribble Paper, Box 3/34). Each of the archives of the seven seceding institutions maintains a copy of these minutes.

19. Ibid.

20. Ibid.

21. Dick Herbert, "The Sports Observer," *News and Observer* (May 12, 1953), 13.

22. Ibid.

23. "Gray Gives Stand on Bowls for New League: Carolina, State Favor Frosh Ban," *News and Observer* (May 12, 1953), 13.

24. Smith Barrier, *Greensboro Daily News* (May 12, 1953), Sports-2.

25. "Following are the Minutes."

26. Ibid.

27. Ibid.

28. "Meeting of the Southern Conference Institutions Which Had Expressed No Desire to Withdraw from the Southern Conference," May 8, 1953 (VT, RG 2/10, Southern Conference, 1953, Box 8).

29. Ibid.

30. Ibid.

31. Ibid.

32. "Following are the Minutes."

33. Ibid.

34. Chauncey Durden, "Sportview," *Richmond Times-Dispatch* (May 9, 1953), 12.

35. "Following are the Minutes."

36. AP, "Seven School Pull Out of Southern

Conference: Gamecocks, Tigers are included in Rebel List, Penney named Group Chairman at NC Meeting," *The State* (May 9, 1953), B,1.

37. *Ibid.*

38. Moses Crutchfield, *Greensboro Daily News* (May 27, 1953), 2–2.

39. Smith Barrier, "New Conference's Details Planned; ECC Considered," *Greensboro Daily News* (May 27, 1953), 2–3.

40. Earle Hellen, "Recording Sports," *Greensboro Record* (May 9, 1953), B-2.

41. Smith Barrier, *Greensboro Daily News* (May 10, 1953), Sports-4.

42. Letter to C.P. Miles from Lee Milford, June 2, 1953 (CU, Athletic Council Records, Box 5, Series 26, ACC, 1953).

43. *Ibid.*

44. Shelley Rolfe, "Timely Dispatches," *Richmond Times-Dispatch* (April 29, 1953), 15.

45. Earle Hellen, "Recording Sports," *Greensboro Record* (May 9, 1953), B-2.

46. Letter to Roy Hawley from Roy Clogston, May 11, 1953 (NCSU Athletics, Subject Files, 1952–1954, Box 3).

47. Letter to Bill Brannin from Roy Clogston, May 19, 1953 (NCSU Athletics, Subject Files, 1952–1954, Box 3).

48. *Ibid.*

49. "Sports in Progress," *Daily Progress* (May 12, 1953), 12.

50. "Sports in Progress," *Daily Progress* (May 19, 1953), 10.

51. *Ibid.*

52. *Ibid.*

53. *Ibid.*

54. Jerry Armstrong, "Views and Previews," *Technician* (May 15, 1953), 6.

55. "Big 5 for the Big 7," *Daily Tar Heel* (May 15, 1953), 2.

56. Charles Wray, "Cameron Discusses Conference Break," *Duke Chronicle* (May 15, 1953), 1.

57. *Ibid.*

58. "A Chance to Start Anew," *Old Gold and Black* (May 18, 1953), 4.

59. Johnny Ray, "Game Time," *The Gamecock* (May 15, 1953), 6.

60. "Trailing the Tiger," *The Tiger* (May 14, 1953), 4.

61. *Diamondback* (May 12, 1953), 1.

62. John Handley, "Cat Tails," *The Davidsonian* (May 8, 1953), 3.

63. John Handley, "Cat Tales," *The Davidsonian* (May 15, 1953), 3. Bill Dole coached at East Carolina College before taking the job at Davidson. He coached Davidson from 1952 through 1964.

64. Dave Rubenstein, "Seven Schools withdraw from Southern Conference," *The Flat Hat* (May 12, 1953), 5.

65. Jim Rudin, "Rudin's Ramblings," *The Hatchet* (September 29, 1953), 8.

66. *Ibid.*

67. *Ibid.*

68. Lucien Hall, "Split of Southern Conference May Prove Help to University," *The Richmond Collegian* (May 15, 1953), 4.

69. *Ibid.* A Quonset hut erected especially for the tournament was one consideration.

70. Charles Hedrick, "Tech Sorts Reveu," *The Virginia Tech* (May 15, 1953), 6. Later, the paper was known as *The Collegian*.

71. *Ibid.*

72. George Keller, "Moseley States Tech Policy towards Sports," *The Virginia Tech* (May 22, 1953), 6.

73. "Kentucky Seeks Membership in Atlantic Coast Conference," *Washington Post* (September 18, 1953), 34.

74. Jake Penland, "In the Press Box with Jake Penland," *The State* (May 10, 1953), B-1.

75. *Ibid.*

76. Jake Penland, "In the Press Box with Jake Penland," *The State* (May 10, 1953), 13.

77. Dick Herbert, "The Sports Observer," *News and Observer* (May 12, 1953), 13.

78. Walker, 55.

79. Earle Hellen, "Recording Sports," *Greensboro Record* (May 12, 1953), B-8.

80. *Ibid.*

81. Bob Quincey, "Nobody's Saying, but Everybody's Thinking (Shhh!) League Split," *Charlotte News* (May 8, 1953), B-10.

82. Dick Herbert, "The Sports Observer," *News and Observer* (May 13, 1953), 13.

83. Hugo Germino, "Do You Agree," *Durham Sun* (May 9, 1953), 12.

84. *Ibid.*

85. Harold Wimmer, "Time for Sports," *Roanoke Times* (May 10, 1953), 25.

86. "Eastern Schools Could Follow Southern Break," *Christian Science Monitor* (May 11, 1953), 14.

87. *Ibid.*

88. Ralph Bernstein, "Dudley would Organize New Football Conference," *Roanoke Times* (November 7, 1953), 12. After leaving Villanova in 1957, Dudley became the founder of the Liberty Bowl, originally played in Philadelphia before moving to Atlantic City and eventually Memphis. In addition, he was well-known at Villanova for selling tickets to Villanova football games through grocery purchases. Villanova dropped football in 1981 only to restart it in 1985.

89. Wilton Garrison, "The Sports Parade," *Charlotte Observer* (May 10, 1953), D-3.

90. Today, the facility is known as Bojangles Coliseum.

91. "Memorandum to President H.C. Byrd, President A. Hollis Edens, Chancellor J.W. Harrelson, Chancellor R.B. House, President Robert F. Poole, President Donald Russell, President Harold W. Tribble," May 20, 1953 (WFU, Tribble Papers, Box 3/34).

92. Letter to Hollis Edens from Harold Tribble, May 26, 1953 (Duke, President's Office, A. Hollis Edens Papers, Atlantic Coast Conference).

93. Smith Barrier, *Greensboro Daily News* (May 10, 1953), Sports-4.
94. Dick Herbert, "The Sports Observer," *News and Observer* (May 13, 1953), 13.
95. *Ibid.*
96. Smith Barrier, *Greensboro Daily News* (May 22, 1953), Sports-1.
97. Letter to Oliver Cornwell from Charles Jordan, June 18, 1953 (Duke, President's Office, A. Hollis Edens Papers, Atlantic Coast Conference).
98. Herman Blackman, "It Looks as if W. Virginia will Join New Conference," *Washington Post* (May 27, 1953), 27.
99. Dave Kelly, "Virginia has Feelers from New League," *Washington Post* (May 29, 1953), 17.
100. *Ibid.*
101. "Virginia Council Won't Talk on League Recommendation," *Washington Post* (June 2, 1953), 17.
102. *Ibid.*
103. Herman Blackman, "7 'Seceders' Meet and Form 'Atlantic Coast Conference,'" *Washington Post* (June 15, 1953), 11.
104. Ken Alyta, "Atlantic Coast Conference Seeks 8th Member," *Charlotte Observer* (June 15, 1953), 14.
105. Bob Brooks, "Name? Eighth Member? Bowls? Face New Conference," *News and Observer* (June 14, 1953), 17.
106. Chauncey Durden, "The Sportview," *Richmond Times-Dispatch* (June 18, 1953), 17.
107. Bob Brooks, "Name? Eighth Member? Bowls? Face New Conference," *News and Observer* (June 14, 1953), 17.
108. Dick Herbert, "The Sports Observer," *News and Observer* (June 15, 1953), 13. Also see Herman Blackman, "Atlantic Conference May Add Class, Power with Penn, Georgia, Florida," *Washington Post* (June 18, 1953), 25.
109. Minutes of Conference Meeting, June 14, 1953 (Duke, ACC, 1953–1956).
110. *Ibid.*
111. Herman Blackman, "7 'Seceders,' 11.
112. "Meeting of Athletic Directors May 25 and 26, 1953" (WF, Tribble Papers, Box 3/34).
113. *Ibid.*
114. "Publicity Group set for A.C.C.," *Greensboro Daily News* (July 12, 1953), 2-2.
115. Smith Barrier, *Greensboro Daily News* (June 16, 1953), 2-2.
116. Minutes of Conference Meeting, June 14, 1953 (Duke University, ACC, 1953–1956).
117. *Ibid.*
118. Ken Alyta, "Final ACC Lineup Seen at Meeting," *News and Observer* (July 24, 1953), 17.
119. Shelley Rolfe, "McDonald, in Personal Opinion, says he's in Favor of U.Va. Joining ACC," *Richmond Times-Dispatch* (July 30, 1953), 23.
120. "Minutes of the Meeting of the Athletic Council of the University of Virginia," May 30, 1953 (UVA, Papers of the President, Colgate Darden, Athletics, July–December 1953, Box 4).
121. *Ibid.*
122. *Ibid.*
123. Julian Scheer, "Darden Cools Virginia's ACC Bid," *Charlotte News* (July 22, 1953), B-6.
124. Dick Pierce, "Speculatin' Sports," *Charlotte Observer* (June 18, 1953), B4.
125. "S.E.C. Coaches Favor Two Platoons, Tech Head Puts Ills on Remoteness," *Greensboro Daily News* (December 13, 1951), 34.
126. *Ibid.*
127. Hawley passed away on March 20, 1954, less than a year after West Virginia had been left out of the new league. Some believed that that disappointment contributed to his death.
128. Herman Blackman, "Darden Pulls Hidden Ball Play on Virginia U. Plans," *Washington Post* (July 23, 1953), 18.
129. *Ibid.*
130. John S. Watterson, "Football at the University of Virginia, 1951–1961: A Perfect Gridiron Storm," *Journal of Sport History* 34 (Fall 2007), 382.
131. Letter to Irvin Stewart from Walter Newman, July 1, 1953 (VT, RG 2/10, Southern Conference Presidents, 1953, Box 8).
132. "2 Virginia Schools or None May be a Problem for ACC," *The Sun* (August 9, 1953), S3.
133. *Ibid.*
134. Shelley Rolfe, "Reviewing Sports," *Richmond Times-Dispatch* (August 9, 1953), IV-1.
135. "Virginia Sifts Plan to Enter Atlantic Loop," *Washington Post* (September 13, 1953), C4.
136. "SC Meeting Slated Here Today," *Roanoke Times* (June 26, 1953), 31.
137. Shelley Rolfe, "Virginia not ready to make up its Mind on ACC Membership," *Richmond Times-Dispatch* (June 24, 1953), 22.
138. "So. Conference Upholds Ban on Freshmen," *Washington Post* (June 28, 1953), 5.
139. Harold Wimmer, "Southern Conference Will Peg Membership at Ten," *Roanoke Times* (June 27, 1953), 11.
140. "Conference Meets Today," *Washington Post* (June 26, 1953), 33.
141. "So. Conference Upholds Ban on Freshmen."
142. Shelley Rolfe, "Sportview," *Richmond Times-Dispatch* (June 28, 1953), D-7.
143. Harold Wimmer, "Time for Sports," *Roanoke Times* (July 1, 1953), 20.
144. In the Virginia Tech Archives, there are letters from individuals and alumni chapters urging this course of action. It almost was unanimous in favor of resigning from the Southern Conference.
145. "Minutes of the Atlantic Coast Conference at Sedgefield Inn, Greensboro, NC August 7, 1953" (WFU, Tribble Papers 3/34).
146. *Ibid.*
147. *Ibid.*
148. *Ibid.*
149. *Ibid.*
150. Earle Hellen, "More Fireworks set at Sedgefield Meeting," *Greensboro Record* (August 7, 1953), B-4.

151. Dick Herbert, "Harmony Marks NCAA Meet," *News and Observer* (January 11, 1953), 27.
152. "Minutes of the Atlantic Coast Conference at Sedgefield Inn, Greensboro, NC August 7, 1953" (WFU, Tribble Papers 3/34).
153. Minutes, August 7, 1953.
154. *Ibid.*
155. *Ibid.* Also see Tim Peeler and Roger Winstead, *NC State Basketball: 100 Years of Innovation* (Chapel Hill: University of North Carolina Press, 2010), 82.
156. Letter to H.A. Fisher from Everett Case, May 25, 1953 (NCSU, Office of the Chancellor, John William Harrelson Records, Chancellor's Meetings, Athletics, Box 46).
157. Letter to H.A. Fisher from Everett Case, June 24, 1953 (NCSU, Office of the Chancellor, John William Harrelson Records, Chancellor's Meetings, Athletics, Box 46).
158. Memo to H.A. Fisher from J.W. Harrelson, June 27, 1953 (NCSU, Committees, Council on Athletics Records, Infractions, Box 40).
159. *Ibid.*
160. *Ibid.*
161. *Ibid.*
162. *Ibid.*
163. Gray's response to allegations against State was volcanic. The documents show a man almost personally wounded.
164. Letter to J.W. Harrelson from Gordon Gray, July 3, 1953 (NCSU, Office of the Chancellor, John William Harrelson Records, Chancellors' Meetings, Athletics, Box 46).
165. Smith Barrier, *Greensboro Daily News* (August 11, 1953), 2-2.
166. Letter to J.W. Harrelson from H.A. Fisher, June 13, 1953 (NCSU, Office of the Chancellor, John William Harrelson Records, Chancellors' Meetings, Athletics, Box 46).
167. Letter to Roy Clogston from Wallace Wade, no date (NCSU, Office of the Chancellor, John William Harrelson Records, Chancellors' Meetings, Athletics, Box 46).
168. Letter to James Penney, September 9, 1953 (WFU, Tribble Papers 3/34).
169. The Gulf States Conference existed until 1971. At that time, it had only seven members.
170. Smith Barrier, "Conference Split brings Problems to Keep Everybody Busy as Ever," *Greensboro Daily News* (May 10, 1953), Sports-2.
171. "Minutes of the Meeting of the Athletic Council," September 25, 1953 (UVA, Papers of the President, Colgate Darden, Athletics, July–December 1953, Box 4).
172. University of Virginia, "Board of Visitors Meeting" (October 9, 1953), http://xtf.lib.virginia.edu/xtf/view?docId=2006_10/uvaGenText/tei/bov_19531009.xml&chunk.id=d3&toc.id=d3&brand=default, accessed on March 15, 2022.
173. *Ibid.*
174. *Ibid.*
175. *Ibid.*
176. *Ibid.* Also see the Papers of Frank Talbott Jr, 1949–1962, housed at the University of Virginia.
177. *Ibid.*
178. Jack Walsh, "Tebell Wins Four-Hour Argument before Board," *Washington Post* (October 10, 1953), 13. Also see "Sports in Progress," *Daily Progress* (October 10, 1953), 10.
179. Omar Marden, "Virginia Becomes Eighth Member of Atlantic Coast Conference," *Richmond Times-Dispatch* (October 10, 1953), 12.
180. "Sports in Progress," *Daily Progress* (October 10, 1953), 10.
181. Walsh, "Tebell Wins."
182. "U.Va. Officials Welcome ACC Tie-Up," *Richmond Times-Dispatch* (October 10, 1953), 13.
183. Chauncey Durden, "The Sportview," *Richmond Times-Dispatch* (October 10, 1953), 12.
184. *Ibid.*
185. *Ibid.*
186. *Ibid.*
187. "Tatum Says Virginia Fills Missing Link; Farrington Chagrined," *Washington Post* (October 10, 1953), 14.
188. Letter to Gordon Gray from Colgate Darden, October 29, 1953 (UVA, Papers of the President, Colgate Darden, Athletics, July–December 1953, Box 4).
189. Letter to Colgate Darden from Gordon Gray, October 30, 1953 (UVA, Papers of the President, Colgate Darden, Athletics, July–December 1953, Box 4).
190. Ken Alyta, "A.C.C. All Ready for Tie-Up with Bowl—but Impatient," *Greensboro Daily News* (September 30, 1953), 2–5.
191. "A.C.C.'s Orange Bowl Pact Set with Big Seven—Tentatively," *Greensboro Daily News* (October 13, 1953), 2–2.
192. "Arrangements Completed for Big Seven—Atlantic Coast Orange Bowl Tie-Up," *New York Times* (October 19, 1953), 26.
193. "Coaches, College Officials Praise Orange Bowl's Conference Tie-Up," *New York Times* (October 20, 1953), 39.
194. "Special Meeting of the Southern Conference," November 16, 1953 (VT, RG 2/10, Southern Conference, 1953, Box 8).
195. *Ibid.*
196. Smith Barrier, *Greensboro Daily News* (November 10, 1953), 2–4.
197. Earle Hellen, "ACC Officials Arrive for Meeting Tomorrow," *Greensboro Record* (December 3, 1953), C-13.
198. "Virginia Rescues A.C.C. from Red," *The Sun* (December 5, 1953), 13.
199. "Minutes of Atlantic Coast Conference Meeting at Sedgefield Inn, Greensboro, N.C., December 4, 1953 (NCSU, Committees, Council on Athletics Records, Atlantic Coast Conference, 1953–1955, Box 22).
200. *Ibid.*
201. Memo to Mr. Gray from William Friday, December 8, 1953 (UNC, General Administration/Consolidated University: Subgroup 2: Consolidated

UNC Campus Files; Series 2: UNC-CH, Subseries 3: Athletic Affairs; General, 1953).

202. *Ibid.*

203. Letter to H.E. Kirby from R.B. House, December 14, 1953 (UNC, Chancellors' Records, R.B. House Series, Atlantic Coast Conference).

204. *Ibid.*

205. Smallwood, "ACC Officially Welcomes."

206. Irwin Smallwood, "Peahead Visits ... SC Meets ACC," *Greensboro Daily News* (December 6, 1953), Sports-5. Red O'Quinn was a dominant receiver at Wake Forest between 1946 and 1949 while playing under Peahead Walker. After a short time in the NFL, O'Quinn joined the Montreal Alouettes of the CFL, becoming one of their greatest pass receivers. He later served as a CFL general manager and as a coach. He was inducted into the CFL Hall of Fame. Alex Webster was one of NC State's greatest players. A running back of tremendous strength and power, Webster played for Montreal before having an outstanding career with the New York Giants with whom he was inducted into their circle of fame.

Chapter 10

1. Chauncey Durden, "The Sportview," *Richmond Times-Dispatch* (July 23, 1963), 16.

2. *Ibid.*

3. *Ibid.*

4. "Moseley is Given Vote of Confidence; New Eight-Year Contract by Tech," *Richmond Times-Dispatch* (August 8, 1953), 10.

5. Stan Jones was an early adherent of strength training, helping him become a fearsome guard and tackle in the NFL, playing on both sides of the ball in some seasons.

6. Dick Herbert, "The Sports Observer," *News and Observer* (October 12, 1953), 13.

7. Smith Barrier, *Greensboro Daily News* (October 9, 1953), Sports-1.

8. Dick Herbert, "The Sports Observer," *News and Observer* (October 19, 1953), 13.

9. Jake Penland, "In the Press Box," *The State* (October 23, 1953), D-1.

10. "Continued Improvement," *The State* (October 23, 1953), 4.

11. Jack Walsh, "Gamecocks Stun West Virginia, 20–14," *Washington Post* (November 15, 1953), C1.

12. Louis M. Hatter, "Maryland," *The Sun* (November 15, 1953), 1.

13. *Ibid.*

14. Grier started for Pittsburgh in the 1956 Sugar Bowl versus Georgia Tech.

15. Dick Herbert, "The Sports Observer," *News and Observer* (November 21, 1953), 11. Also see Dick Herbert, "Underdog Blue Devils Seek Revenge against Engineers," *News and Observer* (November 21, 1953), 11.

16. Letter to Jim Tatum from H.A. Fisher, December 7, 1953 (NCSU, Office of the Chancellor, John William Harrelson Records, Chancellor's Meetings, Athletics, Box 46).

17. Although drafted by San Francisco, Faloney headed to Canada where the Hamilton Tiger-Cats had offered him more money. He starred for the Tiger-Cats, winning three Grey Cups. He enjoyed a spectacular career becoming one of the greatest players in CFL history. After retirement Faloney was inducted into the Canadian Football Hall of Fame in 1974.

18. Dick Herbert, "The Sports Observer," *News and Observer* (November 28, 1953), 11.

19. Chauncey Durden, "The Sportview," *Richmond Times-Dispatch* (January 3, 1954), IV-1.

20. Louis M. Hatter, "Bielski, Irvine Elected 1954 Terp Co-Captain," *The Sun* (January 3, 1954), D-1.

Bibliography

Archival Sources

Clemson University
Athletic Council Records, 1950–1954
Board of Trustees Minutes
Robert F. Poole Presidential Papers

Duke University
Director of Athletics Records, 1939–2007
Edmund M. Cameron Records, 1929–1972
President's Office, A. Hollis Edens Papers, 1949–1960
Wallace Wade Papers

North Carolina State University
Athletics, Director of Athletics Records, 1938–2017
Athletics, Subject Files, 1909–1976
Council on Athletics Records, 1923–2009
Media Guides, Football
Office of the Chancellor, John William Harrelson Records, 1933–1953

University of Maryland
Athletics, General Records
Geary Eppley Papers
Office of the President, Harry C. Byrd Papers

University of North Carolina
Athletic Affairs
Chancellor's Records, R.B. House Series
General Administration/Consolidated Campus Papers
Inauguration of Gordon Gray as President of the Consolidated University of North Carolina, 1950
Records of the Office of the President, Gordon Gray, 1950–1955

University of South Carolina
Daniel W. Hollis, Oral History Interview, February 5, 1987
Office of the President, Donald Russell
Office of the President, Norman Smith

University of Virginia
Board of Visitors Minutes
Papers of the President, Colgate Darden

Virginia Tech
Athletic Records
Football, 1892–1959
General Athletics, 1933–1959
Records of the Office of the President, Walter S. Newman

Wake Forest University
Athletics Director Papers
James H. Weaver Papers
President's Office, Harold Wayland Tribble Papers

Newspapers

Baltimore Sun
Biblical Recorder (Raleigh, NC)
Charlotte Observer
Charlotte Record
Christian Science Monitor
Columbia Record (Columbia, SC)
Daily Press (Newport News)
Daily Progress (Charlottesville, VA)
Durham Morning Herald
Durham Sun
Evening Sun (Baltimore)
Greensboro Daily News
Greenville News (Greenville, SC)
Hartford Courant
Herald Tribune (New York)
New York Times
News and Observer (Raleigh, NC)
News Leader (Richmond, VA)
Oklahoman (Oklahoma City)
Richmond Times-Dispatch
Roanoke Times
Rocky Mount Evening Telegram (Rocky Mount, NC)
The State (Columbia, SC)
Washington Post
Winston-Salem Journal

Collegiate Newspapers

Cadet (Virginia Military Institute)
Cavalier Daily (Virginia)
Chronicle (Duke)
Collegian (Richmond)
Daily Tar Heel (North Carolina)
Davidsonian (Davidson)
Diamondback (Maryland)
Flat Hat (William and Mary)
Gamecock (South Carolina)
Hatchett (George Washington)
Old Gold and Black (Wake Forest)
Paladin (Furman)
Technician (NC State)
Tiger (Clemson)
Virginia Tech

Articles

Abbott, Carl. "College Athletic Conferences and American Regions." *Journal of American Studies* 24 (August 1990): 211–221.

Austin, Brad. "Protecting Athletics and the American Way: Defenses of Intercollegiate Athletics at Ohio State and Across the Big Ten During the Great Depression." *Journal of Sport History* 27 (Summer 2000): 247–270.

Borucki, Wes. "'You're Dixie's Football Pride': American College Football and the Resurgence of Southern Identity." *Identities: Global Studies in Culture and Power* 10 (2003): 477–494.

Bulletin of the American Association of University Professors 37 (Autumn 1951): 476–496.

Carlson, Chad. "'Doing Just What the Others Were Doing': The University of Kentucky Wildcats and the Debate over Commercialized College Athletics, 1946–1954." *The Register of the Kentucky Historical Society* 115 (Autumn 2017): 525–560.

Carvalho, John, and Daisa Baker. "Taming the Monster: The 1929 Carnegie Report on College Athletics." *Southern Quarterly* 56 (Spring 2019): 69–82.

Clark, Daniel. A. "The Two Joes Meet. Joe College, Joe Veteran: The G.I. Bill, College Education, and Postwar American Culture." *History of Education Quarterly* 38 (Summer 1988): 165–189.

Crow, Jeffrey J. "The Paradox and the Dilemma: Gordon Gray and the J. Robert Oppenheimer Security Clearance Hearing." *The North Carolina Historical Review* 85 (April 2008): 163–190.

Dankelson, Annie. "The Postwar Campus Crunch." *Maryland Today* (November 2, 2021). https://today.umd.edu/the-postwar-campus-crunch.

Doyle, Andrew. "'Fighting Whiskey and Immorality' at Auburn: The Politics of Southern Football, 1919–1927." *Southern Cultures* 10 (Fall 2004): 6–30.

———. "Foolish and Useless Sport: The Southern Evangelical Crusade Against Intercollegiate Football." *Journal of Sport History* 24 (Fall 1997): 317–340.

———. "Turning the Tide: College Football and Southern Progressivism." *Southern Cultures* 3 (Fall 1997): 28–51.

Durden, Robert F. "Donnybrook at Duke: The Gross-Edens Affair of 1960: Part I." *The North Carolina Historical Review* 71 (July 1994): 331–357.

Fenhagen, F. Weston, and Alice A. Joyce. "The Birth of the Chancellorship." *Carolina Alumni Review*. November–December 1995: 15–23.

"Football is a Farce." *Life* (September 17, 1951): 38.

Goldberg, David L. "What Price Victory? What Price Honor? Pennsylvania and the Formation of the Ivy League, 1950–1952." *The Pennsylvania Magazine of History and Biography* 112 (April 1988): 227–248.

Holland, Gerald. "Dixie's Yankee Hero." *Sports Illustrated* 7 (December 9, 1957): 75–85.

Inauguration of Gordon Gray as President of the Consolidated University of North Carolina, 1950. Chapel Hill, University of North Carolina, 1950.

Llewellyn, Matthew P., and John Gleaves. "A Universal Dilemma: The British Sporting Life and the Complex, Contested, and Contradictory State of Amateurism." *Journal of Sport History* 41 (Spring 2014): 95–116.

Mallette, Mal. "Jim Tatum of the Tar Heels." *Saturday Evening Post* (November 2, 1957): 30, 90–92.

Martin, Charles H. "Commentary: Bear, Parking, and Football." *Journal of Sport History* 34 (Fall 2007): 397–404.

Miller, Patrick B. "The Manly, the Moral, and the Proficient: College Sport in the New South." *Journal of Sport History* 24 (Fall 1997): 285–316.

Nehls, Christopher C. "Flag-Waving Wahoos: Confederate Symbols at the University of Virginia, 1941–51." *The Virginia Magazine of History and Biography* 110 (2002): 461–488.

Nelli, Humbert S. "Adolph Rupp, the Kentucky Wildcats, and the Basketball Scandal of 1951." *The Register of the Kentucky Historical Society* 84 (Winter 1986): 51–75.

"Next the Board of Visitors." *Bulletin of the American Association of University Professors* 37 (Autumn 1951): 486.

Paxton, Harry T. "Basketball Bites Dixie." *Saturday Evening Post* (March 10, 1951): 31; 111–114.

Peter R. Henriques. "The Byrd Organization Crushes a Liberal Challenge, 1950–1953." *The Virginia Magazine of History and Biography*. 87 (January 1987): 3–29.

Schmidt, Raymond. "The 1929 Iowa Football Scandal: Paying Tribute to the Carnegie Report?" *Journal of Sport History* 34 (Fall 2007): 343–351.

Shapiro, Beth J. "John Hannah and the Growth of Big-Time Intercollegiate Athletics at Michigan State University." *Journal of Sport History* 10 (Winter 1983): 26–40.

Slaton, Amy E. "Engineering Segregation: The University of Maryland in the Twilight of Jim Crow." *OAH Magazine of History* 24 (July 2010): 15–23.

Smith, Ronald A. "The William and Mary Athletic Scandal of 1951: Governance and the Battle

for Academic and Athletic Integrity." *Journal of Sport History* 34 (Fall 2007): 353–373.
Southern, David W. "Beyond Jim Crow Liberalism: Judge Waring's Fight against Segregation in South Carolina, 1942–42." *The Journal of Negro History* 66 (Autumn 1981): 209–227.
"Sport: Lifting the Curtain." *Time* (December 3, 1951).
Sumner, Jim L. "The North Carolina Inter-Collegiate Foot-Ball Association: The Beginnings of College Football in North Carolina." *The North Carolina Historical Review* 65 (July 1988): 263–286.
Swanson, Ryan. "Establishing Proper 'Athletic Relations': The Nascent SEC and the Formation of College Athletic Conferences." *The Alabama Review* 68 (April 2015): 168–188.
Terry, George D., and Catherine Wilson Horne, eds. *The Bridge Builder: Solomon Blatt Reflects on a Lifetime of Service to South Carolina*. Columbia: McKissick Museum of the University of South Carolina, 1986.
Waggoner, Jennings L., Jr., and Robert L. Baxter, Jr. "Higher Education Goes to War: The University of Virginia's Response to World War II." *The Virginia Magazine of History and Biography* 100 (July 1992): 399–428.
Walker, Jonathan, and Rich Gooch. "The Life of Dan Faurot." Harry S. Truman Library.
Watterson, John S. "The Death of Archer Christian: College Presidents and the Reform of College Football." *Journal of Sport History* 22 (Summer 1995): 149–167.
_____. "Football at the University of Virginia, 1951–1961: A Perfect Gridiron Storm." *Journal of Sport History* 34 (Fall 2007): 375–387.
Webster, Bayard. "The Rise and Fall of the University of Maryland." *Harper's Magazine* 213 (October 1, 1956): 64–69.
Whiteford, Mike. "The Road Not Traveled: ACC's 1953 Snub Altered WVU's Sports Direction." *Charleston Gazette* (June 25, 2010): B.1.

Books

Anderson, Christian K., and Amber C. Fallucca. *History of American College Football: Institutional Policy, Culture, and Reform*. New York: Abingdon, 2021.
Barton, Don, and Bob Fulton. *Frank McGuire: The Life and Times of a Coaching Legend*. Columbia: Summerhouse Press, 1995.
Bell, Andrew McIlwaine. *The Origins of Southern College Football: How an Ivy League Game Became a Dixie Tradition*. Baton Rouge: Louisiana State University Press, 2020.
Bowling, Lewis. *Wallace Wade: Championship Years at Alabama and Duke*. Durham: Carolina Academic Press, 2006.
Bradsher, Bethany. *The Classic: How Everett Case and his Tournament Brought Big-Time Basketball to the South*. Houston: Whitecaps Media, 2011.
Brill, Bill, and Ben Cohen. *An Illustrated History of Duke Basketball*. New York: Sports Publishing, 2012.
Brugger, Robert J. *Maryland: A Middle Temperament, 1634–1980*. Baltimore: Johns Hopkins University Press, 1996.
Callcott, George H. *A History of the University of Maryland*. Annapolis: Maryland Historical Society, 1966.
Cardozier, V.R. *Colleges and Universities in World War II*. New York: Praeger, 1993.
Congdon, Lee. *Legendary Sports Writers of the Golden Age: Grantland Rice, Red Smith, Shirley Povich, and W.C. Heinz*. Lanham, MD: Rowman & Littlefield, 2017.
Corrie, Bruce A. *The Atlantic Coast Conference, 1953–1978*. Durham: Carolina Academic Press, 1978.
Dabney, Virginia. *Mr. Jefferson's University*. Charlottesville: University of Virginia Press, 1981.
Durden, Robert Franklin. *The Duke Endowment: Lasting Legacy to the Carolinas, 1924–1994*. Durham: Duke University Press, 1998.
_____. *The Launching of Duke University, 1924–1949*. Durham: Duke University Press, 1993.
Edgar, Walter B. *South Carolina: A History*. Columbia: University of South Carolina Press, 1999.
Fleister, Arthur A., III, Brian L. Goff, and Robert D. Tollison. *The National Collegiate Athletic Association: A Study in Cartel Behavior*. Chicago: University of Chicago Press, 1992.
Friddell, Guy. *Colgate Darden: Conversations with Guy Friddell*. Charlottesville: University Press of Virginia, 1978.
Godson, Susan H., Judwell H. Johnson, Richard B. Sherman, Thad W. Tate, and Helen C. Walker. *The College of William and Mary: A History*. Williamsburg: King and Queen Press, 1993.
Goodman, Matthew. *Triumph, Scandal, and a Legendary Basketball Team*. New York: Ballantine, 2019.
Gray Legacy: How a Family Helped Change a City. Winston-Salem: Wake Forest School of Medicine, n.d.
Grundy, Pamela. *Learning to Win: Sports, Education and Social Change in Twentieth Century North Carolina*. Chapel Hill: University of North Carolina Press, 1993.
Hamer, Fritz P., and John Daye. *A History of College Football in South Carolina: Glory on the Gridiron*. Charleston, SC: Arcadia, 2009.
Heinemann, Ronald L. *Depression and the New Deal in Virginia: The Enduring Dominion*. Charlottesville: University of Virginia Press, 1983.
Hitchcock, Susan Tyler. *The University of Virginia: A Pictorial History*. Charlottesville: University Press of Virginia and University of Virginia Bookstore, 1999.
Hollis, Daniel Walker. *University of South Carolina: College to University*. Vol. II. Columbia: University of South Carolina Press, 1956.
Iamarino, John. *A Proud Athletic History: 100 Years*

of the Southern Conference. Macon: Mercer University Press, 2020.

Jacobs, Barry. *Golden Glory: The First 50 Years of the ACC*. Greensboro: Mann Media, 2002.

Kean, Melissa. *Desegregating Private Higher Education in the South: Duke, Emory, Rice, Tulane, and Vanderbilt*. Baton Rouge: Louisiana State University Press, 2008.

Kemper, Kurt E. *Before March Madness: The War for the Soul of College Basketball*. Urbana: University of Illinois Press, 2020.

———. *College Football and American Culture in the Cold War Era*. Urbana: University of Illinois Press, 2009.

Krause, Jerry, and Ralph Pim. *Lessons from the Legends: Beyond the X's and O's*. Monterey, CA: Coaches Choice, 2006.

Lefler, Hugh Talmedge, and Albert Ray Newsome. *North Carolina: The History of a Southern State*. Chapel Hill: University of North Carolina Press, 1973.

Lesesne, Henry H. *A History of the University of South Carolina, 1940–2000*. Columbia: University of South Carolina Press, 2001.

Lewis, Ronald L. *Aspiring to Greatness: West Virginia University Since World War II*. Morgantown: West Virginia University Press, 2013.

Link, William A. *Frank Porter Graham: Southern Liberal, Citizen of the World*. Chapel Hill: University of North Carolina Press, 2021.

———. *William Friday: Power, Purpose, and American Higher Education*. Chapel Hill: University of North Carolina Press, 1995.

McKinney, Horace "Bones." *Bones: Honk Your Horn If You Love Basketball*. Shrewsbury, MA: Garland, 1988.

Meet the Wolfpack: North Carolina State College Football Information, 1951. Raleigh: North Carolina State College, 1951, 1952.

Mettler, Suzanne. *Soldiers to Citizens: The G.I. Bill and the Making of the Greatest Generation*. Oxford: Oxford University Press, 2005.

Mitchell, Tucker. *Peahead! The Life and Times of a Southern Fried Coach*. Winston-Salem: Library Partners Press, 2018.

Montez de Oca, Jeffrey. *Discipline and Indulgence: College Football Media and the American Way of Life during the Cold War*. New Brunswick: Rutgers University Press, 2013.

North Carolina State College 1952 Football Information. Raleigh: NC State College, 1952.

Noverr, Douglas A., and Lawrence Edward Ziewacz. *The Games They Played: Sports in American History, 1865–1980*. East Lansing: Michigan State University Press, 1983.

Olson, Keith. *The G.I. Bill, the Veterans, and the Colleges*. Lexington: University of Kentucky Press, 1974.

Oriard, Michael. *King Football: Sport and Spectacle in the Golden Age of Radio and Newsreels, Movies and Magazines, the Weekly and the Daily Press*. Chapel Hill: University of North Carolina Press, 2005.

———. *Reading Football: How the Popular Press Created an American Spectacle*. Chapel Hill: University of North Carolina Press, 1993.

Padros, John. *Safe for Democracy: The Secret Wars of the CIA*. Chicago: Ivan R. Dee, 2006.

Palmer, Arnold, and James Dodson. *A Golfer's Life*. New York: Ballantine, 1999.

Paschal, George Washington. *A History of Wake Forest College*. Vol. 3. Wake Forest: Wake Forest College, 1943.

Peeler, Tim. *Legends of N.C. State Basketball*. New York: Sports Publishing, 2015.

———, and Roger Winstead. *NC State Basketball: 100 Years of Innovation*. Chapel Hill: University of North Carolina Press, 2010.

Powell, Adam K. *Border Wars: The First Fifty Years of Atlantic Coast Conference Football*. Lanham, MD: Scarecrow Press, 2004.

———. *University of North Carolina Basketball*. Charleston, SC: Arcadia, 2005.

Puckett, Jenny R. *Fit for Battle: The Story of Wake Forest's Harold W. Tribble*. Bloomington AuthorHouse, 2011.

Reagan, Alice Elizabeth. *North Carolina State University: A Narrative History*. Raleigh: North Carolina State University Foundation and North Carolina State Alumni Association, 1987.

Roth, John. *The Encyclopedia of Duke Basketball*. Durham: Duke University Press, 2006.

Sack, Allen L., and Ellen J. Staurowsky. *College Athletes for Hire: The Evolution and Legacy of the NCAA's Amateur Myth*. Westport, CT: Praeger, 1998.

Shaw, Bynum. *The History of Wake Forest College*. Vol. 4, 1943–1967. Winston-Salem: Wake Forest University, 1988.

Smith, Ronald A. *Pay for Play: A History of Big-Time College Athletic Reform*. Champaign: University of Illinois Press, 2010.

———. *Sports and Freedom: The Rise of Big-Time College Athletics*. New York: Oxford University Press, 1990.

Snider, William D. *Light on the Hill: A History of the University of North Carolina Chapel Hill*. Chapel Hill: University of North Carolina Press, 1992.

Snook, Jeff. *Sooner Nation: Oklahoma's Greatest Players Talk about Sooner Football*. Chicago: Triumph Books, 2015.

Solberg, Winton U. *Creating the Big Ten: Courage, Corruption, and Commercialization*. Champaign: University of Illinois Press, 2018.

Sperber, Murray. *Onward to Victory: The Creation of Modern College Sports*. New York: Henry Holt, 2014.

Stanley, Richard T. *The Eisenhower Years: A Social History of the 1950s*. Bloomington: iUniverse, 2012.

Thelin, John R. *Games Colleges Play: Scandal and Reform in Intercollegiate Athletics*. Baltimore: Johns Hopkins University Press, 1994.

———. *A History of American Higher Education*, 3rd ed. Baltimore: Johns Hopkins University Press, 2019.

Walker, J. Samuel. *ACC Basketball: The Story of the Rivalries, Traditions, and Scandals of the First Two Decades of the Atlantic Coast Conference.* Chapel Hill: University of North Carolina Press, 2011.

Wallenstein, Peter. *Cradle of America: A History of Virginia.* Lawrence: University of Kansas Press, 2014.

Watterson, John Sayle. *College Football: History, Spectacle, Controversy.* Baltimore: Johns Hopkins University Press, 2000.

Whittingham, Richard. *What a Game They Played: An Inside Look at the Golden Era of Pro Football.* Lincoln: University of Nebraska Press, 2001.

Index

Numbers in **_bold italics_** indicate pages with photographs

academics: athletics, redefining the role of 5–7, 73, 90–91; athletics, relationship to 3–4, 20, 29, 48–49, 65–66, 93–94, 98, 225; expansion in the post-war period 4–5; impact of commercialism 223–24; objection to the Sanity Code 40–43, 47
ACC *see* Atlantic Coast Conference (ACC)
ACC Basketball (Walker) 1
ACC Basketball Tournament 205
ACC football, the first season (1953) 207–19
African Americans *see* race/racial issues
Alden, Bob 182
Alley, Lyles 117
alumni pressure and influence: 1, 9, 41, 47, 51, 55–56, 61, 63, 66, 68, 72–73, 83, 89–91, 98, 101, 131, 141, 195, 200–202, 205–6; *see also* commercialism in collegiate sports
amateurism, the myth of 6, 43, 55, 74, 126, 153
American Association of University Presidents 71
American Council on Education (ACE) 126–30, 133–34, 237*n*25, 237*n*27
Anderson, Carl ("Butter") 198
Annapolis, MD *see* U.S. Naval Academy
Appalachian State Teachers College (renamed Appalachian State University) 186, 229*n*77
Army (football team) *see* U.S. Military Academy (West Point)
athletic recruitment 234*n*78; concern over practices in 4, 20, 43, 48, 49, 57, 68, 70, 98, 102, 153; impact of bowl games 126, 186; impact of Korean War 45–46; North Carolina State University 113, 197–99; proposed reforms 98, 129–31, 135; recruiting at Duke 32; recruiting at UNC 36; recruiting by McGuire 159; recruiting by Tatum 30–31;

Sanity Code and 52; University of Iowa 234*n*78; *see also* freshman eligibility
athletic reform 227*preface*1; ACC goals at founding 40, 46–50, 223–24; ACE report on 128–30, 133–34, 237*n*25; attempts in the Southern Conference 65–70, 128–35; de-emphasis and dropping programs 50–53, 72–74, 99–100; initiation of the football bowl ban 67–72; large vs. small school issues 4, 136; role of Byrd 224; role of Edens **_22_**, 65; role of Gray **_18_**, 65, 127–28; role of Hannah 128–29, 224; role of Murray 223; role of Poole 224
athletic scholarships: addressing reform 91, 98–102, 126–31, 134–35; cheating and scandals 59–63, 197; Davidson College 182; Johns Hopkins University 232*n*54; North Carolina State University 198–99; rejection of Sanity Code 41–43; Southern Conference policy 40; University of Maryland 25, 42; University of Virginia 42, 202; UVA Gooch Report 73–74; Vanderbilt University 153–55
Atlanta Constitution 92, 100
Atlantic Christian College (renamed Barton University) 51, 178, 186
Atlantic Coast Conference (ACC): archival documents, lack of 2, 176, 239*n*18; founding, discussions leading to 51–53, 64, 128, 131–36, 171–77; founding member schools 9–12; founding, public reaction to 180–85; leadership in creating 16–39, 221–25; meeting for the first time 177–78; naming and organizing 186–88; NCAA relationship 177, 189, 196, 198; 1954 Orange Bowl 219–21; North Carolina State University basketball probation 198, 242*n*163; policy toward bowl games 196–97, 202–4; selecting

an eighth member 178–80, 187–88, 199–203; selecting more members 204–6; Wade as commissioner 177, 206; Weaver as commissioner 190
The Atlantic Coast Conference, 1953-1978 (Corrie) 1
Auburn University (formerly Alabama Polytechnic Institute) 39–40, 58, 87, 95, 139–40, 151, 216, 218
Auerbach, Arnold Jacob ("Red") 160

Babcock, Mary Reynolds 26
Balka, Dick 147
Barclay, George Thomas: coaching at Washington and Lee 43, 90, 110; as football player at UNC 30, 153; hired to coach at UNC 154, 160; 1953 ACC football season 209–14; *see also* Washington and Lee University
Barger, Jerry 80, 137, 208, 210, 212, 219
Barrier, Harry Smith, Jr. 5, 68–69, 99, 103, 175, 186, 190, 198, 204
Barth, Karl 26
Bartholomew, Bob 138, 208, 210, 219
Bass, Marvin Crosby ("Big Moose") 62, 77–78, 86, 233*n*7
Baylor University 138, 139
Beedin, Brent 190
Before March Madness (Kemper) 1–2
Berreira, Urbino J. ("Bino") 84
Bible, Dana John 155
Big Four Conference 40
Big Six Conference 40
Big Seven Conference 203
Big Ten Conference 129, 134; about the founding of 227*n*2; influence in the NCAA 1; playing against the ACC 211–12; Southern Conference compared to 3, 6, 11, 86, 222, 224; support of Sanity Code 41–43; suspension of Iowa 99, 234*n*78

251

Index

Blackman, Herman 174
Blaik, Earl Henry ("Red") 5, 56
Blair, Joe 190
Blatt, Sol 28, 34, 227n15
Bojangles Coliseum (formerly Charlotte Coliseum) 186, 240n90
Bolling, Douglas 29
Border Wars (Powell) 1
Bostian, Cary 203
Boston College 42, 81–82, 85, 89, 141, 147–48, 155, 185, 215, 217
bowl game controversy: ACC and 203–4; creating the bowl ban policy 67–72; lifting the bowl ban 131–33, 144–46, 156, 195, 204; 1950 Gator Bowl, Maryland and 31; 1951 Orange Bowl, Clemson and 67; 1952 bowl invitations 91–98, 108–10; participation, opposition to 67, 72–74, 125–31, 146, 156; participation, support for 35, 65
Bowl games: Cotton Bowl 93, 109, 140–41, 203; Delta Bowl 59, 231n67; Dixie Bowl 59; Gator Bowl 30–31, 35, 75, 90, 95–96, 107, 109–10, 153, 184, 238n45; Liberty Bowl 240n88; Orange Bowl (the game) 35, 67, 86, 95, 131, 138, 156, 173, 174, 184, 203–4, 214; Orange Bowl (stadium, formerly Burdine Stadium) 234n53; Oyster Bowl 147, 214; Probation Bowl 140; Rose Bowl 13, 33–34, 131, 185; Senior Bowl 101; Sugar Bowl 78, 81, 83, 91–94, 98, 101–2, 108, 127, 138, 156, 184, 203, 216–17, 243n14; Sun Bowl 50, 84
Bowling Green State University (OH) 119
Bowman Gray Fund 17, 97
Bowman Gray School of Medicine 17, 186
Bowman Gray Stadium 14, 152, 210–11
Boxold, Charley 219
Bradley, Francis W. 28
Bradley, Harold ("Hal") 115, 121, 124, 162, 164, 166, 222
Bradley University 54, 107
Brandenburg, Paul 119
Bratkowski, Zeke 81, 213
Brazell, Carl 215
Brigham Young University (BYU) 157
Brooks, Bob 189
Brooks, Eugene Clyde 21
Brown, Paul 36, 75
Brown, Robert N. ("Red") 116–19, 123, 191–92
Bryan, John Stewart 58
Bryant, Paul William ("Bear") 30, 74, 78, 100, 150
Bubas, Victor A. ("Vic") 114, 118, 198
Bullock, Teedie 215

Burdine Stadium (renamed Orange Bowl) 95, 220, 234n53
Burris, Paul ("Buddy") 30
Butts, Wally 75, 81, 142, 212
Byrd, Harold C. ("Curly") 6, **24**, **87**, 228n44; academic control over athletics 40, 49–50, 224; athletic scandals, responding to 55; athletics role in university growth 48; becoming president at Maryland 23–25; challenging bowl ban policy 91–109, 125–31; forming the ACC 174, 184; hiring Tatum as football coach 30–31; interest in leaving Southern Conference 58–62, 131–35; 1952 Sugar Bowl invitation 93–94; opposition to Sanity Code 42; running for governor 195–96, 200, 222, 228n19; *see also* University of Maryland
Byrd, Harry Flood, Sr. 15, 228n50
Byrd Stadium (renamed Maryland Stadium) 51, 79–80, 138, 228n50
Byrnes, Jimmy 28, **105**, 109

Caldwell, Charley 75
Califano, Leonard 197
Cameron, Edmund McCullough ("Eddie") **187**; coaching at Duke 31–32, 35, 75–77, 111; duties as athletic director 115; leaving the Southern Conference 51–53, 128, 155; negotiations for the Orange Bowl 203; plea for athletic reforms 47–49; role in ACC formation 2, 174–78, 181, 186–89; role in ACC leadership 221–24; *see also* Duke University
Canadian Football League (CFL) 206, 231n66, 233n7, 243n17, 243n206
Carmichael, William ("Billy") 18, 20, 97–98, 122, 158, 234n71
Carmichael Auditorium 36, 234n71
Case, Everett **113**; coaching at North Carolina State University 3–4, 222–24; creating a basketball dynasty 36, 99, 159; 1951 basketball season 112–22; 1952 basketball season 156–65; 1952 Dixie Classic 157; 1952 Southern Tournament 122–24; 1953 Southern Tournament 165–70; probation for recruiting violations 197–99; role in ACC formation 184; *see also* North Carolina State University
Casey, Willis 166
Catawba College (NC) 81–82
Chandler, Alvin Duke 61, 72, 127, 130, 136

Charlotte Coliseum (renamed Bojangles Coliseum) 186, 240n90
Christian Science Monitor 57
The Chronicle (Duke student newspaper) 181
The Citadel (aka Military College of South Carolina): dealing with cheating and scandal 62; enrollment and freshman eligibility 46; football bowl ban 103, 125; joining the Southern Conference 3–4, 39–40; membership in Southern Conference 176, 178, 182–83, 195; 1951 football season 57, 79–80, 86; 1952 basketball season 161, 163, 165; 1952 football season 150; 1952 season play 150; 1953 football season 211; rejection of the Sanity Code 41–42, 49
City College of New York (CCNY) 5, 54, 91, 159
civil rights 14
Civil War 9–10, 11, 13, 29
Clemson, Thomas 10
Clemson University (formerly Clemson Agriculture College): ACC founding member 3; creation of the school 10; dealing with cheating and scandal 63; founding of the Southern Conference 39–40; 1951 basketball season 121–24; 1951 football season 82, 84–87; 1952 basketball season 161, 165; 1952 bowl controversy 95–98; 1952 conference probation 99–108, 137; 1952 football season 139, 140, 143, 145, 147–48, 150; 1952 Gator Bowl 109–10; 1953 ACC football season 207–19; Poole selected as president 27–28; *see also* Howard, Frank J.; Milford, Lee W., Sr.; Poole, Robert Franklin ("Frank"/"Sarge")
Clogston, Roy: as athletic director 36, 103, 111, 124, 221, 229n77; controlling fan behavior 162; role in ACC formation 174; selecting the ACC eighth member 179
Clonts, Forrest: academic oversight of athletics 225; role in athletics at Wake Forest 37–38; role in forming the ACC 174–79; role in leadership of ACC 189–90, 221; role in Southern Conference leadership 101; selecting the ACC eighth member 204–6
Coalter, Jim 123
Cole, William P., Jr. **87**, 94, 132
College Football (Watterson) 1
College of William & Mary: academic dishonesty

Index

scandal 5, 59–64, 68, 91, 94, 106–8; football bowl ban 125, 204; joining the Southern Conference 3, 40, 58–59; 1951 basketball season 119–24; 1951 football season 80, 82–83, 86; 1952 basketball season 163; 1952 football season 141, 152; 1953 football season 209; playing during and after the scandal 119, 135–36, 141, 151–52; post-scandal de-emphasis of athletics 72, 99–100, 182; rebuilding the athletic program 73–74, 127
Collins, Chuck 34, 35–36
Columbia University (NY) 29, 118
commercialism in collegiate sports: academics defeated by 223–24; ACC role in controlling 6–7, 201; amateurism, the myth of 6, 43, 55, 74, 126, 153; concern over the growth of 2–4, 40, 52, 55, 66, **67**, 69, 76, 107, 141, 186; de-emphasis as solution to 73–74; money/salary pressures 33, 44–45, 57, 58, 61, 104, 115, 155, 177, 183, 210; post-season play contributing to 71–72, 126, 146–47, 203–4, 219; scandal and relationship to 57, 60; television broadcasting of games 93; *see also* alumni pressure and influence; sportsmanship in athletic competition
communism in American life 14, 18–19, 23, 55, 107, 110
Concord Daily Tribune 99
Continental Football League 233*n*7
Cornell University 30, 118
Cornwell, Oliver: academic oversight of athletics 225; role in athletics at UNC 38; role in forming the ACC 174, 177, 187; role in leadership of ACC 189, 206, 221
Corrie, Bruce 1
Cosgrove, Tom 149
Crozier, Richard 122
Cunningham, John R. 62, 66, 124, 125, 176; *see also* Davidson College

Daily Progress 180, 188
The Daily Tar Heel (UNC student newspaper) 71, 174, 181
D'Angelo, Al 208
Darden, Colgate Whitehead, Jr. **200**; anti-communist stance 23; becoming president at UVA 28–29; dealing with post-war enrollment 15; de-emphasis and academic oversight 73–74, 129, 146, 155; departure from UVA 222; joining the ACC 180, 191–94, 199–203; membership in Southern Conference 45, 47, 128; opposition to Sanity Code 42; relationship of athletics and academics 224; *see also* University of Virginia
Davidson, Hal ("Bull") 142, 143–44
Davidson College: athletic de-emphasis and reform 51–53, 66, 125, 135; enrollment and freshman eligibility 45–46; hiring Dole to coach 240*n*63; membership in Southern Conference 3, 6, 40, 195, 212, 223; membership in the Big 5 Conference 40, 46; 1951 basketball season 120–21; 1951 football season 78–83; 1952 basketball season 156, 158, 165; 1952 football season 138–39, 142–43, 155; reaction to ACC split 181–83; *see also* Cunningham, John R.
Davidsonian 182
The Davidsonian (student newspaper) 181–82
Davis, Lowell 168
Deasy, Howard 118
DeHart, James ("Jimmy") 32
D'Emilio, Rudy 116, 119, 121, 122, 162, 163, 164
DePorter, Al 168–69
desegregation *see* race/racial issues
DeVos, John 168
The Diamondback (Maryland student newspaper) 181
Dixie Bowl (football) 59
Dixie Classic Basketball Tournament 3–4, **114**, 117–18, 157–58, 186, 223, 236*n*12
Dixie Conference 199
Dodd, Robert Lee ("Bobby") 84, 100, 146–47, 217
Dole, Bill 143, 182, 240*n*63
Donovan, Herman 55
Drew, Harold Delbert ("Red") 151, 203
Dudley, Ambrose ("Bud") 185, 240*n*88
Duke, James Buchanan 10
Duke, Washington 10
Duke University (formerly Trinity College): ACC founding member 3, 51–53, 190; creation of the school 10; hiring Bradley to coach basketball 115; hiring Cameron to coach basketball 31–32; hiring Wade to coach football 32–33; joining the Southern Conference 39–40; 1951 basketball season 116–24; 1951 football season 80, 82–86; 1952 basketball season 156, 161–65; 1952 football season 137–38, 142–43, 145–47, 149; 1953 ACC football season 207–19; 1953 Southern Conference Tournament 165–66; war-time V-12 program 12; *see also* Cameron, Edmund McCullough ("Eddie"); Edens, Hollis; Murray, William David ("Bill"); Wade, William Wallace
Duquesne University (PA) 51
Durden, Chauncey 5, 89, 95–96, 100, 102, 127, 149, 173–74, 202, 236*n*28, 239*n*14
Durham Morning Herald 57, 91

East Carolina College (renamed East Carolina University) 178, 195
Eastern College Athletic Conference 185
Eastern Conference 105, 133–34, 180, 185
Edens, Hollis **22**; academic oversight of athletics 4, 46–48, 57, 224; anti-communist stance 23; barring West Point transfers 62; becoming president at Duke 21–23; departure from Duke 222, 228*n*43; football bowl ban 65–67, 71–72, 93, 102–3, 107, 125–34, 144, 171, 204; role in forming the ACC 184–87; selecting the ACC eighth member 193, 203; *see also* Duke University
Elon University 111, 186, 235*nn*141–142
Emory and Henry College (VA) 36, 195
Emory University (GA) 22, 39
Enright, Rex Edward **85**; coaching at USC 33–34, 84–**85**, 145, 221; named Coach of the Year 219; 1952 football season 138, 140, 150–52; 1953 ACC football season 208–19, 211, 213–19; role in forming the ACC 2, 6, 128, 155, 174, 181, 184; role in leadership of ACC 190, 205–6, 224; *see also* University of South Carolina
Eppley, Geary ("Swede") 31, 43, 50, 97, 101, 106, 174, 176–77, 196–97, 203, 205
Erickson, Chuck ("Knute Rockne of North Carolina"): becoming football coach 35–36; move to become athletic director 38, 142, 154, 221; role in forming the ACC 2, 128, 174, 189; role in leadership of ACC 178, 203; *see also* University of North Carolina
Erskine College (SC) 46, 51

Faloney, Bernie 208, 218, 219
Farrington, Max: creation of the Southern Conference 43–45; dividing the Conference for

post-season play 130; facing secession by Conference members 133, 173–78; inviting new schools to join 146; rebuilding the Southern Conference 182–85, 202, 204; as Southern Conference president 48–50, 101, 103; *see also* George Washington University
Faurot, Donald Burrows ("Don") 30, 220, 229n61, 304
Feathers, William Beattie ("Big Chief") 46, 82, **88**, 110–11, 141, 235n139, 235n141
Fetzer, Bob 36, 38, 43, 89
Filipski, Gene 140, 143, 211
financial aid *see* athletic scholarships
Fisher, Hilbert A. 47–48, 70–71, 110, 174–79, 196–99, 205, 218–19
Florida State University 103, 110, 145–46, 178, 195, 199, 219
Fordham University (NY) 118, 150
Fort Jackson, SC 14
Freeman, James Andrew ("Buck") 158–59
freshman eligibility: athletic scholarships 45–46, 66, 69–70, 127, 146, 171, 173, 175, 223; *see also* athletic recruitment
Friday, William ("Bill") 19, 65, 67, 232n7
Fulbright, J. William 57
Fullerton, Ed 79, 109
Furman University: dealing with cheating and scandal 62–63; enrollment and freshman eligibility 46, 66; football bowl ban 103–6, 126; membership in Southern Conference 3–4, 39–40, 182–83, 191, 195, 223; 1951 basketball season 117, 120–22; 1951 football season 82, 86; 1952 basketball season 156, 162–65; 1952 football season 140–42, 151; 1953 football season 211, 218; 1953 Southern Conference Tournament 165–66

gambling *see* point fixing; scandal and corruption
The Gamecock (USC student newspaper) 181
Games Colleges Play (Thelin) 1
Gantt, "Goo Goo" 83
Garrison, Wilton 43, 69, 144, 185
George, Maurice 157, 168
George, Sonny 141, 208
George, William J. ("Bill") 85
George Washington University: Farrington as athletic director 44–45; football bowl ban 124; membership in Southern Conference 4, 44, 176–78, 182, 193, 195, 223; 1949 cheating scandal 54; 1951 basketball season 116–17, 120–23; 1951

football season 80, 84, 86; 1952 basketball season 157–58, 161, 163–64, 166; 1952 football season 105–7, 138, 140–41, 143, 155; 1953 football season 202, 211, 214; 1954 Southern Conference Tournament 183; support of athletic reform 49–51; *see also* Farrington, Max
Georgetown University 50–51, 74, 120, 182
Georgia Institute of Technology (aka Georgia Tech) 11, 39–40, 83–84, 133, 137, 146–47, 151, 155–56, 174, 215, 217–18, 220, 236n17
Germino, Hugo 81, 121, 147, 184
Gerrard, Gerry 115
Gerry Gerard Award 170
Giermak, Chet 166
Glickfield, Lou 149
golf 37, 99, 172–73, 221, 239n17
Gooch, Robert Kent ("Bobby") 29
Gooch Report 45, 73–74, 155
Gordon, Nield 117, 122
Graham, Frank Porter ("Dr. Frank") 18–20, 41–42, 89–90
Gramling, Johnny 138, 142, 145, 147, 208, 211, 213, 215
Gray, Bowman, Sr. 16
Gray, Gordon **18**, **71**; becoming UNC president 16–20; bowl game controversy 68–72, 101–3, 107–8, 144–46, 171, 196, 203–4; compliance with NCAA rules 198; departure from UNC 222; desegregation at UNC 53; disagreement with Sanity Code 41–43; leadership of President's Group 46; North Carolina State University recruiting violations 198–99, 242n163; oversight of athletics 4; position on forming a new conference 132–35; rejection of Tatum as coach 153, 218; role in ACC formation 184–86, 188, 222–24; role in athletic reform 4, 46–50, 63–67, 90–91, 126–30, 175; stance against communism 23; *see also* University of North Carolina
Gray, Jane Boyden Craige 17
Gray, Johnny 212
Greason, Murray 37, 156–57, 159–60, 168–70, 222, 224, 227
Great Depression 11, 21, 28, 34, 172
Greater Greensboro Open 99, 172, 239n7
Greensboro, NC 172, 185
Greensboro Daily News 99
Greensboro Record 156, 204
Greenville Daily News 99
Greenville News 95, 102, 104, 117
Grier, Robert, Sr. ("Bobby") 217, 243n14

Grimaldi, Vince 117
Groat, Dick 115–19, 121–24, 167, 236n22
Groat, Richard Morrow ("Dick") 115–19, 121–24, 166, 167, 236n22
Gross, Paul 228n43
Guepe, Art 75, 90, 143, 145–46, 154–55, 191–93, 210, 214, 238n45
Guilford College (NC) 172, 178
Gulf States Conference 199
Guthrie, Hunter 50

Hair, Billy 82, 84–85, 109, 138, 140, 143, 145, 147–48, 150, 209
Hannah, John A. 128–29, 224
Hanulak, Chet 79
Hargrove, Nathan ("Piggy") 112–13
Harlow, Dick 55
Harper, William Rainey 58, 231n65
Harper's Magazine 25
Harrelson, John W. ("The Colonel") **71**; chancellor at North Carolina State University 20–21; dealing with cheating and scandal 63, 197–98; football bowl ban 91, 144; racial integration at State College 47; relationship of athletics to academics 57, 70–**71**, 74, 224; retirement 203; role in forming the ACC 188; supporting athletic reform 65; *see also* North Carolina State University
Hart, Leon 233n18
Harvard University 19, 22, 55, 91
The Hatchet (GWU student newspaper) 182
Hatter, Louis 216
Hawley, Roy ("Legs") 173, 178, 179, 183, 184, 188, 193, 205, 241n127
Heisman Trophy 89, 109, 138, 218
Hellen, Earle 156, 163, 173, 184, 204
Hemric, Ned Dixon ("Dickie") 117, 118, 124, 157, 160–64, 166–70
Hendrickson, Horace James ("The Horse"): coaching at Elon University 235n142; coaching at North Carolina State University 111, 235n141; hired to coach at State 138; 1952 football season 140–43, 146; 1953 ACC football season 208–18; *see also* North Carolina State University
Herbert, Dick 2, 82, 90, 99, 102–4, 107, 116–18, 130, 134, 165, 173, 184, 213, 219
Hickman, Herman 77
High Point University (NC) 51, 98
Hillenbrand, Bruce 211, 213, 215
Hinkel, John V. 228n45
Hobbs, A.W. 47–48, 50, 174, 179, 189

Holcomb, Stu 153
Hollis, Dan 28
Holter, Edward F. 132
Holup, Joe 157, 166
Holy Cross, College of (MA) 157, 161, 185
Hoover, J. Edgar 52
Horner, Jack 91, 100, 121, 157, 168
Horvath, Paul 118
House, Robert Burton ("Bob") 67; becoming chancellor at Chapel Hill 19–20; football bowl ban 67–69, 91; leadership in Southern Conference 49; oversight of athletics 57, 65, 71, 90; racial integration at UNC 20, 47, 53; role in forming the ACC 6, 128, 130, 174; role in leadership of ACC 196, 221; selecting the ACC eighth member 197, 203, 205; *see also* University of North Carolina
Houston, Clarence 42
Howard, Frank J. **35**; coaching at Clemson 34–35, 75, 95, 104, 221, 229*n*75; football bowl ban 110; 1951 football season 67, 82, 84; 1952 football season 138, 140–41, 143; 1953 ACC football season 208–9, 215; role in forming the ACC 6, 40, 174, 184, 186, 223; support of athletic reform 98, 130–31; *see also* Clemson University
Hundley, Rod 197
Hurricane Florence (1953) 211

Iba, Henry 115–16
Ingrassia, Brian 1
integration *see* race/racial issues
Ivy League 11, 72–74, 91, 118, 127, 134, 185, 189, 200–201

Janicki, Bernie 116, 118–19, 121
Jefferson, Thomas 11
Johns Hopkins University 36, 74, 232*n*54
Johnson, Dick 123
Johnson, Frank 119, 164
Johnson, William ("Hootie") 80, 138
Johnston, Olin 28
Jones, Stan 208, 243*n*5
Jordan, Charles 47–48, 174–77, 187, 189–90
Jordan, Ralph ("Shug") 87, 100
Justice, Charlie ("Choo Choo") 59, 89, 106, 233*n*18

Karmosky, Charles 60–61
Kemper, Kurt 1–2
Kenan, Rand, Jr. 36
King, Don 150, 209
Kitchen Thurman D. 25
Knowles, Eddie 145
Koch, Joe 141
Korean War 42, 44–46, 51, 56, 66
Kovarovic, John 197

Laird, Greene Flake ("Red") 193
Lakatta, Robert 197
LaSalle University 119, 120
Latimer, Carter ("Scoop") 95, 104
Lauricella, Hank 109
Layne, Bobby 237*n*1
Leahy, Frank 36, 89, 146, 216–17
Lear, Johnny 149, 216
Lenoir-Rhyne University (NC) 80
Lewis, Art ("Pappy") 191–92, 215
Life (magazine) 64
Lifson, Al 117
Lindsey, Clark ("Pug") 29
Lipstas, Ray 168
Listopad, Ed 85
Long Island University (LIU) 5, 54, 159
Louisiana State University 14, 39–40, 108
Lutz, Worth ("a million") 137, 141, 145, 147, 208, 210, 212
Lyles, Billy 168, 170

Male, Evan 192
Man, Ted 190
Manhattan College (NY) 54, 107, 118
Marshall, Nelson 59–61
Mary Washington College 11
Maryland College of Medicine 11
Maryland Stadium (formerly Byrd Stadium) 228*n*50
Maryland State College (formerly Maryland Agricultural College) 11
Mazelli, Ronnie 197
McAlister, David S. 43, 101, 176–78
McCallister, Don 33–34
McCray, Ruben 59–61, 231*n*72
McDaniel, R.C. 178
McDonald, Ned L. 155, 188, 191–92, 218, 241*n*119
McFadden, Banks 120–21, 123, 165, 236*n*22
McGuire, Frank 157–59, **159**
McKeldin, Theodore 15, 94, 228*n*19
McKinney, Horace ("Bones") 157, 159–60, 169–70, 222
McKissick, James Rion 28, 229*n*55
Meadows, Ed ("Country") 84, 137, 212, 237*n*1
Mehre, Harry 34
Michigan State University 86, 128–29, 147, 212
Miles, Sally 178–79, 184, 204–5
Milford, Lee W., Sr.: football bowl ban 103–4; 1952 Gator Bowl invitation 95–96; proposal for athletic reform 102, 135; role in forming the ACC 174, 184; role in leadership of ACC 192, 221; role in Southern Conference athletics 38–39; selecting the ACC

eighth member 179; *see also* Clemson University
Millikan, Herman A. ("Bud") 115–16, 120–21, 167, 222
Milliken University (IL) 51
Mills, Warren 161
Mississippi Agricultural and Mechanical College (renamed Mississippi State University) 39–40, 210, 218
Mississippi Southern College (renamed University of Southern Mississippi) 199
Mitchell, Jim 197
Modlin, George 25, 26, 66, 134
Modzelewski, Dick ("Little Mo") 139, 237*n*3
Modzelewski, Ed ("Big Mo") 79, 109, 129, 139, 237*n*3
Morrill Land Grant Act of 1862, 10–11
Morrison, Dwane 119
Moseley, Frank: coaching at Virginia Tech 78, 207; joining the ACC 179, 183, 185, 192–94, 210–11; 1951 football season 80; 1952 football season 139; *see also* Virginia Tech (aka Virginia Polytechnic Institute)
Murray, William David ("Bill") **76**; coaching at Duke 75–77, 80–81, 84–85, 90, 137, 214; coaching in the ACC 207, 209–10, 212; emphasis on sportsmanship 6, 223–24; 1952 Cotton Bowl 141–42; 1953 ACC football season 207–14; 1960 Cotton Bowl 221; role in ACC leadership 221; selecting the ACC eighth member 190–91; *see also* Duke University

Nash, Jay B. 48
National Basketball Association (NBA) 160, 236*nn*18–19
National Collegiate Athletic Association (NCAA): Big Ten Conference and 1; bowl game policy 96–97, 105, 131, 196–97; 1950 Tournament 54; 1951 Convention 41–43; 1952 Convention 128; 1953 Convention 196; 1953 Tournament 170; 1957 Tournament 221; relationship with the ACC 177, 189; rules restrictions 114, 159; Sanity Code 41–47, 52, 69, 74, 103, 224; scandals and corruption 54, 197–99, 222; school compliance with policies 47, 49, 52; scoring record 238*n*12
National Football League (NFL) 85, 89, 208, 233*n*7, 237*n*3, 243*n*5, 243*n*206
National Invitation Tournament (NIT) 54
Navarro, Frank 149

Index

Navy (football team) *see* U.S. Naval Academy
Neely, Jesse Claiborne ("Jess") 34, 82
New York Herald Tribune 55, 57
New York University 36, 48, 117–18, 133–34
Newberry College (SC) 86
Newman, Marshall 140, 215
Newman, Walter S. 63, 67, 130, 134, 171, 173, 176, 192, 194, 215
News & Observer (Raleigh) 68–70, 93, 95, 99, 107, 149
Niagara University (NY) 51
Nielson, Frederick 23
North Carolina Agricultural and Technical University (formerly Negro Agricultural and Technical College) 172
North Carolina Athletic Conference 186
North Carolina College of Agriculture and Mechanic Arts *see* North Carolina State University
North Carolina Department of Conservation and Development 21
North Carolina Historical Commission 19
North Carolina National Guard 21
North Carolina North Carolina State University of Agriculture and Engineering *see* North Carolina State University
North Carolina State College *see* North Carolina State University
North Carolina State University (aka State College): about the name and name changes 10, 227Intro$n$2; ACC founding member 3; compliance with the Sanity Code 41–43; creation of the school 10; founding of the Southern Conference 39–40; Harrelson selected president 20–21; hiring Case to coach 3–4, 99, 112–13; hiring Clogston to coach 36; hiring Feathers to coach 46, 82, 110; hiring Hendrickson to coach 110–11, 138; 1951 basketball season 116–24; 1951 football season 81–83, 86; 1952 basketball season 156, 160–65; 1952 football season 138, 141–43, 145–46, 148; 1953 ACC football season 207–19; 1953 Southern Conference Tournament 165–70; post-war growth and development 21; recruiting violations and probation 197–98, 242n163; *see also* Case, Everett; Harrelson, John W. ("The Colonel"); Hendrickson, Horace James ("Horse")
North State Conference 178
Northwestern University 213

Notre Dame 1, 11, 34, 88–90, 133, 146, 149, 211, 214–18, 220, 225, 233n18
Nugent, Tom 110

off-season (spring) practice 65, 69, 70, 91, 127, 130
Ohio State University 1, 11, 30, 38, 42, 109
O'Keef, Herbert 57, 90, 93, 107
Oklahoma State University (formerly Oklahoma A&M) 59, 115, 220, 231n67
Old Gold and Black (Wake Forest student newspaper) 181
Onward to Victory (Sperber) 1
O'Quinn, Red 206, 243n206
organized crime 5
Oriad, Michael 2
Outland Trophy 79

Pacific Coast Conference 41
Palmer, Arnold 37, 221
Parker, Clarence ("Ace") 75, 232n1
Parker, Larry 83
Pay for Play (Smith) 1
Peacock, Dick 110
Penland, Jake 5, 80, 90, 94, 134, 147, 170, 183–84
Penney, Jim: athletics-academic relationship 37, 94, 225; role in ACC formation 174, 176–77, 179, 184, 201, 204, 206; role in ACC leadership 188–89, 221
Pennsylvania State University (aka Penn State, the Nittany Lions) 55, 119, 130, 133, 173, 185, 193, 195, 216
Pierce, Dick 168, 191
Pitt, Howard 141
Plyler, John 66, 126, 128, 130
point fixing *see* scandal and corruption
Pomfret, John 58–63
Poole, Robert Franklin ("Frank"/"Sarge") *105*; academic oversight of athletics 49, 224; becoming president at Clemson 27–28, 222; football bowl ban 126–27, 144; founding the Southern Conference 6; Gator Bowl invitation 95, 103–9; role in forming the ACC 128, 130–33; *see also* Clemson University
Povich, Shirley 92, 107, 131–32
Powell, Adam K. 1
Presbyterian College (SC) 46, 82, 86, 139, 140, 155, 195, 209, 212
Price, Ed 140
Price, Robert 197
Princeton University 75, 91, 157
Pritchett, Norton 45, 52–53
Purdie, Kenneth S. 178
Purdue University 208, 211–12

Queens College (NY) 70
Quincy, Bob 69–70

race/racial issues: addressed in North Carolina 14; breaking the color barrier 217; integration at Maryland 24, 228n50; integration at North Carolina State University 230n42; integration at UNC 20, 47, 53; integration at UVA 15
Ranzino, Sam 118
Reading Football (Oriad) 2
recruitment *see* athletic recruitment; freshman eligibility
reform 4
Reynolds, Mary Babcock 113
Reynolds, William Neal 113
Reynolds Coliseum 5, 32, 36, 112–13, *114*, 183, 194, 205, 223
Rice University 34, 82
The Richmond Collegian (student newspaper) 182–83
Richmond Times-Dispatch 5, 48, 52, 61, 72, 74, 89, 92, 127, 199
The Rise of Gridiron University (Ingrassia) 1
Rives, Bill 94
R.J. Reynolds Tobacco Company 16
Roanoke Times 92, 96, 99, 106
Robinson, Harvey 210
Rockne, Knut Kenneth 34
Rogers, Tom 77, 81, 85, 138, 139, 152, 175, 209
Rolfe, Shelley 52, 179, 194
Rollins College (Winter Park, FL) 46
Rosenbluth, Lennie 197, 198
Ross, Donald 172, 187
Rotella, Al 110
Royall, Darrell 30
Rudin, Jim 182
Rupp, Adolph 54–55, 117, 197, 199
Russell, Donald: becoming USC president 28, 237n39; relationship of athletics to academics 224; support of bowl games 131

St. Bonaventure University (NY) 59
St. John's University (NY) 156, 158, 159
St. Mary's College of California 51, 70
Sanders, Sam 143
Sanford, Steadman V. 39–40
Sanity Code 41–47, 52, 69, 74, 103, 224
Saturday Evening Post 31, 114–15
scandal and corruption: about the issue in collegiate sports 1–2; bowl games and 91–97, 126; conference enforcement 105–8; impact on the Southern Conference 111; North Carolina State University recruiting violations 198–99; point shaving 5, 54–56, 107, 149, 159;

reforms for ending 4–6, 205–6; Sanity Code and 41; UNC point shaving 222; University of Iowa 99, 234n78; West Point cheating scandal 56–58, 62–63, 140, 143, 212, 231n55; William & Mary cheating scandal 58–62, 136, 151; *see also* athletic reform; sportsmanship in athletic competition
Scarbath, Jack 78–79, 109, 139–40, 149, 151, 208
Scheer, Julian 191
scholarships *see* athletic scholarships
Scott, Tom 116–17, 118, 158, 238n4
Scott, W. Ken 13–14, 122
Scott, Xen 33
Scott Stadium 86, 145–46, 209–10
segregation *see* race/racial issues
Seival, John 197
Sell, Henry B. 232n54
Selvy, Frank 117, 120, 122, 124, 162, 163, 165–66, 236n19
Serkin, Alvin 197
Seven Sinners 42
Shapiro, David 54
Shaughnessy, Clark 31
Shue, Gene 120, 122, 124, 163–64, 166–67, 170, 236n18
Siegel, Morris 91–92, 106–7, 131
Simpson, Jimmy 75
Smallwood, Irwin 174, 239n17, 243n206
Smith, Dick ("Cap'n") 43, 176
Smith, Norman Murray 55; becoming president at USC 26; discussion of ACC formation 128; opposition to bowl games 125; relationship of athletics and academics 70; resignation 28
Smith, Ronald A. 1
Smith, Walter W. ("Red") 55–56, 209, 212
Smith Barrier *see* Barrier, Harry Smith, Jr.
Snavely, Carl (the "Gray Fox") 30, 78, 83, 88–90, 137, 146, 149, 152–54, 233n25, 238n42
Snavely, Carl, Jr. 78
Snidow, Conley 195
Sottile, Jim 119, 124, 157, 166–67
Southeastern Conference: comparison with Big Ten 1; comparison with Southern Conference 11, 100, 156; comparison with the ACC 217, 224; opposition to Sanity Code 41–43; resistance to reforms 91, 126; split from the Southern Conference 3, 39–40, 68–69; teams moving to the ACC 183, 189
Southern Conference: changes brought on by WWII 12–16; commissioner named 33, 43–44; comparison to the ACC 217, 224; the day the conference died 3–7; football bowl ban 67–72, 125–31, 144–46, 156, 196, 204; issuance of athletic scholarships 41–43; joining the ACC 204–5; leadership of Farrington within 44–45; Maryland as the largest member 24–25; member secession, reorganization following 194–95; member secession to a new conference 133–36, 171–80; 1921 founding of the conference 39–40; 1951 bowl ban crisis 90–98; 1951 coaching turnover 75–78; 1951 conference competition 78–88; 1951 meeting of the conference leadership 51–53, 99–108; 1951 meeting of the President's Group 46–50, 64–72; 1952 football season 137–52; 1952 meeting of the conference leadership 128–31; 1952 meeting of the President's Group 127–28; 1953 meeting of the President's Group 171; racial integration 53; recognizing need for athletic reform 46–55; recruiting and freshman eligibility 45–46; rejection of Sanity Code 41–43; relationship with NCAA 47, 49, 52, 114; scandals and corruption 54–63; shutting down athletics due to cost 50–51; stature of Duke athletics in 11, 32; Virginia departure/re-entry into 40, 45, 52–53, 146; withdrawal of Clemson 104; withdrawal of Maryland 131–32
Southern Conference (baseball) 50
Southern Conference (basketball): Case and the changes in 3–4, 99, 112–15, 164; cheating scandals 5, 48, 52, 54–56, 59, 106; fan behavior 162; 1951 season play 116–24; 1952 season play 160–65; North Carolina State University probation 198; post-season tournaments 70, 92–93, 97, 102; post-war growth and development 13; proposed reforms 65–68, 99–101
Southern Conference Tournament 50; dominance of North Carolina State University 3–4; 1949 tournament *114*; 1952 tournament 116, 120, 122, 164; 1953 tournament 158, 165–70; 1954 tournament 183, 194; surviving the ACC split 184
Southern Intercollegiate Athletic Conference 39–40
Southern Methodist University (SMU) 55, 82, 137, 139, 141, 173
Southwest Conference 1, 32, 43
Southwest Missouri State University 115
Southwestern College (renamed Rhodes College) 32
Speight, Bobby 116, 122, 157, 162, 164, 166, 168, 170
Spencer, Larry 141
Sperber, Murray 1
split-T offense 30–31, 80–81, 137–38, 149–50, 154, 208–9, 212, 220
sportsmanship in athletic competition: fan behavior 36, 84, 107, 162, 213, 216; teaching the meaning of 52, 76, 123, 207, 223–24; *see also* commercialism in collegiate sports; scandal and corruption
Stagg, Amos Alonzo 231n65
Stewart, Irvin 48–49, 63, 67, 94, 126, 173, 178, 194
Stoddard, George 131
Streit, Saul 55–56
Summerall, Charles 62
Sweet Briar College (VA) 70
Syracuse University 156

Talbott, Frank 201
Tatum, James Moore ("Big Jim"/"Sunny Jim") *148*; bowl game controversy 91–94, 101, 108–10; coaching at Maryland 4, 6, 25, 63, 88; coaching at Oklahoma 30–31, 229n66; coaching at UNC 30, 132, 221, 233n25; coaching offer from North Carolina State University 217–18; ego and personality 55, 89–90, 147, 153; Maryland athletic recruitment 42–43, 129; named Coach of the Year 98; new conference, support of 6, 127–28; 1950 Gator Bowl 31; 1953 ACC football season 208–18; 1954 Orange Bowl 219–20; role in ACC formation 174, 178, 184, 186, 192, 196, 202, 205, 223; role in ACC leadership 220–21; *see also* University of Maryland
Taylor, Charles A. ("Chuck") 112–13
Teas, Billy 217
Tebell, Gustave K. 135–36, 146, 155, 179–80, 188–92, 200–202, 205, 221
The Technician (North Carolina State University student newspaper) 180
television, sports broadcasting 5, 42–43, 55, 93, 129, 147, 203, 225
Terrill, Lee 116, 124
Terwilliger, Ronald 197
Texas Tech University (TTU) 84, 111, 118, 151
Thelin, John R. 1, 16
Thompson, Mel 116, 118–19, 124, 157, 162, 164, 166
Thurmond, James Strom, Sr. 14

Index

The Tiger (Clemson student newspaper) 181
Tribble, Harold Wayland 27; academic oversight of athletics 4, 57, 77, 104, 224; becoming president at Wake Forest 18, 25–27, 222, 228n53; football bowl ban 126; relationship of athletics and academics 224; reorganizing the Southern Conference 174, 186; role in ACC leadership 222; support of athletic reform 130–31, 171; *see also* Wake Forest University
Tribble, Henry Wise 25–26
Trinity College (formerly Normal College) 10
Truman, Harry S. 18, 127
Tufts University 42
Tulane University 39–40, 95
Turner, Mebane 202
Tusculum University (TN) 51
Twin City Sentinel 17
two-platoon system 46, 66, 70–71, 98, 100, 107–8, 126, 207–8

Underwood, Paul 197
Underwood, Thomas 55
Union Institute Academy (renamed Normal College) 10
U.S. Federal Bureau of Investigation (FBI) 52, 149
U.S. G.I. Bill: impact on post-war higher education 4; increased veteran enrollment 10, 13, 16, 28, 222; veteran graduation and enrollment decline 227n10
U.S. Military Academy (West Point): academic cheating scandal 5, 56–58, 72, 91, 94, 231n55; elimination of football 57; expulsion and transfer of players 61–63, 143, 215; inclusion in a new conference 180, 185; Navy football rivalry 130; post-scandal football performance 140, 212–15
U.S. Naval Academy (Annapolis): Army football rivalry 130; competitive scheduling 106, 139, 174; elimination of football 57; inclusion in a new conference 134, 180, 185; performance on the field 79, 86, 89, 118, 148–51, 155, 214; wartime V-training programs 12–13, 24, 25, 32, 158
University of Alabama 11, 33–34, 39–40, 58, 78, 86, 106, 131, 139–41, 150, 151, 156, 185, 203, 208, 217–18, 220
University of Cincinnati (OH) 158
University of Delaware 76
University of Florida 39, 120, 138, 143, 147, 183, 189
University of Georgia 22, 31, 33–34, 39–40, 81, 87, 90–91, 106, 120, 139, 142–43, 149, 183, 189, 208, 212–14, 229n84
University of Illinois 131
University of Iowa 99, 216, 218, 234n78
University of Kentucky 5, 30, 39–40, 54–55, 75, 78, 101, 138, 149–50, 158, 183, 199
University of Louisville (KY) 26, 118–19
University of Maryland (formerly Maryland State College): ACC founding member 3; Byrd selection as president 23–25; creation of the school 10–11; founding of the Southern Conference 39–40; growth and development during post-war period 15–16; hiring Millikan to coach basketball 115–16; hiring Tatum to coach football 4, 25, 29–31; 1951 football season 78, 80, 83, 86–88; 1952 basketball season 163–64; 1952 bowl controversy 91–98, 101; 1952 conference probation 99–108, 137; 1952 football season 138–39, 140, 149, 151–52; 1952 Sugar Bowl 108–9; 1953 ACC football season 207–19; 1953 Southern Conference Tournament 165–67; 1954 Orange Bowl 214, 218, 219–21; rejection of the Sanity Code 41–42; reorganizing the Southern Conference 50; rivalry with Virginia, creation of 202; withdrawal from Southern Conference 131–32; *see also* Byrd, Harold C. ("Curly"); Tatum, James Moore ("Big Jim"/"Sunny Jim")
University of Miami 95, 104, 109, 199
University of Michigan 11, 42, 225
University of Minnesota 1
University of Mississippi 39–40, 100, 139, 149, 152, 208, 215–16, 220
University of Missouri 34, 86, 139, 209, 211, 214
University of North Carolina (UNC): ACC founding member 3; coaching changes 152–54; creation of the school 9; founding of the Southern Conference 39–40; Graham Plan 41; Gray becomes president 16–19; hiring Erickson as athletic director 35–36; hiring House as chancellor 19–20; hiring McGuire as basketball coach 157–59; 1951 basketball season 118–24; 1951 football season 78–79, 81–83, 86–90; 1952 basketball season 156–58, 160–65; 1952 football season 142, 143–44, 145, 150; 1953 ACC football season 207–19; 1953 Southern Conference Tournament 165–67; post-season bowl appearances 98, 101; post-war academic development 14–16; racial integration 14; Sanity Code compliance 41–43; Snavely as football coach 30, 78, 83, 88–90; war-time V-12 program 12; *see also* Erickson, Chuck; Gray, Gordon; House, Robert Burton ("Bob")
University of North Carolina at Greensboro (formerly Woman's College) 18, 19, 172, 228n31
University of Oklahoma 30–31, 55, 58, 78, 80, 83, 219–20, 221
University of Pennsylvania 11, 31, 56, 73, 111, 133, 161, 180, 183, 185, 189–90, 208, 211, 224
University of Pittsburgh 81, 86, 95, 133, 150, 173, 180, 185, 192–93, 195, 216–17, 220, 243n14
University of Richmond (formerly Richmond College): academic oversight of athletics 66; football bowl ban 125; membership in Southern Conference 3, 40, 179–80, 182–83; Modlin selected president 25; 1949 football season 78; 1950 football season 51; 1951 football season 82; 1952 basketball season 161; 1952 football season 141, 145, 152, 155; 1953 basketball season 161; 1953 football season 135; 1953 Southern Conference Tournament 165–66; reorganizing the Southern Conference 194; war-time V-12 program 12
University of South Carolina (USC, formerly South Carolina College): ACC founding member 3; creation of the school 9; Enright hired to coach basketball 33–34;[1] membership in Southern Conference 40; 1951 football season 80, 82, 85–87; 1952 basketball season 163–65; 1952 football season 138, 139, 140, 146, 152; 1952 season play 150; 1953 ACC football season 207–19; post-war academic development 14–16; war-time V-12 program 12; *see also* Enright, Rex Edward
University of Southern California 118
University of Tennessee 11, 33, 39–40, 55, 81, 86, 88, 92–93, 100, 108–11, 120, 125, 129, 137–43, 147, 173–74, 208, 210
University of Texas 55, 82–83, 108, 138, 140–42, 190, 222
University of the Pacific 84, 95
University of the South 39–40
University of Toledo 54

University of Virginia: acceptance as ACC member 3, 204–5; coaching changes 154–55; creation of the school 11; Darden as president 28–29; de-emphasizing athletics (the Gooch Report) 73–74; departure/re-entry into Southern Conference 40, 45, 52–53, 146; football bowl ban 146, 202; founding of the Southern Conference 39–40; joining the ACC 178–80, 187–94, 197, 199–203; 1952 football season 142–43, 145; post-war growth and anti-integration efforts 15–16; rejection of the Sanity Code 41–42; reorganizing the Southern Conference 50; war-time V-12 program 12; *see also* Darden, Colgate Whitehead, Jr.
University of Wyoming 75

Vanderbilt University 39–40, 93, 100, 134, 149, 154–55, 192, 214, 238*n*45
Vaught, Johnny 100, 149, 153, 216
Villanova University 42, 51, 118–19, 138, 140, 143, 148, 161, 185, 210–11, 240*n*88
Virginia Military Institute 40, 42, 46, 79–80, 105, 126, 145, 179, 202, 223
Virginia Tech (aka Virginia Polytechnic Institute): dealing with cheating and scandal 63; enrollment and freshman eligibility 46; founding of the Southern Conference 39–40; joining the ACC 178–79, 183–85, 189, 192–97, 203–7; membership in Southern Conference 225; Moseley hired as coach 78; Newman as president 130; 1951 football season 79–80, 83; 1952 football season 139, 142–43, 155; 1953 football season 135, 207, 209–10, 216; proposal for athletic reform 171, 173; rejection of the Sanity Code 41–42; reorganizing the Southern Conference 176; *see also* Moseley, Frank
The Virginia Tech (student newspaper) 183
Voyles, Carl 58–59, 231*n*66

Wade, William Wallace **88**; bowl game controversy 94–96, 101–2, 203–5; called into war-time service 32; coaching at Duke 12–13, 32–34, 76–77, 80–81, 141–42; dealing with scandal and corruption 197–99; departure from Duke 75; secession of conference members 176–78; serving as ACC commissioner 177, 206; as Southern Conference commissioner 43–44, 52, 65–67, 162; *see also* Duke University
Wadiak, Steve 80, 82–83, 87, 211
Wake Forest Manual Institute (renamed Wake Forest College) 9–10
Wake Forest University (formerly Wake Forest College): ACC founding member 3, 175; hiring McKinney to coach 157, 159–60; hiring Weaver to coach 36–37; joining the Southern Conference 3, 40; 1951 basketball season 118–24; 1951 football season 81–83, 85–86; 1952 basketball season 157, 161–65; 1952 football season 138, 139, 141, 143, 145, 152; 1953 ACC football season 207–19; 1953 Southern Conference Tournament 165–70; relocation to Winston-Salem 10, 14, 26; Tribble selected as president 25–27; *see also* Tribble, Harold Wayland; Weaver, James Harvey ("Jim")
Walker, Clyde ("Peahead") 30, 34, 57, 77, 81, **88**, 110–11, 175, 206, 218, 233*n*6, 243*n*206
Walker, Ewell Doak 233*n*18
Walker, J. Samuel 1
Walker Doak 233*n*18
Wallace Wade Stadium (formerly Duke Stadium) 88
Washington and Lee University: enrollment and freshman eligibility 223; football bowl ban 67, 125; founding of Southern Conference 39–40; hiring Cameron to coach 31–32; membership in Southern Conference 6, 176, 183, 193; 1950 football season 153–55; 1951 football season 80; 1951 Gator Bowl 75, 90; 1952 basketball season 161; 1952 football season 139, 148, 152, 155, 161, 163; 1953 football season 135, 211; *see also* Barclay, George Thomas
Washington Post 91–92, 174, 188
Washington Star 92
Washington State University 33, 34
Watterson, John Sayle 1, 194
Weaver, Dewitt 111
Weaver, James Harvey ("Jim"): athletic director at Wake Forest 36–37; football bowl ban 103; named Southern Conference commissioner 43–44, 221; named the ACC commissioner 38, 190, 221; 1951 basketball season 122; 1952 basketball season 141; 1953 basketball season 162; role in ACC formation 174; *see also* Wake Forest University
Weber, Jerry 197
Webster, Alexander ("Red") 138, 143, 206, 243*n*206
Welsh, George 192
West Point *see* U.S. Military Academy (West Point)
West Virginia University 236*nn*15–16; academic oversight of athletics 48–49; dealing with cheating and scandal 63; football bowl ban 105–7, 126; Hawley as athletic director 173, 241*n*127; joining a new conference 134–35; joining the ACC 178–80, 187–94, 197, 204–6; membership in Southern Conference 44, 195, 204, 225; 1951 basketball season 116–17, 119–23; 1951 football season 81, 85–86; 1952 basketball season 157, 165; 1952 football season 140–42, 150–52, 155; 1952 Southern Conference Tournament 165–67; 1953 football season 210, 215–18, 220; 1953 Southern Conference Tournament 165–67; 1954 Sugar Bowl 216, 217; reorganizing the Southern Conference 50, 182–83
Western Football League (WFL) 233*n*7
White, Hugh 216
Wilkinson, Charles Burnham ("Bud") 30–31, 229*n*66
Williams, Bob 3
Williams, Jack 155
Williams, Larry 167–70
Wilson, Bernard, Jr. ("Barney") 59–60
Wimmer, Harold 92–93, 105, 109–10, 184–85, 195
Winston-Salem Journal 17
Wofford College (SC) 195
Woman's College of the University of North Carolina 18, 19, 172, 228*n*31
women 10–14, 28, 58, 59
Workman, Mark 116, 117, 119, 123–24, 157, 236*n*15
World War I 19, 21, 27, 29, 73
World War II: enrollment and athletics during 12–13, 44, 66, 113–14; school transformations following 4, 9, 13–16, 21, 28, 54, 137, 166; war-time service by academics and coaches 17, 30–31, 34, 36, 44, 70, 73, 75, 78, 112, 158
Worrell, Flo 150
Wyatt, Bowden 75

Yale University 16, 77, 91
Yurin, Bernie 168

Z. Smith Reynolds Foundation 10